The
Cleveland Browns
The Great Tradition

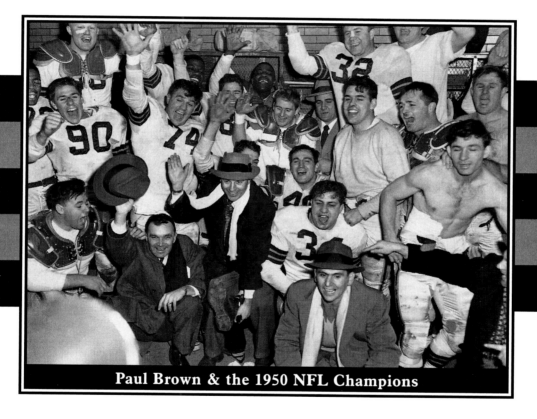

Paul Brown & the 1950 NFL Champions

EDITED AND DESIGNED BY
Bob Moon

CONTRIBUTING WRITERS
Steve Byrne, Jim Campbell, Mark Craig & Bob Moon

PUBLISHED BY
SporTradition Publications
Columbus, Ohio

Brian Sipe

Contents

Published by:
SporTradition Publications
798 Linworth Rd. East   Columbus, Ohio 43235
614-785-0641

Editor & Designer: Bob Moon, SporTradition

Contributing Writers:
Steve Byrne, Jim Campbell, Mark Craig & Bob Moon

Additional Copies:

By Phone: Toll Free 1-888-785-0641 (MC/Visa/Discover)

By Mail: Send a check or money order for $42.95 per book (includes P&H) payable to SporTradition. Ohio residents add $2.13 sales tax per book. Include your name, address and telephone number.

>   **Mail to:** SporTradition Publications
>   798 Linworth Rd. East
>   Columbus, OH 43235

Publisher's Cataloging-in-Publication
The Cleveland Browns : the great tradition / edited by
    Bob Moon ; contributing writers: Steve Byrne, Jim
    Campbell, Mark Craig & Bob Moon. — 3rd ed.
       p. cm.
       Includes bibliographical references.
       ISBN: 0-9667660-1-6

    1. Cleveland Browns (Football team)—History. I. Moon,
Bob. II. Byrne, Steve. III. Campbell, Jim. IV. Craig, Mark.

GV956.C6C54 1999
796.332/64/0977132   QBI99-1382

Foreword

More than 50 years ago, we original Browns established something unique and special in Cleveland—a legacy of success that was rooted in the desire to be the best in the game. Our fans throughout Ohio and all over the world soon identified with that success and bonded with us over the years. Because Browns tradition became a part of their lives, they would not accept the move of the franchise in 1995 and ultimately spoke loudly to cause the NFL to put a new team in Cleveland. As I watch the Browns return to the field in a brand new stadium in 1999, I'm reminded that the game has changed considerably since my day, but take pride in being part of the beginning of that great tradition on the lakefront.

We owe it all to Paul Brown, who taught us how to play the game, understand the game and respect the game. Unquestionably, Paul Brown was a winner and he surrounded himself with winning players and coaches. The challenge of winning—to prove we were champions year after year no matter the obstacle—kept us in the title game 10 straight seasons and eventually sent nine of us from those early teams, including Paul Brown, to the Pro Football Hall of Fame. It's a winning tradition that remains the foundation of Cleveland Browns football.

I'm also proud of the contributions that the Browns of my era made to pro football. Today's game is certainly more specialized and, some people say, more sophisticated. But much of the way the game is played at the end of this century can be found in the innovations, strategy and techniques that were developed and implemented by Paul Brown, his coaches and players more than a half century ago. Everyone, for example, has heard of the West Coast Offense. That's our basic passing attack that Paul brought to Cincinnati where Bill Walsh, who was an assistant there, picked it up and took it to San Francisco.

This book captures and celebrates the history and tradition of the Cleveland Browns in a variety of formats and in more detail than any book I've ever seen. There are chapters about each historic era and stories about the greatest victories and rivalries that represent those eras. There is a section about Paul Brown and the other head coaches, plus position-by-position chapters tracing the history of the Browns' offense, defense and special teams players. I am pleased to be a part of this important volume and proud that the legacy we established made such a book possible.

Dante "Gluefingers" Lavelli

Dante Lavelli
Cleveland Browns, 1946-56
Pro Football Hall of Fame, 1975

McBride's New Enterprise

The man was a radical. We can use that word in the most positive way when describing Arthur B. McBride, the millionaire businessman from Cleveland who wanted to own a football team. The time was the early 1940s, when owning a professional sports franchise was considered nothing more than a rich man's hobby, as most pro sports teams failed to make money. McBride, known to all in Cleveland as Mickey, wasn't looking for another hobby. This man was all business and his football team was going to be a business venture as well, albeit a fun one. How different that attitude was to the rest of the professional football owners' fraternity. Most franchises operated in the red, and attendance was not much better than the average baseball game today. College football was still No. 1 in the hearts of American sports fans and most people accepted that.

Not McBride. Although the National Football League owners were, for the most part, as wealthy as he was, they were content to see their other businesses make up for revenue lost on football. But McBride was never content with losing. He saw no reason why one business should be allowed to lag behind simply because the others were successful. If Mickey were to own a team, the operation would be first class all the way.

McBride had worked his way up from the streets of Chicago, where he sold newspapers as a boy. He made money on the side when his regular customers would give him the free transfers they had just received from the street car conductor. In exchange, McBride would give them newspapers. He then sold the transfers for three cents to people who would normally have to pay five cents—early evidence of his business acumen.

> Architects of a dynasty, Mickey McBride (left) and Paul Brown share a moment of pride after the Browns won their third straight AAFC title in 1948.

COACHING LEGEND: At Ohio State, Paul Brown coached for three seasons (1941-43), winning the national title in '42.

Later, at age 23, McBride was a circulation director of William Randolph Hearst's *Chicago American*. He held that position with the *Cleveland News* from 1913-31 before going into business for himself.

Everything he touched turned to gold. He owned Yellow-Zone Cab Co., Cleveland's only taxi fleet. He owned real estate in Ohio, Florida and Illinois, a radio station, a printing company and a horse race wire syndicate.

Ironically, it was college football that put the notion of owning an NFL franchise into his head. McBride had never been a football fan, or even a sports fan. He liked baseball and boxing, but could hardly be described as a big follower.

But when his son, Arthur Jr., went off to Notre Dame in the fall of 1940, McBride made the pilgrimages to see the Irish play every Saturday, and not just in South Bend, Ind. He followed the Fighting Irish wherever they would play. The love for football at Notre Dame infected McBride in a big way.

Returning to Cleveland the day after he had watched his first Notre Dame game, McBride attended a Cleveland Rams contest, his first NFL game. The man who had never been to a football game in his life would now become a familiar sight both at college and NFL affairs.

Unlike Notre Dame, the Rams were fodder for the Bears, Redskins and other successful clubs. They hadn't had a winning record over their first five seasons after their inception in 1937. The Rams were sold in 1941 to Daniel F. Reeves, and the rumors that the team would eventually leave Cleveland were now flying. McBride was nonetheless convinced that with the right promotion, professional football could sell in Cleveland. He offered to purchase the Rams, but Reeves declined the offer.

Reeves' rebuff led McBride to the office of *Chicago Tribune* sports editor Arch Ward almost two years later, in the winter of 1944. He had heard Ward, who had already started the Major League baseball All-Star game and the all-star football game between top college seniors and the NFL champion, was looking to launch a second pro football league. The Rams had suspended operations in 1943, and McBride wanted to secure a team for Cleveland in the event of the NFL pulling out of town.

Two upstart leagues had already failed in recent years. Ward was determined it wouldn't happen with his. He would have no problem with McBride in that regard. Money was not an issue with McBride, who wanted the best and was willing to pay for it. The two men hit it off as they each understood what the other wanted.

Representatives from six cities met with Ward in a St. Louis hotel room on June 4, 1944, to form the All-America Football Conference. Two more franchises would be added during the summer and, on Sept. 4, it was announced

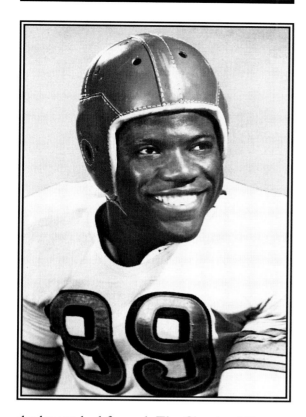

the league had formed. The Cleveland Browns would join the Brooklyn Dodgers, Buffalo Bisons, Chicago Rockets, Los Angeles Dons, Miami Seahawks, New York Yankees and San Francisco 49ers.

McBride was not a very happy man when Reeves, despite the Rams having won the NFL championship in 1945, announced on January 12, 1946, the club was moving to Los Angeles. He thrived on competition and, even though the Browns had yet to play a game, was winning the publicity war against the club in the established league.

McBride had hired Paul Brown, who had coached Ohio State University to a national championship in 1942, to coach the team. He had many OSU and Big Ten alumni and native Ohioans under contract. He held a name-the-team contest during the 1945 season when the Rams were on their way to a 9-1 record and an NFL championship.

The contest winner was a young sailor, John J. Harnett, whose entry of "Panthers" earned him a $1,000 war bond. Several weeks later, a man named George Jones approached McBride

BROWN'S BUCKEYES: Paul Brown signed several of his former Ohio State players when he joined Cleveland's new AAFC franchise. Among them were middle guard Bill Willis (left), receiver Dante Lavelli (right) and place-kicker Lou Groza.

to say he had once owned a semi-pro football team named the "Cleveland Panthers," and requested a fee for the rights to the name.

McBride refused. The team had not been a winner and McBride and Brown agreed that they did not want to be associated with an unsuccessful venture. A second contest was held, this time with a new car as the prize. The name most frequently suggested was "Browns,"

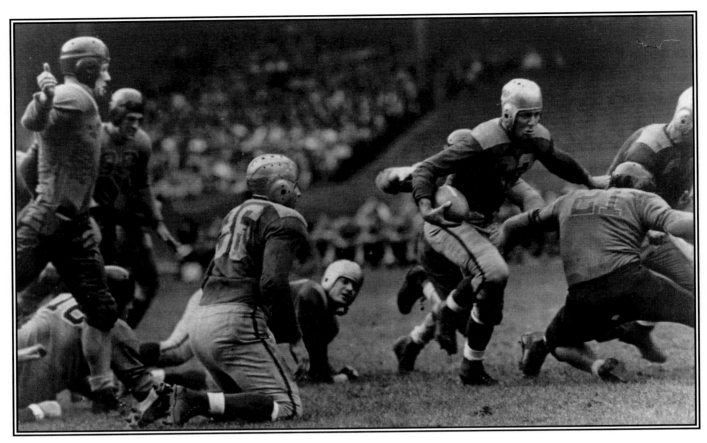

HALL'S FAME: "Bullet" Parker Hall (32) was the Cleveland Rams' most famous name in the pre-World War II years. Hall was a classic tailback who could run, pass and kick. The Rams played in Cleveland from 1937-42 and 1944-45, dropping from the NFL in the war year of '43. They won the '45 championship, beating the Redskins, before moving to Los Angeles in '46.

in recognition of Brown's notoriety throughout Ohio. A three-man selection committee finally agreed that "Browns" would be the choice.

"The Cleveland Browns, who have never played a football game, are already receiving more publicity than the Cleveland Rams, who have just won the world football championship," *Cleveland Plain Dealer* sports columnist James Doyle said.

Despite their success on the field, the Rams drew only 73,000 fans to four home games and 32,178 to the championship in Cleveland Stadium against a team with the biggest name in the game—the Washington Redskins and quarterback Sammy Baugh.

Hiring Brown was McBride's master stroke. The Norwalk, Ohio, native was already a legend in his home state. A graduate of Massillon High

School and Miami University (Ohio), Brown started his marvelous career at 21 when he was hired in 1930 as head coach of Severn Prep, a private school run by the Navy. Two years later, after compiling a 16-1-1 record at Severn, he returned to his alma mater.

Brown rang up an 80-8-2 record in nine seasons at Massillon. During his final six years the Tigers had a 58-1-1 record and were regarded as the finest high school program in the nation.

When Ohio State lost head coach Francis Schmidt after the 1940 season, Brown was the logical choice to replace him. He didn't even have to apply for the job. It was done for him by sportswriters, OSU alumni and the Ohio Football Coaches Association. Brown left Massillon with not only an enviable record, but a 21,000-seat stadium (up from 5,000 when he arrived) named for him.

Brown compiled an 18-8-1 record in three seasons at Ohio State. His record might have been better had World War II not called away most of the younger members of the '43 team, which ended with a losing record (the only one Brown would suffer in his first 26 years of coaching). In the Navy himself in 1944, Lt. Paul Brown coached the Great Lakes Naval Training Center team to a combined 15-5-2 record over two seasons.

Brown, oddly enough, was not McBride's first choice to be head coach. As a Notre Dame zealot, McBride wanted the Irish's dynamic taskmaster, Frank Leahy, who had posted a 24-3-3 record from 1941-43. Notre Dame officials, however, talked him out of it.

McBride then sought the advice of *Plain Dealer* football writer John Dietrich, who did not hesitate to tell him Paul Brown was the man he wanted. Brown, Dietrich said, was young, a winner and popular in the part of the world where the Browns would be drawing fans.

Arch Ward concurred. Saying Brown would "be as good as anyone you could get," Ward offered to make the short trip to Great Lakes Naval Center to solicit him. Brown signed a five-year contract on Feb. 8, 1945, in Ward's office at the *Tribune*. His annual salary would be $25,000 per year. He was only 36 years old.

"Paul was the easiest person I ever hired," McBride said at the time. "I could've signed him for $15,000, but I wanted to make a splash for publicity. I wanted to say my team had the highest-paid coach in America."

The Rams announced their move to Los Angeles less than a month after their finest moment—a 15-14 victory in the NFL Championship game of Dec. 16, 1945. The Browns reportedly would refrain from luring Rams players to stay in Cleveland, but five players and a coach decided not to make the trip west. The decision of one of the players, tackle Chet Adams, caused the Rams to bring a breach of contract suit against the Browns.

The Rams requested U.S. Federal Court Judge Emerich Freed to grant an injunction forbidding Adams to play for the Browns. The Browns, in return, dismissed back Ted Fritsch from training camp. Fritsch had played for the Green Bay Packers since 1942, and the Browns believed cutting him might make the Rams drop their suit. Fritsch rejoined the Packers and stayed with them through 1950.

BUILDING BLOCKS: Paul Brown built the Browns with players and opponents from his past college and service coaching experience. It resulted in scenes such as this after the Browns won the 1948 AAFC title. From left to right are Edgar Jones (Pittsburgh), Lou Saban (Indiana), Otto Graham (Northwestern) and Marion Motley (Great Lakes Naval Training Center).

Freed ruled on Aug. 29, 1946, that Adams could play for the Browns, citing the fact that the Cleveland Rams ceased to exist after Jan. 12 and that Adams and the others were free agents. Adams said his having been signed by Rams assistant coach Red Conkright, the coach who opted to remain in Cleveland, was a factor in his decision to jump leagues.

Adams and the other ex-Rams—backs Don Greenwood and Gaylon Smith, punter-safety Tom Colella and lineman Mike Scarry—were among the few players not hand-picked by Paul Brown. The football world had gotten a glimpse of the Brown method of building a team, and it was something of a shocker.

Brown stuck to people, both players and coaches, with whom he was familiar. Such a method might have smacked of cronyism, but Brown had an uncanny eye for talent, and was determined not to take a man simply because he was a "name" player. The fact that a man had NFL experience made little difference to Brown. He was looking for one specific type of man and was determined to stock the Browns with those people.

Lin Houston, a guard, played for Brown at Massillon and Ohio State. Others who played for Brown at OSU included guards Bill Willis and George Cheroke, tackles Lou Groza and Jim Daniell, fullback Gene Fekete and end Dante Lavelli. Playing for Brown at Great Lakes were fullback Marion Motley and defensive end George Young.

Brown also had an excellent memory for opponents. He recalled from his Ohio State years a halfback named Edgar "Special Delivery" Jones from the University of Pittsburgh. He had made a mental note on a big receiver from Utah named Mac Speedie, who had played for the Fort Warren team against Brown's Great Lakes squad.

The most important opponent Brown would remember was Otto Graham, a multi-sport star at Northwestern University. Recruited primarily for his prowess as a high school basketball player, Graham was not even invited to try out for the football team as a freshman. He got a chance the next year only because rumors had reached the varsity that a guy playing in the intramural league could really throw the ball.

Graham's football career progressed slowly, but by 1943 he was as renowned as a gridder as he was as a basketball player. He led the Wildcats to an 8-2 record that year, second in the Big Ten, and was chosen All-America. When he left Northwestern, he had received three letters each in football and basketball and two letters in baseball.

If Brown's desire to bring Graham on board surprised anyone, it was possibly because Brown had made it known he would run the offense out of the T formation. Graham had only learned that offense in the service, with the North Carolina Pre-Flight. But Graham had all that Paul Brown wanted in a player, both athletically and personally. He became

> **Otto Graham was a multi-sport star at Northwestern who became the Browns' first and highest-paid player, earning a $7,500 salary in 1946.**

SPEEDIE MOVES: Mac Speedie snares a pass near the sideline against the Dodgers at Ebbets Field in 1948. Speedie had played for the Fort Warren team against Paul Brown's Great Lakes squad during World War II. Brown remembered the big receiver from Utah when putting together his first Browns team in 1946.

the Browns' first, and highest-paid, player, earning $7,500 in 1946.

"The two things I insisted on were that I would be in charge of the football end of the business and that I would have an absolute free hand in selecting my players," Brown once said. "I wanted them all to be high class, and I picked them on the basis of personality as well as ability. I'd always lived by the rule that you don't win with dogs and, to me, it's a rule that never has changed."

The Rise & Fall of the AAFC

When the Cleveland Browns opened their first training camp on July 28, 1946, at Bowling Green State University in northwest Ohio, an experiment within an experiment was launched. First, there was the experiment of whether another professional league could make a go of it beside the established National Football League, in operation more than 25 years. But within the experiment that was the All-America Football Conference, there was the question of whether Paul Brown's novel way of running a team, with the head coach in complete control of all football operations, would succeed. Preparation was a Brown trademark. As was his style, he had been meticulous in his personnel selections for the Browns' first team. Not only did he choose his new players based on personal experiences with them, but he selected his coaches the same way.

The new staff included familiar names from many eras in Brown's coaching career: Fritz Heisler played for Brown at Massillon High School and was a member of Brown's staff at Massillon and Ohio State. John L. Brickels played against Brown as a student at Wittenberg College and coached against him at New Philadelphia (Ohio) High School when Brown was at Massillon. Blanton Collier, a highly successful high school football and basketball coach from Paris, Ky., was on Brown's staff at Great Lakes and helped develop the T formation there. Bob Voigts was an assistant at Great Lakes under coach Tony Hinkle, who preceded Brown.

As with his players, Brown insisted the coaches were people who knew what he wanted. What Brown wanted most of all was perfection. Mental discipline was as important as physical conditioning. The coach didn't want, as he said "just a bunch of tough guys who can take it." To that end he instituted the use of film clips to study an opponent's tendencies as well as

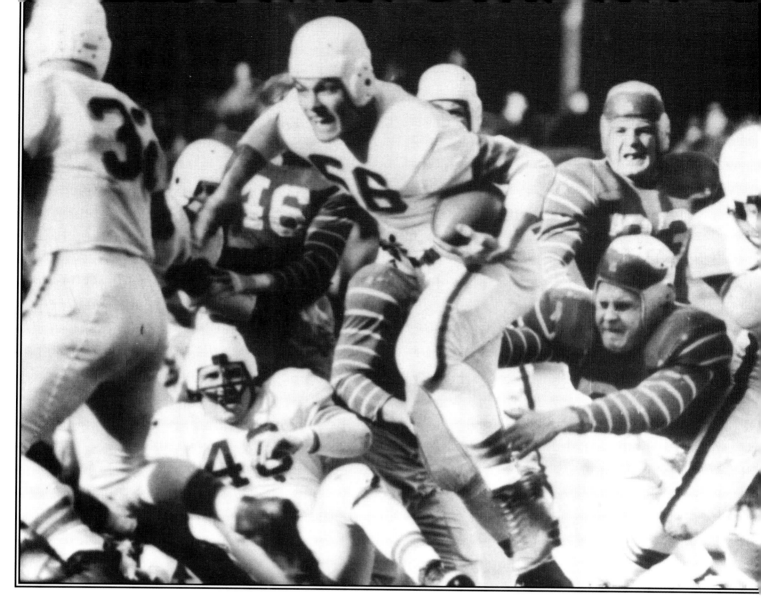

Dante Lavelli charges through a herd of Buffalo Bison in a 42-17 Browns win at Cleveland Stadium on Nov. 24, 1946.

grade his own players, notebooks and classroom sessions. He was the first coach to keep his players sequestered in a hotel the night before a game. He developed a passing game designed to locate holes in the defense and a defensive strategy to counter opponents' passing attacks. Brown was the first coach to use intelligence tests to determine a player's coach-ability. "Somewhere along the line the dumb guy will get your football team in trouble, probably on the field, maybe off," Brown said in a 1953 interview. "We can't afford to fool around with him."

Brown's men, he said, would love playing football for the game itself first and the paycheck second. He spoke with great pride when declaring he had "the most amateurish professional football team in the country" and "nothing more than a glorified college team." The Cleveland Browns were amateurs in spirit, but hardly in reality.

Perhaps the greatest testament to Brown's system was the number of men who became successful head coaches after playing or coaching for Brown.

CAMP CONFERENCE: Paul Brown gives instructions at Bowling Green State University, site of the Browns' training camp from 1946-51. Players lived in a sorority house and practiced next to a local cemetery (above), but the relaxed campus atmosphere was favored by Brown, who later moved the site to Hiram College. The Browns' traditional seal brown and burnt orange colors were adapted by Brown from BGSU's color scheme.

Chuck Noll, Bill Walsh, Don Shula and Weeb Ewbank won Super Bowls. Blanton Collier coached the Browns to the 1964 NFL title. Lou Rymkus and Lou Saban each coached back-to-back AFL champions—Rymkus in Houston and Saban in Buffalo. Ara Parseghian coached Notre Dame to two NCAA national championships. Otto Graham, Walt Michaels, Abe Gibron, Mike McCormack, Mac Speedie, Paul Wiggin, Sam Wyche and Bruce Coslet also played under Brown and later became NFL or AFL head coaches

Brown insisted that everyone who worked for him display a decorum in practice and in public. Players were expected to come to practice in clean T-shirts and be as well groomed when they arrived as when they left. In public, the Browns had to wear jackets, slacks and polished shoes. Drunkenness and brawling were, naturally, forbidden.

The practice, while possibly new to pro football, might have been an idea Brown borrowed from baseball's Joe McCarthy, the New York Yankees manager from 1931-46, who made his players wear jackets and ties while staying at the team's hotel during spring training. Both teams dominated their respective sports.

One illustrative story concerns a talented young college lineman in whom the Browns were interested. But when the player arrived at the team's training camp uncombed, unshaven and dressed like a laborer, Brown told him a mistake had been made and the man should visit the business manager, who would give him money for transportation home. Brown didn't even give the player a chance to right his own ship. The coach wasn't there to teach you to be a gentleman. You either came to him as one or didn't come at all.

But while Brown demanded that his players be gentlemen, the coach himself engaged in practices that in 1946 were hardly considered gentlemanly. He refused to agree not to raid the NFL or to pursue NFL veterans who had yet to be discharged from the armed services. While there was no rule barring black players from the league, Brown would have no part of any gentleman's agreement keeping blacks out of the AAFC.

The latter decision led Brown to offer tryouts to Bill Willis and Marion Motley a few days after the first training camp opened. It forced the NFL's hand, as the senior league anticipated the hiring of black players. The Rams had signed Kenny Washington and Woody Strode, the first black men in the league in 13 years, in the spring prior to the '46 season.

Brown's decision to court players with remaining college eligibility was even more controversial and caused a rift between him and his former employer, Ohio State, which was the main pool of his talent. Brown, however, insisted he only went after players who had no plans of returning to school. "We're not trying to snatch athletes who want to return to college," Brown said. "We are going to run our business aggressively—that means to win."

Such was the case of Lou Groza, who had only one season of college football experience when he joined the Browns. Groza lettered for the Buckeyes as a freshman in 1942 before entering the Army, but played no football during his time in the service. OSU head coach Carroll Widdoes accused Brown of raiding the Buckeyes, although Groza and Jim Daniell, who also had remaining eligibility, had said they would return as students only.

If Groza was a risk for lack of experience, so too was Dante Lavelli, who suffered a season-ending injury in his second year at Ohio State (1942), then joined the Army in 1943 and, like Groza, played no football while a serviceman. But Brown knew a football player when he saw

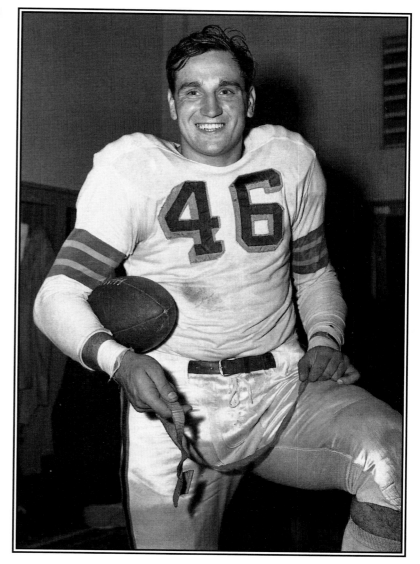

GLAD GROZA: After three years in World War II, Lou Groza was happy to be with the Browns in 1946. But Ohio State coach Carroll Widdoes was unhappy with Paul Brown for signing former Buckeyes such as Groza with eligibility remaining. Here Groza displays the guide tape he used to align his kicking form.

one and Lavelli caught 386 passes over his 11 seasons with 6,488 yards and 62 touchdowns. Lavelli did not start in the first exhibition game of the first AAFC season on Aug. 30, 1946. Nor did Mac Speedie, the left end who would join Lavelli as one of the most prolific receivers in Browns history with 349 combined AAFC-NFL receptions from 1946-52.

Cliff Lewis, a local product (Lakewood) and star at Duke University, was the starting quarterback, as Otto Graham was just joining the Browns after leading the College All-Stars to a

FIRST STARTER: Cliff Lewis, not Otto Graham, was the starting quarterback when the Browns opened the 1946 season by beating the Miami Seahawks, 44-0. Lewis became Graham's backup, but his major contribution was as a defensive back.

16-0 victory over the Rams on Aug. 24. Gene Fekete started at fullback over Marion Motley, who had only been in camp since Aug. 9.

The game was played in the Akron Rubber Bowl against the Brooklyn Dodgers in front of 35,964. The Browns won, 35-20, after overcoming a 13-0 deficit. Fred "Dippy" Evans, a star halfback for Notre Dame's unbeaten 1941 team, scored the first touchdown on a pass from Lewis. Evans also scored on an interception return, while Speedie and George Young caught touchdown passes from Graham. John Rokisky returned a fumble for a TD.

It was the only exhibition game of the inaugural season. One week later the Browns hosted the Miami Seahawks before a crowd that was only about 13,000 below what the Rams drew for four home dates in 1945 and almost double the size of the crowd that saw them beat the Redskins at Cleveland Stadium for the title. The legwork McBride did to drum up interest in the Browns worked far beyond anybody's dreams, as 60,135 witnessed the first-ever regular-season Browns game.

Mac Speedie and Alton Coppage replaced Rokisky and John Yonakor as starting ends. The rest of the first string was a repeat of their exhibition game, with Jim Daniell and Chet Adams at tackles, Bill Willis and Ed Ulinski at guards, Mike Scarry at center, Edgar Jones and Don Greenwood at halfbacks, Gene Fekete at fullback and Cliff Lewis at quarterback.

The game was a sign of things to come in the future. It was simply no contest, just as the AAFC would be for the Browns for four seasons. Speedie scored the first touchdown on a 19-yard pass from Lewis. Graham and Lavelli combined on a TD pass and Tom Colella and Greenwood scored on runs. Ray Terrell added a TD on a 76-yard interception return and Groza kicked three field goals. The final score was Browns 44, Seahawks 0.

Motley started ahead of Fekete at fullback for the second game, played before 51,962 at Soldier Field in Chicago, a record for a professional game there. It was in this one that the Browns may have established themselves as the class of the league. Motley's 122 yards rushing, Greenwood's 41-yard touchdown gallop and a defense that held Elroy "Crazylegs" Hirsch, the Rockets' star halfback, to minus-one yard rushing lifted the Browns to a 20-6 win. The Browns scored another shutout, 28-0, against the Buffalo Bisons, in Week 3, and rolled through the first half of the schedule unbeaten, outscoring opponents by a combined 180-34. Four home games averaged 58,000 fans.

Next, the San Francisco 49ers, behind quarterback Frankie Albert and his favorite target, Alyn Beals, handed the Browns their first loss, 34-20, before 70,385 at Cleveland Stadium. Albert, an All-America at Stanford and a master of the T formation, was surprisingly hot and cold

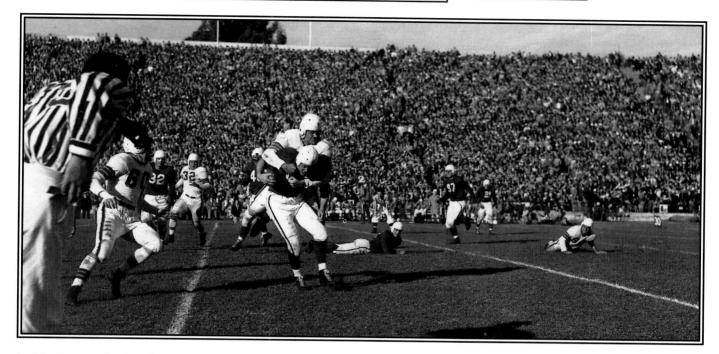

in his first professional season. But he was hot on that Oct. 27 day and so was the defense, as the Browns rushed for just 34 yards. The Los Angeles Dons beat the Browns the following week, 17-16, on a late field goal.

That was it for losing for one season. The Browns avenged the loss to the Niners, 14-7, on Nov. 10, and averaged 48 points a game over the last four contests. They finished the season with a 12-2 record and had outscored their rivals by an average of 30-10.

The championship game was played Dec. 22 against the New York Yankees, who outclassed the Eastern Division via a 10-3-1 record, a seven-game lead over the other three clubs in the circuit. New York was coached by Ray Flaherty, who had coached the Washington Redskins to two NFL titles and a seven-year record of 56-23-3. Flaherty never hid his disdain for Paul Brown. After the Browns whipped the Yankees, 24-7, on Sept. 29, Flaherty verbally attacked his players for losing to a team "from podunk led by a high school coach."

The Yankees were a talented club, especially on defense, where Flaherty assembled two lines that alternated quarters. Bruce Alford, Bruiser Kinard, Derrell Palmer and Perry Schwartz were its top stars. On offense, halfback Spec

Sanders led the league in rushing (709 yards, six TDs). Quarterback Ace Parker was considered the equal of Graham and Albert.

Brown made the most controversial move of his coaching career just as the Browns were preparing for the biggest battle of the campaign. Jim Daniell, a starting tackle and team captain who played for Brown at Ohio State, was involved in an altercation with Cleveland police and charged with public intoxication. Daniell's companions, Mac Speedie and Lou Rymkus, were charged with disorderly conduct. Brown shocked the team and the community by firing Daniell before the next day's practice, while allowing Speedie and Rymkus to stay with the club. Brown insisted he was not playing favorites. Daniell had specifically violated Brown's ironclad rule against drinking during the football season.

"It is up to the players to observe the rules or take the consequences," Brown explained.

FIRST CHAMPIONS: Tired but proud, Otto Graham, Dante Lavelli, Paul Brown and Mac Speedie (l-r) relax after defeating the New York Yankees, 14-9, for the 1946 AAFC championship. The Browns received $931.57 apiece as their winners share, considerably less than the value of a Super Bowl ring in the 1990s.

"Daniell is not being made an example. He's simply getting what's coming to him."

Daniell was later cleared of the intoxication charge, but Brown did not invite him to return. He gave the rights to Daniell to the Chicago Rockets, but Daniell never played another professional football game.

As for the game, Motley, who gained 98 yards on 13 carries, gave the Browns a 7-3 lead on a one-yard touchdown run. The Yankees went up 9-7 as Sanders capped an 80-yard drive with a two-yard TD run. The Browns regained the lead in the fourth quarter and won, 14-9.

The winning drive started at their own 24-yard line. Graham passed to Edgar Jones, who made a diving catch at the Yankees' 42-yard line. Jones took a lateral from Graham and passed to Lavelli to the 28. Lavelli scored the go-ahead TD when he got behind Jack Russell at the seven-yard line, caught Graham's pass and stumbled the rest of the way to the end zone. Graham, who engineered the winning score, sealed the victory when he intercepted a

Parker pass at the Cleveland 30-yard line. The "high school coach" had been vindicated.

"My satisfaction was proving my principles," Brown said afterward, "proving that the same ideals that won in high school and college could win in professional ball."

The Browns had defeated the Yankees three times and even Flaherty conceded, saying the Browns were just as good as the NFL-champion Chicago Bears. It wasn't long before others were copying the Browns' trap plays, on which Motley used his incredible starting speed to get through a hole in the middle of the line and then use his 230 pounds to plow over defenders; and their sideline passing routes that took advantage of the speed and cutting abilities of Speedie and Lavelli, and Graham's knack for reading defenses.

The AAFC was a rousing success in 1946. Only the Miami Seahawks and the Brooklyn Dodgers did not have healthy attendance. The average AAFC game outdrew the average NFL affair by about 1,000. It appeared as if the dream of Arch Ward, to have two leagues operating separately, with a championship game at the end of the campaign, would come true.

But the league was victim of its own success. Salaries, especially for rookies, were escalating beyond some teams' ability to pay. The ongoing raiding of the rival league's rosters only upped the ante. The expense of air travel, something the AAFC did from the beginning, was a huge drain on budgets.

The league was also a victim of the Browns' success. The Browns put up a record of 52-4-3 in the four years of the AAFC's existence. They lost to only two of the seven other teams (Los Angeles and San Francisco each beat the Browns twice). They were the only champion the AAFC ever had. Included in the Browns'

With snowflakes falling at Cleveland Stadium, Don Greenwood attempts to intercept a pass intended for New York's Jack Russell in the 1946 AAFC championship game.

STREAKING: The Browns were undefeated in 1948, including this 34-21 victory over New York on Nov. 21 at Yankee Stadium. At left, Ara Parseghian tackles Spec Sanders while defensive end John Yonakor backs up the play. At right, receiver Horace Gillom goes up to battle a Yankee defender for the ball.

incomparable record were a 16-game regular-season winning streak and a 29-game streak without a loss. The Browns went from Oct. 12, 1947, to Oct. 9, 1949, without a defeat. It included another championship win over New York, 14-3, in 1947, and 14-0 record and 49-7 title-game victory over Buffalo in 1948. And it made the Browns one of only two pro football teams to ever go through a season unbeaten and untied. (The 1972 Dolphins are the other.)

Although Paul Brown's coaching methods were never predictable, the results were, and that led to a lack of fan interest. The Browns were simply too good, so good that attendance was steadily backsliding. The home crowds that had averaged 57,000 in 1946 were 31,000 in '49.

The Browns were a bigger draw away from Cleveland Stadium in the final season of the AAFC, averaging 37,000 on the road (but only 5,000 showed up for the season finale against the Hornets, formerly the Rockets, in Chicago).

Oddly enough, it was the most humiliating defeat the Browns experienced in their AAFC years that resulted in the only decent crowd in Cleveland Stadium in 1949. The Browns had been embarrassed by the 49ers, 56-28, in San Francisco on Oct. 9. It marked the end of their two-year unbeaten streak. It would be 41 seasons before the record for opponents' points in one game would be broken.

Brown, while seemingly unperturbed at the end of the game, boiled over when the team got to its hotel in Los Angeles for the Oct. 14 game versus the Dons. Brown berated his club in no uncertain terms, saying he would break up the team if certain people stopped playing to their abilities. The Dons paid the price: the Browns returned to Cleveland with a 61-14 victory.

PLUNGING AHEAD: Otto Graham (60) watches Edgar Jones plow through for the first TD in the Browns' 49-7 1948 AAFC title-game win over Buffalo at Cleveland Stadium. The victory capped the Browns' undefeated season. Blocking for Jones are Eddie Ulinski (36), Lou Groza (46) and Frank Gatski (22).

There were 72,189 on hand at Cleveland Stadium 16 days later when the 49ers came to town for the second meeting with the Browns that season. Albert passed to Len Eshmont for the first scoring of the contest, but the Browns led, 30-21, when the 49ers scored their final TD with just 15 seconds to go. San Francisco Hall-of-Fame halfback Joe "the Jet" Perry, who had gained 156 yards on 16 attempts on Oct. 9, was held to 28 yards on 10 carries.

The beating the Browns took in the first contest against the Niners might have been a case of overconfidence. They had been down 28-7 to the Bills in the opening game of the season, but rallied in the fourth quarter on three Graham TD passes, one to Horace Gillom and two to Mac Speedie, to escape with a 28-28 tie.

The remainder of the season became anticlimactic, even though the Browns and 49ers would meet again in Cleveland for the AAFC title. A mere 16,506 attended the Nov. 6 game against Chicago, a record low for a Browns

game in Cleveland. Only 22,550 fans paid to attend the 1949 championship game, a 21-7 Browns victory on Dec 11.

Mickey McBride was determined to see the AAFC survive. The Browns were profitable and McBride offered financial help to the struggling franchises. It was really to no avail. Most teams in both leagues were in the red as the bidding war for talent escalated. There also were rumors that Paul Brown would accept a college coaching position. After he signed a new seven-year contract on Jan. 1, 1949, those rumors were quashed.

But the Browns-49ers rivalry was fierce. Their matchups drew an average of 64,164. No NFL teams could make that claim. It wasn't

WINNING GAMES, LOSING APPEAL: Empty seats are the backdrop as Dub Jones runs into two Brooklyn-New York Yankees defenders in a 14-3 victory at Cleveland Stadium in 1949. The Browns' domination of the AAFC saw fan interest drop dramatically as the league headed toward extinction.

lost on the NFL. When merger talks were held in Chicago in January of 1949, the senior league agreed to take Cleveland and San Francisco, and let the other AAFC franchises fall by the wayside. McBride rebelled. He was not willing to see his new friends "thrown to the vultures" as he put it.

McBride had become close to Ben Lindheimer of the Dons and Jim Breuil of the Bills in particular, and balked at the idea that five of the seven AAFC teams should simply fold their tents. But the handwriting was on the wall. As long as the Cleveland Browns continued to remain unchallenged for supremacy, things could only get worse for the league.

It was clear the Browns needed a new challenge. Brown, as always, anticipated it would come. Two days before the Browns defeated the 49ers, the leagues announced an end to the war. The National Football League would admit the

Browns, the 49ers and the Baltimore Colts. The remaining players from the four defunct teams would be put in a pool from which all other NFL clubs could choose.

Brown and McBride made sure the truce wasn't a victory for the NFL. The two demanded the AAFC receive fair treatment, or the NFL could do without the Browns. Bert Bell was on the Browns' side and stated the Browns should be treated as members of the NFL, not losers in a war. No doubt, Bell saw the Browns' entry into the older league as a great drawing card. "[The] merger is a victory for the public," Bell said, "and we'll treat it that way."

Brown insisted his club be put in a division with other eastern teams and fully expected to see the Browns take on the Philadelphia Eagles, the two-time defending NFL champion, in their first game in their new league.

There was nothing more for the Browns to prove except whether they could compete in the NFL, which was considered by most to be where the superior talent lay. Despite what the Browns and the entire AAFC had accomplished, there was still a prevailing attitude among a few that any NFL team could beat any AAFC team, and that the Browns were no exception. Many believed they'd get their comeuppance against the big-leaguers.

END OF THE LINE: The bench was full, but the stands were not when the Browns beat Buffalo (top) in a December 1949 playoff game at Cleveland Stadium. Only 17,270 showed up, the Browns' second smallest home crowd in their four-year AAFC existence. A week later (above), Paul Brown rides Edgar Jones' shoulders as he and his players celebrate their final AAFC title, a 21-7 victory over the San Francisco 49ers.

Making Believers of the NFL

Earle "Greasy" Neale might have been the only one with a right to scoff at the Cleveland Browns and the All-America Football Conference, and he did so, right after his Philadelphia Eagles won the National Football League championship on Dec. 18, 1949. "[The Browns] are a basketball team," Neale told a reporter after declaring there was no one left to challenge his Eagles. "All they do is throw the ball." Neale had taken note of the Browns' pass-oriented offense featuring Otto Graham throwing to Dante Lavelli, Mac Speedie and Dub Jones. But maybe no one could fault Neale for his cockiness. Philadelphia had shut out the Los Angeles Rams, the finest passing team the NFL could offer, 14-0. The Eagles gained 343 yards to the Rams' 119 and held Los Angeles quarterback Bob Waterfield to only 10-of-28 passing with two interceptions.

Philadelphia could do a little passing itself. Quarterback Tommy Thompson completed 54 percent of his throws that year with 16 touchdowns and only 11 interceptions. He'd had a couple of great receivers with whom to work in Pete Pihos and Jack Ferrante. But it was Steve Van Buren, the NFL's leading rusher four of the previous five seasons, who made Philadelphia what it was. He continued to prove it in the title game with 196 yards on 31 carries on a rain-drenched Los Angeles Coliseum field.

To the surprise of almost no one, least of all Paul Brown, the first game of the 1950 season would pit the two champions—Saturday, Sept. 16 in Philadelphia.

Rumors were Neale was secretly worried about the Browns' passing game. The Browns had sailed unbeaten through five exhibition games against their new NFL opponents, averaging 35 points a game. Mort Berry, a sports reporter for the *Philadelphia Inquirer*, was sent to follow the Browns throughout the preseason. He spoke in glowing terms of Cleveland's

talent, but most dismissed his assertions as nothing more than an attempt to spur on ticket sales for the upcoming opener. If the Eagles' coach was indeed worried about the champions of the All-America Football Conference, it wasn't enough to make him scout them. Scouting was considered unnecessary in the NFL of the 1940s. The teams all played each other, twice a year in most cases, and were usually familiar with the opponents' various offensive and defensive tendencies.

But the Browns had never played a game in the NFL. While everyone expected the Clevelanders to get a strong lesson in reality from the Eagles, Paul Brown was busy making sure they wouldn't. When the Eagles and Rams were sloshing through the mud in the 1949 title game, Browns assistant coaches Fritz Heisler and Blanton Collier were somewhere in the crowd, taking note of every nuance of these division champions. The Browns had film of the Eagles and had nine months to study the club they knew they would play in Game No. 1.

READY TO GO: The Browns' offense lines up in Philadelphia's Municipal Stadium, site of the Army-Navy game, prior to the 1950 opener versus the Eagles. Standing in the backfield are (left to right): HB Dub Jones, FB Marion Motley, QB Otto Graham and HB Rex Bumgardner. On the line are RE Dante Lavelli, RT Lou Rymkus, RG Lin Houston, C Frank Gatski, LG Weldon Humble, LT Lou Groza and LE Mac Speedie.

Neale's pride and joy was the defense he had invented, an alignment of five linemen, four defensive backs and two linebackers who made contact with the receivers just beyond the line of scrimmage. Almost every other team copied it to the point it became known as the "Eagle" defense. Brown, however, saw serious flaws in the fact the defense had no middle linebacker. The Eagles stopped the run by clogging the line of scrimmage while the outside men swooped onto the quarterback.

Brown and his staff decided that if their offensive linemen could be spaced farther apart on the line of scrimmage, the Eagles' defenders would follow them when they moved out. The defense would, unwittingly, open wide holes for the Browns' ball carriers, Marion Motley, Dub Jones and Rex Bumgardner.

Such a plan was all well and good, provided a team had the talent on a par with the Eagles. Brown made sure the Browns did, and secured some much-needed players for the 1950 season. There were holes to fill when three key members of the club that dominated the AAFC—halfback Edgar "Special Delivery" Jones, linebacker Lou Saban and guard Ed Ulinski—retired after the 1949 campaign. Brown also decided that the play of John Yonakor, a starting defensive end since 1946, had deteriorated and traded him to the NFL's New York Yanks.

Another deal with the Buffalo Bills brought the Browns three players exempt from the AAFC draft pool: halfback Rex Bumgardner, defensive tackle John Kissell and guard Abe Gibron. Bumgardner offset the loss of Jones and Gibron replaced Ulinski. To take Yonakor's position, the Browns acquired Len Ford, who had been with the Los Angeles Dons since '48, in the pool. Ford went on to become All-Pro four times, one of the best defensive ends ever and a Pro Football Hall of Famer.

As well as the Browns did in the off-season before their maiden trip through the NFL, the conference-rival New York Giants did even better. In a deal with the Brooklyn-New York Yankees, the Giants took four players, all defensive starters, for head coach Steve Owen's Umbrella Defense. The Giants were the only team to consistently give Paul Brown's offense trouble in Cleveland's early years in the NFL.

That was because the core of the Browns' point-scoring machine was still around from Day One. Eight offensive starters on the 1950 team had been at the Browns' first training camp in '46. Quarterback Otto Graham, fullback Marion Motley, ends Mac Speedie and Dante Lavelli, center Frank Gatski, tackles Lou Groza and Lou Rymkus and guard Lin Houston were original Browns, as were three defensive stars—end George Young, middle guard Bill Willis and safety Cliff Lewis.

A new offensive standout had joined the Browns in 1948. Dub Jones had been with the AAFC's Brooklyn Dodgers, where he was a star in the defensive backfield. Brown was willing to trade the draft rights to Michigan's All-America halfback, Bob Chappuis, to acquire Jones to bolster the Browns' secondary.

It became apparent, however, that Jones' strength was as a running back and receiver. At 6-foot-4, he was, obviously, much larger than defensive backs who tried to cover him. Paul Brown would one day refer to him as the team's best all-around offensive player.

Jones started slowly in Cleveland. He had only nine catches and 33 carries in 1948. That increased to 12 receptions and 77 carries in 1949. In the Browns' first season in the NFL, Jones blossomed—83 carries, 31 catches and a team-leading 11 touchdowns.

The Browns roared through their five 1950 preseason games, winning them all, with only the Chicago Bears giving them any trouble. That, perhaps, made the regular-season opening that much more of a draw, and 71,237 piled into Philadelphia's Municipal Stadium to see the four-time champions of a "Humpty Dumpty" league get a lesson from the two-time kings of the real professional league.

"We've been taunted and disparaged for playing in an inferior league" Brown told his

FORWARD PROGRESS: Otto Graham dives goal-ward during a 20-14 victory over the Redskins on Nov. 20, 1950. It was the Browns' fourth straight win en route to six straight to close out the regular season. Also pictured are guard Weldon Humble (38), center Frank Gatski (22) and receiver Mac Speedie (58).

team before its first preseason game, against Green Bay in Toledo. "There's not only this season at stake, but four years of achievement. I'm asking you to dedicate yourselves to preserving the reputation the Browns have made."

The Browns gained a new reputation on that humid Saturday night in Philadelphia. They pummeled the Eagles, 35-10. Granted, the Eagles were without fullback Steve Van Buren and starting halfback Bosh Pritchard, but the famed "Eagle Defense" couldn't handle the Browns' halfback-in-motion offense and was left vulnerable to the speed of Cleveland's receivers in one-on-one coverage.

Graham tossed touchdown passes 59, 26 and 12 yards to Jones, Lavelli and Speedie, respectively. Graham and Bumgardner each scored on one-yard runs in the fourth quarter. Kicking for an injured Lou Groza, Chubby Grigg successfully converted all five PAT attempts.

THE PERFECT TOE: Lou Groza kicks a field goal to put the Browns in front, 3-0, in the 1950 playoff game against the New York Giants. Sneaker-clad tackle Forrest "Chubby" Grigg (48) loses his helmet on the frozen field at Cleveland Stadium.

The Eagles were not a power that year. After posting a 31-8-1 mark over the previous three seasons and winning NFL championships in 1948 and '49, Philadelphia slipped to 6-6 in 1950. The Giants were the only team owning a winning record the Browns would play that year and the New Yorkers defeated them two times. It wouldn't be until post-season action that the Browns would finally make believers of almost everyone.

The Giants had won 6-0 in Cleveland and 17-13 in New York. The first meeting spoiled the Browns' home opener and NFL debut in the Stadium. New York's umbrella defense permitted the ends in a six-man front to drop back and cover receivers, thus allowing seven men (two ends, a middle linebacker and four defensive backs) to defend against the pass.

Graham & Co. was stifled in the first half of the first game against the Giants but moved the

ball at times in the second half. It simply could not get the ball in the end zone against Owen's umbrella. They got to the New York 10-yard line during one series, but Graham and Motley collided on a hand-off attempt, fumbled and the Giants then recovered. The Browns were shut out for the first time in their existence, and would not suffer another for 22 years.

Perhaps the Giants prepared for the Browns at the expense of other duties. They followed their victories over Cleveland with losses to decidedly inferior clubs, the Steelers and Cardinals. But both the Giants and Browns rolled through the second half of the season undefeated, creating a tie for the American Conference title, each with 10-2 records.

The conference title game was played at Cleveland Stadium in 10-degree weather, with a wind-chill factor well below zero. The Browns wore rubber-soled shoes except for Groza, who wore a rubber-soled shoe on his left foot and a football shoe with cleats removed on his right kicking foot. The idea worked. Groza kicked a field goal in the first half and another one with 58 seconds left to snap a 3-3 tie.

The hero of the game, however, was Bill Willis. The star middle guard chased down Gene "Choo Choo" Roberts, who had broken off the line of scrimmage and into the clear 47 yards from the Browns' goal line in the fourth period. Willis made up 20 yards and caught Roberts from behind at the Cleveland four-yard stripe. The defense held and the Giants were denied what probably would have been the game-winning TD. A safety made the final score 8-3, Cleveland.

The 1950 NFL Championship game might have marked the beginning of an era in pro football history. The league's most sophisticated passing teams, the Browns and the Los Angeles Rams, were to meet in the title game. Like the Browns, the Rams had finished in a tie in their conference and beat a team in a playoff, the Chicago Bears, that had defeated them twice in the regular season. The game would mark the first time the Rams would play in Cleveland Stadium since they beat the Wash-

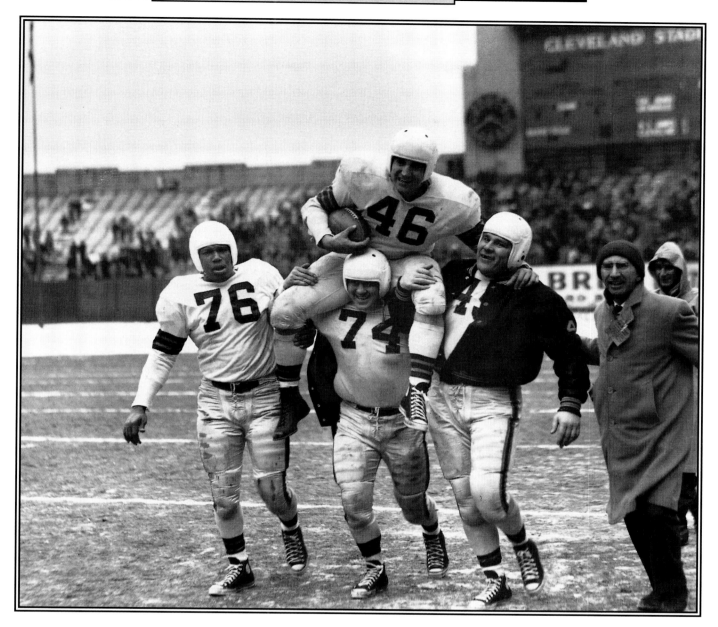

UNMATCHED SUCCESS: Wearing a football shoe on his right kicking foot and a sneaker on his left, Lou Groza is carried off the Cleveland Stadium field after booting two field goals to beat the Giants in the 1950 playoff game. His escorts are (l-r) Marion Motley, Tony Adamle and John Kissell.

ington Redskins for the title in 1945, before abandoning Cleveland for the West Coast.

The Rams' offense could certainly match the Browns' attack, and do it with more people. Los Angeles had two outstanding quarterbacks, Bob Waterfield and young Norm Van Brocklin. They could match the Browns' Jones, Speedie and Lavelli with Tom Fears, Elroy "Crazylegs" Hirsch, V.T. Smith and Glenn Davis.

The Rams' running game was powered by Dick Hoerner, Paul "Tank" Younger and Dan Towler. Logically, the experts predicted a high-scoring game and they were right. Graham and

Waterfield combined for 64 passes, 40 completions and five touchdown passes (four by Graham). The Browns won it in the last minute, 30-28, on a 16-yard field goal by Groza.

Paul Brown, although he never used such language, figuratively told the NFL what it could do with its superior-league theory in

31

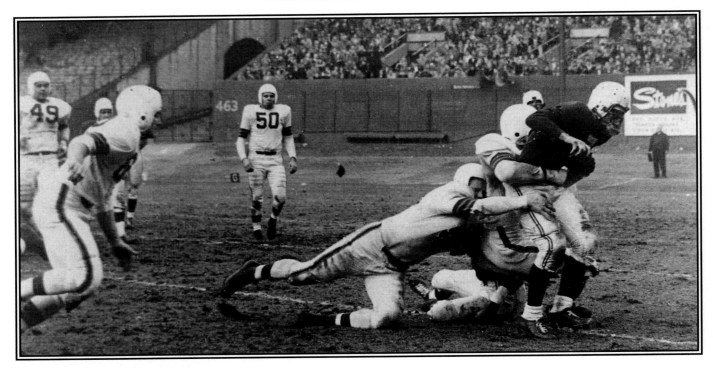

CAPTURED CARDINAL: Running back Elmer Angsman is tackled by Tommy Thompson and Bill Willis at Cleveland Stadium in December 1951. Chicago scored 28 points that afternoon, the most by a regular-season opponent in the Browns' brief NFL history. The Browns prevailed, 49-28, part of an 11-game winning streak after an opening-game loss to the 49ers.

1950. It would be hard to figure, then, why Brown would have considered any other job after becoming master of all he surveyed.

Whether he actually considered leaving the Browns is still unknown. Brown himself was typically close-mouthed about whether he'd said he wanted another job. Nevertheless, he was asked by the University of Southern California and interviewed by his former employer, Ohio State, for their head coaching positions.

Brown turned down the USC job, citing the fact he couldn't share in the profits the way he could as a professional coach. As far as Ohio State was concerned, however, a strong "Bring Back Brown" movement was said to have raised a huge sum for a signing bonus.

But Brown still had his enemies at OSU. He told Gordon Cobbledick, *Plain Dealer* sports editor, that he didn't ask nor was he offered a job at the interview he had in the winter of 1951

and that he knew many people at Ohio State still held a grudge against him for taking Lou Groza and Dante Lavelli to the AAFC when they still had college eligibility remaining.

In any event, the OSU Athletic Board recommended Miami University coach Woody Hayes for the position. A fight was expected to ensue among the board of trustees for the final hiring of a coach, but the trustees followed the athletic board's recommendation and offered the job to Hayes.

Things worked out for the best. Hayes held the OSU post until 1978, becoming one of the winningest coaches in college football history. Brown won six more conference titles and two league crowns over the next 12 seasons.

Brown came up with two more innovations in his first few years of coaching in the NFL. Although he had used a messenger guard for bringing in plays in the AAFC days, he began to go to it far more often in 1951 and beyond. Otto Graham was not always happy about it, and often failed to use Brown's messengered plays because he believed the players on the field knew best what to do. Still, it was merely a case of agreeing to disagree between coach and quarterback—not any raging controversy.

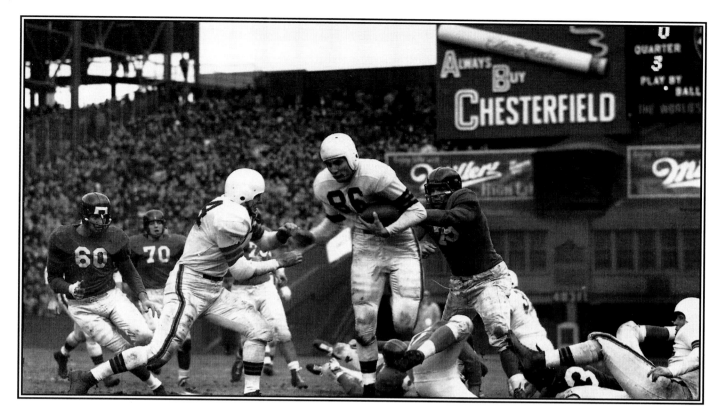

The other innovation was to put a thin plastic bar across the helmet to protect a player's mouth, a forerunner of the face mask now worn by all NFL players. The idea came courtesy of 49ers rookie middle guard Art Michalik, who severely cut Graham's mouth on a hit out of bounds during a 1953 game in Cleveland, won by the Browns, 23-21.

Everything else remained the same. Brown still worked his players hard in training camp, but kept practices light between regular-season games. There was still plenty of classroom work, and rookies who couldn't follow Brown's system were not kept around no matter how highly touted they were coming out of college.

The Browns lost to the 49ers in the 1951 season opener, then rolled over 11 straight foes en route to an 11-1 record, and another American Conference title. Cleveland's defense was outstanding, with linebacker Tony Adamle, middle guard Bill Willis and end Len Ford getting Pro Bowl nods. The secondary featured future Pro Bowlers Warren Lahr and Tommy James at cornerback and veteran Cliff Lewis alternating with a rookie named Don Shula at safety.

The opponent for the NFL Championship game was again the Rams, a team the Browns whipped 38-23 in Game 2 of the regular season. Things wouldn't go so well the second time around. Norm Van Brocklin, who had hardly played in the 1950 title game, connected with Tom Fears on a 73-yard touchdown reception to break a 17-17 tie and give the Rams a 24-17 win at Los Angeles Coliseum.

Although the Van Brocklin-to-Fears pass embarrassed the defense, a pair of rookies—Andy Robustelli and Norb Hecker—did the same to the Browns' offense. Robustelli, an end who would go on to a Hall-of-Fame career, beat Marion Motley on a rush and scooped up a fumble caused when Larry Brink sacked Graham. Robustelli fumbled himself, but the ball somehow fell back in his arms as he was going down at the Browns' two-yard line.

Hecker, a Cleveland native and an alumnus of Baldwin-Wallace College (in Berea, Ohio, where the Browns now have their headquar-

NEW FACES OF THE FIFTIES: Rebuilding an aging roster, Paul Brown found fiercely-competitive new talent as shown here. Top: Chick Jagade saw time at fullback as Marion Motley's knees gave out. Left: Halfback-receiver Ray Renfro succeeded Dub Jones. Right: Ken Konz joined as a defensive back and punter.

ters) put the nail in the Browns' coffin by sniffing out a screen pass intended for Dub Jones on Cleveland's final drive and smacking Jones two yards behind the line of scrimmage.

It was Paul Brown's first loss in a championship game. It was the first year since 1944 that the city of Cleveland could not boast of a pro football champion.

Cleveland won another American Conference championship in 1952, but without the same smooth-running engine. Graham had his poorest year and several players (Jones, Lavelli, Speedie, Motley) were suffering injuries. On defense, tackle Chubby Grigg had moved on to the Dallas Texans and safety Cliff Lewis had retired. They were replaced by rookies Bob Gain and Bert Rechichar respectively.

The Browns were 8-3 and one game ahead of the Eagles going into the last game of the season, against the Giants. New York won, but the Browns caught a break when the Washington Redskins upset the Eagles to give Cleveland another conference title.

But the Browns did not redeem themselves for a lackluster season in the 1952 title game. The newest NFL powerhouse, the Detroit Lions, had just beaten the Rams in a playoff for the National Conference crown.

Detroit's offense was led by Hall-of-Fame quarterback Bobby Layne, who was definitely not Paul Brown's kind of guy. Layne was well known as a braggart and as one who enjoyed the nightlife. He demanded the respect of his teammates as much as he earned it. He bullied anyone he thought was not putting out 100 percent to the point where many considered him to be more of a coach than the real head coach, Buddy Parker.

Two critical Cleveland fumbles led to two Detroit touchdowns. The Browns were on the Lions' two-yard line with a first down and a chance to tie the score at 14-14, but a five-yard loss, a 12-yard sack and a one-yard gain killed the drive. The final score at Cleveland Stadium was Lions 17, Browns 7.

It was clear by the end of the 1952 campaign that Mickey McBride was tiring of owning a

OTTO'S INJURY: Otto Graham rolls right before being knocked out of bounds versus the 49ers in November 1953. A late elbow hit in the mouth by middle guard Art Michalik forced Graham from the game. He returned in the second half with 15 stitches and a Paul Brown-invented plastic face bar on his helmet, a forerunner of today's high-tech face masks.

pro football team. He sold the club to a syndicate headed by longtime steel magnate David Jones, former Cleveland Indians president Ellis Ryan, Randall Park Raceway owner Saul Silberman and Homer Marshman, who had founded the Cleveland Rams in 1937. The selling price was a record $600,000.

"I never made anything (from owning the Browns)," McBride said, "but I didn't lose anything either, except maybe a few thousand dollars. I've simply had my fling at pro football and convinced myself Cleveland will always buy the best. Now I'm getting out. I have a few other things to keep me busy."

LAST ORIGINALS: Paul Brown poses in 1953 training camp with seven of the eight players remaining on the Browns' roster from his first team in 1946. From left to right are Dante Lavelli, Bill Willis, Marion Motley, Frank Gatski, Otto Graham, Lou Groza and George Young. (Not pictured: Lin Houston.)

McBride wasn't the only man to walk away from the Browns after the 1952 season. Mac Speedie, the club's all-time leading receiver at the time and the man who led the AAFC in receptions three times and the NFL once, signed with a Canadian Football League team. Defensive tackle John Kissell also went to the CFL, but rejoined the Browns in 1954. None of these changes seemed to have any effect on the club. Rumors the Browns were slipping in 1953 were quashed as the team won its first 11 games and was set to become the first in the NFL since the 1942 Chicago Bears to sail through a regular season unbeaten and first ever to win every game of the year.

It didn't happen. On the last weekend of the season, a Browns defense that hadn't allowed more than 21 points in a game suddenly caved in to the Eagles in a 42-27 loss. The championship battle, again versus Detroit, was closer, but no better. Jim Doran caught a 33-yard touchdown pass from a scrambling Bobby Layne with two minutes to go to give the Lions a 17-16 victory in Detroit.

It was Doran's only touchdown of the year. Doran, a starting defensive end, came in to play offense because star receiver Leon Hart suffered a twisted knee in the first period. It was Paul Brown's third straight championship loss. Although Brown was bitter after the defeat, the '53 season was perhaps a vindication of his system. Many of the original Browns—Speedie, Cliff Lewis, George Young, Lin Houston, Lou Rymkus—were either gone or relegated to backup roles. But Brown knew talent and was able to rebuild while still contending. In place of the originals came Bob Gain, Don Colo, Walter Michaels, Doug Atkins, Ken Gorgal, Ken Konz, John Sandusky, Ray Renfro and others.

Marion Motley, slowed by injuries and age, finally had to share fullback duties with Harry "Chick" Jagade. Motley played his last game for the Browns in '53. He sat out 1954 and came back with the Steelers as a linebacker in 1955 after being traded for fullback Ed Modzelewski.

Also retiring after the 1953 season were Dub Jones, Bill Willis, guard Lin Houston, linebacker Tommy Thompson and defensive tackle Derrell Palmer. Jones would later un-retire.

Prior to the 1953 season, Brown had made the biggest trade in NFL history, a 15-player deal with the Baltimore Colts. The Browns sent 10 men to the Colts, including starting defensive backs Bert Rechichar and Don Shula, in

OVER AND OUT: Otto Graham scores the final touchdown of his 10-year career on a one-yard run in the third quarter of Cleveland's 38-14 victory over the Rams in the 1955 NFL title game. Graham retired again, but this time it was permanent.

exchange for five players, three of whom were serving in the military. Defensive tackle Don Colo and middle guard Mike McCormack were the key pickups for the Browns. After one season as the successor to Bill Willis, McCormack moved to right offensive tackle in 1955 where he remained through 1962.

The Browns were back in the NFL championship game in 1954 with a 9-3 record, despite having given up 55 points in a loss to the otherwise mediocre Steelers. For the third year in a row they would meet the Lions, who had defeated Cleveland 14-10 on the last weekend of the season, on another Layne-to-Doran pass.

This time was much different. The Browns slaughtered the Detroiters, 56-10, before 43,827 at Cleveland Stadium. Graham, who had completed only two of 15 passes in the 1953 title game, was 9-of-12 with three touchdown passes and three TD runs in the avalanche.

A 9-2-1 record in 1955 got the Browns to the championship game an unprecedented sixth straight season. They had little trouble beating the Rams, 38-14, at the Los Angeles Coliseum for their third NFL crown.

Graham, who had tried to retire after the '54 campaign only to be coaxed back by Brown, called it quits for good after the '55 title game. The retirement signaled the end of an era that may never be equaled. With a 31-team league now it would be nearly impossible for any team to win seven championships in 10 seasons.

Unquestionably, the Browns were the team of the 1950s just as the Packers, Steelers and 49ers were the teams of the '60s, '70s and '80s, respectively. And like Bart Starr with Green Bay, Terry Bradshaw with Pittsburgh and Joe Montana with San Francisco, Otto Graham was the on-field symbol of a football dynasty.

Paul Brown, with his snap-brim fedora and camel hair coat, was as familiar a sight on the sidelines as the Packers' Vince Lombardi with his dark-rimmed glasses, the Steelers' Chuck Noll with his square jaw and the 49ers' Bill Walsh with his white hair and sweaters.

A Team & Times in Transition

The retirement of Otto Graham was the symbolic end of the "dynasty" years of the Cleveland Browns franchise. For the next seven seasons, the Browns would bear little resemblance to their predecessors. Perennial contenders, yes, but no longer were they the dominant team of the NFL, or even the Eastern Conference—the New York Giants assumed that role. Everything changed. Instead of Graham, there was Ratterman, then O'Connell, then Plum, then Ninowski, then Ryan. By 1956, the familiar names of the '40s and early '50s were retired or nearly so. Although Paul Brown did a skillful job of rebuilding, the new talent did not respond as well to his old ways. That, combined with the lack of championships, helped lead to Brown's dismissal. By 1963, the changes included a new coach, a new owner and a new symbol of greatness: Jim Brown.

The arrival of Brown in 1957 coincided with the emergence of professional football as a television sport. After baseball's Giants and Dodgers left New York for the West Coast after the '57 season, the New York media focused attention on the football Giants, NFL champs in 1956 and loaded with quality talent. The major exposure given the Giants, their famed overtime battle with the Baltimore Colts in the 1958 championship game and their revitalized rivalry with the Browns, helped spark new interest in the NFL with television viewers nationwide. Brown provided a perfect show for television. His moves, his style, his wide sweeps around end, his long runs, his tackle-breaking power—they exemplified NFL football at its entertaining and professional best.

While Brown was the one constant in the 1956-62 era, the rest of the roster was in transition. By Brown's first season, the Browns were in the second year of an ongoing search for Otto Graham's successor. The process had begun in 1954 when Paul Brown traded Bob Gar-

rett, a quarterback from Stanford and the Browns' bonus selection in the draft, to Green Bay for veteran quarterback Vito "Babe" Parilli, whom he expected would be the Browns' No. 1 quarterback for the 1956 season. Parilli had two years of solid

NFL experience, having split time with Tobin Rote with the Packers in 1952-53. George Ratterman had scant experience as Graham's backup. But Parilli had real trouble learning Brown's system and Ratterman, who had four years of bench time to pick it up, was ahead of Parilli and became the starter.

Brown, ever the innovator, brought to the game a new technological device—a citizen's band radio, set in Ratterman's helmet, with an FCC-assigned frequency between Brown and his quarterback for the purpose of feeding Ratterman the plays. The system, developed by Cleveland resident George Sarles in his basement, worked OK, but the Browns lost 31-14 to the Lions on its maiden voyage. The whole thing finally blew up.

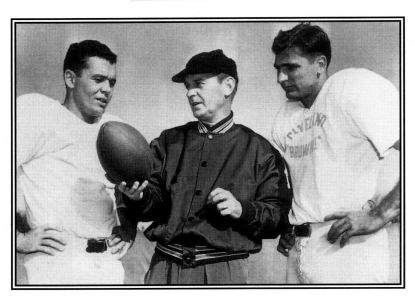

A QUARTERBACK CARROUSEL: George Ratterman (right photo) began the 1956 season as Otto Graham's successor, but his career ended on a knee injury in Game 4. It left Paul Brown (above) to work with Tommy O'Connell (left) and Babe Parilli.

The Cardinals, who beat the Browns in the season opener, claimed to have had their own electronic play-calling system via a wire buried just below the ground surrounding the sidelines, whose signal was picked up by hearing aids worn by the team captains.

The Giants claimed they were intercepting the Browns' signals with a receiver on their bench and knew what the Browns would do on every play (a violation of FCC signal-stealing law). The Giants later admitted they planted the story about signal stealing just to ridicule the whole idea of electronic communication between coach and quarterback.

Whatever, the Browns abandoned that system and commissioner Bert Bell declared all electronic devices in helmets illegal. But the '56 season was just as disastrous. Brown had only his second losing campaign in 27 years of

coaching as the Browns finished 5-7. A victory over the eventual NFL-champion Giants was the lone bright spot.

Ratterman suffered a career-ending knee injury in the fourth game. Brown was down to one quarterback. He found another in a man cast off by the Bears, Tommy O'Connell.

Like the quarterback position, the entire offense was in transition. The line was solid, but aging with veterans Frank Gatski, Abe Gibron, Mike McCormack and Lou Groza still in position. Pete Brewster and Ray Renfro were quality receivers, but Dante Lavelli was at the end of his Hall-of-Fame career.

Rookie Preston Carpenter led the team in rushing as part of a backfield that featured a wide variety of performers: Maurice Bassett, Ed Modzelewski and Fred "Curly" Morrison. The club that had scored 349 points in 1955 scored half that many in '56. The Browns needed help.

Enter Jim Brown.

If a case could be made for a greatest athlete of all time, Jim Brown would be an excellent candidate. In his senior year at Manhassett,

TRANSITION TALENT: Entering the mid 1950s, Lou Groza (76) was one of the solid, but aging, veterans remaining on the offensive line. Maurice Bassett (30) was one of a variety of backfield performers in the post-Motley, pre-Brown period.

N.Y., High School, Brown averaged 14.9 yards per carry on the football team and 38 points a game on the basketball squad.

At Syracuse University, he was a member of the varsity football, basketball, lacrosse and track teams. In that latter sport he finished 10th in a national AAU meet, despite not having the time to train due to his other athletic endeavors. It's highly likely that had he dedicated himself to the decathlon, Brown would have posed a serious challenge to Olympian Rafer Johnson at that meet.

On the recreational side, Brown consistently shot in the low 80s on the golf course, bowled games of 200 or better and earned the rank of marksman on the rifle range. He was offered a chance to become a professional boxer and was invited to a tryout with the Cleveland Indians.

But Paul Brown wasn't looking for a new fullback when the draft rolled around. Quarterback was the Browns' primary concern after the 1956 season and there were a number of good ones available in the draft. Unfortunately, other teams were shopping for them, too.

The Packers chose Paul Hornung, the Heisman Trophy winner from Notre Dame. San Francisco took a local product, Stanford's John Brodie. The Browns figured they'd take Len Dawson of Purdue, a local kid of their own from Alliance, Ohio. But a flip of the coin to determine if the Browns or the Steelers would get the fifth draft choice didn't go Cleveland's way, and Pittsburgh selected Dawson. The Browns had to "settle" for Jim Brown.

Brown gained 942 yards (78.5 per game) on 202 carries (16.8 per game) with nine touchdowns as a rookie in 1957. He gained 89 yards in his NFL debut against the Giants and had a league-record 237 against the Rams in Game 9.

More importantly, the Browns won the Eastern Conference at 9-2-1 and beat the previous year's champions, the Giants, twice. It may have been Paul Brown's best coaching job. He

MAULED BY LIONS: Tommy O'Connell's injured ankle and Milt Plum's pulled hamstring put the Browns in a quarterback crisis for the 1957 title game. Detroit overpowered the Browns, 59-14. Plum (16), played in the second half of what would be Paul Brown's final championship game as a pro football coach.

did it without Otto Graham. Only offensive tackle Lou Groza remained from the 1946 original Browns. Only Groza, defensive end Len Ford and defensive back Warren Lahr were starters from the 1950 NFL champions.

The title game was another matter. The Lions, who rallied from a 27-7 halftime deficit to beat the 49ers in a playoff for the Western Conference crown, were peaking. The Browns,

on the other hand, had lost Tommy O'Connell to a broken ankle in Game 10 and saw his back-up, rookie Milt Plum, pull a hamstring in practice during game week. Although both played against the Lions, neither was effective and Detroit rolled to a 59-14 victory.

The Lions were without Bobby Layne, but had an adequate backup in former Packers starter Tobin Rote. They also had Frank Gatski, one of the original Browns, starting at center on an outstanding offensive line.

That game would be the last NFL title contest in which Paul Brown would coach. The 1958 team finished 9-3 and tied with the Giants for first place. The Browns had lost to

New York in the final regular-season contest on a last-minute field goal by Pat Summerall, then were beaten again by the Giants, 10-0, in the playoff game.

Paul Brown would never lead the Browns to first place again. He did finish first two more times as head coach of the Cincinnati Bengals in the 1970s, but the Browns finished second in 1959 and '60 and third in 1961 and '62.

ton, wide receiver Gary Collins, offensive tackle Dick Schafrath, guards Gene Hickerson and John Wooten and defensive back Ross Fichtner were all Paul Brown's draft selections.

But it was Jim Brown in those years who made the Browns a glamour team. In fact, it was Brown and the 1958 Giants-Colts championship contest (alias "The Greatest Game Ever Played") that did more to make the league so

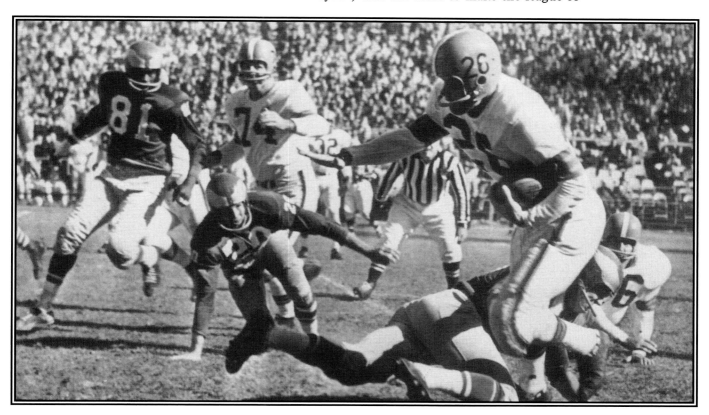

The Browns certainly were not without top talent in the years 1956-62. Jim Brown made the Pro Bowl every year in his nine-year career. Offensive tackle Mike McCormack, defensive tackle Bob Gain and guard Jim Ray Smith made it five times each. Walter Michaels was a four-time Pro Bowler. Cornerback Don Paul made it three times. Quarterback Milt Plum, linebacker Galen Fiss and receiver Ray Renfro were chosen twice.

The transition years also saw the drafting of the players who would lead the Browns back to glory in the mid '60s. Middle linebacker Vince Costello, cornerback Bernie Parrish, defensive end Paul Wiggin, outside linebacker Jim Hous-

RELIABLE: Ray Renfro (26) provided veteran stability during the influx of new players from 1956-62. He gained most of his 5,508 receiving yards during those years, retiring after the '63 season. His total is second only to Ozzie Newsome's 7,980.

attractive to television. Brown led the league in rushing in all but one of his nine seasons. He retired as the all-time touchdown leader with 126, a record that stood for 29 years until Jerry Rice of the 49ers broke it in 1994.

The Browns' principal rival in the years 1956-62 was the New York Giants, and the battles between Jim Brown and Sam Huff, the Giants' outspoken middle linebacker, became media events within the games.

CONFRONTATION: The Jim Brown-Sam Huff battles provided visual imagery made for pro football's rise to popularity on television. Huff is the winner on this play from a 1961 Giants victory at Yankee Stadium. Jim Ray Smith (64), Milt Plum (16), Bobby Mitchell (49) and Mike McCormack (74), plus New York's Rosey Grier (76) get a close-up view.

Huff was a folksy West Virginian who had joined the Giants in 1956 and started at middle linebacker that season. In 1960, a TV documentary entitled "The Violent World of Sam Huff," a brutal, profanity-laced program in which Huff was wired for sound, helped glamorize the game by showing it at its most unglamorous. There were no gallant open-field touchdown runs or cheerleaders mobbing a quarterback— just players with dirt and grass stains all over

themselves slugging it out. Naturally, the Huff-Brown wars were the highlight of the program.

In truth, Brown won the majority of those battles. The subsequent years have shown Huff to be a good linebacker, but not in the class with the top men at that position such as the Lions' Joe Schmidt or the Bears' Bill George.

But the games often went to the Giants. New York possessed a team of stars led by two Pro Bowl quarterbacks, Charlie Conerly and Y.A. Tittle. They threw to Del Shofner, Kyle Rote and Bob Schnelker; and handed off to Frank Gifford, Mel Triplett and Alex Webster. Blocking for them were Rosey Brown, Jack Stroud, Ray Wietecha and Darrell Dess.

A defense that included linemen Andy Robustelli, Dick Modzelewski, Rosey Grier and

Jim Katcavage, linebacker Cliff Livingston and defensive backs Emlen Tunnell, Jim Patton, Erich Barnes and Dick Lynch was tough on all offensive stars, not just Jim Brown. The series went 9-5-1 in favor of the Giants during Paul Brown's last seven seasons (1956-62).

The biggest change in the Browns occurred on March 21, 1961, when a young advertising executive named Art Modell headed a syndicate that paid almost $4 million for the franchise. Modell, only 35 years old, envisioned pro football and television as a marriage made in heaven. He had hit it big in realizing how to use daytime television to market products to housewives, and dreamed of using TV to market the NFL to fans nationwide.

Pro football was Modell's passion. It was his only diversion from the go-go world of Madison Avenue. He followed the NFL religiously. One of the men he most admired was Paul Brown. Modell got word the Browns were for sale on a tip from former Brown Curly Morrison, communicated by a mutual acquaintance, theatrical agent Vince Andrews, in October of 1960. Modell wasted no time in putting together the financing to acquire the club.

It was ironic that Modell, who was a big fan of Paul Brown, would be the man to relieve Brown of his coaching duties. Unlike Mickey McBride or David Jones and their partners, Modell would not be a spectator in the daily operations of his team.

The 1962 season wasn't a happy one. Paul Brown coveted Heisman Trophy winner Ernie Davis of Syracuse University, which would give the Browns a 1-2 punch in the backfield much like the champion Packers enjoyed with Paul Hornung and Jim Taylor. Brown traded halfback Bobby Mitchell and the Browns' second first-round pick in the '62 draft, running back

GIANT LEAP: Milt Plum fires over defensive tackle Dick Modzelewski's charging pass rush in 1960, typical of the hard-fought Browns-Giants rivalry. "Mo" later became a key member of the 1964 championship team's defensive line.

Leroy Jackson, to the Redskins for the rights to Davis. It was an excellent deal for the Redskins, who were under increasing pressure from the other teams, civil rights groups and the federal government to integrate. Mitchell became the first black to play in a Redskins uniform.

The deal resulted in second-guessing in Cleveland. Mitchell had averaged 32 receptions and 106 carries in his four years with the Browns. He had scored 38 touchdowns. He was dealt for someone who had never been in a National Football League game.

Worst of all, Brown didn't tell Modell what he was doing. The owner wasn't pleased. He did tell the boss about trading quarterback Milt Plum, who had publicly criticized Brown for not allowing audibles. (All plays were being brought in from the coaching staff.) Modell OK'd the deal, which sent Plum to the Detroit

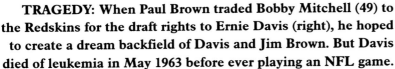

TRAGEDY: When Paul Brown traded Bobby Mitchell (49) to the Redskins for the draft rights to Ernie Davis (right), he hoped to create a dream backfield of Davis and Jim Brown. But Davis died of leukemia in May 1963 before ever playing an NFL game.

Lions for quarterback Jim Ninowski, whom Brown promised would be the starter. A later trade brought Frank Ryan, a Phi Beta Kappa (Rice), from the Rams to back up Ninowski.

Ninowski had served as Plum's backup in 1958-59 before being dealt to the Lions prior to the 1960 season for linebacker Bob Long and a third-round draft choice. Ninowski replaced Earl Morrall as the starter in '60 but was not as effective in '61. Presumably, life would be better the second time around in Cleveland for the ex-Michigan State star, but it was not to be.

Ninowski was flattened on a passing attempt in the second quarter of the seventh game by Pittsburgh's Gene "Big Daddy" Lipscomb, suffering a dislocated shoulder and broken collarbone. He was replaced by Ryan who directed the Browns to a 41-14 victory that day and three

more wins that season. Ryan never looked back, leading the Browns to five straight winning seasons (1963-67) and the NFL championship in 1964. Ninowski became Ryan's backup through '66, taking over when the score was out of reach and often adding a touchdown or two.

Davis never played for the Browns. He was diagnosed with leukemia and missed all of the 1962 season. He died on May 18, 1963. Ernie Green, acquired from the Green Bay Packers during 1962 training camp, eventually became Jim Brown's and Leroy Kelly's backfield mate.

As for Paul Brown, the dissatisfaction was growing. Several players went to Modell and complained about the way Brown was handling personnel. Losing was not the problem, they said, but Brown's attitude was. The coach who had been football's greatest innovator, unfortunately, had failed to remain one step ahead of the competition. Every head coach was imitating Paul Brown, but some were doing it with better players and/or building on what Brown had started 17 years earlier.

RYAN'S ROLE: Opening the 1962 season as the starting quarterback, Jim Ninowski (above) passes to Ray Renfro versus Baltimore in Game 5. Two weeks later, Ninowski suffered a broken collarbone and separated shoulder against Pittsburgh. It took Frank Ryan off the sideline (left) and into the starter's role.

After playing in title games in 11 of their first 12 seasons, the Browns had failed to reach a championship contest for five straight years. The Giants and the emerging Green Bay Packers were the new symbols of NFL domination.

Modell announced on Jan. 9, 1963, that Paul Brown had been relieved of his coaching and general manager duties. He would be paid for the remaining six years on his contract and given "other duties." Blanton Collier, who had rejoined the Browns in 1962 as offensive backfield coach, replaced Brown. All other assistant coaches were rehired.

The Paul Brown era was over, the Art Modell era had begun and the Cleveland Browns were about to enter a new period of consistent title contention.

New Success in the Sixties

After 17 seasons, the Cleveland Browns entered 1963 for the first time ever without Paul Brown in charge. But if anyone could take the sting out of Brown's dismissal, it was Blanton Collier. He had been a Paul Brown assistant for the team's first eight seasons and the head coach at the University of Kentucky before rejoining the Browns as a backfield coach in 1962. He was 56 years old when he became an NFL head coach for the first time. But it was not just experience that made Collier what he was. He was ready to follow Paul Brown's legend because he knew Brown's coaching system inside out, although almost a complete opposite of his mentor personality-wise. "We're going to be watched by the entire football world in the coming season," Collier told his players at the start of training camp, "and we will be judged on only one basis: if we win or lose.

"The world doesn't want the nice guy," he continued. "I think the world would sort of like a winner to be a nice guy, but first he's got to be a winner. Each year you have to produce or get out. That's not Collier's law or Modell's law. It's the law of professional sports. I won't be mild mannered or easygoing. I do not know how I acquired that reputation. I'm not a tough person, and I don't try to be. But I get fired up about things, especially lack of effort and lack of attention. What you do and how soon you do it will determine how dedicated you are."

Collier professed to being as tough as his predecessor, but everyone saw a coach dedicated to winning without being dedicated to a style that many believed had become passe. Perhaps no player noticed it more than Frank Ryan, the cerebral quarterback who had taken over the starting role eight games into the 1962 season following an injury to Jim Ninowski.

> Despite his mild-mannered demeanor, Blanton Collier made it clear that he could get "fired up" when necessary.

Under Collier, Ryan was now allowed to call his own plays, and was given the freedom to change a play at the line of scrimmage if he saw the defense was stacked against it. Without the messenger system, Ryan was able to use his intelligence as effectively as he was able to use his physical talent.

The Browns also had to deal with three players' deaths in preseason. Ernie Davis' death in May followed that of Tom Bloom, a cornerback from Purdue drafted in Round 6. Bloom was killed in an automobile accident

COMMUNICATION: Head Coach Blanton Collier confers with Jim Brown during the 1963 training camp. There was an excellent rapport between the two men and Brown responded with 1,863 yards rushing that season, the best of his career.

Jan. 18. Don Fleming, a starting safety and a Browns player since 1960, died when he was electrocuted on June 4 while working at a construction site in Florida. The turbulence and tragedy of the off-season was put on hold as Collier and the assistant coaches set about to tinker with their talented club, while adding a new measure of youth to the mix as well.

On offense, second-year wide receiver Gary Collins (22) replaced veteran Ray Renfro (32). Ernie Green (24) and Ken Webb (27), acquisitions from the Packers and Lions, respectively, shared duties as Jim Brown's backfield mate.

John Wooten (26), a fifth-year vet, moved from right to left guard, replacing Jim Ray Smith (30), who had been traded to Dallas for Monte Clark (26). (Clark became a starting right tackle in 1965.) The move allowed Gene Hickerson to take over the right guard spot that he held through 1971. Second-year right tackle John Brown (24) succeeded the retired Mike McCormack.

On defense, Jim Houston (25), a No. 1 draft choice in 1960, was inserted in the lineup at left linebacker after having played defensive end his first three years. Left linebacker Galen Fiss was switched to the right while Vince Costello remained in the middle.

Collier and staff also worked a 21-year-old rookie, Jim Kanicki, into the defensive line for Bob Gain (34) who suffered an injury-plagued year. In the secondary, veterans Bernie Parrish and Jim Shofner remained at the corners. Ross Fichtner moved from left to right safety, allowing rookie Larry Benz (22) to take over the left.

Collier appeared to have made all the right moves as the Browns now had most of the personnel in place for their run of five playoff appearances over the next six seasons.

The 1963 season saw no Browns player respond more positively to the change of coaches than Jim Brown, who in 1962 had failed to gain 1,000 yards for the first time since his rookie season and for the first time in a six-year career had failed to lead the league in rushing. (Jim Taylor, the fullback of the league-champion Packers, did it.) Jim Brown had been running primarily between the tackles during Paul Brown's last few years. Under Collier, he had the whole field with which to work.

"In Paul's latter years . . . we were just so conservative, it was as if we were afraid," Jim Brown said. "Then Blanton came, and it wasn't a dictatorship anymore. Any play that would give me an easy opportunity to move the ball, Blanton was all for it, and he came up with those plays."

"I have never seen anyone [have] a relationship with a superstar like Blanton had with Jim," Wooten said. "From the time Blanton

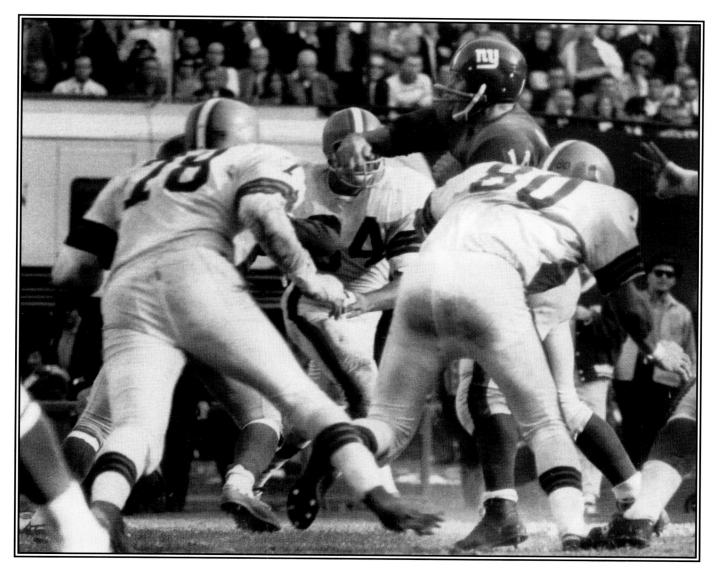

returned to Cleveland he and Jim had liked and respected each other. Blanton could motivate anyone, from a superstar such as Jim Brown, to the most insecure man, to all of us in between."

Brown improved his rushing yardage from 996 in 1962 to 1,863 in '63, with a staggering 6.4 yards-per-carry average. The team itself went from 7-6-1 to 10-4, but still finished a game behind New York in the Eastern Conference race. The Browns, Giants and Cardinals were tied at 8-3 with three games to go.

Cleveland beat the Cards in Week 12, but were annihilated by Detroit on the next-to-last weekend to fall from a first-place tie with New York. The Giants won their last three games, clinching it via a victory over Pittsburgh, a team that routed them 31-0 in the second week of the season.

CLOSING IN: Frank Parker (78), Paul Wiggin (84) and Bill Glass (80) surround New York's Y.A. Tittle in a 1963 Browns victory. The Browns nearly won the Eastern Conference that season, finishing at 10-4, a game behind the Giants, whose dynasty would end when the Browns won the crown in 1964.

Y.A. Tittle had been brilliant in 1963. He completed 60 percent of his attempts and threw 36 touchdown passes to only 14 interceptions. Only John Unitas of the Baltimore Colts had a year equal to Tittle's. But 1963 was a last hurrah for an old team that had created a mini-dynasty in its conference. Tittle was 37 years old. The club was loaded with players with 10 or more years of service.

It all unraveled in a hurry for the Giants. The team plunged to 2-10-2 in 1964 and weren't a force again in the league until 1970. By that

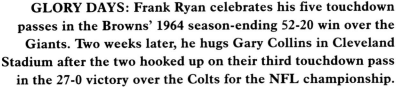

GLORY DAYS: Frank Ryan celebrates his five touchdown passes in the Browns' 1964 season-ending 52-20 win over the Giants. Two weeks later, he hugs Gary Collins in Cleveland Stadium after the two hooked up on their third touchdown pass in the 27-0 victory over the Colts for the NFL championship.

time the National Football League and American Football League had merged, and the Browns found themselves as one of the three teams switched from the older league to the AFL. The merger destroyed the once-fierce Browns-Giants rivalry for good.

The Browns won the Eastern Conference in 1964, but had trouble earning respect for doing it despite the fact the club was in a hot race with the St. Louis Cardinals all season. It was thought the Browns simply won the conference through attrition, rather than on merit. The Giants had fallen, so who else BUT Cleveland should win the East? Not only that, but the Baltimore Colts began tearing up the Western Con-

ference. An opening-day loss was followed by 10 straight victories. They smashed the Chicago Bears, the NFL champions in the previous year, 52-0, in the third game of the season. They defeated Vince Lombardi's Packers twice, and racked up 428 points to just 225 for their opponents. John Unitas threw 19 touchdown passes and a mere six interceptions.

Baltimore was coached by Don Shula, 34, one of the youngest heads in NFL history. He had grown up in Painesville, Ohio, just outside of Cleveland, played college football at John Carroll University in Cleveland Heights, Ohio, and started his NFL career with the Browns in 1951. Shula had also been an assistant under Collier at Kentucky and replaced another former Browns assistant coach, Weeb Ewbank, with the Colts.

The Baltimore defense, led by veteran Gino Marchetti, led the league in fewest points allowed and fewest touchdowns allowed (28).

The linebacking was solid, with 12-year veteran Bill Pellington in the middle and young veterans Jackie Burkett and Don Shinnick on the outside. Cornerback Bobby Boyd was the leader of a revamped secondary.

Blockers for Unitas included future Hall of Famer Jim Parker, a first-round draft choice from Ohio State in that banner year of 1957. Parker had moved to guard in 1963 because young Bob Vogel was a budding star at left tackle. Dick Szymanski was the All-Pro center, and on the right side of the line were two men who had been starters when Baltimore won back-to-back NFL crowns in 1958-59—Alex Sandusky and George Preas.

Unitas' arsenal of pass receivers included Raymond Berry, double-threat halfback Lenny Moore, tall flanker Jimmy Orr, and John Mackey, considered by many the first superstar tight end in NFL history. Unitas, Berry, Moore and Mackey all became Hall of Famers.

Moore led the Colts in rushing and in touchdowns with 16 by run and three by reception. Jerry Hill, Tony Lorick and converted quarterback Tom Matte, another Ohio Stater, shared the fullback duties.

Oddly enough, it was the Giants who might have given the Browns a shot at the title. One of New York's two victories and one of its two ties were against St. Louis, despite the latter's superior record. The Browns beat the Giants twice, including the last game of the season, to edge the Cards by a half game for the conference crown. The Browns had a tie and a loss in their two games against St. Louis. The Colts probably helped, too, by punishing the Cardinals, 47-27, in their regular-season meeting.

Everyone expected the Colts to do the same to Cleveland in the championship game. The offenses were considered equally explosive, but

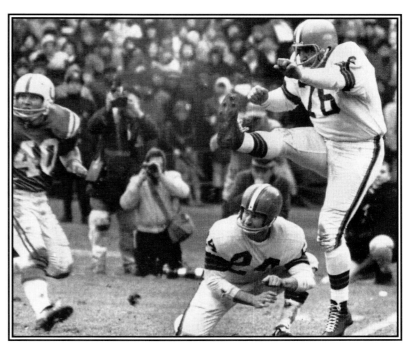

BOOTING BALTIMORE: Lou Groza kicks a 43-yard third-quarter field goal to open the scoring in the 1964 title game against the Colts. Bobby Franklin is Groza's holder.

the Colts' vaunted defense was supposed to provide the difference. Almost all experts had a high-scoring game in sight.

It was a high-scoring game: for the Browns in the last two quarters, because that is when they scored all their points in a 27-0 triumph. Frank Ryan fired three touchdown passes to Gary Collins and Lou Groza kicked two field goals as the Browns dominated the second half before almost 80,000 in Cleveland Stadium. Collins gained 130 yards receiving. Jim Brown had 114 yards rushing on 28 carries. But it was the defense that got itself some respect that Dec. 27 day by limiting Unitas to 96 yards passing and intercepting him twice.

The Browns ruled the Eastern Conference again in 1965 with an 11-3 record, their best

mark ever in a 14-game season. They were four games ahead of the Dallas Cowboys and the New York Giants, who finished tied for second place. They did this without Paul Warfield, the wide receiver who had had such a great rookie year in '64, for 10 games because of a broken shoulder suffered in the annual preseason game between the defending NFL champion and the College All-Stars.

Frank Ryan wasn't the healthiest man in 1965, either. Gino Marchetti of the Colts separated Ryan's shoulder in the Pro Bowl, and Ryan was in a cast for most of the off-season. He was injured again in Game 2 of the regular season, a 49-13 loss to St. Louis. Jim Ninowski came in to lead the Browns to a victory over Philadelphia the next week, and Ryan returned the following Saturday to fire a 44-yard TD pass to Collins in a 24-19 win over the Steelers.

THE UNFROZEN TUNDRA: The Browns slogged through the second half of the 1965 championship game in a mud bath at Green Bay's Lambeau Field. Above, Vince Costello stops the Packers' Jim Taylor for a short gain. Opposite page, Frank Ryan and Jim Brown head to the sideline after a frustrating series. The 23-12 defeat became Brown's final game.

The championship game was against the Packers in Green Bay. Nature wasn't kind to the Browns that day, as a morning snowfall started to melt during the game. The field had been hard and dry the day before as the Browns went through their final tune-up, but it was a mud bath in the second half. Jim Brown's running was rendered a non-factor by such a dreadful surface and the Browns fell, 23-12, after trailing by just one point, 13-12, at halftime.

The title was the third of five head coach Vince Lombardi would win with the Packers

UNBREAKABLE: Galen Fiss was a member of the Browns' Rubber Band Defense of the '60s, dubiously dubbed because it "stretched, but didn't break." Fiss, Vince Costello and Jim Houston formed a solid corps of linebackers, joined at various times by Dale Lindsey, Johnny Brewer and Sidney Williams.

So the best-paid football player of 1965 (Brown was earning $80,000) walked away from the game at the age of 30, informing Collier he was "no longer mentally prepared to play."

But the Browns kept winning. With little time to prepare for the Post-Jim Brown Era, the Browns finished 9-5, tied for second in the division. Leroy Kelly, a three-year veteran who had mainly been a punt returner over his first two seasons, gained 1,141 yards rushing and led the league in yards-per-carry average at 5.5, and touchdowns rushing with 15. Only Gale Sayers of Chicago had more yards rushing than Kelly.

"I don't expect to replace [Jim Brown]," Collier said. "Runners such as Jim come along once in a lifetime. But I do expect someone from this squad to make a name for himself."

Ernie Green, who had been better known as the guy who blocked for Jim Brown, made a bit of a name for himself in 1966 as well. Green gained 750 yards that season, 224 more than his previous best year (1963) and caught 45 passes, 17 more than his career high (also 1963).

The Browns finished at 9-5 again in 1967 and won their division, the Century, in the new NFL alignment that had four four-team divisions. They were crushed, however, 52-14, by the rising star of the Eastern Conference, Capitol Division champion Dallas.

The next two seasons were more successful as the Browns ruled the Century Division again with records of 10-4 and 10-3-1. They reached the championship games in 1968 and '69, but were blown out both times by the Western Conference champions, the Colts, 34-0, in 1968, and the Vikings, 27-7, in 1969.

While the Browns were maintaining their winning tradition, their old division rivals, the Giants, Eagles and Cardinals, were experiencing periods of inconsistency. New York never finished better than 7-7 in the last six years of the decade. Philadelphia had only one winning season from 1962-77. The Cardinals rallied in 1968 to finish 9-4-1 and one-half game behind the Browns, after new head coach Charley Winner's housecleaning following ugly racial confrontations, but fell back to 4-9-1 the next year.

in the 1960s, as Green Bay became the team of that decade just as the Browns had been the team of the '50s. As for the Browns, they would be the underdog in two more NFL championship contests before the decade would end. They would do it without Jim Brown.

On July 14, 1966, Brown became the second football legend with that name to leave the Cleveland Browns in 3 1/2 years. He was in England, shooting a film called "The Dirty Dozen" at the time. He had assured the Browns he would be back, and it was owner Art Modell's Hollywood connections that had helped Brown land a role in that film in the first place.

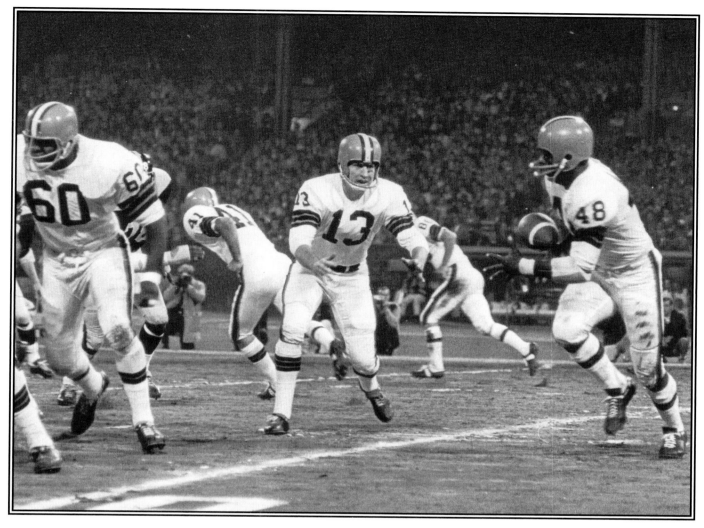

IMPORTANT COG: Frank Ryan pitches to Ernie Green as left guard John Wooten (60) clears a path. Green provided consistency and versatility in the Browns' backfield through most of the 1960s, paired first with Jim Brown as a halfback, then moving to fullback in 1966 to team with Leroy Kelly.

The new power became the Dallas Cowboys, coached by Tom Landry since the team's birth in 1960. Landry had been a Browns nemesis for many years, first as a defensive back in the AAFC with the Brooklyn-New York Yankees, then as a member of coach Steve Owen's New York Giants Umbrella Defense of the early '50s, then as an assistant coach on the Giants teams that knocked the Browns from Eastern Conference dominance in the late '50s, and finally as head coach of Dallas.

The Cowboys made it to the championship game in 1966 and '67, only to lose close ones to the Packers. Landry himself presented an interesting contrast to the intimidating Vince Lombardi of Green Bay. Both men were assistants with the Giants in the glory days of the '50s, but Landry was more in the Paul Brown mold. He was a quiet, stoic, gentlemanly figure who had an uncanny eye for talent.

In truth, there were no reasons the Browns should have fallen off the radar screen. They put eight players in the Pro Bowl every season from 1966-69. It was the same number who went after the 1965 season and one more than made it after their NFL championship year. Right guard Gene Hickerson was All-Pro five consecutive years from 1966-70. Leroy Kelly made All-Pro each year from 1966-69. Paul Warfield and Gary Collins were All-Pro twice.

Collier was never afraid to tinker with success. When longtime right linebacker Galen Fiss neared the end of his brilliant 11-year career in 1966, Collier replaced him with tight

LEAPS AND BOUNDS: Leroy Kelly (above) led the NFL in rushing for the second straight season in 1968 with a career-high 1,239 yards, his third straight 1,000-yard effort. That same season, Milt Morin (right) moved into the lineup to become the first full-time pass-catching tight end in team history.

end Johnny Brewer, a rugged blocker and just as sure a tackler. Brewer responded to the move and made the Pro Bowl after the 1966 season.

The switch paved the way for the team to put Milt Morin in Brewer's tight end position. After dividing his time with Ralph "Catfish" Smith in 1966-67, Morin held the job through 1975 and became the first pass-catching tight end in Browns history.

Defensive players were moved from one side of the line to the other with great frequency. Defensive ends Paul Wiggin and Bill Glass were flip-flopped with regularity. So were tackles Jim Kanicki and Walter Johnson.

The linebackers became even more interchangeable. It was usually Jim Houston at left linebacker, except when it was John Garlington or Bob Matheson. Houston would then be in the middle, because middle linebackers Matheson and Dale Lindsey would be elsewhere. If Houston was in the middle, Lindsey would be at right linebacker, unless it was Garlington there. Only the right linebacker, Billy Andrews, wasn't constantly on the move.

Also on the move was Leroy Kelly. The man who had carried the ball just 43 times in the two years he and Jim Brown were members of the team, led the league in rushing in 1967 and '68, scoring 27 touchdowns in those seasons.

Not all Browns stars in the '60s were home-grown. Defensive end Bill Glass came over in the Milt Plum trade in 1962 and was selected for the Pro Bowl four times with his new club. Erich Barnes, who'd worn out his welcome

first with the Bears and then with the Giants, found a home in the Browns' secondary and made the Pro Bowl after the 1968 season.

Frank Ryan left the Browns just before the start of the 1969 season. It was not a real surprise, as Ryan had earned a doctorate in mathematics and had been teaching the subject at Case Western Reserve University. The Browns acquired Bill Nelsen from the Steelers in anticipation Ryan would call it quits. Nelsen was

ALMOST GREAT IN '68: Rookie defensive tackle Marvin Upshaw (above) gets in the face of Dallas quarterback Craig Morton in the Browns' 31-20 victory in the 1968 Eastern Confernce Championship game on Dec. 21. A week later, Bill Nelsen (left) and the offense could not get untracked as the Colts won, 34-0, to advance to Super Bowl III against the Jets.

Pittsburgh's No. 1 quarterback in 1965, but injuries plagued his career there and he was dealt for Cleveland's backup quarterback, Dick Shiner. Ryan made his way to the Washington Redskins, where he played two seasons.

Nelsen performed far above expectations in both 1968 and '69, leading the Browns to two straight upsets of the Cowboys in divisional playoff games. In the '68 game, interceptions by Mike Howell, Ben Davis, Dale Lindsey and Erich Barnes helped Nelsen's cause considerably in a 31-20 victory. In the '69 game, Nelsen completed 18 of 28 passes, with six third-down completions resulting in first downs, as the Browns won, 38-14.

But Nelsen had a history of knee problems and was never considered the club's long-term answer. The team was in the market for a top-flight quarterback for the 1970 season.

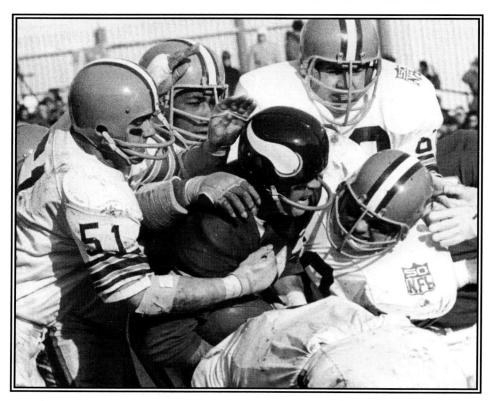

GANG TACKLE: Dale Lindsey, Walter Johnson, Jim Kanicki and Jim Houston (l-r) surround quarterback Joe Kapp in the 1969 NFL Championship game on Jan. 4, 1970, in Bloomington, Minn. The Vikings won, 27-7, in eight-degree temperatures to advance to Super Bowl IV against Kansas City.

Miami had wanted all along. Its running back stable already included Larry Csonka, Jim Kiick and Mercury Morris. Kelly was not needed, but a deep threat like Warfield, to make the trio of running backs more potent, was.

Warfield had enjoyed his best season in 1968 with 50 receptions and career highs in yards (1,067) and touchdowns (12). He followed that with 42 catches, 886 yards and 10 touchdowns in 1969.

Reaction to the deal was one of shock. Warfield had been one of the most popular Browns ever. He was a native of Warren, Ohio, and was an Ohio State alumnus. Bill Nelsen said the news made him feel as if he had been traded. The Browns' community reacted as if a family member had left home.

At 10-3-1, however, the Browns were far down in the draft order. There was no way they could get the two quarterbacks who had been considered "can't miss" future NFL stars— Louisiana Tech's Terry Bradshaw or Purdue's Mike Phipps—without trading with a weaker team. Pittsburgh had the first selection and said it would take Bradshaw. Green Bay, which was in need of defensive linemen, announced it would select Mike McCoy of Notre Dame. Miami was next and no one was certain what general manager Joe Thomas would do.

What he did was tell the Browns the price for his club's first-round draft choice was either Leroy Kelly or Paul Warfield. How badly DID the Browns, Art Modell and Blanton Collier want that quarterback? Badly enough, apparently. Warfield went to the Dolphins and the Browns drafted Phipps. Warfield was the one

Business was business, however, and Paul Warfield was a Dolphin as the 1970 season, the first in which the NFL and AFL would operate as one league, rolled around. The Browns tried to fill the void with ex-Giants speedster Homer Jones, who caught 184 passes for 4,054 yards and 29 touchdowns over the previous four seasons. Cleveland dealt two starters, fullback Ron Johnson and defensive tackle Jim Kanicki, to acquire him. But Jones lasted just one season and the job eventually went to Fair Hooker.

The trade of Paul Warfield, one of the symbols of the successful 1960s, marked the end of an era in Browns history as much as the passing of a decade and the entrance to a new alignment of the league had for many other teams. Soon, losing a coach would be added to that list. The Cleveland Browns and the National Football League were about to begin a period in which almost nothing would be the same.

> **The trade of Paul Warfield to Miami marked the symbolic finish to the Browns' contending years of the 1960s.**

Realignment & Rivalries

ollowing the 1970 NFL season, the Browns' first in the American Foot[ball] Conference of the realigned NFL, team owner Art Modell had this to sa[y]. "We were not prepared for the American Football League. That was my fault. We were just not prepared for their style of play, and had a so-so year." The Browns finished 7-7 that season and lost the Central Division title to Paul Brown's third-year Cincinnati Bengals. It was the only non-winning record in Blanton Collier's eight years as the Browns' head coach. But maybe no one, even the big winners, was prepared for 1970. The National Football [League, standing] the same stand in its two-division format since 1933, and the American [Football League,] the six-year-old challenger, had formally merged in 1966, but television con[tracts would] allow permanent inter-league play until their 1970 expiration.

[The] pro football as we know it—two conferences of three divisions each, a two-[tiered playoff sche]dule (since expanded to three) culminating in a world-championship game, [at a neutra]l site. That's the way it has been for more than 25 years, the longest stretch [that the] NFL has gone without a major upheaval.

[The r]ecord the Browns managed in the first season might have been the only [thing that] made Art Modell ashamed in 1970. The former ad man from Brooklyn [had come to] the NFL in almost no time. Granted, Modell was a man who knew [money and TV, and he came] into the league at a time when TV was helping all sports become [rich. But he brought] more than knowledge to the table. Modell was a shrewd negotiator [who, as chairman] on the [NFL']s television committee, made TV and pro football wealthy.

[But it was a move Mo]dell's made in the spring of 1969 that had the most impact, both [on and off the field]s. Negotiations over the makeup of the new NFL were at an

Realignment & Rivalries

F ollowing the 1970 NFL season, the Browns' first in the American Football Conference of the realigned NFL, team owner Art Modell had this to say: "We were not prepared for the American Football League. That was my fault. We were just not prepared for their style of play, and had a so-so year." The Browns finished 7-7 that season and lost the Central Division title to Paul Brown's third-year Cincinnati Bengals. It was the only non-winning record in Blanton Collier's eight years as the Browns' head coach. But maybe no one, even the big winners, was prepared for 1970. The National Football League, working the same stand in its two-division format since 1933, and the American Football League, the six-year-old challenger, had formally merged in 1966, but television contracts did not allow permanent inter-league play until their 1970 expiration.

With it came pro football as we know it—two conferences of three divisions each, a two-week playoff schedule (since expanded to three) culminating in a world-championship game, played at a neutral site. That's the way it has been for more than 25 years, the longest stretch through which the NFL has gone without a major upheaval.

The break-even record the Browns managed in the first season might have been the only thing that could have made Art Modell ashamed in 1970. The former ad man from Brooklyn became a major player in the NFL in almost no time. Granted, Modell was a man who knew television and who came into the league at a time when TV was helping all sports become lucrative, but he brought more than knowledge to the table. Modell was a shrewd negotiator who, as chairman of the NFL's television committee, made TV and pro football wealthy.

But it was a decision of Modell's made in the spring of 1969 that had the most impact, both on the league and on the Browns. Negotiations over the makeup of the new NFL were at an

impasse. The AFL owners wanted the conferences to have equal numbers of teams and have AFL and NFL franchises mixing within the divisions.

Quarterback Mike Phipps was the Browns' hope for the future when they joined the AFC's Central Division.

Leading this group was Paul Brown, now the vice president, general manager and head coach of the Cincinnati Bengals, who joined the AFL in 1968. NFL owners wanted to maintain the old alignments, which meant the 16 teams of the senior league would make up one conference and the 10 AFL clubs would form another, with the latter catching up through expansion.

Modell proposed a compromise in which the Browns, Steelers and Cardinals would join the conference composed of AFL teams and stay in the same division. The Bengals, with whom the Browns would have a ready-made rivalry, would be the fourth team in the circuit. The Browns, Modell said, wouldn't move unless Art Rooney, owner of the archrival Steelers, would agree to it. Rooney agreed, but Bill and Stormy Bidwell, owners of the St. Louis Cardinals, would not.

ARE YOU READY FOR SOME FOOTBALL?: The Browns opened the 1970 season in the first-ever ABC Monday Night Football game, beating the Jets, 31-21, at Cleveland Stadium. Gary Collins (right) catches a 55-yard pass from Bill Nelsen for the first touchdown in Monday Night history. Billy Andrews (above) seals the victory in the fourth quarter by racing 25 yards for a touchdown after picking off a Joe Namath pass.

The whole ordeal took a toll on Modell, and the Browns' owner was hospitalized with a bleeding ulcer by the time the other owners eventually reached an agreement (only because NFL commissioner Pete Rozelle locked them in their New York hotel meeting room until they did). Modell's plan finally was approved, although it was the Colts who became the third NFL club to switch to the AFL, now called the American Football Conference. Baltimore was put in the AFC East, while the Houston Oilers became the fourth team in the AFC Central with Cleveland, Pittsburgh and Cincinnati.

The Browns were rewarded by being named one of the teams to play in the first regular Monday night football game in league history. The Cardinals had been playing one game per season on Monday nights for several years, and now the idea was adopted as a weekly game in which all teams could participate. Once again, Modell was instrumental in hammering out the details for the game. The Columbia Broadcasting System had the rights to the NFC, stemming from its having broadcast the NFL for years, and the National Broadcasting Co., which televised the AFL since 1965, was given domain over AFC contests. The Monday night games, however, went to the American Broad-

casting Co., which at first had the AFL (1960-64), but was better known for its telecasts of college football. The Browns' opponent in that first "Monday Night Football" game was the New York Jets. The matchup, played on Sept. 21, 1970, was a natural. One of the winningest teams of the NFL would play an old-line member of the AFL, as both teams were now cousins in the new AFC.

Not only that, but the Jets had stunned the pro football world by upsetting the 19-point favorite Baltimore Colts in Super Bowl III two seasons earlier to give the young league the respectability it had sought for nine years. Joe

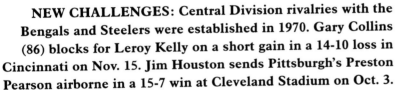

NEW CHALLENGES: Central Division rivalries with the Bengals and Steelers were established in 1970. Gary Collins (86) blocks for Leroy Kelly on a short gain in a 14-10 loss in Cincinnati on Nov. 15. Jim Houston sends Pittsburgh's Preston Pearson airborne in a 15-7 win at Cleveland Stadium on Oct. 3.

Namath, the Jets' brash and talented quarterback who had "guaranteed" the Super Bowl victory, was the big drawing card for the game, to be played at Cleveland Stadium.

Namath was brilliant, completing 19 of 32 passes for 299 yards. But it was the Browns' defense, which intercepted Namath three times and recovered a Jets fumble, that was responsible for Cleveland's 31-21 victory despite a 445-221 disadvantage in total yardage. Browns right linebacker Billy Andrews picked off a Namath pass and returned it 25 yards for a touchdown to ice it for Cleveland. Gary Collins put his name in the trivia books when he caught a 55-yard pass from Bill Nelsen to score the first touchdown in a "Monday Night" game.

Perhaps a more important and significant game was actually played in the 1970 preseason when the Browns met their intrastate rivals,

the Cincinnati Bengals, for the first time. The Bengals won that game, 31-24.

The first regular-season Browns-Bengals game took place on Oct. 11 in Cleveland, site of Paul Brown's greatest success as coach of the Browns for 17 years. The game will most be remembered for the deafening boos that greeted Brown on his first visit to Cleveland Stadium as a coach in eight years. Brown did not shake hands with Blanton Collier after the preseason game in Cincinnati and declined to do so after the first regular-season meeting as well, won by the Browns, 30-27.

A rivalry was born. Cincinnati won the second regular-season contest, 14-10. The game was the second victory in a seven-game winning streak the Bengals put together en route to an 8-6 record and the AFC Central Division championship. Two weeks following the season, Blanton Collier announced he would retire.

The announcement came after the Steelers game, which the Browns lost, 28-9. Cleveland's record was 5-6 at the time, one game behind Cincinnati in the division standings. However, Collier said it was not a ploy to motivate his

club. The fact was the coach's hearing, which had always been impaired, was getting worse. He could barely hear on the sideline and feared the affliction would affect his ability to coach.

The Browns did finish the season with a bang, although not enough of one to allow Blanton Collier to depart as a champion. They sandwiched road-game victories over Houston and Denver around their most heartbreaking loss of the season, 6-2 to the Cowboys at home. Dallas got two field goals in the second half to win it, but it was the Browns' mistakes—three interceptions, a blocked punt to set up one field

DON'T LOVE YA BLUE: Walter Johnson (71) and Rich "Tombstone" Jackson (87) chase Houston quarterback Dan Pastorini in a 20-0 victory on Nov. 5, 1972. The Browns dominated the Oilers in the early years of their Central Division rivalry, winning the first nine, and 12 of 16 through 1977.

goal, a fumble by Gary Collins inside the Cowboys' 10-yard line, two offensive interference calls on Collins—that sunk the Browns.

Offensive coordinator Nick Skorich was named to replace Collier. Skorich had previously been head coach of the Philadelphia Eagles from 1961-63 and remains in 1999 the

SHERK ATTACK: If Mike Phipps was a first-round bust in the 1970 college draft, Jerry Sherk was more than a boon in the second round. Sherk provided strength, stability and intensity at defensive tackle throughout the decade. Top photo, Sherk puts a punishing pounce on Franco Harris. Above left, Terry Bradshaw can't avoid Sherk's menacing presence. Above right, Sherk charges through traffic in pursuit of O.J. Simpson.

only man the Browns ever hired for the head coaching job who had previous NFL head coaching experience.

The Browns rebounded in 1971 to win the Central Division with a 9-5 record, then lost to the Colts, 20-3, in the playoffs. However, the Browns would not win another division cham-

pionship for nine seasons (1980). They actually improved to 10-4 in 1972 and entered the playoffs as a Wild Card team, but lost to the Miami Dolphins, 20-14.

The rise of the Pittsburgh Steelers, which had begun in 1969 with the hiring of former Browns linebacker-guard Chuck Noll, would be realized in 1972 and completed two years later with a Super Bowl victory. The rivalry, which the Browns had until then dominated (33 victories to the Steelers' 11) was suddenly one of the hottest in the league.

The Browns beat the Steelers, 26-24, in Week 10 of 1972 on a 26-yard field goal by Don

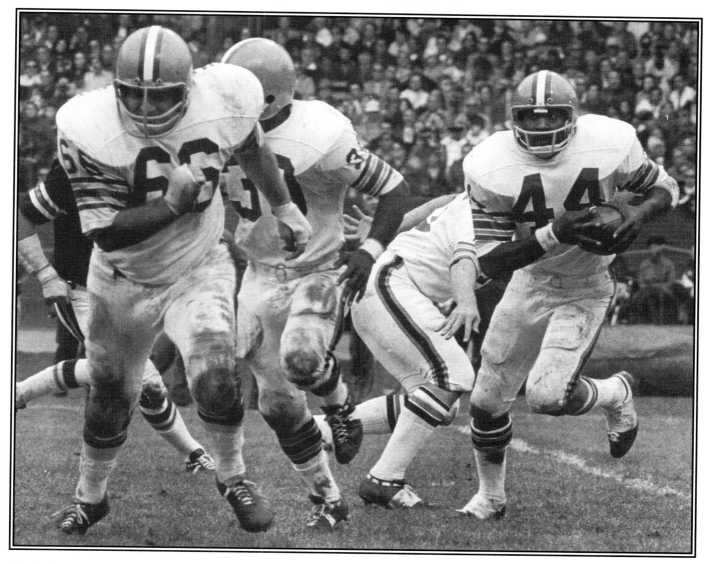

Cockroft with 13 seconds to play, to leave each team at 7-3. But the Steelers slapped a 30-0 loss on the Browns two weeks later in Pittsburgh. Both teams won their last two games easily, as Pittsburgh won the Central championship, its first title of any kind in 40 years of National Football League membership.

The Steelers dominated the Browns in the standings, but not always on the field. Though the Browns would lose 16 straight at Three Rivers Stadium from 1970-85, they would win five games at Cleveland Stadium from 1970-77.

The Browns fell to 7-5-2 in 1973 and 4-10 in 1974. Skorich was fired and replaced by offensive line coach Forrest Gregg on Jan. 22, 1975. Gregg had been an All-Pro offensive tackle for

TRANSITION: The veteran pillars of the 1960s playoff teams moved on in the '70s, making way for new talent to emerge in the Kardiac Kids era. Gene Hickerson and Leroy Kelly (above) departed after the 1973 season. Walter Johnson (opposite page) left after the 1976 campaign to play a final year in Cincinnati.

the Green Bay Packers from 1956-70 and was only 42 years old when Art Modell picked him to be the fourth head coach in Browns history. Gregg soon brought Blanton Collier, 69, out of retirement to coach the quarterbacks.

Gregg, known as a stern, gruff man and a true taskmaster, didn't produce results immediately. The Browns were 3-11 in 1975, their poorest season in history until 1990, but bounced back to go 9-5 in '76. Cleveland even

ARRIVALS: Safety Thom Darden (above), a No. 1 pick in 1972, and running back Greg Pruitt (right), a second-round selection in 1973, were two of a long line of successful high-round draft choices that formed the nucleus of the Kardiac Kids of 1979-80.

had a shot at the Central Division title on the last week of the season.

The Browns, Bengals and Steelers were 9-4 entering the final game, but Cleveland was stunned by Kansas City, 4-9 at that point, by a score of 39-14. Pittsburgh and Cincinnati, meanwhile, were burying weak opponents, the Oilers and Jets, by a combined score of 63-3. The Steelers won the division because they had swept the season series with the Bengals.

The years 1970-77 saw the departure of most of the team's stars of the 1960s. Leaving were receiver Gary Collins and halfback Leroy Kelly, who each played briefly in the World Football League. Retiring were guard Gene Hickerson, offensive tackle Dick Schafrath, linebacker Jim Houston, defensive back Erich Barnes and tight end Milt Morin. Defensive tackle Walter Johnson moved on to Cincinnati.

Also retiring would be wide receiver Paul Warfield, who had left the Dolphins for the WFL, then returned to the Browns for his final two seasons (1976-77) after the league went out of business in 1975.

In their positions came many of the players who would form the Kardiac Kids outfit that won the AFC Central in 1980. Defensive tackle Jerry Sherk arrived with the 1970 draft. The 1971 draft produced defensive back Clarence Scott, linebacker Charlie Hall and, in the sixth round, offensive tackle Doug Dieken.

Defensive back Thom Darden was the first-round pick of 1972 and running back Greg Pruitt was a No. 2 choice in 1973. Linebacker Dick Ambrose arrived in 1975. Fullback Mike Pruitt and receiver Dave Logan were selected

in 1976. Outside linebacker Robert L. Jackson was the Browns' top choice in '77.

Coming to the Browns via trades or free agency were wide receiver Reggie Rucker, center Tom DeLeone, guard-center Robert E. Jackson and cornerback Ron Bolton.

Perhaps the biggest disappointment of the years 1970-77 was that Mike Phipps never became the quarterback almost everyone said he would be. Bill Nelsen remained the starter in Phipps' first two seasons. Following a shoulder separation suffered in the 1976 opener, Phipps was no longer a starter. He'd had only one year in which he completed more than 50 percent of his passes and threw 81 interceptions to 37 touchdown passes. He was traded to the Bears in 1977 for Chicago's fourth-round draft selection that year and its first-round pick in '78.

It wasn't Phipps who benefited most by the return of Blanton Collier as quarterback coach in 1975 and '76. The old master was more of a help to a player few predicted would be a star when the Browns nabbed him in the 13th round of the 1972 draft.

Rutigliano & the Kardiac Kids

There might never be two men in the same profession more different than Forrest Gregg, the tough disciplinarian who coached the Browns from 1975-77, and his successor, the kinder, gentler Sam Rutigliano, who took over in 1978. Gregg was known as a stern taskmaster who got the most out of young players with a no-nonsense, demanding approach. He was a Hall-of-Fame offensive tackle for Vince Lombardi in the glory days of the Green Bay Packers when they were dominating professional football in the 1960s. But while Lombardi, the ultimate tough-guy coach, could still motivate veteran players, Gregg had his problems with the guys who had been there and done that. He was dismissed by Art Modell and replaced by Dick Modzelewski with one game to go in the 1977 regular season, which ended with a 6-8 record after a 5-2 start.

"Forrest was a Hall of Famer," former Browns wide receiver Reggie Rucker said. "You have to look at his background. You have to take into consideration that the apple doesn't fall far from the tree. He played for Vince Lombardi. I think in the '70s you had a different kind of athlete. You couldn't just tell a player what to do. The player wanted to know why he was doing it, and that just wasn't Forrest's way."

In his place came Rutigliano. Unlike Gregg, Nick Skorich and Blanton Collier, Rutigliano had not served as an assistant coach with the Browns when Modell hired him as the only the fifth full-time head coach in team history on Dec. 28, 1977. Like Gregg, Collier and Paul Brown, however, Rutigliano had no previous head coaching experience in the NFL. Cleveland, in fact, was one of the few places Rutigliano had never lived.

> Quarterback Brian Sipe led the Browns to a steady climb in the AFC Central and to some of the most memorable wins in franchise history.

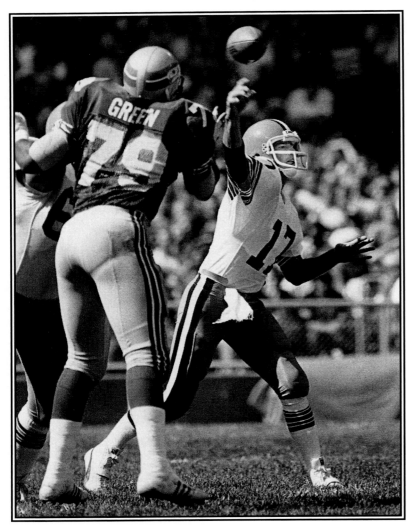

OVER THE TOP: Although short by NFL standards at 6-1, Brian Sipe took Cleveland's passing statistics to new heights. He is the Browns' all-time leader in passing attempts (3,439), completions (1,944), yardage (23,713) and TD passes (154).

A son of an Italian immigrant from the Sheepshead Bay section of Brooklyn, Rutigliano had gone to junior college in Decatur, Miss., and to four-year college at the universities of Tennessee and Tulsa. He was an end on the 1951 NCAA championship team at UT as a junior before moving to Tulsa for his senior season. He was back in New York for his first coaching job, Lafayette High School, while he attended Columbia University at night.

After several years in the preps, he accepted college assistant coach's jobs at the universities of Connecticut and Maryland, the latter position working under the former Browns linebacker of the 1940s, Lou Saban.

In 1967, when Saban was named head coach and general manager of the Broncos, Rutigliano joined his staff. The Patriots, Jets and Saints were his next employers. He coached with four teams in a stretch of 11 seasons. "He bounced around pretty good," Modell said of Rutigliano, but added that he believed he had the next Blanton Collier as his new head coach.

"He's a teacher by background," the Cleveland owner said, "just like Collier was. Beyond that, he relates with today's attitudes. He's contemporary in his relationship with players. I could have gotten a name coach, but that's not what I wanted."

What Modell really wanted to do was start from scratch. The old order would no longer exist. Everything would be different.

Different it was. Where Forrest Gregg had been intensity and boiling blood, Rutigliano was a coach who wanted to make sure that the players avoided emotional peaks and valleys. Rutigliano was fond of saying you can't have players swinging from the rafters one day and expect to have them calm down the next.

"You were dealing with a team that was frazzled and unsure of its direction," Rucker explained. "I remember I asked Peter Hadhazy [Browns executive vice president], 'Why don't you get Sam?' The team couldn't use another dictator. It needed someone to bring a new flavor. I knew Sam from when I was a player and he was coach for the Patriots, and when Sam came in, I knew the guys would love him. He could be firm, but he wasn't into telling adults how to conduct their lives."

One thing that did not change was the Browns' commitment to Brian Sipe at quarterback. Sipe was a 13th-round draft choice in 1972 from San Diego State, where he was NCAA passing champion. He did not make the Browns' roster until 1974 and was never expected to oust Mike Phipps, the club's No. 1 draft choice in 1970, and the player for whom the Browns traded future Hall of Fame inductee Paul Warfield to acquire.

Phipps never became the star the experts said he would be, and when he broke a shoulder in the first regular season game of 1976, Sipe went in and never went out. The slender Californian who guided the Browns to a 9-5 record played well enough to spur the club to trade Phipps to the Bears on May 3, 1977.

It was a long road for Brian Sipe. Sure, he had set all those records at San Diego State, but that was when he was playing for the pass-happy head coach Don Coryell in the pro-set offense. Sipe was considered small by quarterback standards (6-1, 195 pounds) and didn't possess a strong arm.

But Coryell would later take another quarterback considered lacking in physical skills, Dan Fouts, and see him make a mockery of many old NFL passing records with the San Diego Chargers.

Rutigliano liked Sipe. Watching films of the quarterback in Modell's basement, the Browns' head-coach candidate said he was impressed by the fact that Sipe never missed open receivers, never turned his shoulders when he set up to pass and would move in the pocket only to find his receivers and not out of panic.

A broken shoulder blade knocked Sipe out for the second half of the 1977 season, but he came back in 1978, Rutigliano's first year as head coach, to become the most prolific passer in Browns history. He set team records for attempts and completions in '78 and broke them both for two years running.

There was plenty of talent around Sipe. The offensive line of Doug Dieken and Barry Darrow at tackles, Henry Sheppard and Robert E. Jackson at guards and Tom DeLeone at center had played together for two seasons. Reggie Rucker was a quality veteran wide receiver and young, athletic Dave Logan was ready to move into the other wide receiver spot being vacated by the aging Paul Warfield (who had rejoined the Browns in 1976 after five years with the Dolphins and one year in the World Football League). Greg Pruitt was an All-Pro in the Cleveland backfield.

The holes to fill were at tight end and fullback. Milt Morin's last season with the Browns was 1975. His replacements at tight end, Oscar

CALM COMMUNICATOR: Head Coach Sam Rutigliano's ability to relate to modern-day players helped the talented Browns to mature into a cohesive unit. It culminated in the Kardiac Kids' dramatic close-win seasons of 1979-80.

Roan and Gary Parris, had only 20 receptions combined in 1977. Cleo Miller, a free agent pickup from the Kansas City Chiefs, who also got him as a free agent, was starting at fullback while No. 1 draft choice Mike Pruitt was mostly sitting. Pruitt carried only 99 times over his first two seasons, as he was not a favorite of Forrest Gregg.

To resolve the tight end problem, Rutigliano drafted a wide receiver, Ozzie Newsome of Alabama, in the first round of 1978. Crimson Tide head coach Paul "Bear" Bryant had called Newsome the best receiver he had ever coached, and Rutigliano was convinced his draftee would be a tight end with the moves of a wide receiver.

He wasn't wrong. Newsome caught 38 passes as a rookie for a 15.5-yard average per catch. He increased that to 55 receptions and nine touchdowns in 1979.

The fullback situation was solved by making Mike Pruitt the starter over Cleo Miller. Pruitt greatly increased his number of carries from 47 in 1977 to 135 the next season. Miller's dropped from 163 to 89 in the same period. Pruitt would have his breakout season in '79 with 264 carries for 1,294 yards (4.9 yards per carry), 41 receptions and 11 touchdowns.

There was talent on defense, too. Defensive tackle Jerry Sherk and free safety Thom Darden were All-Pros. Cornerback Clarence Scott had been a starter since 1971 and outside linebacker Charlie Hall had been one since 1972. Dick Ambrose was solid at middle linebacker and Ron Bolton had started at cornerback since 1973, first with the Patriots and since 1976 with the Browns.

But with two first-round draft choices in 1978, Rutigliano had the luxury of drafting a

PRUITTS DO IT: Under Sam Rutigliano, Greg Pruitt (opposite page) was joined by Mike Pruitt (above) in the Browns' backfield with immediate success. In 1979, Mike Pruitt's 1,294 rushing yards was the best total since Jim Brown's 1,544 in 1965.

defensive player as well as a tight end. Clay Matthews of Southern Cal became the Browns' No. 1 pick. He started two games in 1978 and all 16 the following year.

The Browns improved to an 8-8 record in 1978. Sipe threw for 2,906 yards and 21 touchdowns. Greg Pruitt was carrying the ball less, but with more success. He had 60 fewer carries while improving his rushing average from 4.6 yards a carry to 5.5.

Sipe was even more impressive in 1979. He had coolly directed the Browns to come-from-behind victories in the first three regular-season contests with fourth-quarter rallies, then watched the defense put it all together in a 26-7 victory over the Dallas Cowboys, the defending NFC champion, in a Monday night game at Cleveland Stadium.

TRIO OF TARGETS: The 1980 Kardiac Kids featured three clutch pass receivers who caught the majority of quarterback Brian Sipe's team-record 337 completions. From left to right are Reggie Rucker, Ozzie Newsome and Dave Logan.

Then reality set in. Three straight losses made the Browns 4-3. They were still 9-5, with a shot at a Wild Card playoff berth, but no late heroics were in order in a 19-14 loss to the Oakland Raiders in Week 15 and a 16-12 setback to the Cincinnati Bengals in the finale.

Still, 12 of the 16 games were decided by a touchdown or less. The thrilling finishes to so many games earned the Browns the nickname "Kardiac Kids" for their ability to induce heart failure among the team's followers.

They did it without Greg Pruitt for the most part. He suffered a sprained knee in the victory over the Cowboys and re-injured it in Week 9, finishing him for the year. Pruitt was limited to 62 rushing attempts and 14 receptions. Calvin Hill, an 11-year veteran who had starred with the Dallas Cowboys from 1969-74 before spending two seasons in Washington, played mostly in Pruitt's place.

Even more serious was the health of Jerry Sherk. A staph infection in his left leg, diagnosed after the 10th game of the season, put the defensive tackle in the Cleveland Clinic for five weeks. His condition was listed as critical and it wasn't known whether he'd even survive. He did, but spent the off-season rehabilitating the leg and trying to regain the strength he lost from a 35-pound drop in his weight.

Consequently, 1980 hardly looked like a season that was going to live in the memories of Browns fans for eternity. The defense was considered porous, having yielded 22 points a contest. To improve the situation, Rutigliano hired Marty Schottenheimer as defensive coordinator. An ex-linebacker with the Bills and Patriots who had been linebackers coach at Detroit the previous two seasons, Schottenheimer set about to create a 3-4 alignment. The four-linebacker setup was intended to stop the run, but would not provide much of a pass rush.

It would have to be accomplished without Jerry Sherk, who left after two quarters of the

LINE MATES: The offensive line for the 1979 Kardiac Kids included (above, l-r) right tackle Henry Sheppard, right guard Robert E. Jackson, center Tom DeLeone and left guard Cody Risien. They were joined by left tackle Doug Dieken (right).

first regular-season game and did not play again in 1980. Sherk had 10 1/2 sacks in 1979, thus reducing the Browns' pass-rushing ability.

Lyle Alzado, an All-Pro with the Denver Broncos who was acquired for the start of the 1979 season, also had 10 1/2 sacks that year. He was the only starting defensive lineman in '79 who would keep his job in '80. Henry Bradley, who was cut in training camp of '79 and was driving a truck in Cleveland when he was called back to the club to replace Sherk after the 10th game, became the nose tackle in the 3-4 defense. Marshall Harris, a second-year veteran acquired from the Jets, was the other defensive end. Harris took over for Jack Gregory, the 1979 starter who retired after a 13-year career.

Robert L. Jackson, the Browns' No. 1 draft selection in 1977, moved into the starting line-up as the fourth linebacker. Charlie Hall and Clay Matthews played outside while Jackson and Dick Ambrose were the inside linebackers.

But the biggest deal the Browns pulled was to get an offensive star, Buffalo Bills guard Joe DeLamielleure, to join an already strong line that included solid veterans Doug Dieken, Tom DeLeone, Henry Sheppard, Robert E. Jackson, Cody Risien and Gerry Sullivan.

DeLamielleure was unhappy with the Bills and boycotted their training camp. Although the general consensus was that defensive players should be the top priority, the team said it couldn't pass up a player with DeLamielleure's credentials, which included never missing a start since his rookie season of 1973, five straight Pro Bowl selections and blocking for record-setting rusher O.J. Simpson.

What Rutigliano had assembled was a team without a big name, even though Sipe would become the living symbol of the Kardiac Kids. The Browns were a collection of talented, low-profile players who never let individual success cloud the purpose of the season-long mission, or let the occasional failures knock them off their even keel. It was Sam's way, and he insisted it was working.

The 1980 preseason, however, was a disaster. The Browns won just one of four games and gave up a combined 111 points in three of them. The offense was no great shakes either, averaging 13 points a game. The regular season started just as badly. Cleveland was beaten by the Patriots, 34-17, in the opener and lost the home debut the next week, 16-7, to the Oilers.

Then came the turnaround. Sipe marched the Browns 66 yards in four plays to shatter a 13-13 tie in the third quarter of a 20-13 win over Kansas City. A touchdown pass to No. 1 draft choice Charles White was the winner.

Next, Sipe completed 13 straight passes, a club record, in a victory over Tampa Bay, 34-27. Calvin Hill's 43-yard TD catch in the fourth quarter gave the Browns a 31-27 lead. A loss to the Broncos was followed by five straight vic-

FIRED UP: Former Broncos defensive end Lyle Alzado brought his emotional brand of leadership to the Browns' line in the 1980 playoff season. He was joined by end Marshall Harris and nose tackle Henry Bradley in the 3-4 alignment.

tories, with a 27-26 conquest of the defending Super Bowl champion Steelers being the highlight as the Browns erased a 26-14 deficit in less than four minutes.

On Nov. 30, the Browns moved into first place by themselves at 9-4 with a 17-14 victory over the Oilers. They fell back into a tie with Houston two weeks later, but won the AFC Central title with a 27-24 triumph over the Bengals in Cincinnati on the last week of the campaign. Don Cockroft's 22-yard field goal with 1:25 to play broke a 24-24 tie.

The Browns and Oilers both finished 11-5, but Cleveland was the division champion on the strength of an 8-4 record among AFC foes to Houston's 7-5 mark.

SEASONED VETERANS: Running back Calvin Hill (top), defensive tackle Jerry Sherk (right) and safety Clarence Scott (above) added 10, nine and eight years of NFL experience, respectively, to Sam Rutigliano's first "Kardiac Kids" team of 1979.

Sipe was later named NFL Most Valuable Player. He had passed for 4,132 yards, second in league history at the time to San Diego's Dan Fouts. He became only the third quarterback to ever eclipse the 4,000-yards passing plateau (Joe Namath did it with the Jets in 1967). Sipe broke his own team records for pass attempts (554) and completions (337), and threw for 30 touchdowns and just 14 interceptions. Mike Pruitt had the second of his four 1,000-yard rushing seasons and also led the team with 63 receptions.

Once again, 12 of the 16 games were decided by a touchdown or less. This time, however, the Kardiac Kids won nine of those close ones. And the fans were ecstatic. There were 15,000 of them at Hopkins Airport when the team arrived from Cincinnati. Cleveland mayor George Voinovich was one of them, as he called the Browns' AFC Central championship the most important thing to happen to the community since he'd been in office. The eight-year playoff drought was over. All was now good in Brownsland.

The Kardiac Kids would play one more close game, although it would not result in heart failure, but rather heartbreak. The Oakland Raiders had crushed Houston, 27-7, in a

BEHIND THE LINE: Robert L. Jackson (56), Dick Ambrose (52) and Clay Matthews (57) formed three-fourths the 1980 linebacking corps. They were joined by Charlie Hall.

Wild Card playoff game for the right to visit Cleveland and take on the Browns. Had the Oilers won, the Browns would have hosted the AFC East champion Buffalo Bills, as the league attempted not to match teams from the same division in the playoffs until the conference championship.

The Cleveland area was going through two weeks of Browns madness. The 20,000 tickets available for the playoff battle were sold in two hours. Fans camped all night in front of ticket outlets, waiting for the 10 a.m. window opening. Christmas shoppers were buying Browns merchandise as fast as the shopkeepers could put it out for them.

The area needed this. Like many northern cities that had been manufacturing giants in the late 19th and early 20th centuries, and a magnet for European immigrants, Cleveland's future was precarious. Jobs in the smokestack industries were vanishing and the population was dwindling. Clevelanders were leaving the city in droves, both to the ever-sprawling suburbs and to the ballooning "Sun Belt" states.

RED RIGHT 88: In the nightmare ending to a dream season, Oakland's Mike Davis intercepts Brian Sipe's end-zone pass to Ozzie Newsome (82) at Cleveland Stadium. The play halted the Kardiac Kids' hopes to advance in the 1980 AFC playoffs.

Worse yet, "Cleveland" jokes were becoming popular, as the city became the nationwide symbol of the declining Northeast-Midwest industrial corridor.

In Oakland, the Raiders had been consistent winners for more than a decade. Jim Plunkett, the 1970 Heisman Trophy winner, had resurrected his career with the Raiders. So had vicious defensive end John Matuszak, the first overall draft choice of 1973 whose unruliness almost swept him out of the league until he joined the Raiders in '76.

The defense was extremely tough. Cornerback Lester Hayes, who led the NFL with 13 interceptions, and veteran linebacker Ted Hendricks were All-Pro. On offense, Plunkett had two excellent wide receivers in Cliff Branch and Raymond Chester and a budding young star at tight end, Todd Christensen. Plunkett could hand off to running backs Mark van Eeghen and Kenny King behind an outstanding offensive line with veterans such as Gene Upshaw, Art Shell and Dave Dalby.

Game day was bitterly cold in Cleveland, with temperatures around zero. Still, 77,000 fans decided not to watch the game on television and come to the Stadium. Nothing could dampen, or chill, this party.

The Browns scored first when Ron Bolton intercepted Plunkett's pass and returned it 42 yards for a touchdown. Hendricks blocked Don Cockroft's extra-point attempt and Cleveland led, 6-0. Van Eeghen scored on a one-yard run just before halftime to put Oakland ahead, 7-6, at the intermission.

Cockroft kicked two field goals in the third quarter to make it 12-7 Browns, but van Eeghen scored again, with 9:22 remaining, to put the Raiders ahead, 14-12.

FRUSTRATION: Sam Rutigliano paces the Astrodome sideline during a 34-27 loss to Houston in 1983. Although the Browns finished at 9-7 that season, the close-win Kardiac Kids era would reverse itself in 1984 with seven losses in the first eight games, six by 10 points or less, leading to Rutigliano's dismissal.

The Browns stopped Oakland at the Cleveland 15-yard line with 2:22 to play. Sipe then drove them 72 yards to the Raiders' 13, at the open end of the stadium. But on second down, instead of going for a risky field goal attempt into a strong cross wind, Sipe threw to Ozzie Newsome in the end zone where it was intercepted by defensive back Mike Davis. The season was over and the play, known as "Red Right 88," would forever live in Browns infamy.

Plunkett defended the decision to try to get a touchdown, even though it seemed as if they were well within field goal range. He said all the points, with the exception of Bolton's interception return, were scored in the closed end of the stadium. He added that a field goal into the open end would not have been a sure thing from any distance.

It was some consolation that the Browns gave the Raiders their toughest playoff game. Oakland went on to defeat the Philadelphia Eagles, 27-10, in Super Bowl XV.

The 1980 season was the last hurrah for the Kardiac Kids. They fell to 5-11 in 1981 as the Bengals, with Forrest Gregg as coach, won the Central and went to the Super Bowl.

The Browns went 4-5 in the strike-shortened 1982 season and made the playoffs under the league's makeshift post-season schedule. They were 9-7 in 1983, which became the last for Brian Sipe in the NFL as he was lured away by the new United States Football League. In 1984, after the Browns lost seven of their first eight, Rutigliano was dismissed and replaced by Marty Schottenheimer. The Kardiac Kids era unofficially concluded with Sipe's jumping leagues. It was time for a new period in Browns history as hearts were soon replaced by bones.

Kosar, Canines & Contenders

Hanford Dixon would probably be remembered anyway. The Browns' No. 1 draft choice of 1981 was a three-time All-Pro and, with Frank Minnifield, formed what was regarded as the best cornerback tandem in the late 1980s NFL. But Dixon's on-field accomplishments in his nine-year career may be overshadowed by what he brought to the atmosphere surrounding the Browns and their fans. All the barking, all the canine masks, all the Milk Bones scattered in the end zone nearest the Cleveland Stadium bleachers, you can thank Hanford Dixon for that. "I was just trying to fire up our defensive linemen," Dixon recalled. "We weren't known for our pass rush, and we needed a good pass rush. All teams need a good pass rush. I started telling the media our linemen were going to run after the quarterback like a pack of dogs chasing a cat. Then I told Frank Minnifield we should start barking at the linemen, you know, to get them fired up. Pretty soon the fans started barking, and you know the rest."

The rest is that the Cleveland Browns' fans adopted Dixon's persona faster than Walter Payton could hit a hole off left tackle. For every game in the latter half of the 1980s otherwise rational folks would behave like dogs (or, as it came to be spelled, "Dawgs," in imitation of Dixon's Alabama drawl). The bleachers, where the most dedicated barkers held seats, became the "Dawg Pound." Fans poured into the Stadium wearing masks that made them look like bulldogs, bloodhounds, golden retrievers, et al. They carried bones, both real ones and replicas, and wore clothing adorned with dog references as the apparel manufacturers moved quickly to take advantage of the situation.

It was infectious. The image of the good-timing, slightly rowdy football fan sitting in a 55-year-old stadium with a grass field, barking like a maniac, caught on across the nation.

Fans who had never been within an all-day drive of Cleveland suddenly found a team with which they could identify. The emotional outlet of the Dawg phenomenon was unprecedented. Nearly 15 years after its beginning, the Dawg Pound has become synonymous with Browns football.

The Oakland Raiders had cultivated an image for themselves in the 1970s. They were the nasty boys of pro football who looked like Paul Brown's worst nightmare—unshaven, unshorn and dressed like motorcycle gang members. Characters like Ken Stabler, Jack "Assassin" Tatum, John Matuszak, Ted Hendricks, Otis Sistrunk and George Atkinson glamorized the "silver and black" for people who followed the NFL on television.

Their opposite number was the Dallas Cowboys, who were clean-cut and businesslike and never approached games as if they were street rumbles. While Oakland was coached by super-animated John Madden, Dallas had taciturn Tom Landry and quarterback Roger Staubach, an Annapolis graduate who made the Cowboys "America's Team."

MARTY'S MAGIC: Marty Schottenheimer guided the Browns to their best run of success since the 1960s. From 1985-88, the Browns won three Central Division titles, appeared in the AFC Championship game twice and in 1986 enjoyed their highest win total (12) since the 14-0 undefeated AAFC season of 1948.

The Chicago Bears became an image team about the time the Browns were beginning the Dawg shtick. Chicago had recognizable figures such as the tough-guy coach (Mike Ditka), the iconoclastic quarterback (Jim McMahon) and the endomorphic rookie (defensive tackle William "The Refrigerator" Perry).

But in all those cases it was the players who upheld the image. With the Browns, their fans were the show, and the media were quick to play it up. John Thompson, alias "Big Dawg," had as familiar a face to football fans nationwide as Art Modell, even if it was hidden by a bloodhound mask. Standing in the front row of the bleachers, the Big Dawg's exhorting the team to victory was constantly being captured by the TV cameras and shown on highlight films on Sunday nights.

It was harmless, for the most part. But the Browns occasionally had to curb their Dawgs. The throwing of real marrow bones on the field was halted for the safety of the players, and the team attempted to better police the Pound after reports of unruliness increased. Oddly enough, however, Dixon and Minnifield weren't the best known, or even the best loved, of the Browns in the late 1980s. That honor went to quarterback Bernie Kosar, the Northeast Ohio native who led the Miami Hurricanes to an NCAA title in 1983, then said in 1985 that he would skip his last two years of college eligibility if he could fulfill his lifelong dream of playing for Cleveland.

The Browns were happy to oblige. Brian Sipe had jumped to the USFL after the 1983 season. His replacement, Paul McDonald, had a dismal year in 1984 despite having four seasons as Sipe's backup. McDonald threw 23 interceptions to just 14 touchdown passes.

He wasn't helped by Mike Pruitt's knee problems, which sidelined the All-Pro rusher for four games after undergoing arthroscopic surgery. Pruitt had his worst season with 506 yards and a 3.1 per-carry rate, and was released before the start of the 1985 campaign.

Age and injury caught up to the offensive line. Left tackle Doug Dieken played in his 14th (and final) season in 1984. Right tackle Cody Risien missed all of the '84 season following a preseason knee injury. Joe DeLamielleure was released after 12 years in the league.

Head Coach Sam Rutigliano was fired eight games into the season, as the Browns were 1-7.

> **Bernie Kosar was a lifelong Browns fan from Boardman, Ohio, who gave up his last two years of college eligibility to be selected by Cleveland in the 1985 supplemental draft. By 1989 (right), he was leading the team to its fifth straight trip to the playoffs and third AFC Championship game.**

IMMEDIATE IMPACT: With rookie Bernie Kosar taking control, the Browns returned to the playoffs in 1985. In Game 13 (above), Kosar and the Browns beat the Giants, 35-33, on their way to an 8-8 record and the AFC Central Division title.

It was the first time that Art Modell had ever replaced a head coach in mid season. Defensive coordinator Marty Schottenheimer took over. The team won four more games to finish 5-11.

The club spared no expense to get Kosar. They gave the Buffalo Bills their first draft choices in 1985 and '86, a third choice in '85 and a sixth pick in '86 for the Bills' first choice in the supplemental draft of 1985. The Browns picked up another quarterback, Gary Danielson of Detroit, for a third-round draft pick in 1986. Danielson had been in professional football since 1974, first in the World Football League and two years later with the Lions.

Danielson started the first five games of '85 before injuring his right shoulder. Kosar got the nod and led the Browns to an 8-8 record and the first of three consecutive AFC Central championships. Kosar completed half of his passes (124 of 248) with eight touchdowns to seven interceptions.

While the quarterbacking was in transition, the Browns were mainly a running team. Fullback Kevin Mack gained 1,104 yards and Earnest Byner added 1,002. Mack and Byner became the third pair of running backs on the same team to each gain 1,000 yards in the same season (Miami's Larry Csonka and Eugene "Mercury" Morris in '72, and Franco Harris and Rocky Bleier of Pittsburgh in '76). Their combined yardage was second in team history to Jim Brown and Ernie Green in 1963.

Byner had a great game in the 1985 divisional playoff game versus Miami: 161 yards to break the club's record for yards rushing (114 by Jim Brown in 1964) in a playoff game. His 66-yard run was also a Browns playoff record for longest gain rushing. But Cleveland lost, 24-21, after leading 21-3 at one time. After the game Kosar criticized the coaching staff for using an offensive plan he considered too conservative, and said something had to be done.

What was done was the hiring of Lindy Infante as offensive coordinator. Infante, most recently the coach of the Jacksonville Bulls in the USFL, was considered one of the greatest offensive minds in pro football. He was better known to Browns fans as designer of the 1981 AFC-champion Cincinnati offense, led by Ken Anderson passing to Isaac Curtis, Cris Collinsworth and Dan Ross. Infante installed a new offense to highlight Kosar's assets (reading defenses, accuracy) and disguise his weaknesses (a basic lack of mobility, average offensive line).

HIGH FIVE: Under defensive specialist Marty Schottenheimer's direction, this became a common scene of celebration. In 1985 (above), starters included defensive end Reggie Camp (96), linebackers Eddie Johnson (51) and Tom Cousineau (50), and defensive backs Frank Minnifield (31) and Don Rogers (20).

The Browns also set about to find a wide receiver, though they didn't have a first-round draft choice. Former Brown Paul Warfield was assigned to scout the nation to find one with speed and good hands the Browns could draft in Round 2. Warfield recommended San Diego State's Webster Slaughter.

The team obviously did something right. The Browns compiled a 12-4 record in 1986, best in the AFC, and improved their scoring by 104 points over 1985. After an opening-day loss to the defending Super Bowl champion Chicago Bears, and a Week 3 pounding by the Bengals, the Browns started soaring. They won their last five games, eight of their final nine and 11 of the last 13.

Kosar had career highs in passing attempts (531), completions (310) and yards (3,854). Suddenly there was a new contingent of quality receivers. Third-year veteran Brian Brennan led the club with 55 catches and six touchdowns. Slaughter had a great rookie year with 40 catches and four TDs. Tight end Ozzie Newsome and second-year man Reggie Langhorne had 39 receptions each. The running backs got into the act, too. Herman Fontenot grabbed 47 passes, Earnest Byner had 37 catches and fullback Kevin Mack had 28 receptions.

Mack and Byner had each surpassed 1,000 yards rushing in 1985, but the running game took a back seat in '86 to Infante's pass offense. Mack led the team in rushing with 665 yards.

REVAMPED RECEIVING: Three new wide receivers joined tight end Ozzie Newsome as Bernie Kosar's targets in the '80s. Brian Brennan (above), Reggie Langhorne (left) and Webster Slaughter (top) became Browns in 1984, '85 and '86, respectively.

The offensive line provided good protection for Kosar and quality blocking for Mack and Byner. Starters were Rickey Bolden or Paul Farren at left tackle, Farren or Larry Williams at left guard, Mike Baab at center, Dan Fike at right guard and Cody Risien at right tackle.

The Dawg Defense, meanwhile, solidified around four Pro Bowl veterans: nose tackle Bob Golic, outside linebacker Chip Banks and cornerbacks Dixon and Minnifield. Outside linebacker Clay Matthews was reaching his prime, while defensive ends Reggie Camp and Carl Hairston provided solid play along with inside linebackers Anthony Griggs and Eddie Johnson, and safeties Ray Ellis and Chris Rockins.

The 1986 season was the Kardiac Kids all over again. Brownsmania was everywhere. The record, coupled with the Dawg persona, had the area delirious with Super Bowl dreaming. Songs by professional and amateur recording artists started popping up on radio stations with ever greater regularity. Nowhere could a

BACKFIELD BRILLIANCE: Kevin Mack (left) and Earnest Byner (right) provided a power rushing attack not seen since the '60s. In 1985, the pair each gained more than 1,000 yards as the offense featured a new emphasis on the running game.

Northeast Ohio resident get away from the Browns in the last months of 1986.

But, as with every other season, the Super Bowl would have to wait for the Browns. The road almost took a detour in the AFC Divisional playoffs as the Browns rallied from 10 points behind late in the fourth quarter to pull out a 23-20 double-overtime victory over the Jets on Mark Moseley's dramatic 27-yard field goal.

But if the Browns had won one they should have lost that week, they lost one they should have won the following week in the AFC championship contest at Cleveland Stadium. The Denver Broncos came to town fresh off a divisional playoff victory over the defending AFC champion Patriots. The Broncos were led by quarterback John Elway, one of the best all-

ECSTASY AND AGONY: Chip Banks sacks Jets quarterback Pat Ryan (right) in the Browns' 23-20 double-overtime win at Cleveland Stadium in the 1986 AFC playoffs. The following week (above) Bernie Kosar avoids pursuit in the AFC Championship game against Denver, also at the Stadium. Kosar directed the Browns to a fourth-quarter 20-13 lead, only to be tied on "The Drive" and beaten in overtime on a Rich Karlis field goal.

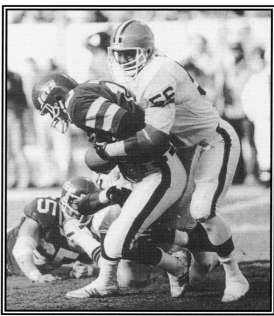

around athletes in the NFL, and a stubborn defense led by Pro Bowlers Rulon Jones, Karl Mecklenburg and Dennis Smith.

A field goal by Mark Moseley with 20 seconds left in the first half tied the game at 10-10. It was 13-13 with 5:43 remaining in the fourth quarter when Kosar found Brian Brennan behind the Denver defense and threw a 48-yard touchdown pass to him to put the Browns ahead, 20-13. Celebrating was premature, however, because Marty Schottenheimer's prevent defense couldn't prevent Elway and the Broncos from embarking on a 98-yard, 15-play drive that managed the clock to perfection. "The Drive," ended on a five-yard pass to Mark Jackson with 37 seconds remaining to tie the score and force the Browns into overtime for the second playoff game in a row.

Cleveland won the coin toss to begin the overtime and elected to receive. The Denver defense stopped them and Jeff Gossett punted to the 24-yard line. The Broncos then marched

60 yards to set up Rich Karlis' 33-yard game-winning field goal with 5:48 to go. The final: 23-20 Denver, the same score by which the Browns beat the Jets a week earlier.

In 1987, the Browns won the AFC Central again despite a strike by the players' union that cancelled one game and had the teams using replacement players for three others. The regular Browns had an 8-4 record and the replacements won two of three games. Kosar enjoyed another banner year, leading the league in completion rate (62 percent) and topping the AFC in quarterback rating (95.4).

The Browns and the Broncos met for the AFC championship again in 1987, but this time it was in Denver. The Broncos jumped to a 21-3 halftime lead and were up 28-10 at one point in the third period. But two touchdowns by Earnest Byner, one on a pass and the other via rushing, cut the margin to 28-24. Rich Karlis nailed a 38-yard field goal with 10 seconds left in the third quarter to make it 31-24.

Cleveland tied it with 4:12 gone in the final period on a four-yard pass from Kosar to Webster Slaughter. Denver untied it with 4:01 left on a 20-yarder from Elway to Sammy Winder.

The Browns were driving for another tying score when disaster hit. They were at the Broncos' eight-yard line when Kosar handed to Byner, who pushed ahead to the three, but was stripped of the ball by Jeremiah Castille, who recovered with 1:12 to play. A safety when Broncos punter Mike Horan ran out of the back of the end zone was meaningless.

The Broncos had won again, 38-33. "The Drive" of the '86 season had been followed by "The Fumble" of '87. Added to "Red Right 88" of the 1980 season and the Browns' most painful playoff memories of the 1980s forever had memorable monikers.

THE FUMBLE: Denver's Jeremiah Castille prepares to strip Earnest Byner of the ball on the Broncos' three-yard line in the fourth quarter of the 1987 AFC Championship game at Mile High Stadium. The Browns were driving for a tying touchdown, but instead were again denied a trip to the Super Bowl.

The 1988 season might be forever remembered by Browns fans as the Year of the Injured Quarterback. Bernie Kosar took a shot to the elbow of his throwing arm in a 6-3 win over the Chiefs in Game 1. The next week, Gary Danielson was lost when he broke his left ankle in a 23-3 loss to the Jets. Mike Pagel went down in the sixth game, a 16-10 loss to Seattle.

Thirty-eight-year-old Don Strock, who was brought out of retirement and signed following Danielson's injury, became the quarterback. He responded by leading the Browns to an upset of Philadelphia in Week 7 and by playing an outstanding second half as the Browns defeated the Oilers, 28-23, in Week 16.

The latter contest got the Browns a Wild Card playoff berth. They had been trailing the entire game and were behind, 23-7, when Hous-

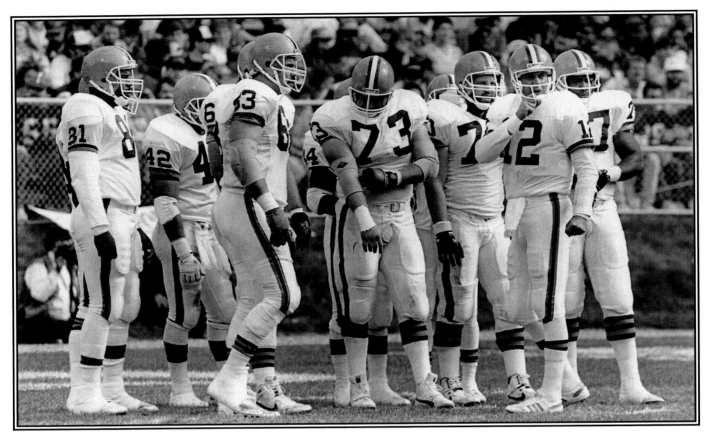

WRIST TAKER: Don Strock (12) became the fourth starting quarterback in 1988 following injuries to Bernie Kosar, Gary Danielson and Mike Pagel. Strock took plays into the huddle strapped to his wrist, then took the Browns to the playoffs.

ton's Warren Moon fired a seven-yard TD pass to Haywood Jeffires at the six-minute mark of the third quarter.

But Strock led the Browns back. A two-yard touchdown pass to Earnest Byner at 6:06 left in the third period was followed by two-yard TD run by Byner two minutes into the fourth stanza. The game-winner was a 22-yard pass from Strock to Slaughter at the 8:37 mark. The drive featured three catches by Reggie Langhorne for 47 yards. The final second-half figures for Strock showed 16-for-23 passing for 215 yards, two touchdowns and no interceptions.

There was no such miracle rally the following week when the two teams met again at Cleveland Stadium for their Wild Card playoff game. Strock suffered a hand injury trying to recover his own fumble in the first quarter and

Mike Pagel, just activated off the injured reserve list (shoulder separation) was called to duty. Pagel did well, completing 17 of 25 passes for 179 yards and two touchdowns, but the Oilers went home after two straight weekends in Cleveland with a 24-23 victory.

Pagel's 14-yard touchdown pass to Webster Slaughter in the third quarter put the Browns ahead, 16-14, but Houston came back on a touchdown run by Lorenzo White and a 49-yard field goal by Tony Zendejas with 1:54 remaining to take a 24-16 edge.

Slaughter caught another touchdown pass from Pagel with 31 seconds remaining, but the Browns' onside kick was recovered by the Oilers as time expired.

The game would be the last one Marty Schottenheimer would coach with the Browns. A growing philosophical gap between Schottenheimer and owner Art Modell led to an agreement that the head coach would step down. Schottenheimer was quickly hired to coach the Kansas City Chiefs.

BIG DADDY & FAMILY: Browns defenders demonstrate the intensity typical of the Browns-Bengals battles of the late '80s. End Carl "Big Daddy" Hairston (left) wraps up quarterback Boomer Esiason. Nose tackle Bob Golic (below) does likewise. Above, linebackers Clay Matthews (57) and Mike Johnson (59), and safety Felix Wright (22) tackle running back Ickey Woods.

In his place came Bud Carson, a longtime defensive coach who was being given his first shot at a head coaching position at the age of 58.

Carson was the architect of the Pittsburgh Steelers' "Steel Curtain" defense of the 1970s, which helped them win Super Bowl titles in 1974 and '75. He was defensive coordinator for the Rams in 1978-79 and helped them to an NFC championship. Along the way, Carson's Rams defense held the Seattle Seahawks to minus-seven yards in a game, an all-time low in NFL history. He also was defensive coordinator of the Jets in 1985-88, where he improved that club's defense from No. 23 overall in 1984 to eighth the following season.

Carson's first season as coach in 1989 was an odd one. In the regular-season opener versus the Steelers, the Browns set club records for the most lopsided shutout score and the fewest yards of total offense allowed (53) in a 51-0 rout. The Browns forced eight turnovers and had seven sacks.

The Browns were 7-3 at one point. They had beaten their archrivals, the Broncos, but

TOP DAWG'S EXIT: Hanford Dixon's nine-year career ended following the 1989 season. He retired as a three-time leader in Browns interceptions, a three-time Pro Bowl pick and the one-time creator of the symbol of "rabid" Browns fans: the Dawg.

lost an overtime battle to Miami and dropped their rematch with the Steelers. Things started to look really bleak when they could only reach a 10-10 tie in a home game against the Chiefs and former coach Marty Schottenheimer, who was rebuilding the fortunes of Kansas City. That was followed by three consecutive losses and the Browns were 7-6-1.

But the Browns next beat the Minnesota Vikings in overtime with a bit of trickery. Matt

Bahr set up for what looked to be a 31-yard field goal try in overtime, but holder Mike Pagel took the ball, stood up and hit linebacker Van Waiters with a 23-yard pass in the end zone to win a game by that means for the first time in 12 years.

Bahr had sent the game into overtime with a 32-yard field goal with 24 seconds to play. The triumph set up a showdown for the divisional title with the Oilers in Houston.

The Browns built a 17-3 advantage by half-time, but Warren Moon and the Oilers dominated the second half. A field goal by Tony Zendejas was sandwiched by touchdown passes to Drew Hill to give the Oilers a 20-17 lead.

The second TD pass to Hill happened one play after one of the most bizarre events in Browns history. Moon, operating from a shotgun formation, had the snap go over his head. Clay Matthews recovered, but tried to lateral to a teammate. The ball was loose and recovered by Hill at the Browns' 27-yard line.

Kevin Mack finally gave the Browns the victory on a four-yard run with 39 seconds to go. Mack, who played only four games in 1989, did the bulk of the running on the winning drive and finished with 62 yards on 12 carries.

The divisional playoff game was another wild affair as the Buffalo Bills visited Cleveland. The Browns led for good when Bernie Kosar tossed a three-yard touchdown pass to Ron Middleton with 1:06 to go in the first half to make the score 17-14. The Browns were ahead, 34-24, when Thurman Thomas grabbed a TD pass from Jim Kelly with four minutes to play. The extra-point try was no good, which forced the Bills to have to go for a touchdown if they were in the position to win.

They got in the position, but couldn't convert. Ronnie Harmon dropped a 14-yard pass from Kelly in the end zone and Clay Matthews intercepted a Kelly pass on the one-yard line with nine seconds left. Matthews didn't attempt a lateral that time and the Browns survived with a 34-30 victory.

Survived is the word. The defense allowed Kelly 405 passing yards, a Cleveland playoff record. The 656 passing yards by both clubs was also a record for a regulation-length playoff game, as were the seven touchdown passes the two teams threw.

But for the third time in four seasons the Browns were defeated by the Broncos in the AFC Championship game. This time it wasn't close. Denver outscored Cleveland 13-0 in the fourth quarter at Mile High Stadium to register a 37-21 win. John Elway threw four touchdown passes, including a 70-yarder to Mike Young and two to running back Sammy Winder. Brian Brennan had two touchdown catches for the Browns as Cleveland scored all its points in the third period.

DEFENSIVE DIRECTION: Head Coach Bud Carson guided the Browns to a 9-6-1 mark in 1989 and a playoff win over Buffalo before losing to Denver in the AFC title game. The architect of Pittsburgh's Steel Curtain defense of the 1970s, Carson saw his defense shut out the Steelers in the '89 opener, 51-0.

The loss made the Browns 0-5 in games that could have sent them to the Super Bowl: NFL championship games in 1968 and '69, and AFC title games in 1986, '87 and '89.

It would be another five years before the team reached a playoff game. They would do it without Bernie Kosar. The young man from Boardman who wanted to lead his boyhood favorite team to Super Bowl glory was released in 1993. The loyalty and devotion Browns fans had for Kosar made the end of the line much more difficult to face.

Hanford Dixon retired following the '89 season, but the Dawgs did not retire. The image he and fellow cornerback Frank Minnifield created is around today—with an official logo—but a bit more more controlled than when the "Corner Brothers," as Minnifield and Dixon called themselves, were patrolling the secondary.

Rebuilding in the New NFL

Bill Belichick knew that the Cleveland Browns were a team in trouble long before he was named their head coach on Feb. 5, 1991. He figured as much based on conversations with Browns front office personnel such as Ozzie Newsome, Mike Lombardi, Ernie Accorsi, Jim Shofner and team owner Art Modell. But seeing it on the field was a whole different experience for the 38-year-old who 10 days earlier had won his second Super Bowl ring as the New York Giants' defensive coordinator. "Sure, I talked to Art about building the team and the organization," Belichick said. "But when the reality of it all hit me was in training camp in 1991. That's when I remember going into Art's office and telling him that it was going to take five years." Cleveland won six games in 1991. Before the 1995 season, Belichick said the team was "lucky" it won that many.

Of the 3-13 team from 1990 that Belichick inherited, he said: "It was just a mess. Just look at the players who were here at the time—Paul Farren, Mike Baab, Ralph Tamm, Ben Jefferson, Tim Manoa, Bob Buczkowski, who we traded, John Talley, Ken Reeves, Van Waiters."

Belichick pointed out that few players from the 1991 Browns team were still active in the league as early as three years later. Even Bernie Kosar, the popular quarterback who was released in Belichick's most controversial decision on Nov. 8, 1993, had become no more than a backup in Dallas and Miami.

"Of the ones who were still in pro football in 1994, very few were still playing," Belichick said. "Kosar, Scott Galbraith, Ralph Tamm, guys like that are still hanging on in the league. Now a guy like [wide receiver] Webster Slaughter, that's different. It's unfortunate that we lost him, but he just got turned loose [as a free agent] by the courts in 1992. We didn't really have a chance to keep him."

When the Browns prepared for the 1995 season, only four players remained from when Belichick took over: running back Leroy Hoard, offensive left tackle Tony Jones and defensive ends Anthony Pleasant and Rob Burnett. "When you're as bad as we were in 1991, it's going to take more than one or two moves to make it happen," Belichick said in May of '95. "It's going to take some time. Unfortunately, I don't know how you can speed up the process."

Modell accepted Belichick's reasoning. He gave Belichick a five-year contract in 1991 and extended it by two years in 1993. "We were in a tailspin before Bill Belichick arrived," Modell said. "We were going nowhere very, very fast. We had to change our whole approach."

Such was the story of the five-year Bill Belichick era: continual, seemingly endless rebuilding along with annual optimism—from Modell or the coach himself—that the team was making strides, plus pleas for patience. With only one winning season, however, the Belichick era marked the longest stretch of non-contending teams in Browns history.

PLAN B POSITIVE: Former Giant Matt Stover was one of the Browns' better Plan B free agent acquisitions after signing in 1991. In 1994, he became the most accurate field goal kicker in team history by closing out the season with a record 20 straight.

When Belichick started, he had four basic ways to acquire new players: the draft, trades, the waiver wire and Plan B free agency, which was the earliest form of free agency that made every NFL team's fringe players free to switch teams. Two years later, the league's new seven-year collective bargaining agreement drastically changed the rules of the NFL.

"In the old days, you drafted a guy and he played for you for 12 years," Belichick said. "As long as he was good enough to make the team, you kept paying him and he kept playing."

Unrestricted free agency for players after their fourth season and an unyielding salary cap that kicked in for the 1994 season ended that sort of stability. "The way the game is in this era, you have to be flexible," Belichick explained. "It's a little bit like being a college coach because you know no matter what you do, you just can't keep a team together."

The new system was far from perfect when it took effect, but Belichick said that at least everybody began playing by the same rules.

"The playing field is level now," Belichick said. "Whoever is the best is a reflection of the best organization, from management to ownership to coaching to scouting. If you compare that to the 1993 season, you'll see what I mean. That was the year before the salary cap, but the year everyone was keeping cap figures. You had teams like Miami and New Orleans with $50 million payrolls, and ours was at $32 million. That's a big difference."

In 1994, the year the cap and free agency came together, the Browns reached the playoffs for the first time since 1989. Their 11-5 record was the best since 1988, good for second in the AFC Central Division. They beat New England in the opening round of the playoffs before losing to Pittsburgh in the second round.

In the 1990s era of pro football, the Browns, like all teams, had to make tough decisions. Long gone were the days when talent was the only thing a coach looked for. "A player's worth is just as important as whether he can make your team or not," Belichick said. "It's like you have to appraise real estate. If you appraise it wrong, then that's going to hurt your football team competitively."

Modell believed the collective bargaining agreement signed in 1993 raised the NFL to a level of competition unmatched to that point. And with players moving around, a salary cap to deal with and off-season activity being scrutinized as closely as the regular-season games, Modell also said the pressure to win became higher than ever before.

"It's more demanding now in the Belichick era than it was in the Paul Brown era," Modell explained. "The pressure is public pressure, peer pressure, self-imposed pressure and, most importantly, media pressure. This was not the case when I first bought the team in 1961. It's overwhelming."

Modell was happy with the way Belichick stood up to the pressure of finding players in the most difficult era of player acquisition.

HOLDOVERS: After four years of rebuilding the Browns' roster, only four players remained in 1995 from head coach Bill Belichick's first season of 1991: defensive ends Rob Burnett (90) and Anthony Pleasant (98), running back Leroy Hoard (33) and offensive tackle Tony Jones (66).

BUILDING BLOCKS: First-round draft choices were the pride of head coach Bill Belichick. Safety Eric Turner (opposite page) was the top pick in 1991 followed by running back Tommy Vardell (above) in '92, center Steve Everitt (above right) in '93, cornerback Antonio Langham (right) and receiver Derrick Alexander in '94, and linebacker Craig Powell in '95.

"Belichick's greatest strength is his ability to judge talent," Modell said. "Say what you want about his X's and O's, and his motivational abilities and player relations. Putting all that aside, I haven't had anybody in a long, long time who has the ability to judge talent as he has. Look at his No. 1 draft picks from 1991 to '95. The proof is in the pudding. There it is. History has shown the job he's done."

In 1995, Belichick said he was most proud of his first-round draft picks. He picked safety Eric Turner second overall in 1991, running back Tommy Vardell ninth in 1992, center Steve Everitt 14th in 1993, cornerback Antonio Langham and wide receiver Derrick Alexander ninth and 29th, respectively, in 1994, and linebacker Craig Powell 30th in 1995.

"Nobody really had us taking Turner as the second player in 1991," he said. "We took some criticism for taking him, but I never had any doubts he would be an outstanding player in this league, and I think he became clearly one of the top defensive players in the league.

"It may have seemed easy, with him being the second pick, but there were a lot of misses in that draft. Pittsburgh took Huey Richardson [15th], Tampa Bay got Charles McRae [seventh], and Atlanta used the third pick on Bruce

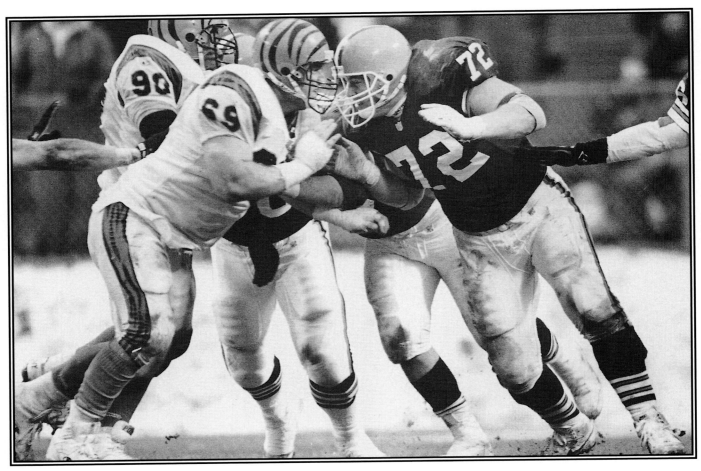

UNWAIVERING CONSISTENCY: Guard Bob Dahl squares off against Cincinnati's Tim Krumrie. Dahl was waived by the Bengals and Steelers before the Browns signed him in 1992. Entering 1995, he had started 41 straight games for the Browns.

Pickens. I think we got a good player in that draft out of a guy people thought was a reach, a guy that a number of people wouldn't have taken in the spot we were sitting."

Turner tied for the league lead in interceptions with nine in 1994. He had 17 in his first four seasons.

The draft was not the only tool the Browns used in hopes of finding a winning formula in the 1990s. Plan B free agents, unrestricted free agents, waiver wire castoffs and players picked up through trades all became part of the mix.

The Browns took care of their place-kicking needs when they signed Matt Stover as a Plan B free agent from the New York Giants in 1991. Stover had not kicked in a regular-season game,

but by 1994 he had moved ahead of Matt Bahr as the most accurate field goal kicker in Browns history, including a team-record 20 straight to close out the season.

In 1992, safety Stevon Moore was signed as a Plan B free agent. Basically thrown away by Don Shula's Dolphins, Moore joined Turner to give the Browns one of the strongest safety tandems in the league in 1994.

When the unrestricted free agent market opened in 1993, the Browns signed, among others, wide receiver Mark Carrier and quarterback Vinny Testaverde in 1993, linebacker Carl Banks and cornerback Don Griffin in 1994, and receiver Andre Rison and running back Lorenzo White in 1995.

Belichick also plucked running back Randy Baldwin from Minnesota's practice squad in 1991. By 1993, he was one of the league's most dangerous kick returners and one of the best downfield tacklers on the special teams.

In 1992, the Browns found offensive lineman Bob Dahl on the waiver wire after both Cincinnati and Pittsburgh had given up on him. Dahl, a defensive lineman at the University of Notre Dame, was drafted in the third round of the 1991 draft by Cincinnati. He landed on the Bengals' practice squad and was released that season. The Steelers picked him up and put him on their practice squad as they tried to convert him to offense. They gave up too early and released Dahl.

The Browns then picked him up before the 1992 season and put him on their practice squad until activating him on Halloween that year. Ironically, he made his first start the following week against Cincinnati. Heading into the 1995 season, Dahl had started 41 straight games for the Browns.

Belichick also agreed to take in linebacker Pepper Johnson when the Giants were rebuilding their linebacking corps in 1993. A year

GIANT ACQUISITIONS: Bill Belichick's rebuilding efforts included former New York Giants familiar to him when he was defensive coordinator for the Giants' Super Bowl champs of the 1986 and '90 seasons. Linebackers Carl Banks (left) and Pepper Johnson (right) joined the Browns in 1994 and '93, respectively.

later, Johnson moved into the starting middle linebacker position in Cleveland. He registered more than 200 tackles and was a team leader.

The Browns also found a mammoth offensive tackle that everyone overlooked in the 1993 draft. Orlando Brown, a 6-7, 325-pounder from South Carolina State, was signed as a free agent in 1993. By mid season a year later, he had developed into a solid player at right tackle.

In the way of trades, the Browns picked up a couple starters for mid-to-low draft picks in 1992 and 1993. In '92, they gave the Rams an eighth-round pick for linebacker Frank Stams. In 1993, they acquired Miami offensive lineman Gene Williams for a fourth-round pick.

MOVING ON: Eric Metcalf provided spectacular thrills as a Browns kick returner and running back from 1989-94. But as part of what would become a trend in the mid 1990s, he was traded to Atlanta in '95 as the Browns cleared room under the salary cap to sign perennial All-Pro receiver Andre Rison.

"There are a lot of things you'd like to do over again," Belichick said. "Obviously, the [defensive tackle] Jerry Ball trade in 1993 didn't go particularly well for us. I'd say that's the biggest mistake, only because we gave up something for him. We gave up a third-round pick."

Other personnel decisions haven't worked out, but Belichick isn't as upset about them because the price the team paid was low.

"A guy like [offensive tackle] Freddie Childress obviously didn't work out, but all we gave

up for Childress was an eighth-round pick. So what," Belichick said. "Those are the kinds of moves you've got to make when you're not very good. Freddie Childress didn't work out, but Randy Baldwin did, Frank Stams did, Matt Stover did, and so did a lot of others."

Punter Tom Tupa is a classic case. He came to the Browns as an NFL quarterback who also was Ohio State's all-time leading punter. He lasted five seasons (1988-92) with the Cardinals and Colts, playing in 45 games with 13 starts at quarterback. He punted the ball only six times, averaging 46.7 yards.

Tupa signed with the Browns for two games in 1993, but didn't see any action and was released. They brought him back in the spring of '94, made him their full-time punter and were not disappointed in the fall.

"To win in the NFL, you have to find good players," Belichick said. "You can't think you're going to out-trick or out-coach everybody at this level. It doesn't work. You have the new rules, and you have eight rounds in the draft as compared to 12. There are fewer four-year college players and a lot more junior college guys. You have more ground to cover, but it's just something you work your way through."

The Browns, he added, became much more thorough in that department since player personnel director Mike Lombardi took over the department in 1992. "The 1991 and 1992 drafts weren't very good drafts for us," Belichick said. "I think we did OK early in the draft when we really knew what we were doing, but we blew some picks in the later rounds."

In 1992, the Browns drafted a player by the name of Marcus Lowe, a defensive tackle from Baylor, in the 10th round. Guys like Lowe are long shots to begin with, but Lowe was a man who spent only one day in Cleveland. He rode the stationary bike for a day and was told to go home and come back when he wasn't the size of the Goodyear blimp. Marcus never returned, and was cut because he was simply too large.

A guy like Lowe taught Belichick a lesson he will never forget. "There were a couple cases in the later rounds in 1991 and 1992 where I

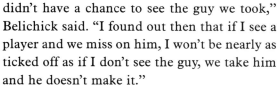

SUCCESSFUL SIGNINGS: The Browns utilized free agency to rebuild all aspects of the roster. Former Colt and Cardinal Tom Tupa (left) became the punter, kick holder and backup quarterback in 1994. Ex-Buccaneer Vinny Testaverde (right) succeeded Bernie Kosar as the starting quarterback in 1993.

didn't have a chance to see the guy we took," Belichick said. "I found out then that if I see a player and we miss on him, I won't be nearly as ticked off as if I don't see the guy, we take him and he doesn't make it."

By the 1993 draft, Belichick said the organization had been pretty well-schooled in what he wanted in a football player. "We're definitely going in the same direction," Belichick said. "The information from the scouting department is a lot better. The quality of the scouts is a lot better. The scouts adhering to the philosophy of the football team is a lot better. And the players are a lot better."

The work left Belichick and his staff with basically two weeks off a year. They would take a two-week vacation before the start of training camp. He believed it was worth the effort.

"I think we have basically rebuilt the whole team," Belichick said. "Four years later, I don't look at any area and think we're deficient. Obviously, we could always be better. But provided we can stay healthy and the younger players can continue to improve as the ones who

have been here before have, I think we're going to have a good team for quite a few years."

In May of 1995, Belichick looked back on his training-camp meeting with Art Modell in 1991 and shook his head.

"The biggest thing this organization has to be proud of is coming off a 3-13 season, then going 6-10 when we probably were lucky to be 6-10 and ending up 12-6, including the playoffs, in 1994," Belichick said. "In four years, we took a team that was second worst in the league to the fourth-best record in the league. It was slow and it was steady, and maybe it wasn't spectacular, but we built a team. And it's a team that I think will last. I don't think it's going to be a team that goes 11-5 one year and 4-12 the next."

But Belichick's rebuilt team did not last—either as a winner or in the city of Cleveland.

An Ending and a Mending

A fter their 11-5 finish in 1994 (one win behind the Central Division champion Steelers) and advancing to the second round of the AFC playoffs, the Browns were bursting with optimism as they approached the 1995 season. Year Five of Bill Belichick's rebuilding program was expected to produce a Super Bowl contender. In September, Art Modell called it "the best [Browns] team in years, and nothing happened in the preseason to discourage me from that opinion." The club, he said, had speed, depth and good conditioning. He cited "the best receiving corps in memory, great, great running backs," and a solid offensive line. He praised a formidable defense that had allowed an NFL-low 204 points in '94. Modell viewed the acquisition of free agent running back Lorenzo White, wide receiver Andre Rison and defensive tackle Tim Goad as "key moves."

The owner's optimism seemed to partially explain why, in June, he declared a moratorium on discussing an issue critical to the Browns' future—the projected $175 million renovation of Cleveland Stadium, the financing of which had not been resolved by Cuyahoga County commissioners. Funding called for an extension of the sin tax on cigarettes and alcohol first used for the Gateway project that resulted in Jacobs Field for the baseball Indians and Gund Arena for the basketball Cavaliers. Modell said he would not discuss the matter until the '95 season ended. After the commissioners placed the sin tax extension (Issue 5) on the Nov. 7 ballot, he continued his silence.

Many believed Modell's moratorium was simply to keep the media focused on the Super Bowl-bound Browns. "As an organization, we're obsessed with [the Super Bowl]," he said in September.

> **Pepper Johnson celebrates his second-half interception in the final game at Cleveland Stadium on Dec. 17, 1995. The Browns beat Cincinnati, 26-10.**

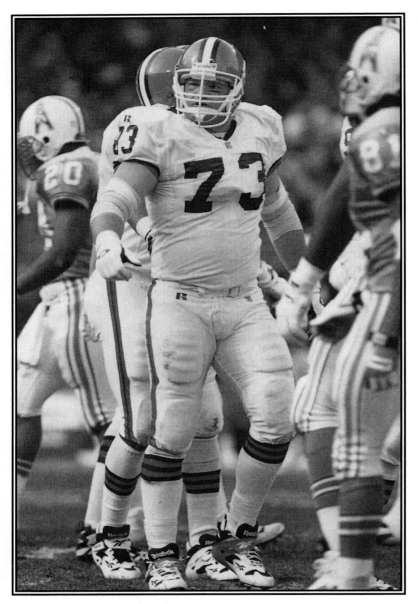

KEY MOVE: Defensive tackle Tim Goad was one of several free agent acquisitions expected to pay dividends in 1995.

The Browns, in fact, were so confident of their chances that Modell said much of the organization's off-season planning had been geared toward guaranteeing the team home-field advantage throughout the playoffs.

But this was the final time that Art Modell would ever speak with optimism about the Cleveland Browns. Two months later he would be speaking of a different homefield advantage, one that would guarantee his franchise a new $200 million home—in Baltimore.

The deal had been brewing since September. Negotiating with the Maryland Stadium

Authority, Modell was offered a package that included a rent-free 70,000-seat open-air downtown stadium next to Camden Yards (to be completed in 1998), plus $30 million a year in annual stadium revenues and $75 million for expenses and a new training facility.

Meanwhile, Modell was privately expressing his concern about Cleveland's stadium renovation proposal. According to the *Cleveland Plain Dealer* Modell wrote to Ohio Governor George Voinovich and to Cleveland Mayor Michael R. White on Oct. 5, urging them to inform the public that extending the sin tax did not guarantee he would keep the Browns in Cleveland. Neither White nor Voinovich had informed the public of the letter said the *Plain Dealer*.

On Oct. 27, Modell finalized a contract with the Maryland Stadium Authority at the Baltimore-Washington International Airport aboard the private jet of Browns minority owner Alfred Lerner. Rumors soon circulated in Baltimore that a deal had been struck.

On Nov. 3, Modell finally broke his silence and spoke with Cleveland-area sports reporters during a late-night conference call. He would neither confirm nor deny the move, stating that he would have more to say in three days.

But the proverbial handwriting was on the wall. And when the Browns played the Houston Oilers the following Sunday, the handwriting was also on the numerous signs brought to Cleveland Stadium by 57,881 confused, angry and betrayed Browns fans:

"Art's Legacy: The Drive, The Fumble, The Move."

"Hey Art—Please Stay. Cleveland Has and Will Support You."

"You're Breaking My Heart, Art."

Fans also displayed signs given to them by proponents of Issue 5: "No Way, Baltimore. Our Browns are Here To Stay" and "Sorry— These Dawgs Are Not For Sale."

Anti-Modell chants erupted from the stands in the fourth quarter, but he never heard them. "For security reasons," Modell was not in attendance—the first time he ever missed a home game in 35 years as owner. The Browns, 4-4 at the time and tied with Pittsburgh for the Central Division lead, were beaten, 37-10.

Speculation ended on Monday, Nov. 6, on a platform in downtown Baltimore. With Oriole Park at Camden Yards as a backdrop, Maryland Governor Parris N. Glendening waved the contract and confirmed that "the Browns indeed are coming to Baltimore."

He introduced Modell as owner of "the Baltimore Browns," and happily proclaimed that the legendary history of Otto Graham, Marion Motley, Jim Brown and other Hall of Famers were now a part of Baltimore.

"The fans have supported the Browns for years," said Modell, "but frankly, it came down to a simple proposition. I had no choice."

Modell's decision was the culmination of years of debate, discussion and proposals for the renovation of Cleveland Stadium. In February 1989, Modell rejected participation in the Gateway project, opting to stay at the Stadium. In September 1993, he called for a meeting with Mayor White to discuss stadium renovations, stressing that the Browns had five years remaining on their lease. He would honor the lease, "but after that I don't know."

In February 1994, Modell said he planned to keep the Browns in Cleveland, but wanted a better facility. A renovation would be acceptable. "The Cleveland Browns, as an organization, will expect only fair treatment. There will be no demands made," he said. "If they can't give us fair treatment, which means we can't be competitive, then that's something we have to take into consideration."

Two months later the Indians moved into Jacobs Field, the crown jewel of the $455 million Gateway project. Modell stated that he had not objected to Gateway, asking only that "something also be done for the Browns." But his Cleveland Stadium Corporation, which operated the Stadium, had lost revenue by releasing its primary tenant, the Indians, to Jacobs Field. Without the Indians, loge sales declined, further straining finances. And the NFL's era of player free agency was dramatically increasing the need for new revenue streams.

SIGNS OF DISAPPROVAL: One day before the move was officially announced, fans expressed their feelings at Cleveland Stadium during the Browns' 37-10 loss to the Houston Oilers.

It was now critical to Modell that the then-63-year-old stadium be completely renovated for the Browns to financially succeed in the modern NFL. His patience had run out. Then months of indecision, altered proposals and missed or extended deadlines by the city finally appeared to push him over the edge in 1995.

He had witnessed the ongoing political debate over who should pay for stadium renovations and how they would be financed. He had waited since December 1994 for a stadium task force report that was ultimately turned in several months overdue, then returned for revisions by Mayor White.

Modell was also concerned that the city's financial resources were strained by cost overruns on Gateway and that county commissioners, in spite of their authority to do so, were reluctant to extend the sin tax for stadium renovations until the Gateway debt was paid. And he watched as the sin tax extension was ultimately placed on the Nov. 7 ballot, thus jeopardizing the funding altogether.

While this was happening, the Los Angeles Rams and Los Angeles Raiders accepted rich stadium deals to relocate to St. Louis and Oakland, respectively. Another deal—from Baltimore—had been rejected by the Cincinnati Bengals. It was only a matter of time before someone else would grab it.

"All I will say, without any details, is that information has been supplied to the government officials for the last two years in volumes—on what is going on in this country and in our society. This is not an eleventh-hour shock to anybody that I have a problem here in Cleveland. They have had information for months. Volumes and volumes of information."

Mayor White's response to Modell's statements was immediate and definitive. He quickly promised a "no-holds-barred" campaign to keep the Browns in Cleveland. "What does it say of an organization to kick a city in the teeth that has been so supportive?" he asked.

The battle for the Browns had begun. The city moved forward on several fronts, each of which was to show that the city had the money, the wherewithal, the persistence and the fighting spirit to keep the Browns in Cleveland.

The first move was to file legal action seeking a restraining order to block the move until a hearing could be held regarding the Browns' attempt to break their lease with Cleveland Stadium. Cuyahoga County Common Pleas Judge Kenneth Callahan issued the order on Nov. 6. After the hearing on Nov. 24, Callahan ruled the franchise could not move to Baltimore unless it won a trial on whether its lease binds it to playing in the Stadium through 1998. A trial date was set for February.

Second, the sin tax passed, thus enabling a revised stadium revenue plan that the city felt was competitive with Baltimore's offer. White presented it to the Browns on Nov. 8 and to the NFL in early December.

Third, the city launched a campaign—"Save Our Browns"—appealing to Browns fans and fan clubs nationwide to start a massive letter writing effort to persuade NFL club owners to vote against the move. The organization would distribute telephone and fax numbers of NFL team offices with a goal of generating at least 10,000 messages to each owner.

Save Our Browns soon became the most visible symbol of efforts to keep the Browns in Cleveland. Wearing orange ribbons and carrying signs, they appeared wherever there was an

QUESTIONABLE CALL: The 1995 Browns lost three out of four at mid season after head coach Bill Belichick replaced quarterback Vinny Testaverde with rookie Eric Zeier (above).

But Modell, of course, had pledged to not move the Browns. "As long as I owned the team, and as long as I was given any cooperation at all, but the game has changed considerably," Modell said to the reporters on Nov. 3. "The Cleveland Browns have had some tremendous financial difficulties since the free agency market opened up. And the ballgame has changed. So as far as my proclamation that I would not move the team, that's null and void."

"We've suffered enormous losses in the last four years," he added. "We've lost a bundle in recent years. All I want to do is compete. I'm not in this thing to make money. I'm not in it to go broke either. I have to do whatever I have to do to protect my family, my franchise and my employees."

Modell was asked why, if the stadium tax proposal was insufficient, he had not publicly stated, or demanded, exactly what he did want.

opportunity to protest—and get media coverage. When the Browns played the Steelers on Monday Night Football on Nov. 26, Save Our Browns rallied outside Three Rivers Stadium. When a U.S. Senate subcommittee met in late November to consider how Congress should respond to the recent rash of sports franchises shifting cities, Save Our Browns rallied on the lawn of the Capitol. When the Browns played their final home game at the Stadium against the Bengals on Dec. 17, they rallied once again.

"The assault waged to block Modell is unprecedented," said columnist Tony Grossi in the *Plain Dealer*. "No city, no fandom, has bombarded NFL fax machines and telephone lines like this one. No city's lead official has logged as many miles and working hours to stop a franchise from deserting its home as Mayor Michael R. White. As White and his tireless staff galvanize support nationwide and in Congress, the NFL ponders a solution to a mess of its own creation."

By early December, efforts were aimed at the Jan. 17 owners meeting in Atlanta where a vote would be taken on the move. Clearly, however, significant progress had been made. On Dec. 10, NFL commissioner Paul Tagliabue was interviewed by NBC television:

"I think our challenge as a league is to keep a team in Cleveland and get a team to Baltimore," he said. "We're going to respect the [Browns] fans. We'll stick with those fans and we'll find a way to get that done. The specifics are what we're working on now."

Lawsuits, proposals and political posturing aside, Tagliabue's statement was the first genuine ray of hope that somehow the franchise would stay.

On the field, meanwhile, the Browns were slogging through a sorrowful season. The "best team in years" was heading toward the worst performance since the 3-13 campaign of 1990. Their 3-1 start had been promising, especially after defeating Kansas City (the AFC's winningest team in '95) in Week 4. But then came a Monday night game at the Stadium on Oct. 2 against the Buffalo Bills.

HURTING: Running back Leroy Hoard, a Pro Bowler in 1994 with 890 yards, gained 547 in '95 after playing with injuries.

Tied 19-19 in the closing seconds, the Bills' Steve Christie missed the probable game-winning field goal, only to get a second chance when officials ruled the Browns had called time out before the play. Christie then connected for a 22-19 win. The Browns were emotionally drained and never recharged. They would win only two more games, both against Cincinnati.

In addition to the distractions of the move, the most notable factor in the Browns' demise was the benching of quarterback Vinny Testaverde. In the midst of the best start of his career—10 touchdown passes and just three interceptions—Testaverde did not start against

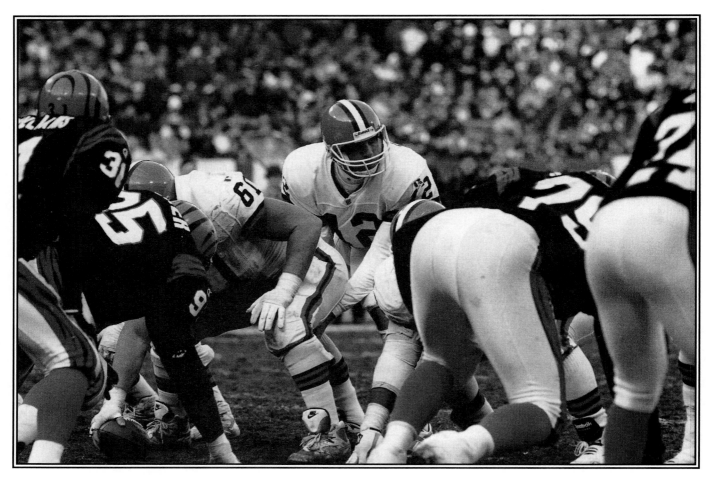

DOWNFIELD DIRECTION: Vinny Testaverde calls signals during the Browns' final scoring drive in the last game at Cleveland Stadium on Dec. 17, 1995. It resulted in a field goal by Matt Stover. The Browns beat the Cincinnati Bengals, 26-10.

the Bengals on Oct. 29, presumably because he was not hitting his expensive target, Rison, the $17 million pass-catching investment.

Rookie Eric Zeier replaced Testaverde and led the Browns to a 29-26 overtime victory. He started the next three (Houston, Pittsburgh and Green Bay), but all were losses. Testaverde returned in the second half of the Green Bay game to complete 16 of 22 passes, but the Browns fell to 4-7, well behind the 7-4 Steelers in the division.

Rison was a major disappointment, finishing as the team's third leading receiver. Not only did the Browns not find a way to utilize his skills—best suited to the run-and-shoot offense of his former club, the Atlanta Falcons—but when Rison criticized fans for booing the team during the Packer game, he

became the subject of boos for the balance of the season, a focal point of the fans' anger.

The running game was marginal as Leroy Hoard played through injuries, forcing the aging Earnest Byner to pick up most of the slack. Lorenzo White barely saw action.

Because of Tim Goad's lack of size and Dan Footman's lack of experience, the defensive line missed the presence of Michael Dean Perry and James Jones, both of whom had departed for Denver following the 1994 season. The defensive secondary missed Eric Turner, who was lost for the year after a back injury in Game 8.

On special teams, place-kicker Matt Stover and punter Tom Tupa had solid seasons, but the Browns struggled to find replacements for two returners who had left after '94—Randy Baldwin (free agency) and Eric Metcalf (trade).

On Dec. 17, the Browns played their final home game against the Bengals—Paul Brown's other team—a franchise that might never have been founded had Modell not fired Brown in 1963. Save Our Browns rallied outside the Stadium while inside sat Paul's son, Mike Brown, the Bengals' president and general manager who had turned down Baltimore's stadium deal because he "wanted to find a way to make it work in Cincinnati."

Brown and orange apparel was never more prevalent than that worn by the 55,875 fans. Handmade signs were everywhere, but scoreboard signs were missing—sponsors had pulled their advertising in protest weeks before.

If the Houston game in November had been a wake, this game was a revival. Without knowing if the Browns would be saved, but with a glimmer of hope, the fans responded as fans—cheering the Browns to a 26-10 victory.

In the final minutes, many began dismantling rows of stadium seats, raising them high above their heads for a national TV audience to see. It was the only real sign of disobedience. At the game's end, Browns players headed for the Dawg Pound, shaking hands and hugging the fans who had supported them for so long.

One week later, the Browns played their final game in Jacksonville. The expansion Jaguars would wrap up their first season while the Browns would wrap up their last. Trailing 21-14 late in the game, Testaverde scored on a one-yard run with 1:13 remaining. Instead of going for a two-point conversion and possible victory, Belichick elected to go for the extra point to tie it at 21. The Jaguars responded with a 34-yard field goal as the gun sounded. The Browns had lost their final game on the final play.

Belichick had been correct in May of 1995 when he said the Browns were not a team that would go "11-5 one year and 4-12 the next." They finished at 5-11.

With two weeks remaining before league owners would meet in Atlanta to vote on the move, Save Our Browns announced a "Two-Minute Warning" campaign. Fans were urged to fax their opinions to the owners the following Friday. A door-to-door drive would collect signatures on petitions that would be displayed to the owners. Drawings by Cleveland school children, expressing their sentiments about the Browns, would be displayed at City Hall.

POUND FOR POUND: John "Big Dawg" Thompson (No. 98) and friends lost their original Dawg Pound as part of the agreement with the NFL to demolish Cleveland Stadium. But they would later occupy their own 10,000-seat section in the new Browns stadium of 1999. (No personal seat licenses allowed.)

A full-page ad would appear in *USA Today* supporting the Save Our Browns cause. Finally, a rally would be held in Atlanta prior to the owners meeting.

On Jan. 16, Save Our Browns convened at the Georgia International Convention Center in Atlanta to unfurl a scroll of 2.2 million signatures opposing the move. Later, at the Stouffer Renaissance Hotel, site of the owners meeting, a flashlight vigil was held.

But no decision was made on Jan. 17. The vote was postponed for three weeks. White asked that Browns fans halt the flood of faxes to NFL owners because he had begun "constructive dialogue." A deal was in the works.

White's battle cry had been "Our Team, Our Name, Our Colors." The Browns must remain in Cleveland. He would not settle for anything else, especially not a relocated team, the candidates of which included Tampa Bay, Seattle, Cincinnati and San Francisco.

In the end, White got two out of three. Our Name and Our Colors remained, but Our Team (Modell's franchise) was permitted to move. Instead, White received a new version of Our Team—a guarantee that the NFL would put a team in Cleveland by 1999. The team would be

HIRAM: Players and fans mingle at the Hiram College reunion of former Browns on July 14, 1996. Milt Plum (top), Tommy James (above) and Ernie Kellermann (right) sign autographs.

known as the Browns, wear brown and orange, and play in a brand new stadium.

NFL owners approved the agreement on Feb. 8 at the O'Hare Hilton in Chicago. The vote was 25-2-3. Modell could move his franchise to Baltimore, but the league would guarantee Cleveland a team—an existing one or an expansion team—by 1999. The Browns name and colors would remain in Cleveland, along with the history, heritage, records and memorabilia from 50 seasons.

"[The team] will bear the name of the Cleveland Browns," said White. "They will wear the colors of the Cleveland Browns. They will be the Cleveland Browns."

Cleveland would demolish Cleveland Stadium and build a new 72,000-seat facility. The NFL would advance the city $28-$48 million to build it. The new Browns owner, not the city, would repay the money to the league. No public money would be used to build the stadium beyond the $175 million renovation package proposed for Cleveland Stadium. The new stadium would have a 10,000-seat Dawg Pound section that would not require personal seat licenses. Modell would pay the city $9.3 million for legal expenses, administrative costs and loss of revenues it would have received from its lease with the Browns.

"The way to come to a solution was to respect the loyalty of the fans of Cleveland [and] to keep the Browns' tradition in Cleveland," said Tagliabue. "To keep the Browns in Cleveland and yet respect the fans of Baltimore—their past loyalty and commitment to the NFL. I think this agreement in a unique and innovative way does that."

Fast forward to July 1996—a warm, sunny summer Sunday on the campus of Hiram College near Cleveland. Former Browns players have gathered for a reunion at the site of the team's training camp from 1952-74. Thousands of fans have joined the festivities to purchase memorabilia, or to wait patiently in countless lines for autographs from more than 80 former Browns in attendance.

No owners, commissioners, mayors, politicians, lawyers, judges or private jets. No protest signs, rallies or petitions. Just the real Cleveland Browns: the players and the fans who had worn—and bled—the brown and orange for 50 years. The healing had begun.

Late that afternoon, fans filed into the football stadium to witness a ceremony in which each player was presented a replica of his jersey. Dignitaries spoke with enthusiasm about the new Browns and new stadium to arrive in 1999. Jim Brown choked with emotion when he told the crowd that "I am a Cleveland Brown."

Several months later, Brown looked at the future: "We've got the name, we've got the colors and we've got the legends that all belong to Cleveland—the Cleveland Browns," he said. "We've got the fans. We're getting a new stadium. We're getting new players because you're always getting new players. We haven't lost a doggone thing. If we look at it in a positive way, we can develop great teams, win some championships and never look back."

NUMBER 32: As a consultant during the 1990s, Jim Brown became a symbol of the Browns' winning past whenever he appeared on the Cleveland Stadium sideline. After the move, Brown became a vocal advocate for Browns fans and tradition.

Orange & Brown Returns to Town

With the deal between the city and the league ironclad, attention turned to two subjects—the construction of the new stadium and whether Cleveland's new NFL entry would be an expansion team or an existing club having difficulties in its current home city. The former subject was more the worry of the politicians and league officials than of Mr. and Ms. Fan, some of whom still doubted whether the NFL, which had allowed one of the most popular and well supported franchises to move because of the owner's financial woes, would honor the agreement. The fans were far more concerned with getting a team, and surveys showed overwhelming support for a brand new club. Few wanted to inherit some other troubled franchise that might do the same thing to Cleveland some day. As far as stadium issues were concerned, demolition of the old home of the Browns began Nov. 25, 1996, approximately two months after the Browns Trust, the NFL and the city hosted "The Final Play," for fans to take one last tour of Cleveland Stadium. The two-day event welcomed 65,000 visitors.

The design of the new stadium was approved by the city's Design Review Committee on Dec. 19 and by the City Planning Commission the following day. It was revealed the stadium would be an open-air facility and would have a mainly glass-and-stainless-steel facade. Most seats would be closer to the action than the seats at the old stadium. Cost was estimated at $242.8 million. Mayor Michael White unveiled the final stadium design, complete with landscaping. The building would be primarily glass, steel and concrete and wouldn't clash with the two other showcases on the lakefront—the Great Lakes Science Center and the Rock & Roll Hall of Fame.

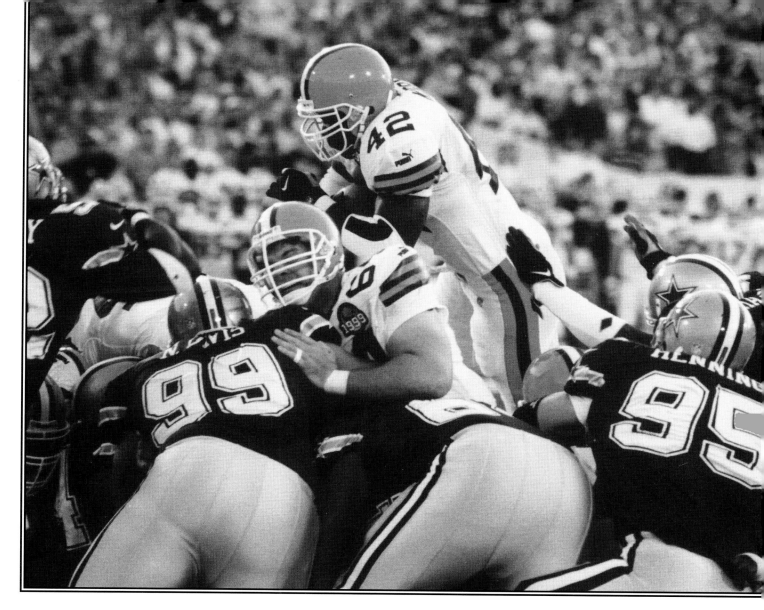

The stadium was to be a bowl-shaped, 12-story structure with a seating capacity of 72,000. Included would be approximately 22,000 seats in the lower and middle decks, 14,000 seats in the upper deck

and 10,000 in the new Dawg Pound at the east end of the field. The field would be grass, with a system of glycol tubes 10 feet underneath to prevent the field from freezing and extend the grass-growing season.

As far as a team to play in the stadium, signs were beginning to point toward an expansion team. Not all owners favored expansion, as the league had done that in 1995 when it brought Carolina and Jacksonville into the NFL. Commissioner Paul Tagliabue, however, was in favor of expansion for Cleveland. Although Modell's move to Baltimore and Al Davis' relocation of the Raiders from Oakland to Los Angeles in 1982 proved the commissioner could not stop teams from switching cities, Tagliabue said he was opposed to any more relocation.

BLAST FROM THE PAST: The Browns' Anthony Pleasant sacks Houston quarterback Warren Moon in the early 1990s. NFL Commissioner Paul Tagliabue was opposed to franchise relocation, but the revolving door found the Browns in Baltimore and the Oilers in Tennessee by the middle of the decade.

Not only had the Browns abandoned Cleveland, but the Houston Oilers moved to Tennessee, the Rams departed Anaheim for St. Louis and the Raiders moved back to Oakland.

Tagliabue had the question put to him by a reporter two days before Super Bowl XXXI in 1997. The reporter asked the commissioner if the terms of the deal with Cleveland could be met by moving an existing team. Tagliabue made it clear relocation of a current NFL member was not what he wanted to see. "[I hope] we can accomplish [these] goals together—team stability, no more moves and teams in Cleveland and Los Angeles," Tagliabue said.

Among the teams seeking new stadiums or better deals on existing ones were the Bengals, Colts, Seahawks, Buccaneers, Vikings, Bills, Patriots, 49ers and Cardinals. It seemed Cleveland was the leverage for teams to get what they wanted from the politicians and the voters.

Expansion, however, remained the goal of Mayor White, which led to speculation as to who would eventually own the new Browns. White announced there were six "suitors," as he termed them. The most talked about prospective owner was Bernie Kosar, the popular ex-Browns quarterback who retired from a 12-year NFL career following the 1996 season.

"I'm definitely interested in bringing the Browns back," Kosar said. "I've spoken with people in the NFL and I keep giving the NFL chances to tell me to back off, and they don't."

Meanwhile, ground was broken for the new stadium on May 15, 1997, with Mayor White turning over the first shovel of dirt. To fans watching the ceremony, White assured them they could be back there in 828 days "in the greatest football facility in the entire world."

By the time of the groundbreaking, estimated cost of the stadium had risen $4.2 million, to $248 million. White kept the faith, repeating his promise the project would be finished "on time and on budget." In September, however, White announced that the project was now over budget by $12.8 million. The overrun was due largely to the delay in the awarding of the contract for the cast-in-place concrete of the stadium's frame. White vowed to close the gap between the estimated price tag and what the real cost had become through "value engineering," i.e. the deletion of some features of the stadium deemed unnecessary.

The first concrete pouring for the stadium's superstructure took place on Oct. 13, 1997. It was expected to be finished by the summer. Season ticket sales, it was announced, were going much more smoothly than stadium construction. It was announced in October of 1997 that 52,000 season tickets had been sold.

But while politicians debated cost overruns, the "suitors" of which White spoke were coming to the door. In January 1998, real estate developer Bart Wolstein announced that he was a candidate to be owner of the Browns. He was aligned with ex-Browns Jim Brown, Dick Schafrath and Mike McCormack, plus former Ohio State and Giants standout John Hicks.

Wolstein and Bernie Kosar were the only announced candidates for the ownership. It was believed Kosar was in partnership with billionaire banker Al Lerner, who had been a minority owner of the Browns when Modell moved the club. Lerner, who has strong political ties in Maryland and was said to be a major player in the Browns' relocation, had not announced his ownership intentions.

Expansion became more likely as the Bengals and Vikings joined the Colts in having their stadium-ownership problems fixed. There were still a few teams that were having problems with their cities, but that all became moot when Paul Tagliabue announced on March 23, 1998, at Orlando's Grand Cypress Hotel, that Cleveland would get an expansion team, the NFL's 31st franchise.

OWNERSHIP SUITORS: Bernie Kosar (left) and Jim Brown (right) were among a number of former Browns looking to become part of the ownership of the new franchise of 1999.

The deadline for announcing such a decision had been November of 1998, and it was looking more likely that owners, many of whom were cool to expansion anyway, would wait that long. Through the efforts of Tagliabue and Mayor White, however, owners unanimously voted in favor of expansion.

"We'll proceed immediately to begin taking steps to make [the new team] a reality," Tagliabue said, "including work on the screening process to select an owner."

And that would dominate Browns news for months. Whoever the lucky party would be, the new owner was likely to get not only a new sta-

BRAIN TRUST: Browns owner Al Lerner and team president Carmen Policy confer at the expansion draft in February 1999. Along with director of football operations Dwight Clark and head coach Chris Palmer, the management team was in place.

dium, but the same salary cap (estimated at $60 million) all other NFL teams had and a stocking plan as generous as the one that allowed the last two expansion clubs, the Panthers and Jaguars, to become contenders quickly.

Joe Mack, former assistant general manager of the Panthers, was named by the league as Browns' player personnel director. His main job was to hire a scouting staff that would enable the eventual owner to get a head start on evaluating talent.

And who will that owner be? Commissioner Tagliabue had said that the league desired the new ownership to be composed of local people, but he announced at the league meetings in May of 1998 that the race for the Browns was now open to all—Ohioans and non-Ohioans. By that time there were four groups, not counting Bernie Kosar (it was believed he would ally himself with another group at some time), actively seeking Browns ownership in the summer of '98. Not included was Al Lerner, though most thought he was simply waiting in the wings until the time was right.

And the right time, it seemed, would be when the price the NFL was charging for the franchise would become too dear for everyone else. The NFL, it was said, would charge a new owner at least $500 million for the Browns. Raiders boss Al Davis talked seriously of making the price $1 billion.

Despite some big hitters on the list, none was richer than Lerner, who was rumored to be one of the six richest individuals in America and possibly the wealthiest man that most people had never heard of. Unlike Bill Gates, Donald Trump et al., Lerner was low-profile.

Outside of Lerner the most formidable bidder seemed to be the Dolan brothers—Charles, founder and chairman of cable television giant Cablevision, and Lawrence, a Cleveland attorney. The Dolans also had actor-comedian Bill Cosby and retired Dolphins head coach and Northeast Ohio native Don Shula as investors.

Lerner finally came out of hiding on July 23, announcing he was seeking ownership of the Browns and also announcing his partner would be Carmen Policy, who had recently resigned as president of the San Francisco 49ers. In eight seasons, Policy had made the business decisions that had helped the 49ers remain a powerhouse (1994 Super Bowl champion). He also was considered a wizard with the salary cap, enabling the 49ers to acquire new talent and keep the old talent while remaining within the letter of the salary cap rules.

Lerner, however, had some baggage. He was, after all, the go-between during negotiations to move the Browns, owned by his close friend Art Modell, to Baltimore, in a state where he had strong connections politically. Lerner's private jet was the scene of several meetings between Browns representatives and Maryland governor Parris Glendening to discuss the deal that eventually moved the Browns.

Still, Lerner's very deep pockets made him the front runner. MBNA, the nation's second-largest issuer of credit cards, was said to be worth $60 billion. Having Policy, a Youngstown native and a "superstar" among corporate attorneys, made Lerner even more attractive.

Meanwhile, the NFL owners approved a stocking plan for the Browns that included an expansion draft in February and 14 selections, including the first pick in all seven rounds, for the college draft.

On Sept. 8, 1998, the NFL owners approved the Lerner-Policy group over the Dolan group to become the new owners of the Browns. The vote was 29-0-1 (with Al Davis abstaining). Lerner would pay $530 million for the club, by far a record price for a sports franchise.

From the moment it was learned that Carmen Policy would be involved with the Browns should Al Lerner get the franchise, rumors abounded that he would bring Dwight Clark with him from the 49ers to be the Browns' director of football operations. Clark, a star wide receiver on the Niners from 1979-87, held a similar job with that club, but hadn't been under contract in 1998. Clark did join the Browns, making it official on Nov. 30.

A triumvirate was now in place for the new Cleveland Browns—Lerner's wealth, Policy's business savvy and Clark's football expertise. There was one more big hiring to come.

Every year, toward the end of every football season, the same names pop up for every head coaching vacancy. Following the 1998 campaign those names included Vikings offensive coordinator Brian Billick, who fashioned the top offense in the league in a year when the Vikes would post a 15-1 record; Broncos offensive coordinator Gary Kubiak, who held that job for the two years the club won its Super Bowl titles; former Raiders head coach Art Shell, who had become the NFC-champion Falcons' offensive line coach; Jaguars offensive coordinator Chris Palmer, regarded as a brilliant molder of quarterbacks; and Raiders defensive coordinator Willie Shaw.

Each was interviewed by the Browns brain trust, replete with a post-interview press conference featuring a positive statement or two about the candidate by Policy.

Kubiak was rumored to be the top candidate both with the Browns and for the head coaching job at the University of Colorado, but

TEACHER: New head coach Chris Palmer gives instructions at the Browns' mini-camp in May 1999. His success in developing young quarterbacks while offensive coordinator at Jacksonville was a major factor in Palmer's hiring on Jan. 21, 1999.

decided to stay with the Broncos instead. Billick became a front runner, but was eliminated at the last minute allegedly because of "significant philosophical differences" with Policy. Shortly thereafter he took the head coaching job with the Ravens.

Palmer thus became the leading candidate. He was hired on Jan. 21, 1999, for five years and approximately $5 million plus incentives. The Cleveland Browns, a shadow franchise for three years, now looked once again like a full-fledged member of the NFL.

ON THE LINE: The Browns sought help on both lines in the expansion draft on Feb. 9, 1999. Lions guard Jim Pyne (left), Cowboys defensive end Hurvin McCormack (right) and Patriots guard-tackle Scott Rehberg were the first three selections.

The Browns were not given a lot of time to get a team together, but things moved quickly with trades and free agency. On Feb. 12, Policy acquired a pair of players from his former team, the 49ers—tight end Irv Smith and defensive end Roy Barker—for "past considerations."

On Feb. 16, the Browns signed Patriots center Dave Wohlabaugh and Colts punter Chris Gardocki. Next came offensive tackle Orlando Brown from the Ravens on Feb. 17 and Vikings defensive back Corey Fuller on Feb. 18.

Meanwhile, Palmer hired a staff of assistant coaches: Clarence Brooks (defensive line), Jerry Butler (wide receivers), Keith Butler (linebackers), Billy Davis (defensive quality control), Jerry Holmes (defensive backs), John Hufnagel (quarterbacks), Tim Jorgensen (strength), Mark Michaels (special teams quality control), Bob

Palcic (offensive line), Ray Perkins (tight ends), Dick Portee (running backs), Bob Slowik (defensive coordinator), Aril Smith (assistant strength), Tony Sparano (offensive quality control) and Ken Whisenhunt (special teams).

But the big day for the Browns, and especially for their fans, was Feb. 9. That was the expansion draft, held in the Canton Civic Center. The Browns chose 37 players from NFL rosters and, with few exceptions, picked youth and low pay over the "name" players past their primes and carrying bloated salaries.

The first selection was a no-brainer. Guard Jim Pyne, 27, who had started every game for Detroit in 1998, was available. Pyne had asked to be put on the expansion draft list, as he was unhappy with his situation. The Lions, looking to clear room for the salary cap, obliged.

The Browns' first five selections were flown to Canton the night before the draft, in order to greet the fans—4,000 of them—during the selection party. The next four were Cowboys defensive end Hurvin McCormack, Patriots

guard Scott Rehberg, Bengals wide receiver Damon Gibson and 49ers center Steve Gordon.

In all, the Browns took 10 defensive backs, nine offensive linemen, five linebackers, four defensive linemen, four wide receivers, four running backs and one quarterback. On the final pick, the team took Antonio Langham, the Browns' No. 1 draft choice in 1994 and the NFL's Defensive Rookie of the Year. But since leaving Cleveland his once promising career had foundered. He started only six games for the 49ers at right cornerback in 1998 despite drawing a $3.02 million salary.

Even more exciting was the college draft, where one of the richest crops of prospects—particularly on offense—awaited. Texas running back Ricky Williams, the Heisman Trophy winner, was considered the premier talent in the draft. But as the team with the first selection, it had become clear that the Browns were on the prowl for a topflight quarterback. At that position there was a smorgasbord of "can't miss" candidates.

EXPERIENCED PROS: Free agents were signed at a fast pace to build the Browns' roster. Safety Marquez Pope (left) was a seven-year veteran from San Francisco. Left tackle Lomas Brown (right) came from Arizona after 14 years in the NFL.

Tim Couch, who had set six NCAA and 10 Southeastern Conference passing records at Kentucky, was considered furlongs ahead in the derby to be the Browns' top draft choice. He had even expressed an eagerness to join the Browns. But as draft day neared, it looked as though Couch had gotten ahead of himself. Akili Smith from Oregon, not highly regarded when the season started, had come on strong in the latter half of the season and had knocked out scouts at the Indianapolis combines with his athletic ability. Suddenly there was no sure thing with Couch.

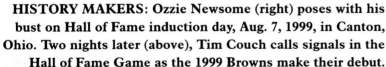

HISTORY MAKERS: Ozzie Newsome (right) poses with his bust on Hall of Fame induction day, Aug. 7, 1999, in Canton, Ohio. Two nights later (above), Tim Couch calls signals in the Hall of Fame Game as the 1999 Browns make their debut.

As it turned out, Couch was the Browns' choice all along. Couch, who skipped his senior year to enter the NFL draft, had operated in a pro-style offense with the Wildcats, and was considered less of a risk than Smith, who had not had the consistent career Couch enjoyed.

With the second choice came speedy (40 yards in 4.31 seconds) wide receiver Kevin Johnson of Syracuse. After him it was Clemson linebacker Rahim Abdullah, Southern California cornerback Daylon McCutcheon, California safety Marquis Smith, Virginia linebacker Wali Rainer, Colorado wide receiver Darrin Chiaverini, Troy State defensive tackle Marcus Spriggs, Maryland linebacker Kendall Ogle, Tarleton (Texas) State tight end James Dearth and Arkansas running back Madre Hill.

Free agents continued to arrive in March and April. The Browns signed offensive tackle Lomas Brown (Cardinals), safety Marquez Pope (49ers) running back Terry Kirby (49ers), defensive tackle John Jurkovic (Jaguars), defensive end Derrick Alexander (Vikings), wide receiver Leslie Shepherd (Redskins), defensive tackle Jerry Ball (Vikings) and defensive tackle Darius Holland (Lions).

Arriving via trades were quarterback Ty Detmer (49ers), fullback Marc Edwards (49ers) and running back Sedrick Shaw (Patriots).

The plum free-agent acquisition came in May when the team signed outside linebacker Jamir Miller of the Cardinals. Miller, 25, was a five-year veteran who had started every game over the previous three seasons. He led the Cards in tackles in '98 with 150.

Miller signed a one-year deal for $1.3 million plus incentives. That should have been considered a steal, but other teams had avoided Miller because of some legal trouble in his life. He had served a four-game suspension in 1995 for violating the team's substance abuse policy. Palmer, however, was confident that Miller had matured and the proof was that the Cardinals

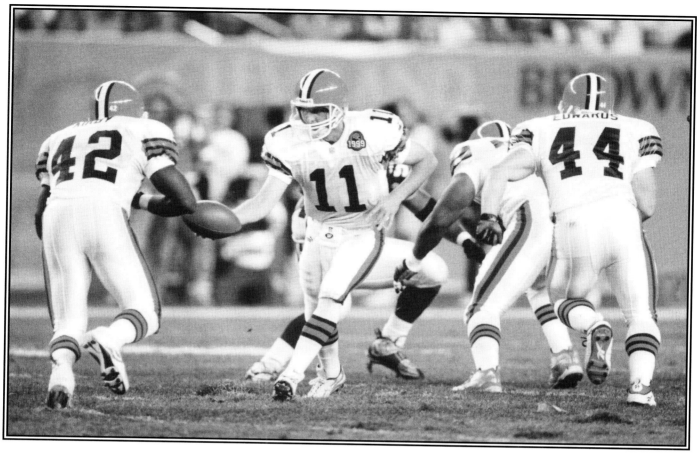

HOME AGAIN: Above, Ty Detmer hands off to Terry Kirby in the Browns' first game at Cleveland Browns Stadium against the Vikings on Aug. 21, 1999. Detmer, Kirby and fullback Marc Edwards (44) arrived from San Francisco as Dwight Clark built the Browns around a nucleus of familiar players from his days in the 49ers' front office. Left, linebacker Jamir Miller was the Browns' premier free agent acquisition after signing in May.

wanted to re-sign him (at less than the two-year $6 million deal Miller wanted).

The Browns conducted four mini-camps in April, May and June. Training camp opened for 34 rookies on July 21 and four veterans—bringing the total in camp to 89—on July 24.

On Aug. 7, Browns fans watched as longtime tight end Ozzie Newsome was inducted into the Pro Football Hall of Fame. Two nights later, the Browns of a new generation took to the field for the first time in the annual Hall of Fame Game before 25,156 at Fawcett Stadium in Canton, Ohio. They defeated the Cowboys, 20-17, on a field goal in overtime by Phil Dawson.

After a 30-3 loss in Tampa Bay the following Saturday, the Browns returned home to open brand new Cleveland Browns Stadium against the Vikings on Aug. 21. The Browns were defeated, 24-17, and looked every bit like an expansion team for most of the game. But to the 71,398 fans in attendance—including the John "Big Dawg" Thompson-led Dawg Pound—the only thing that really mattered was that the Browns were finally back in business.

The **Greatest**

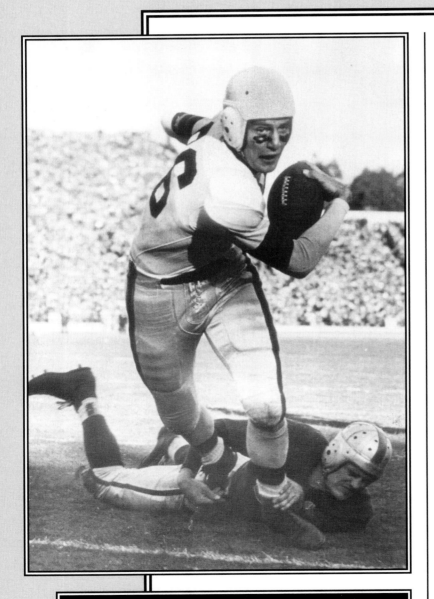

Dub Jones' 20-yard second-half touchdown reception from Otto Graham put the Browns ahead, 24-21.

The 1948 Cleveland Browns were the first major professional football team to go through an entire season undefeated. The 1972 Miami Dolphins have been the only one since. The Chicago Bears twice had been unbeaten in the regular season, only to lose the NFL Championship game each time.

Although the Dolphins are well remembered for their 17-0 mark in '72, they never had to face a schedule such as the Browns saw in late November of 1948. Their last four games were on the road, and three of them were played over an eight-day stretch.

Cleveland beat the New York Yankees, 34-21, on a Sunday, then flew to Los Angeles for a Thanksgiving Day game. They defeated the Dons, 31-14, but Otto Graham injured a knee and was considered doubtful for the Browns' next contest, which would be only three days away in San Francisco.

The Browns were in trouble. Not only were they carrying a 12-0 record that season, but had a 21-game unbeaten streak put in jeopardy by Graham's injured knee, which stiffened in the days following the Dons game. And the 49ers were 11-1 themselves, as only a 14-7 loss to the Browns on Nov. 14 had marred their season.

For the first time in their history, the Browns were underdogs. There was even talk that they wanted to finish tied for the division championship to force a playoff, and another big gate, in Cleveland.

With his knee heavily taped, Graham put on his uniform on Sunday, but told head coach Paul Brown he couldn't play. But when

Victories

49ers return man Forrest Hall fumbled the kickoff and the Browns recovered, Graham and his head coach both seemed to forget about what the quarterback had said. Graham went out with the offensive unit and, on the first play, threw a 28-yard touchdown pass to Dante Lavelli.

Although Graham was able to play the whole game, his customary mobility was not there. After a field goal by Lou Groza gave the Browns a 10-0 advantage, San Francisco answered with a TD run by Joe Perry and a scoring pass from Frankie Albert to Alyn Beals to give the 49ers a 14-10 halftime lead.

Graham attempted a quarterback sneak on fourth down in the third period, but with his knee immobilized, it failed. The Niners tacked on another Albert-to-Beals touchdown and it was 21-10. Graham then led one of the finest comebacks in Browns history. He completed a 24-yard pass to Edgar "Special Delivery" Jones that set up a one-yard touchdown run by Marion Motley on the succeeding drive.

On the Browns' next possession, Graham threw a 20-yard touchdown pass to Dub Jones to put Cleveland in front, 24-21. San Francisco attempted a halfback option pass on the next drive, but defensive back Tom Colella intercepted for the Browns.

Graham then threw 33 yards to Edgar Jones for a touchdown that gave Cleveland a 10-point lead, 31-21. Perry scored again to decrease the Browns' advantage to three points with seven minutes to play. The Browns proceeded to hold possession for the next six minutes.

The 49ers eventually got the ball back at their own 12-yard line with a mere 50 seconds remaining. Albert was sacked by Tony Adamle and the Western Division title of the All-America Football Conference was Cleveland's for the third straight year. The Browns had won three games and scored 96 points in eight days.

Number 1
November 28, 1948

Keeping the Streak Alive

Browns 31
49ers 28

Otto Graham plays with an injured knee, but the Browns are winners for the third time in eight days.

Their unbeaten streak had reached 22 games. They would maintain it for seven more before finally experiencing defeat, a 56-28 loss to the 49ers on Oct. 9, 1949.

Graham finished the 1948 championship season as the AAFC's leading passer for the second of three consecutive campaigns.

His 173 completions on 333 attempts were both the second-highest totals of his 10-year career, surpassed only in 1952 (181-364). Graham's 25 touchdown passes equaled his career-best set the previous season.

Considering the Browns' four-year run of success in the All-America Football Conference, it is difficult to believe that anyone could look at their first game in the National Football League objectively and predict a blowout in favor of their opponent: the Philadelphia Eagles.

Sure, but who would have thought the game would end the way it did, with the Browns routing the two-time defending NFL champions by a 35-10 score?

Probably no one, not even the Browns themselves, thought the latter would come true. But most

In a League of Their Own

Browns 35
Eagles 10

The Browns are already the class of the NFL, beating the confident champs in the season opener.

fans, and almost everyone not connected to the old AAFC expected the former.

Philadelphia, the NFL champions of 1948 and '49, was installed as the seven-point favorite, but many believed that was much too conservative. Some were talking seriously of 50-0. This against a team that had not only made a mockery of its league, going unbeaten only two years before, but one that had strengthened itself considerably in the off-season through a separate transaction with a member of the defunct league and through a common draft of players from the former AAFC teams.

Halfback Rex Bumgardner, defensive tackle John Kissell and guard Abe Gibron came from Buffalo when Bills owner Jim Breuil became part owner of the Browns, then brought the trio with him as part of the

deal. The Browns added defensive end Len Ford (Los Angeles) and linebacker Hal Herring (Buffalo) through the draft.

After the game, Frank "Bucko" Kilroy, the Eagles' All-Pro tackle, called attention to Cleveland's revised roster. Noting the influx of new talent, Kilroy said the Browns had become a team of AAFC all-stars and that Philadelphia wasn't up to beating an all-star team.

But the Browns were up to beating the NFL champions because head coach Paul Brown had prepared for the game down to the last detail. When the Eagles played the Rams for the 1949 title, Browns assistant coaches Blanton Collier and Fritz Heisler were sitting in the L.A. Coliseum stands. Their notes would provide the foundation of Paul Brown's pre-game preparation.

It was only natural the Browns' maiden flight in their new league should be against the other champion. It was like a Super Bowl, with nine months and a training camp in between.

That's where the Eagles might have lost it. Fullback Steve Van Buren, the leading rusher in the NFL four of the previous five seasons, injured a toe on his right foot in Philadelphia's 17-7 loss to the College All-Stars and missed all of the Eagles' other pre-season games.

All-Pro tackle Alvin Wistert suffered a knee injury and halfback Bosh Pritchard injured a shoulder. Still, there was no indication that Van Buren wouldn't play, and the sorry showing the Eagles made in the preseason didn't seem to give a hint of what was to come.

The Browns, meanwhile, had beaten four old-line NFL teams during their exhibition-game schedule. The victory over the Detroit Lions was most critical because it essentially served as a dress rehearsal for the game with the Eagles.

The Lions employed the famed "Eagle Defense," Neale's innovative formation designed to slow opposition passing attacks while still providing plenty of pressure on quarterbacks and the running game.

The Eagle Defense featured a five-man line, two linebackers to jam the receivers as they started their routes, and four defensive backs to enable double coverage on the receivers. Against the Lions, Brown first experimented with a double-wing formation that sent halfback Bumgardner in motion on each play. The additional receiver forced single coverage by the Lions' secondary on Dub Jones.

Secondly, Brown took advantage of the lack of a middle linebacker in the Eagle Defense. By spreading the Cleveland tackles further apart on each play, the defensive tackles followed suit, thus isolating their middle guard and opening up the middle for the Browns' running game, particularly the trap plays to Marion Motley.

There were 71,237 spectators in Philadelphia's Municipal Stadium (site of the Army-Navy game) on Sept. 16, 1950, for the opening of the NFL season and what commissioner Bert Bell said was "the most talked about game in the history of the NFL."

The Browns lost offensive left tackle Lou Groza, also pro football's best field goal kicker, when he hurt a shoulder on the first series. The Browns looked to be in trouble. Kicking was one area in which even the staunchest defenders of NFL superiority believed the Browns had an edge.

That edge was lost, and the Browns proved it on their second series. Eagles second-year punt returner Clyde "Smackover" Scott fumbled Horace Gillom's punt at the Philadelphia 39. Rookie Jim Martin recovered the ball for Cleveland and the Browns moved to the Eagles' 16-yard line. Stalled there, defensive tackle and backup kicker Chubby Grigg, who had not kicked a field goal since high school, was called to give the Browns the lead. His 25-yard attempt was tipped at the line of scrimmage.

The Eagles got to the Cleveland eight-yard line and made it 3-0 on Cliff Patton's field goal. Each team stopped the other on the next two series, but the brilliant but one-dimensional Eagles defense suffered a lapse. As Paul Brown had planned, Cleveland halfback Rex Bumgardner had been going in motion to draw linebacker Joe

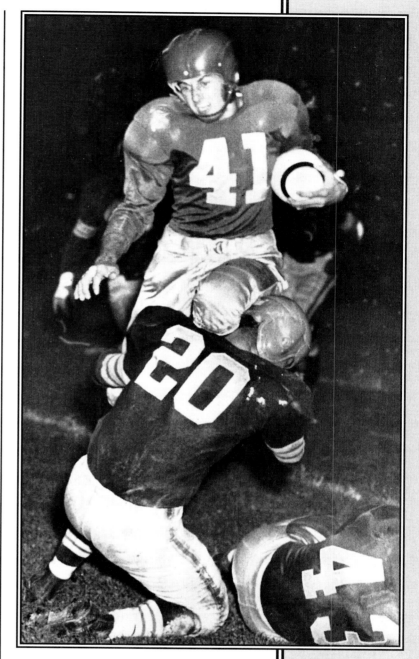

Muha to the sidelines, thus forcing single coverage on Dub Jones.

Jones, who had been running sideline patterns all evening, caught defensive back Russ Craft cheating up on him. When Craft inched his way up, Jones suddenly turned and headed downfield. He was 10 yards in front when Craft realized his mistake, and Otto Graham got him the ball on the Eagles'

Linebacker Hal Herring, one of several ex-AAFC players to join the 1950 Browns, tackles the Eagles' Frank Ziegler.

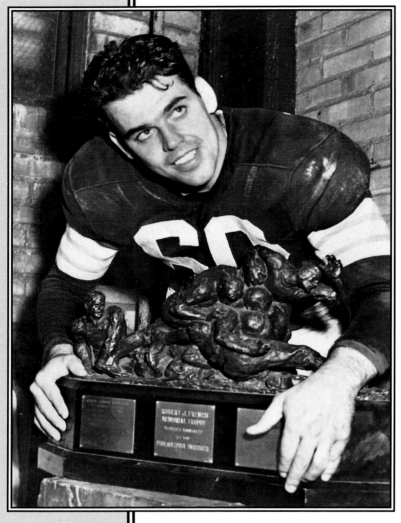

Otto Graham, who threw three touchdown passes and ran for another, received this trophy as the game's best player.

found him for a 26-yard touchdown pass. The Browns led, 14-3, at halftime.

Mac Speedie made it 21-3 six plays into the second half. The big left end was far too tall for Philadelphia's diminutive defensive backs while possessing just as much speed. Speedie caught a 12-yard touchdown pass after a leaping grab at the two.

The Eagles then started double-covering Lavelli and Speedie, so Cleveland started throwing to its running backs. Graham and Bumgardner found each other three straight times before Philly gave up double coverage to pick up the backs.

The Eagles got their only touchdown when All-Pro Pete Pihos beat Cliff Lewis and Hal Herring on a pass from Bill Mackrides, who replaced starter Tommy Thompson, from 17 yards away with 14:17 to play.

Any hopes Eagles fans had of watching their favorites come back were dashed when the Browns used a bruising running game to waste time. The famous trap to Marion Motley, which Cleveland had disdained at first in favor of a passing attack, began to churn away yards and time precious to the Eagles. Graham ended the drive with one-yard TD run to make it Browns 28, Eagles 10.

Warren Lahr intercepted a pass on Philadelphia's next series. Jones then swept 57 yards to the Eagles' seven before defensive back Frankie Reagan stopped him. Bumgardner took it the rest of the way to the end zone on the next play. Final score: Browns 35, Eagles 10.

The game not only proved that the Browns were a team with which the older league had to reckon, but also proved Paul Brown's system was the wave of the future. Brown and his staff had Philadelphia scouted to a fare-thee-well, while the Eagles simply remained with what had worked so effectively in the past.

Likewise, the Eagles' run of success was now in the past as they would not win another conference crown for 10 years. The new standards of excellence in coaching, innovations, and on-field play would now be set by Paul Brown and his Browns.

25. Jones scored easily and the score was 7-3 in favor of the inferior league's champion with 1:37 remaining in the first quarter.

Things got worse for the Eagles. Scott suffered a broken shoulder as Philadelphia was driving on the Browns. That meant the three Eagles ball carriers were gone. Their running game, with which they thought they could dominate the Browns even without Van Buren and Pritchard, was finished. Four plays from the Cleveland 14-yard line netted only three yards.

Swift Browns right end Dante Lavelli was in a mismatch versus linebacker Alex Wojciechowicz, a 13-year veteran. On the following series Lavelli outran Wojciechowicz and got to the end zone where Graham

Were there still any disbelievers three months and eight days following the Browns' whipping of the Philadelphia Eagles, the defending NFL champions, in their first game in a "real" professional league?

Oh sure there were. The Browns, after all, were 10-0 in 1950 against teams with losing records. They played only one team with a winning mark, the New York Giants, and were 1-2 against them. That revolutionary passing game Paul Brown had used to make a shambles of the All-America Football Conference had been grounded by the Giants' "Umbrella Defense." New York yielded only 19 points and one touchdown to the Browns' offense over three games.

However, the Giants had scored only 26 points themselves and had lost their playoff game to the Clevelanders, 8-3, on Dec. 17 at Cleveland Stadium. The Browns *had* won only against teams with losing or break-even records, but they also hadn't lost to any of those clubs, either.

Now Cleveland would take on a powerhouse, the Los Angeles Rams, who had survived a playoff of their own against the Chicago Bears on the same day the Browns were dispatching the Giants. Just like New York, Chicago had beaten the Rams twice in the regular season.

There could hardly have been a better matchup for the crown. From a local angle, the game featured Cleveland's current team against the team it had replaced. Five years earlier, the "Cleveland" Rams defeated the Washington Redskins at Cleveland Stadium for the NFL crown, then packed up and moved to Los Angeles.

From a national angle, had the Browns not made such a splash in their first season in the league, it would have been the Rams the NFL would have canonized in 1950. Regardless, this was to be a battle of wide-open, innovative passing offenses featuring future Hall of Famers from both sides.

Los Angeles, under new head coach Joe Stydahar, set 22 league records and scored a whopping 490 points. No team could hold them to fewer than 14 points in any one

game. Three times they topped 50 points in a game. They scorched Baltimore for 70 points and Detroit for 65. Their two quarterbacks, Bob Waterfield and Norm Van Brocklin, both made the Pro Bowl.

Van Brocklin had been first in passing efficiency that year, with Otto Graham rated No. 2. But the battle within the battle never took place because Van Brocklin had broken a rib in the playoff victory over the Bears. Stydahar had to go with Waterfield, a dilemma any head coach would gladly face.

Waterfield was, however, also the Rams' punter and place-kicker and an injury would have put Los

Number 3

December 24, 1950

The Crowning Achievement

Browns 30
Rams 28

The Browns cap their first NFL season with a fourth-quarter comeback to win the championship.

Angeles at a disadvantage at three positions.

The Rams had lost to Philadelphia in the 1949 championship game on a rain-drenched Los Angeles Coliseum field that inhibited their highly-sophisticated passing attack of Van Brocklin and Waterfield throwing to their outstanding receivers such as Tom Fears and Elroy Hirsch.

With the '50 game in the American Conference champion's city (the NFL used National/American Conference names from 1950-52), no doubt Stydahar had the field conditions on his mind. He started with a big backfield of Paul "Tank" Younger and rookie "Deacon" Dan Towler at halfbacks, rather than the usual smaller, quicker halfback duo of Glenn Davis and V.T. Smith. The coach believed that Younger, also a star linebacker, and Towler, really a fullback,

wouldn't need a hard, dry field to do well against the Browns' defense.

And that defense was almost without one of its most vital cogs. End Len Ford had been on the sidelines since Oct. 15 after a collision with fullback Pat Harder of the Chicago Cardinals. Ford was given clearance to play, but was 15 pounds underweight at game time.

The condition of the playing field was not unlike that of the championship game the previous year. A warming trend hit Cleveland and thawed the frozen ground at the Stadium. A light rain fell in the morning and made the footing softer than it should have been.

So was the Browns' defense, on the game's first play. Perhaps overly conscious of Tom Fears, the Los Angeles end who had a record 84 receptions that year, Glenn Davis slipped out of the backfield unnoticed and caught an 82-yard touchdown pass.

But it took the Browns only six plays to get an equalizer. Graham gained 21 yards rushing and completed three passes on the drive, the final one to Dub Jones for a 31-yard touchdown.

The Rams needed eight plays to get the game's third touchdown on an afternoon when offense was king. Dick Hoerner, the Rams' top rusher and a man once drafted by the Browns, finished the march with a three-yard run. Fears had a 44-yard reception on the drive.

Back came the Browns. A pass interference call against Rams rookie Woodley Lewis and a 17-yard pass to left end Mac Speedie got the Browns from their own 35-yard line to the Los Angeles 26.

Graham then hooked up with Dante Lavelli for Cleveland's second touchdown early in the second quarter. The score, however, stayed 14-13 as the PAT failed when the snap to holder Tommy James was high.

James attempted a pass to Tony Adamle in the end zone, but Adamle dropped it.

It was now time for the Browns' defense to stiffen. The Rams used their running game to march to the Cleveland seven, but V.T. Smith was charged with holding and Ken Gorgal intercepted a Waterfield pass to end the drive.

a passing game and Motley was used mainly as a blocker. Plus, the Rams' defense was heavily geared to stopping him and he was getting hammered at the line of scrimmage on almost every play.

Warren Lahr intercepted a pass at the end of the third quarter, giving Graham the opportunity to begin one of the most pres-

The Browns offense stalled again and punter Horace Gillom uncharacteristically shanked one for only nine yards to the Browns' 46. The Rams got to the Cleveland 12, but could gain only four more yards on the next three plays. Waterfield then missed a 15-yard field goal attempt.

After entering the game in place of rookie Jim Martin, Len Ford was particularly effective in shutting down the Rams. On one series Ford threw V.T. Smith for a 14-yard loss, sacked Waterfield for an 11-yard setback and tackled Glenn Davis 13 yards behind the line of scrimmage.

In the third quarter, Graham connected with Lavelli on another scoring pass, a 39-yarder, to give the Browns their first lead of the game, 20-14. But the Rams responded with two of their own, just 25 seconds apart. Hoerner hit the end zone from a yard away and Larry Brink picked up Marion Motley's fumble and ran it six yards for a score.

Motley was not a strong factor in carrying the ball. The Browns had decided to go with

sure-filled drives in the 50-year history of the Browns.

Twice the Browns converted on fourth down: on a seven-yard pass on fourth-and-four from Graham to Lavelli, and on a quarterback sneak. Graham found Rex Bumgardner on a 14-yard pass play to the back of the end zone for the score. The last play was the only one in the drive in which Graham did not either run himself or throw underneath the Los Angeles defense.

Graham and the Browns were driving for a touchdown again when the quarterback was hit on his blind side and fumbled. Linebacker Mike Lazetich recovered and it looked as if the Rams had the game in the bag. A first down would allow them to run out the clock.

They did not get it. Cliff Lewis took Waterfield's 51-yard punt at the Browns' 19 and ran out of bounds 13 yards later, with

Cleveland's ground game was minimized in favor of a passing attack, but Marion Motley picked up 12 yards on this fourth-quarter play before being tackled by Tank Younger.

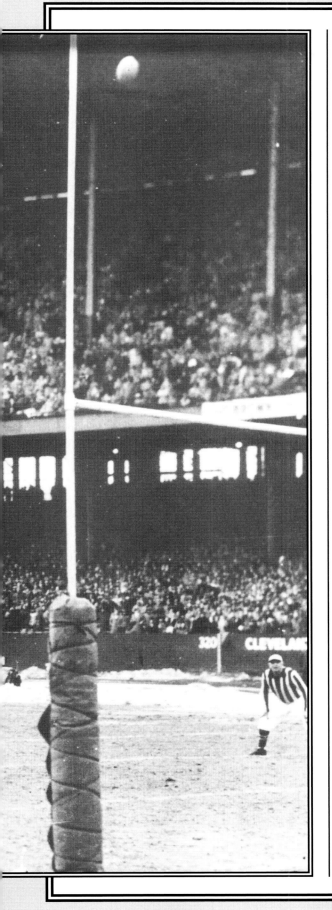

With shoulder pad exposed after a hard day at left tackle, Lou Groza (left) watches his game-winning field goal cross the uprights. In a second view (above), all eyes are focused skyward on the ball.

1:50 left to play. Graham gained 14 yards on a scramble, completed passes of 15 to Bumgardner, 16 to Jones and 12 to Bumgardner. Then Graham ran it to the 10, making sure he was in the middle of the field to set up Groza's field goal attempt.

With a strong 30-mile-per-hour wind at his back, Groza made his most memorable kick, a 16-yarder with 28 seconds left.

After the kickoff, the Rams gained possession on their own 46. Although Waterfield had completed 18 of 22 passes, Stydahar inserted the broken-ribbed Van Brocklin for the final possession. On the first play, Van Brocklin's pass was picked off by Lahr, Cleveland's fourth of the day. The Browns had a 30-28 victory and a championship in their first season in the NFL.

Otto Graham scores one of his three touchdowns on a day that was supposed to be his last in pro football. He also threw two touchdown passes to Ray Renfro and one to Pete Brewster.

There was a brand new look to the Browns for 1954. Only 10 starters remained from the team that won the NFL title in 1950. One-third of the 1954 roster was new as Paul Brown rebuilt the team while keeping the Browns in contention. Two things had not changed—the Browns were still champions of the Eastern Conference and they were still having trouble beating the Detroit Lions.

Detroit had beaten Cleveland in the last two championship games. The Lions would win again on the final weekend of the '54 regular season, Dec. 19, in Cleveland. A week later, the teams were to meet at Cleveland Stadium for another title match. The Lions' 14-10 victory a week before had Browns fans

hoping for the best, but preparing for the worst. Including the preseason, Detroit had an eight-game unbeaten streak against the Browns and were confident their devil-may-care approach was superior to Brown's reliance on a system.

Lions quarterback Bobby Layne had thrown 37 passes in the win on Dec. 19 while the Browns' Otto Graham had passed only six times. Graham had not thrown a TD pass in the four previous meetings between the two NFL powers.

After beating the Browns 17-7 in 1952 and 17-16 in '53, the Lions were ready to become the first club in NFL history to win three consecutive league titles.

Head Coach Buddy Parker had installed a pass-oriented offense similar to the Browns and the Los Angeles Rams. Layne threw to players like Leon Hart, Doak Walker, Dorne Dibble, Cloyce Box, Jug Girard and Jim Doran. Lew Carpenter and ex-AAFC star Bob Hoernschemeyer were dependable ball carriers for the Lions.

Several Browns veterans reportedly met in private during the week between the games to discuss how to overrule the coaches and use the plays they knew were needed to beat the Lions. They would, in effect, be staging a mini-rebellion against Paul Brown's system of sending in plays through a messenger guard rotation.

Brown, too, sensed the old ways would never beat Detroit. So instead of flanking the halfbacks on the outside, which showed a defense just what the Browns were planning to do, Brown decided to run out of a T formation that was the standard in the NFL in the 1950s. He would also turn Graham loose and open up the offense, attacking the Lions before being attacked.

It looked like more of the same in the first quarter, however, when Lions linebacker Joe Schmidt intercepted Graham's pass and Doak Walker was good on a 36-yard field goal to open the scoring.

But it was all Browns from there. Gil Mains was called for roughing punter Horace Gillom on the Browns' first possession and Graham made the Lions pay by tossing a pass through the Detroit secondary to Ray Renfro for an easy touchdown.

Then came the deluge. Don Paul intercepted Layne's pass and returned it 33 yards to the eight. Graham passed to Pete Brewster in the end zone for a 14-3 lead.

In the second quarter, the Lions had to punt and Billy Reynolds returned it to Detroit's 12. Soon after, Graham scored from the one, his first of three touchdowns on the ground. Rookie running back Bill Bowman then scored Detroit's final TD on a five-yard run to make it 21-10.

But before the half ended, the Browns would score twice more for a 25-point halftime lead. To make it 28-10, middle guard Mike McCormack ripped the ball from Layne's cocked arm, setting up Graham's second touchdown run, a five-yarder.

Next, linebacker Walt Michaels intercepted Layne at the Lions' 31 and Graham immediately went to Renfro, who beat All-Pro defensive back Jack Christiansen at the three and plunged into the end zone. At halftime, the score was Browns 35, Lions 10.

In the third quarter, Graham scored his third touchdown, a one-yard run, following a 43-yard completion to Brewster. Next, Ken Konz intercepted a pass and returned it to Detroit's 13-yard line to set up a TD run by Fred "Curly" Morrison that made it 49-10. Finally, in the fourth quarter, a second Konz interception led to a 19-yard touchdown run by Chet "the Jet" Hanulak.

The final score was 56-10. The Browns forced seven Lions turnovers. Cleveland had its receivers running amok through the Detroit secondary as the Lions had to abandon their seven-man rush that once had shackled Graham.

Taming Layne and the Lions

Browns 56
Lions 10

After back-to-back title-game losses, Graham and the Browns finally dominate their nemesis.

Graham had one of his greatest games ever, running for three touchdowns and passing for three more. After completing nine of 12 passes for 163 yards, he left the field in the fourth quarter to a standing ovation. Following the game, the 33-year-old veteran confirmed what had been rumored all season: that he was retiring.

He said he would "go out on top." But he returned, of course, in 1955 to lead the Browns to another championship.

The game was a watershed for the Browns. Talk of the team getting too old to win another NFL championship was put to rest. In fact, the game, and the 1954 season, signalled what appeared to be a successful transition to new talent. On offense, third-year man Ray Renfro became a full-time receiver. Pete Brewster finished his second

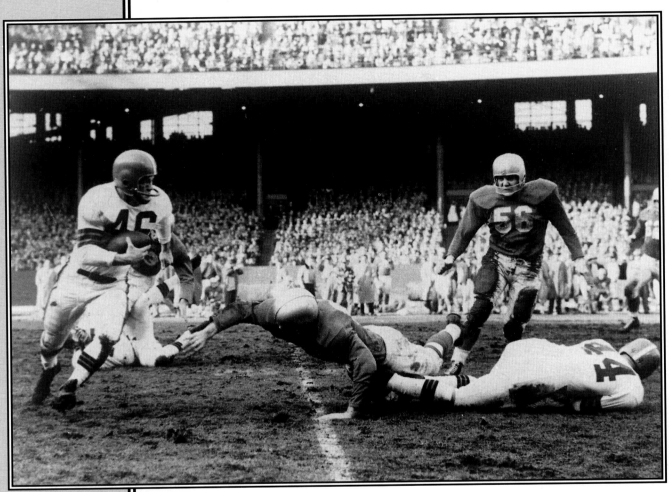

Billy Reynolds runs back a kick with the help of a block by Chet "the Jet" Hanulak (44). Future Hall of Famer Joe Schmidt (56) pursues on the right.

season at left end as Mac Speedie's successor. And rookie Maurice Bassett, in Paul Brown's opinion, had become a better inside runner than Marion Motley, whose aging knees led to retirement in the 1954 preseason (though he returned in '55 to play a final season in Pittsburgh).

On defense, middle guard Mike McCormack, who was acquired in the 1953 10-for-five deal with Baltimore, provided a power-ful pass rush to offset the retirement of veteran Bill Willis. Tackle Don Colo and linebacker Tom Catlin, also acquired from the Colts, had become "bruising defensive players" according to Brown.

Rookie Carlton Massey played so well at defensive end that opposing offenses could no longer simply plan to avoid the other end, Len Ford, as the safest running route. And finally, second-year safety Ken Konz, teamed with seven-year man Tommy James, played like a savvy veteran, intercepting seven passes in 1954, including two for touchdowns.

Furthermore, the newfound aggressiveness exhibited by the Browns in the championship game made Buddy Parker eat his words of Dec. 19, when he said "I only wish it was next Sunday."

In contrast, his post-game comments after the 56-10 thrashing included this statement: "I hope I never have to go through another one like this. If I do, I'll probably be out picking cotton."

Through the 1998 season, neither Parker, nor any other NFL head coach, has had to "go through another one like this" since that day in 1954. Although the 45-point differentials in the Browns' loss to Detroit in 1957 (59-14) and the 49ers' victory over the Broncos in Super Bowl XXIV (55-10) were nearly as great, no team since the 1954 Lions has lost an NFL championship game by a margin that wide. In fact, in the history of the NFL, only the 1940 Bears' 73-0 win over the Redskins was more lopsided.

Everything went right for the Browns. When Pete Brewster attempted this catch inside the Lions' five yard line, the ball was knocked into the air and caught by Ray Renfro.

Baltimore's overtime victory over the New York Giants in the 1958 NFL championship contest in which quarterback John Unitas led the Colts on two rallies, one to tie the score in regulation play and one to win, is generally credited as the consummation of the marriage between the NFL and network television.

So how could either have asked for anything more less than a year later when Unitas' Colts hosted the Cleveland Browns and the best running back in the league—Jim Brown?

The Browns and the Colts had not played each

Jim Brown Jolts the Colts

Browns 38
Colts 31

Big Daddy, Gino and Fatso are no match for the Cleveland fullback's five-touchdown performance.

other since 1956. Unitas was a rookie, and a good one, although his young team would be only 5-7 that year. Brown was a senior at Syracuse University in the fall of 1956, as his future club was also 5-7 and learning how to live without quarterback Otto Graham, who retired the year before.

But Unitas and Brown were NFL superstars three years later and they proved it convincingly on Nov. 1, 1959. Brown scored five touchdowns, a career high, while rushing for 178 yards on 32 carries. Unitas tossed four touchdown passes.

There were 57,557 in the stands at Baltimore's Memorial Stadium to see the greatest offensive players in the NFL match brilliance in an inter-conference battle. The final score was 38-31, as defense wasn't the order of the day. It was much more like a tennis match, as heads turned from side to side while the teams marched up and down the field at will.

But it was a defensive play that "broke the serve." Cleveland safety Junior Wren intercepted a Unitas pass early in the third quarter with the Browns ahead, 17-10. That set up a short touchdown by Brown to give Cleveland a 24-10 lead. The teams alternated touchdowns from that time, just as they had done in the first half.

The Browns kicked a field goal on their first possession. The Colts answered with a three-pointer from Steve Myhra. Brown then gave Cleveland a 10-3 lead with his most impressive run of the day. Taking a pitch from quarterback Milt Plum, Brown escaped several potential tacklers, bowled over defensive back Ray Brown and took off on what became a 70-yard touchdown run. Milt Davis, the Colts' right cornerback, had a chance to catch Brown, but Bobby Mitchell threw a block to keep Davis at bay.

All of Unitas' scoring passes were from short yardage. Baltimore came back with a touchdown pass to Lenny Moore from three yards away to tie the score at 10-10. Brown then gave Cleveland its halftime lead with a 17-yard run.

After Wren's interception and Brown's third touchdown run, Unitas returned with an eight-yard scoring pass to Jerry Richardson. Brown then scored from a yard away and Unitas hit Raymond Berry from 11 yards out to make it 31-24.

Then came the only punt of the afternoon, by Wren, early in the fourth quarter. The Colts marched to the Cleveland seven-yard line, but Unitas' pass intended for Richardson in the end zone was picked off, again by Wren, to keep the Browns ahead.

The fifth Jim Brown TD was on a one-yard plunge. Baltimore scored its final touchdown as Unitas fired a five-yarder to Jim Mutscheller.

Unitas completed 23 of 41 passes for 397 yards, an excellent effort by any measurement. Because the Colts were always behind, pressure mounted on Unitas to keep his team within striking distance. Unitas called just 19 runs for the game, and Bal-

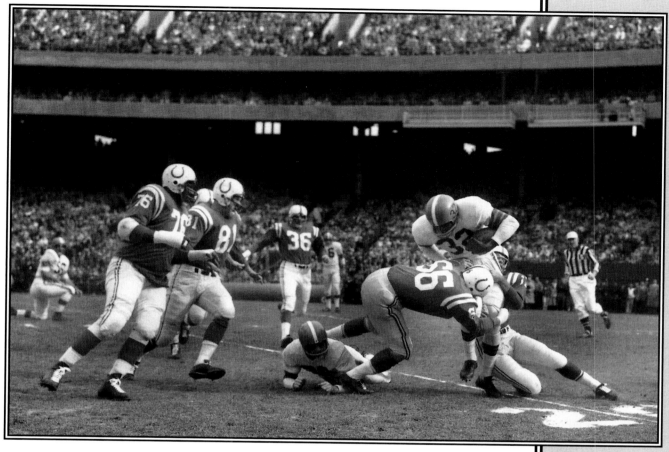

timore's own standout fullback, Alan "the Horse" Ameche, gained only 18 yards on nine attempts.

Milt Plum had an excellent day likewise, going 14-for-23 for 200 yards. Bernie Parrish, a rookie cornerback, intercepted a Unitas pass on the Browns' four-yard line in the second frame. Mitchell caught five passes for 66 yards for the Browns, while Berry made 11 grabs for 156 yards and Moore caught five for 115 yards for Baltimore.

All of that was overshadowed by Brown and his quintet of touchdown runs. It was made more impressive by the fact it was done versus the defending NFL champion, which possessed an awesome defensive front four that included future Pro Football Hall of Famers Gino Marchetti and Art "Fatso" Donovan, plus Don Joyce and Eugene "Big Daddy" Lipscomb.

"He's everything everybody's said, and more," said Weeb Ewbank, the head coach of the Colts and a Browns assistant coach from 1949-53. "We did not tackle as well as

It usually took two or more defenders to tackle Jim Brown. Ray Brown and Don Shinnick (66) make an attempt while Big Daddy Lipscomb (76) and Ordell Braase (81) provide reinforcement.

usual, but maybe that's because we were trying to bring down Jim Brown."

The offensive line had something to do with it. Willie Davis, later to become a star defensive end and Hall of Famer with the Packers, replaced Lou Groza in the first quarter after Groza hurt his back. The rest of the offensive line had another future Hall of Famer, Mike McCormack, at right tackle, Gene Hickerson and Jim Ray Smith at the guards and Art Hunter at center.

"I guess this is my most satisfying day," said Jim Brown, who would win the 1959 league rushing championship with 1,329 yards. "There's nothing like beating the champs. I just might have been hitting with a little something extra today."

Losing to the powerful Baltimore Colts would not have been a disgrace in 1964. Only twice in that autumn did Colts fans not see their favorites win. Baltimore finished 12-2, the third-highest scoring team in NFL history at the time. Only the Vikings and the Lions had beaten the Colts.

Few expected anything special from the Cleveland Browns, champions of the Eastern Conference. The Browns finished at 10-3-1 in 1964, only a half-game better than the year before. Some said the '64 Browns did not look much different from the team that finished second the previous season, and maybe they had only won the title because the New York Giants, who had captured the East six times in the last eight years, had completely collapsed, falling to dead last at 2-10-2.

Besides, the Western Conference was clearly thought to be superior. It had won the NFL championship six times in the last seven seasons. The Colts, Green Bay Packers and Chicago Bears were considered the league's dominating teams.

But on this December day in 1964, the word "domination" would belong to the Cleveland Browns. Their defense, adequate, but not nearly in a class with the Colts, Packers or Bears, shut down a strong Baltimore offense loaded with future Hall of Famers: Johnny Unitas, Lenny Moore, Raymond Berry, John Mackey and Jim Parker.

On offense, quarterback Frank Ryan and receiver Gary Collins had their greatest days as Browns, hooking up on three second-half touchdown passes that, along with Lou Groza's two field goals, gave Cleveland its first NFL championship since 1955—the final year of Otto Graham—and the last title of its first 50 seasons.

Collins, in only his second full season as a starter, was the Browns' most visibly confident player going into the game. During the week preceding the contest, he boasted to a Cleveland television interviewer that the Browns would "win big." And the night before the game, he told teammate Paul Wiggin that he would catch three touchdown passes and win MVP honors.

The game was supposed to be interesting only because Jim Brown, the league's premier running back, would play. Brown had almost singlehandedly demolished the defending champion Colts in a regular-season tilt in 1959 with 178 yards rushing and five touchdowns, but was shackled in a 1962 game, with only 11 yards on 14 carries.

Whether or not Brown had a good game was not supposed to matter. It was on defense where the difference would lay. The Colts had the finest defense in the NFL, giving up a league-low 215 points. Cleveland, on the other hand, gave up more yardage to its opponents than any other club in the circuit. The Browns had yielded 293 points.

There wasn't much the defense was supposed to be able to do against John Unitas, the best quarterback of his day. Unitas was also battle-tested. He had paced the Colts to an overtime victory in the 1958 NFL championship game, also known as "The Greatest Game Ever Played," and led them to victory again in the 1959 title contest. Frank Ryan, meanwhile, had never played in a championship game. Nor had the majority of his Browns teammates.

But some players had. Brown, linebackers Galen Fiss and Vince Costello and defensive end Paul Wiggin were around when the Browns lost to the Detroit Lions in the 1957 title game. Kicker Lou Groza had been with the club (minus the '60 season) since the first day in 1946, while defensive tackle Bob Gain was a starter on the Browns' 1955 champions.

However, it was a player for whom the Browns traded, veteran defensive tackle Dick Modzelewski, who owned the most recent stretch of title-game experience: six over the previous eight seasons with his former team, the Giants, including the NFL championship in 1956. Modzelewski had

become available after Giants head coach Allie Sherman embarked on a housecleaning mission on his aging defense. Already he had dealt tackle Rosey Grier to the Rams and linebacker Sam Huff to the Redskins.

When Modzelewski became available, Blanton Collier and Art Modell were more than willing to give up split end Bobby Crespino for the veteran lineman. Along with his experience, Modzelewski brought enthusiasm and a winning attitude to Cleveland.

Furthermore, in addition to the acquisition of Modzelewski, it was clear that in spite of a 10-4 record in 1963 and three defenders—Galen Fiss, Bill Glass and Bernie Parrish—making the Pro Bowl team, a number of defensive improvements were necessary to overcome New York in the standings.

Gain, a five-time Pro Bowl selection, was winding down his fine career. Collier already had begun working second-year man Jim Kanicki into that position. And shortage of speed in the defensive secondary led Collier to insert another two-year player, Walter Beach, at cornerback in place of veteran Jim Shofner. It also led to a great amount of zone defense because the Browns could not consistently depend on man-to-man coverage.

Heading into the championship game, Baltimore was installed as a seven-point favorite. And why not? Hadn't Charley Johnson, the Cardinals' fourth-year quarterback, scored 61 points on the Browns' defense in

The Ultimate Championship

Browns 27
Colts 0

The underrated Browns overpower and shut down the favored Colts in all phases of the game.

The Browns sacked John Unitas six times. Dick Modzelewski (74), Bill Glass (80), and Jim Kanicki (69) corral the Colts' QB in the first quarter.

Browns' advantage. The Colts were supposed to score points in bunches against this so-so defense and failure to do so was frustrating the visitors.

Baltimore elected to receive the second-half kickoff and the Browns chose to defend the open end of the Stadium, to have the wind behind them in the third quarter. The gamble paid off when Tom Gilburg's punt traveled only to the Browns' 48-yard line. Cleveland could make only 14 yards from there, but with the wind at his back Groza kicked a 43-yard field goal. The scoreless deadlock had been broken, and the momentum was clearly with the Browns.

The defense continued to play the game of its life. Baltimore punted again, this time to Cleveland's 34. Jim Brown swept around left end for 46 yards and Frank Ryan found Gary Collins for an 18-yard pass and the game's first touchdown.

On the next series, the defense held the Colts without a first down. Gilburg again had trouble punting, and a 28-yarder into the wind put the ball at the Baltimore 40. From the 42, Ryan and Collins connected again and the Browns had a 17-0 lead.

Lenny Moore fumbled near midfield and Paul Wiggin recovered. Ryan tossed passes to tight end Johnny Brewer and receiver Paul Warfield. Brown added a 23-yard run to get the Browns to the Baltimore two. Groza's second field goal, in the early moments of the fourth quarter made it 20-0.

Next, Ryan and Collins did it for a third time, from 51 yards away, to give the Browns a 27-0 lead. That's how the game ended, making it one of the most stunning upsets in NFL championship history and proving the Browns' defense was not to be taken lightly.

The Browns sacked Unitas six times. Jim Kanicki led the charge with consistent pene-

two games that year? Johnson was considered a decent passer, but hardly on par with Unitas. Most teams, in fact, were able to score on the Browns that season as they gave up 20 or more points in 10 of 14 games.

The weather in Cleveland Stadium was cold, windy and overcast. Passing into the wind would be a challenge. Neither team could get its offense in gear in the first two quarters, but that was to the

tration despite going against a future Hall of Famer, guard Jim Parker, most of the day.

The offensive line was great, too. Right tackle Monte Clark, who was acquired in a trade with Dallas in '63 for Jim Ray Smith, played the best game of his life against left defensive end Gino Marchetti. Clark was playing because regular right tackle John Brown injured his left knee at mid season. The Colts had 57 sacks in '64, but could not get to Ryan.

Jim Brown gained 114 yards on 27 carries. The entire Baltimore club had 101 yards rushing. Unitas completed 12 of 20 passes for only 96 yards. His outstanding receiving tandem of Raymond Berry and Jimmy Orr caught only five passes for 69 yards. Ryan was 11-of-18 passing for 208 yards. Collins had five receptions for 130 yards.

The doubters had called the Browns "Laugh Champs." The Colts found nothing funny on that December day in 1964.

Frank Ryan throws his third touchdown pass of the day to Gary Collins, a 51-yarder in the fourth quarter. Guard John Wooten (60) provides protection in front.

Paul Brown and Blanton Collier had always been best friends in the days they were making the Cleveland Browns the premier franchise in the All-America Conference and later the NFL. But Brown, Collier's old boss, didn't act like much of a chum after a 1970 preseason game in which the Bengals beat the Browns in Cincinnati. Brown was now head coach of the Bengals, a team the Browns had to play twice a year as a member of the new Central Division of the American Conference in the realigned NFL.

Collier, who took the Browns' head coaching job

Number 7

October 11, 1970

The Unhappy Homecoming

Browns 30
Bengals 27

Paul Brown's return to Cleveland ends in defeat and a cascade of deafening boos after the game.

following Brown's firing by new owner Art Modell in 1963, walked across the field to shake hands with the man for whom he had been an assistant coach for nine seasons. But Brown chose to disappear into the Cincinnati dressing room without even acknowledging the man who had done so much to help him make the Browns the scourge of two leagues. Collier was standing alone in the middle of the field after being jilted.

Would he do it after the Browns and Bengals met for the first time in a regular-season clash, which would also be the first game Brown would coach in Cleveland since 1962? No one was sure. Brown said it was his custom to exchange greetings before a game, not after.

"Blanton knows that," Brown said. "I haven't done it since the league sent out a directive many years ago, when I was still [in Cleveland], that the practice [of walking across the field to shake hands with an opposing coach] should be eliminated. You never know when someone is going to come out and take a swing at you."

Directive or not, the action didn't sit well with Browns fans. Brown, to them, was a sore loser who should just swallow his pride and do what the rest of the league's coaches do. Some thought he would do that in Cleveland, and that he only did it before because he was on his home turf and it was only an exhibition game.

Collier and Brown met before the game. Collier said he told Brown the critical brickbats after the no-shake incident in preseason had not been instigated by him. Collier said Brown believed they were not.

The Browns won the game, 30-27, and at the moment everyone was waiting for, Paul Brown did not shake hands with Blanton Collier. The boos cascaded, deafening, throughout Cleveland Stadium. But Collier claimed he understood.

"It has to do with the way he, or anyone, deals with defeat," Collier said. "He feels worse immediately afterward, and as time goes on he deals with it better. I'm the opposite. I feel badly enough at first but as time goes on it gnaws on me more and more, and I feel worse and worse."

The Browns were 10-point favorites, although it was a hard game to handicap. Cleveland's quarterback, Bill Nelsen, was suffering from a knee injury and played with a heavy bandage wrapping the injury. The starting running backs, Leroy Kelly and Bo Scott, were also suffering from minor injuries and did very little practicing during the week.

The Bengals were having real quarterback troubles. Greg Cook, who'd been the AFL Rookie of the Year in 1969, underwent arm surgery over the summer and was lost for the first part of the '70 season.

His backup, Sam Wyche, who had led Cincinnati to an upset of the Raiders in the first game of the regular season, had failed to move the Bengals' offense in the following two games and was replaced by Virgil

Carter, who had been acquired recently from the Chicago Bears.

In the first quarter, Cincinnati built a 10-0 lead on a 50-yard field goal by Horst Muhlmann and a two-yard touchdown run by Jess Phillips. Then Walter Johnson tackled Carter in the end zone for a safety to give the Browns their initial points.

The Bengals held a slim lead over the middle quarters. Kelly and Nelsen hooked up on a three-yard touchdown to make it 10-9. Bengals defensive end Royce Berry returned a fumble 58 yards for a TD and Nelsen found Milt Morin on a four-yard scoring pass to make the score 17-16 Bengals at halftime.

Muhlmann added another field goal in the third quarter, the only scoring of that period, but also missed a 39-yard attempt in the third. Meanwhile, the Browns' defense, shaky in the first quarter, was starting to assert itself. The Bengals' offense scored three points in the middle quarters and saw Carter sacked five times.

Kelly finally gave the Browns the lead on a one-yard TD run in the fourth quarter. Erich Barnes then intercepted Carter's pass and returned it 20 yards to the Cincinnati six. Two plays after that, Bo Scott ran into the end zone from a yard out.

Carter brought the Bengals back with a 16-yard TD pass to Speedy Thomas. The Browns were faced with third down and three on their 38-yard line with 1:50 to play—plenty of time for the Bengals to get Muhlmann in position to kick a tying field goal—but Gary Collins caught Nelsen's sideline pass and stepped out of bounds at the Cleveland 46, enabling the Browns to run out the clock for a 30-27 triumph.

Nelsen, despite his injured knee, completed 17 of 29 passes for 226 yards as the Browns outgained the Bengals 346-236. Cincinnati had virtually nothing on the ground (54 yards rushing, 20 attempts), but Virgil Carter solidified his hold on the starting quarterback job by completing 20 of 28 passes for 218 yards.

The victory gave the Browns a 3-1 record and made the Bengals 1-3. The Bengals won the rematch in Cincinnati on Nov. 15, 14-10.

A gimpy backfield put the Browns at a disadvantage. Bill Nelsen, Leroy Kelly and Bo Scott were all hurting prior to the contest. Scott (above) picks up eight yards early in the first quarter.

The narrow point margins of both games foretold a pattern of tight, hard-fought contests that would characterize the Browns-Bengals rivalry.

In the Bengals' locker room following the game, Brown was visited by three of his longtime Cleveland stars: Otto Graham, Dante Lavelli and Tommy James. He said he was proud of both of *his* teams, praising the Bengals and Browns equally.

"It looked as if it might have been an intra-squad game," Brown said. "We both knew each other's styles. We've used the same numbering system and much of our football is the same."

The Bengals would go on to win the AFC Central Division championship with an 8-6 record in only their third year of existence. Clearly Paul Brown's coaching genius was now at work in southern Ohio.

Receiver Ricky Feacher is hoisted by Willis Adams following one of his two touchdown catches.

Cincinnati Bengals general manager Paul Brown and his head coach, Forrest Gregg, could have gotten some personal satisfaction with a Bengals victory over the Browns on the last day of the 1980 season. Both men had been fired by Browns owner Art Modell, and there was little doubt both would have enjoyed a pay back.

The Browns had a 10-5 record and a 7-4 conference mark when they visited Cincinnati's Riverfront Stadium. A victory would not just get them their first playoff berth

since 1972, but would give them their first AFC Central championship in nine years. The Browns and Oilers each had 10-5 records going into that day, but the Oilers were done with their conference slate, having compiled a 4-2 record in their division, 7-5 in the AFC.

A win would have left the Browns 4-2 in the Central Division, but a game in front of Houston conference-wise. A defeat and the Browns would be facing elimination as the Steelers, also 4-2 in the Central, were playing San Diego in a Monday night game. Pittsburgh was 9-6 at the time, while the Chargers were 10-5 and in need of a victory to rule the AFC West over the Raiders.

The Steelers were obviously in the most unenviable situation, having to battle an opponent with a division title on its mind at their place. The Oilers were meeting the Vikings, who had already clinched their divisional crown. The Browns were meeting a team with a 6-9 slate that had fallen 31-7 four weeks earlier in one of only two lopsided victories for the Browns that season.

But Cleveland had to be leery of playing away from home against an opponent led by men for whom there was no love lost between them and Art Modell. For the Bengals, last place in the Central Division would have been a little easier to accept had they been able to throw a monkey wrench into the Browns' playoff plans.

But this was the season of the "Kardiac Kids" and, as was the rule in 1980, the outcome was not determined until the closing moments. Don Cockroft kicked a field goal with 1:25 to play to snap a 24-24 tie, and defensive back Ron Bolton halted the final drive by tackling Bengals wide receiver Steve Kreider in bounds at the Cleveland 14 with time running out.

"I could have intercepted the ball, or even knocked it down," Bolton said. "But I didn't want to take any chances. If the pass had been incomplete, [the Bengals] would have had another play. I knew if he caught it and I could keep him in bounds, the game would be over."

The Bengals had used all of their time outs, and could neither set up a field goal try nor run another play from scrimmage. The game ended 27-24 Browns, giving the Clevelanders their Central Division title. Houston had downed the Vikings, making the triumph that much more essential.

It looked as though it would never happen at first. The Bengals' Jim Breech kicked a 42-yard field goal and backup quarterback Jack Thompson scored on a 13-yard run to make it 10-0 Cincinnati. Brian Sipe, the Browns' quarterback, had fumbled to set up Thompson's touchdown with 10 minutes to go before halftime.

Sipe came back and threw a 42-yard scoring pass to Reggie Rucker, then Dino Hall's recovery of a fumbled punt return set up Cockroft's 26-yard field goal with 14 seconds left in the first half. Halftime score: Browns 10, Bengals 10.

In the third quarter, Ray Griffin intercepted Sipe and returned it 52 yards for a TD to put the Bengals ahead 17-10, but the Browns came back with two touchdowns on 35- and 34-yard passes from Sipe to Ricky Feacher, who played for injured starter Dave Logan, to grab a 24-17 lead.

Bengals receiver Pat McInally, who lay on the field for about 10 minutes in the first quarter after being clobbered by Browns free safety Thom Darden, gained revenge when he caught a 59-yard third-quarter TD pass from Thompson to tie the game for the third time. McInally had been carried off the field on a stretcher, but returned to grab three passes for 86 yards.

Cleveland's winning drive began at its own 46-yard line and 6:04 remaining. The running game, which had been ineffective against the Cincinnati defense, suddenly became the primary weapon. Mike Pruitt got most of the calls and finished the game with 51 yards to end the season with 1,034.

The Browns were at the three-yard line on third and goal when Sipe called what head coach Sam Rutigliano called a "feast or famine" bootleg. The quarterback elected to keep the ball rather than pitch it to Cleo Miller. The play fooled everyone except Cincinnati cornerback Ken "The Rattler" Riley, who came up to nail Sipe behind the line of scrimmage.

Not to worry. The Browns still had Cockroft, who had been kicking for them since 1968. Cincinnati called a time out to unnerve Cockroft, but to no avail as the veteran made it perfect and the Bengals' use of a time out came back to haunt them when they had none for the final possession. Cockroft had gone through a trying season, having been bothered by a sciatic nerve injury since the second regular-season game.

The Bengals still had 1:18 to move from their own 32-yard line into field goal range. Quarterback Ken Anderson, who would lead Cincinnati to the Super Bowl a year later, moved the Ben-

Palpitating Performance

Browns 27 Bengals 24

The Kardiac Kids win the AFC Central Division with one more exciting, heart-stopping finale.

gals to the Browns' 34. He then threw out of bounds to stop the clock. Finally, his 20-yard pass to Kreider was complete at the 14, but Bolton tackled Kreider in bounds and time expired. The Kardiac Kids had won the Central with yet another palpitating performance.

"The Bengals were only 6-9, but they wanted to salvage something and they almost did," Browns veteran offensive tackle Doug Dieken said after the game. "Because they had nothing to lose it was a defensive lineman's holiday."

Sipe had 308 yards passing that day to conclude the year with 4,132 yards, still a club record in 1999. At the time it was only the fourth time in league history a quarterback had thrown for more than 4,000 yards. His effort would be recognized with the NFL's Most Valuable Player award.

Little did Browns fans realize after their favorites upset the mighty Dallas Cowboys, 38-14, on Dec. 28, 1969, that it would be another 17 years before the Browns would again see victory in a playoff game. Cleveland had landed in the playoffs five times between that 1969 conference playoff game with Dallas and their divisional tilt against the New York Jets at Cleveland Stadium on Jan. 3, 1987, but had always departed early.

The 1986 season was different, however.

The Browns posted a 12-4 regular-season record, the best in the AFC, and were rolling. They had flattened

Dramatic Win in Double OT

Browns 23
Jets 20

A Kosar-led comeback, an undaunted defense and Moseley's kicks give the Browns a thrilling victory.

the San Diego Chargers by 30 points in their final contest. The week before that, they had handed the Cincinnati Bengals, who had defeated them earlier in the season, a 34-3 walloping at Riverfront Stadium.

The Browns had won their last five games and eight of their final nine. They had even defeated the Steelers in Pittsburgh for the first time since 1969, the same year they had last won a playoff contest.

But there were low spots that season. The Browns lost at home to the then-winless Green Bay Packers in Game 7, after leading 14-3 at halftime. They were lucky to escape Houston and Minnesota with 23-20 victories. They needed overtime to beat the Steelers and the Oilers in Cleveland. While the Browns were impressive, they were hardly a juggernaut.

The Jets weren't either, although they had looked like one when the 1986 season commenced. Head Coach Joe Walton's team enjoyed the best record in the league with a 10-1 record. Quarterback Ken O'Brien, who had thrown for 3,888 yards with 25 touchdowns and only eight interceptions the year before, was lighting up the passing lanes via a 62.2-percent completion rate. Al Toon was catching 85 passes and Freeman McNeil, who had 1,331 yards rushing in '85, was on his way to another four-digit season.

Then came the crash. The Jets lost their next five and barely made it past Seattle and Cincinnati to be one of the two Wild Card playoff entries.

But just when New York was given up for dead, No. 2 quarterback Pat Ryan, who Walton started over O'Brien in hopes of giving the Jets a psychological lift, completed 16 of 23 passes, with three touchdowns and no interceptions, in a 35-15 smashing of the Kansas City Chiefs in the Wild Card game. Suddenly the Browns were facing a team that had again found its confidence.

It found more than that in the second half. With the Jets leading 13-10 in the fourth quarter, Browns quarterback Bernie Kosar moved the team to the Jets' two-yard line. But Kosar, in his first full season as a starter, tried to force a pass to Webster Slaughter in the end zone as Slaughter was double-covered. Russell Carter intercepted.

It was the first interception Kosar had suffered since November, but it would be the first of two that quarter. After the defense held and the Browns took possession at their own 17, Kosar was picked off by Jerry Holmes. Kosar had never thrown two consecutive interceptions before that.

Freeman McNeil, who didn't get his 1,000-yard season but had burned the Chiefs for 135 yards and two TDs the week before, then went 25 yards around the right side for a touchdown and a 20-10 Jets lead. It forced many of the 78,106 fans to get up and leave. Only 4:08 was on the clock and suddenly visions of the 1980 playoff loss to the Raiders, which ended on an interception in the end zone, and the previous year's loss to Miami, in which the Browns squandered a 21-3 lead at halftime, were haunting the long-suffering Browns supporters.

Kosar, however, would reward them for their persevering faith. Mark Gastineau was called on a roughing-the-passer penalty on the first play, which so obviously occurred after Kosar released the ball that many believed it cost the Jets the victory, to put the ball at the Cleveland 33-yard line.

Kosar then threw five completions to Reggie Langhorne, Brian Brennan (two each) and Curtis Dickey to get the Browns to the one-yard line at the two-minute warning. Fullback Kevin Mack plunged in for the touchdown on the next play. It was now 20-17, Jets.

The defense held the Jets without a first down, and the Browns took over at their own 33 with 51 seconds to go. A 25-yard pass interference penalty and a Kosar-to-Slaughter completion got Cleveland to the Jets' five-yard line where Mark Moseley hammered home a 22-yard field goal to put the game into overtime.

The 38-year-old veteran Moseley, a former Washington Redskin who once kicked a then-NFL-record 23 straight field goals over a two-season span (1981-82), had been signed by Cleveland in the last week of November after a leg injury to Matt Bahr.

Moseley would miss a 23-yard attempt in the first overtime, but the Browns' defense then smothered the Jets. The feeling that Moseley would have another chance was so strong the players could taste it. "We thought if we could keep getting the ball in Bernie's hands, we'd win," defensive end Carl Hairston said.

Cleveland took over for the final time at its own 31 with 2:38 to play in the second extra period. Kosar went to the ground, especially to Kevin Mack, who gained 44 yards on the effort. Receiver Brian Brennan, however, might have been the biggest hero as he broke up what looked to be a certain interception at the Jets' 42.

The Browns were at the nine-yard mark when Moseley came onto the field again. This time, he made good from 27 yards away, the Browns took a 23-20 victory with 12:58 to go in the second overtime.

Mark Moseley kicked one field goal to put the game into overtime, then kicked another (above) to win it in the second overtime.

Kosar threw 64 times with 33 completions for 489 yards—all playoff records. Jets punter Dave Jennings was called to duty a playoff-record 14 times.

The victory was likely the most stirring comeback the Browns had seen since the 1950 championship game, a 30-28 win over the Rams. The 1980 Browns were the Kardiac Kids, but that Jan. 3, 1987, double-overtime triumph had too many fans' hearts pounding much too quickly.

"Bernie comes into the huddle and says to us 'We're going to take this game.' It was incredible the way he brought us together one play at a time," offensive tackle Paul Farren said about the closing minutes.

"There were people going home in their cars who wish they'd stayed for the finish," linebacker Scott Nicholas said. You have to wonder if they were at least listening to the thrills on the radio.

159

Things looked pretty dismal for the Cleveland Browns between Dec. 4 and Dec. 10, 1994. What was up until then a sparkling season, their first winning one since 1989, appeared to be going downhill. Cleveland had lost to the New York Giants, a decidedly average outfit, on Dec. 4.

The Browns had fallen out of first place for the first time all season, held a record of 9-4 and now had to visit the home field of the Dallas Cowboys, the two-time defending Super Bowl champs. The Cowboys were awesome. Their record at the time was 11-2, tied for the

How 'Bout Them Browns!

**Browns 19
Cowboys 14**

The improving Browns get a little respect in Big D from the defending Super Bowl champs.

best in the league with the San Francisco 49ers. One of their losses had been to the Niners and those teams were in a heated race for homefield advantage during the playoffs.

The Cowboys certainly were not about to take anybody lightly through the rest of the 1994 season, let alone the Browns, a team that had allowed the fewest points in the NFL through 13 games (164).

The main criticism the Browns had to endure through the '94 season was that their schedule was full of patsies. By the time of the 14th game, Cleveland had only beaten one team with a winning record, the 8-6 Patriots, and had lost to the two other winners on the slate, the Pittsburgh Steelers and Kansas City Chiefs.

The Browns, however, had been given credit for avoiding being upset, but that was prior to the Giants surprising them, 16-13, at Cleveland Stadium. "We don't make the schedule," Browns safety Eric Turner said. "We just play it." Added linebacker Carl Banks: "I can't say those who were skeptical about us were not justified. We have been inconsistent at times."

Skeptics became believers on Dec. 10. The Browns defeated the Cowboys, 19-14, at Texas Stadium to lock up a playoff berth for themselves and throw a serious roadblock into Dallas' plans of homefield advantage in their march to an unprecedented third consecutive Super Bowl championship.

As with most upsets, a little bit of luck played a big part in this one. It looked as if the last play of the game was going to be a game-winning six-yard touchdown pass from Dallas quarterback Troy Aikman to his All-Pro tight end, Jay Novacek. Browns linebacker Mike Caldwell overran the coverage of Novacek, and Aikman spotted him alone over the middle.

But as the Dallas tight end was making his turn to waltz freely into the end zone, he slipped on the AstroTurf and hit the deck. Novacek was immediately covered by Turner, who was playing the game in spite of an injured shoulder. The play started with 10 seconds on the clock and it ended with time having expired and the ball no more than three inches from the goal line.

A smaller piece of luck occurred earlier on the Cowboys' potential winning drive when receiver Michael Irvin failed to step out of bounds and stop the clock after catching a pass at the Browns' 25-yard line.

Irvin, according to the Browns, had gotten away with a pass interference on cornerback Don Griffin, who was knocked to the carpet by Irvin as the latter ran his route. With Griffin fallen, Irvin suspected he might be able to score. But Griffin recovered and Browns safety Stevon Moore came over to help as Irvin was tackled in bounds at the 21.

Aikman spiked the ball to stop the clock with 28 seconds to go, but a few precious ticks had gone off before the Cowboys could line up and down the ball.

Kevin Williams caught a 15-yard pass from Aikman over the middle to get the

Cowboys to the six-yard line. Aikman again spiked the ball to stop the clock, this time with 10 seconds left. The Browns called time out to discuss their defense, and decided to try a matchup zone rather than risk blitzing the high-powered Dallas offense .

"If one guy gets beaten, then that's the game," Browns defensive coordinator Nick Saban said. "You have a greater chance to make a big play [when you blitz], but you're also more susceptible to getting beaten."

The Browns were beaten, but a fortuitous slip saved the day. It was as if fate had thrown an invisible banana peel into Jay Novacek's path to the end zone.

But there was plenty of bad luck on the Browns' side, too. Defenders, for example, dropped five sure interceptions. Running back Leroy Hoard seemed to have a clear path to the end zone on the Browns' first series, but Cowboys All-Pro Charles Haley, who had been blocked to the ground as he rushed quarterback Vinny Testaverde, recovered, chased down Hoard from behind and knocked the ball loose at the Cowboys' two-yard line. The ball was recovered by Dallas in the end zone for a touchback.

The Cowboys took advantage of the break and went 80 yards on 13 plays to take a 7-0 lead. Emmitt Smith, who had won three straight NFL rushing titles, scored on a pass from Aikman from seven yards out.

The Browns answered on their next series when wide receiver Michael Jackson caught Testaverde's pass from two yards away to tie the score, 7-7, as time ran out on the first quarter.

Three possessions had produced three impressive drives, and it looked as if the game might be high-scoring. Not so. The Browns stifled the Cowboys at every turn. Griffin and Turner intercepted Aikman and the Browns recovered two Dallas fumbles. They could not manage any touchdowns, but did get into range for Matt Stover to kick field goals of 34, 32 and 43 yards to make it 16-7 with 12:44 to go.

The Cowboys then followed Stover's third field goal with a 12-play, 78-yard 6:23 scoring drive. Smith did the honors on a four-yard touchdown run.

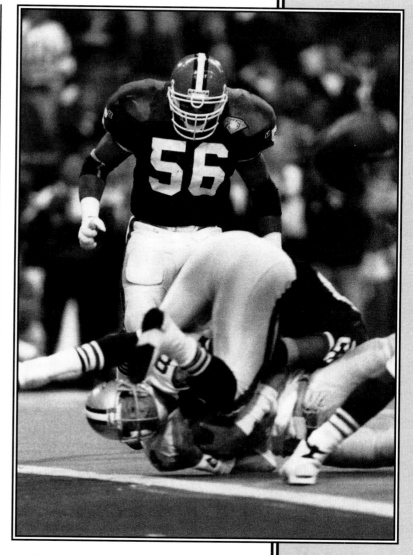

Stover, who closed the '94 season with a Browns-record 20 consecutive field goals without a miss, made it 19-14 with a 32-yarder with 1:49 remaining.

Defensive tackle Bill Johnson recovered a Cowboys fumble at the Dallas 16. Though the Browns failed to move the ball, Stover's kick put the Cowboys in the unenviable position of needing a touchdown rather than a field goal to win the game.

"I don't think we need to ask for respect any more because we got it now," Eric Turner said after the victory. "We beat the Super Bowl champs so everybody has to eat their words a little bit."

Jay Novacek's shoulder lands just short of the goal line on the game's final play. Eric Turner covers him while Mike Caldwell (56) approaches.

How many times have you had to hear a pro football television broadcaster say this prior to a game?: "These two teams just plain don't like each other very much." A major ingredient in any rivalry is good old-fashioned animosity. In the Browns' first 50 seasons, the hostility extended nationwide, to both coasts. Without question, however, the biggest share of ill feelings will forever remain concentrated in the hundred-mile-plus corridor between Cleveland and Pittsburgh.

the Cincinnati Bengals and Houston Oilers. In the late '80s, of course, there was John Elway and the dreaded Denver Broncos.

There are those who will tell you that when it came to the AAFC, the Browns had no rivals. The conventional wisdom went something like this: "The Browns were so much better than any other team in the AAFC that they caused the league to fold. There simply was no competition!" That's not entirely true, although it isn't entirely fiction either. Clearly, Cleveland was better than any other team in the AAFC.

The Rivalries

Although a good rivalry in the 1950s and '60s, the Browns-Steelers battles seldom mattered in the standings as Pittsburgh was never a power. That all changed when the two teams moved to the AFC's Central Division in 1970 just as the Steelers were beginning to emerge as Super Bowl contenders.

Suddenly, the Browns, still solid contenders themselves, were matched against future Hall of Famers such as Terry Bradshaw, Franco Harris, Mean Joe Greene, Jack Lambert, Jack Ham and Mel Blount. The intensity level reached a fever pitch throughout the '70s, '80s and '90s—so much so that when schedule-makers were assembling the 1999 slate, owner Al Lerner successfully lobbied for the Steelers to be the new Browns' first regular-season foe.

Other Browns rivals have included the New York Yankees and San Francisco 49ers in the All-America Conference years; the Los Angeles Rams and Detroit Lions in the 1950-57 playoff era; the Dallas Cowboys in the '60s; and, beginning with the AFL-NFL realignment of 1970,

They lost four games in the four years of "the All-American," as some of the players called, and still call, their league. And there was the 1948 season when the Browns were undefeated, a nearly impossible feat in pro sports.

Of the four losses from 1946-49, San Francisco inflicted two of them: 34-20 in 1946 and 56-28 in 1949. In the '48 undefeated season, the closest call the Browns had was a 31-28 battle with the 49ers in San Francisco, a game in which Otto Graham played with an injured knee and the Browns played on just three days rest after a Thanksgiving day victory over Los Angeles. The 56-28 defeat in 1949, also in San Francisco, ended the Browns' 29-game unbeaten streak which had begun in 1947.

Despite the losses, the Browns maintained the upper hand, beating the 49ers seven times, including the 1949 AAFC title game. In four

Linebacker Billy Andrews wraps up Pittsburgh's Franco Harris.

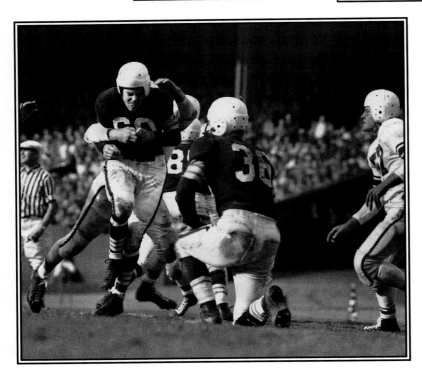

NINER NEMESIS: The Browns lost four games in their four AAFC seasons, two of which were to Western Division rival San Francisco. Otto Graham is sacked in their first-ever meeting, a 34-20 49er win at Cleveland Stadium on Oct. 27, 1946.

years, the 49ers finished second behind the Browns each season: three times in the Western Division (1946-48) and again in '49 when the league played its final season as a seven-team circuit without divisions.

When the teams joined the NFL in 1950 and were placed in different conferences, the rivalry lost some of its intensity. But a tense moment, nevertheless, occurred in the 1953 game at Cleveland Stadium when Otto Graham rolled right, was forced out of bounds and then took an elbow in the mouth by the 49ers' Art Michalik. Graham returned in the second half with a Paul Brown-invented thin plastic bar bolted to his helmet. The device was a forerunner of the modern-day face mask.

That occurence in 1953 probably aggravated Brown as much as having to watch quarterback Y.A. Tittle perform in a 49er uniform. In 1948, the Baltimore Colts were the weakest link in the AAFC, both on the field and at the gate. Their troubles resulted in the league conduct-

ing two April "restocking" drafts for the Colts in which the seven other clubs gave up players to whom they held the rights, but would receive no compensation.

One of the two players the Browns sacrificed was Tittle, who had been a Cleveland draftee and had just signed his first contract with the team. Brown had hoped to groom Tittle as the eventual successor to Graham, but instead watched Tittle launch a Hall-of-Fame career with the Colts, 49ers and Giants.

When it came to the AAFC championship game, the Browns were unbeatable. In the first two years they victimized the New York Yankees, then the Buffalo Bills, and finally the 49ers. The 1946 Yankees were almost the equal of the Browns. They finished 10-3-1 in the Eastern Division and had quarterback Ace Parker and tackle Bruiser Kinard (two future Hall of Famers), plus tailback Spec Sanders and receiver Jack Russell.

The Yankees scored first in the title game at Cleveland Stadium on a field goal, but Motley's short plunge and Lou Groza's PAT put the Browns ahead, 7-3. Sanders scored for New York, but Lou Rymkus blocked the extra point: New York 9, Cleveland 7.

In the final five minutes, Graham led the Browns on a steady march, topping it off with a 16-yard TD pass to Lavelli. Groza converted and the final score stood at 14-9. Motley rushed for 100 yards on 13 carries. Graham threw for 213 yards on 16 of 27. Lavelli and Speedie each caught six passes.

In the 1947 rematch, this time at Yankee Stadium, the Browns scored first on a sneak by Graham. The score was set up by Motley's 51-yard dash around right end. Groza kicked the PAT. New York scored a field goal, but Special Delivery Jones blasted into the end zone from four yards in the third period. Lou Saban's extra point completed the scoring for the day: Cleveland 14, New York 3.

Although the Browns defeated the Yankees seven of the eight times they met in the regular season, that one non-victory, a 28-28 tie in 1947, serves as one of the greatest comebacks in

Browns history. The game was played at Yankee Stadium on Nov. 23, 1947, before the largest New York pro football crowd (70,060) to that date. The Yankees worked especially hard on film study and Browns play diagramming, and felt they could snap the Browns' four-game winning streak in the series. At first, it looked as though coach Ray Flaherty's off-field prepping would pay off. The Yankees were ahead, 28-0, after only 23 minutes of play.

Then Otto Graham went to work! First he connected with Bill Boedeker for a 34-yard scoring pass late in the second quarter. Late in the third, Graham found Marion Motley for a 12-yard TD strike. This score was set up when the Browns' defense stopped New York a yard short of the goal line. Then, throwing from his own end zone, Graham collaborated with Mac Speedie for 82 yards.

Three minutes later, Motley scored again, this time on a 10-yard run. In the final minutes of the fourth quarter, Graham's passing set up Jim Dewar's four-yard quick-opening touchdown thrust. As he did three previous times, Lou Saban, filling in for an injured Lou Groza, was true on the fourth and tying extra point. Browns 28, Yankees 28.

COMEBACK: Tom Colella misses, but Marion Motley, playing linebacker, is on target to tackle Buddy Young in the first quarter of the Browns-Yankees battle at Yankee Stadium on Nov. 23, 1947. The Yankees built a 28-0 first-half lead before the Browns, in one of their greatest comebacks, erased the deficit for a 28-28 tie. Motley scored twice: on a 12-yard catch and a 10-yard run.

But the game was not over yet! With 1:30 left to play, behind the running of Sanders and Buddy Young, New York drove 50 yards to the Cleveland 30. But time finally expired as the Browns' defense covered all Yankees receivers and Sanders couldn't unload to stop the clock with an incompletion.

Writing in the *New York Times*, Louis Effrat called the Browns' comeback "one of the greatest, most spectacular comebacks in many a year." While "only a tie," the game proved that no lead was safe against the powerful Browns.

When the AAFC merged with the NFL in 1950, a draft was held to redistribute players from the defunct AAFC franchises. As part of the maneuvering, the New York Giants were given first choice of players from the Brooklyn-New York Yankees (the Yankees had merged with the Brooklyn Dodgers for the AAFC's final season in '49). Although many of the ex-

HARD-FOUGHT FIFTIES: Fierce clashes between talent-laden teams characterized the early years of the Browns-Giants rivalry. Above, Marion Motley battles for 11 yards in the 1950 playoff game. Right, Roosevelt Brown (79), future Brown Dick Modzelewski (77) and Don Colo (70) have harsh words in 1956.

Yankees became members of the NFL's newly-formed New York Yanks in 1950, the Giants took some of the very best, including three defensive backs: Harmon Rowe, Otto Schnellbacher and Tom Landry, plus future Hall-of-Fame defensive tackle Arnie Weinmeister.

Landry, Rowe and Schnellbacher became three of the four spokes in the Giants' "Umbrella Defense," designed by head coach Steve Owen and featuring an arc of linebackers and defensive backs geared to stopping the passing efforts of Otto Graham. The scheme worked to near perfection as the Giants beat the Browns twice in the 1950 regular season. New York shut out the Browns in Cleveland (6-0), then held them in check three weeks later at the Polo Grounds (17-13). Both teams finished 10-2 and a playoff was needed to determine the American Conference title.

The game was played on Dec. 17 at Cleveland Stadium in 10-degree temperatures. Only 33,054 fans braved the wind chill factor to see what would become typical of the series: a hard-fought, low-scoring game. Browns and Giants alike wore sneakers to get a foothold on the frozen field, except for Lou Groza, who

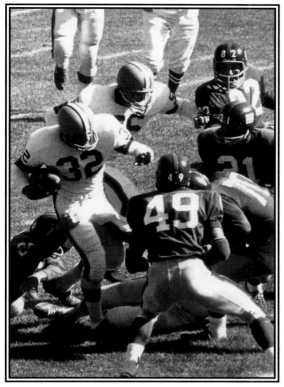

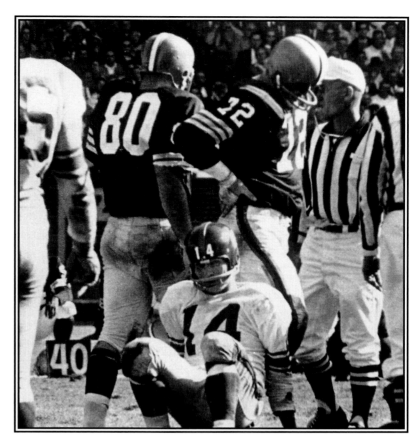

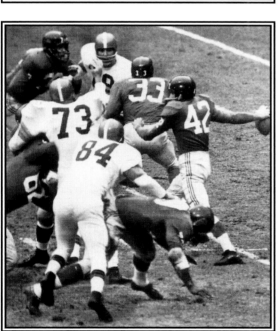

A GIANT EDGE: The Giants dominated the latter years of the rivalry, going 9-3-1 from 1958-63 while winning five Eastern Conference championships. Left, Paul Wiggin (84), Floyd Peters (73) and Bob Gain chase Charlie Conerly in 1959. Above left, Sam Huff (70) and four other Giants take their best shot at Jim Brown in 1963. Above right, Peters (72) and Bill Glass (80) walk away after putting Y.A. Tittle in a down mood in '62.

wore a sneaker on his left foot and a football shoe (minus cleats) on his right kicking foot. Going into the final quarter the Browns were ahead, 3-0. Then the Giants nearly scored when halfback Gene "Choo-Choo" Roberts broke free at the 37-yard line and headed for a touchdown. But suddenly, in one of the most memorable plays in Browns history, Bill Willis, the cat-like middle guard, made up 20 yards on Roberts and caught him at the four. The defense held, actually pushing the Giants back to where Randy Clay kicked a tying field goal to match Groza's.

In the final minute, Groza broke the tie with his second field goal. Then, shortly thereafter, Willis broke through to sack Charlie Conerly in the end zone for a safety and an 8-3 victory.

For the next six seasons, the Browns held the edge in the rivalry, going 8-3-1 against the Giants from 1951-56. But as the Browns were winding down their streak of six straight NFL title games, the Giants were gearing up as their successor, winning the NFL championship in 1956, the Browns' first year without Otto Graham leading the offense.

RAM RIVALRY: A year after the Browns beat the Rams for the 1950 NFL championship, defensive back Cliff Lewis is too late to stop Elroy "Crazylegs" Hirsch from making this catch in the 1951 title game at the L.A. Coliseum, won by the Rams, 24-17.

From 1958-63, the Giants won the Eastern Conference championship five times while the Browns finished second or third each season. By the mid '60s, the Giants' dynasty had ended and the Browns gained the upper hand, keeping it until the merger reduced the frequency of the once titanic struggles to that of a presidential election.

During the early years of the 1950s, the Los Angeles Rams, a team that had won the 1945 NFL title as the Cleveland Rams before relocating to the West Coast in '46, were one of the few teams that could match the Browns' offensive firepower with Bob Waterfield, Norm Van Brocklin, Tom Fears, Deacon Dan Towler, Elroy "Crazylegs" Hirsch and Paul "Tank" Younger. Their defense, however, was not able to match that of the Browns.

The teams met in the 1950 NFL title game. On the first play from scrimmage, Waterfield threw an 82-yard touchdown pass to Glenn Davis, "Mr. Outside" of Army fame. Graham countered with a 31-yard scoring strike to Dub Jones. He later threw scores to Dante Lavelli twice and to Rex Bumgardner. But in the end it was Groza's educated toe that spelled victory. His 16-yard field goal with 28 seconds to play lifted the Browns to the 30-28 win.

As often happened in the pre-free agency days, there was a title rematch in 1951. This time the Rams won, 24-17, at the Los Angeles Coliseum. The back-breaker was a 73-yard pass to Fears from Van Brocklin, one of two Hall-of-Fame quarterbacks (Waterfield was the other) who alternated at the position for the Rams. It broke a 17-17 tie.

With Graham coaxed back for another year after announcing his retirement in 1954, the Browns defeated the Rams, 38-14, in the 1955 championship. Graham threw two TD passes (Lavelli, 50 yards and Ray Renfro, 35 yards) and ran for two scores, but equally important were six Cleveland interceptions. The Browns generated 24 points—the margin of victory—from the turnovers. Don Paul set a champi-

Then, in 1957, came Jim Brown! The new-found rivalry within a rivalry (fullback Brown vs. middle linebacker Sam Huff) became the stuff of which legends and TV documentaries are made. Shielded from Browns blockers by his front-four, Huff was free to "dog" Brown on nearly every play. He did more than today's "spies," he simply tackled Brown whether or not he had the ball. Mostly he did. An example of the effectiveness of this strategy was the 1958 Eastern Conference playoff. The Giants won the right to face the Colts in the famed "sudden death" title game by beating the Browns, 10-0. Huff and friends held Brown to eight yards on seven carries. But there was a toll charge. Huff said, "Tackling Jimmy Brown was like running into an oak tree in the dark."

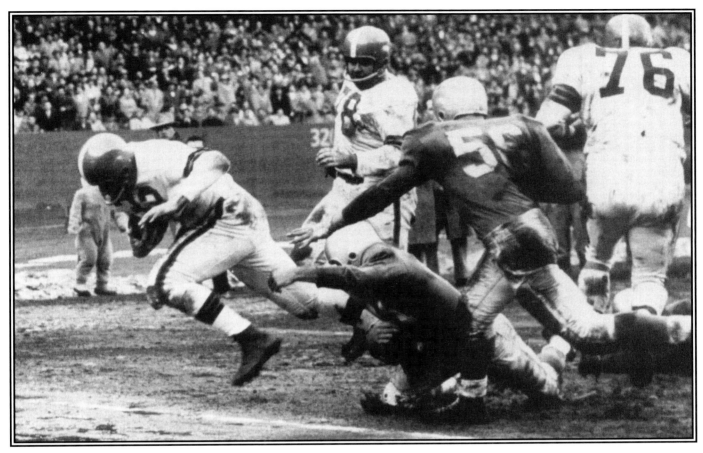

onship record with his 65-yard interception return for a touchdown.

What more could a football fan ask for than a matchup of Hall-of-Fame quarterbacks: the Lions' Bobby Layne and the Browns' Otto Graham? If you're a fan of the Browns, probably three times as much. In 1952, '53, '54, and '57, the two teams met for the NFL championship. In the first three, it was Layne vs. Graham, with Layne winning in '52 and '53.

Buddy Parker was about the only coach to ever get the best of Paul Brown in head-to-head competition. It must have been particularly galling to Brown since Parker's use of football's renegades was the opposite of Brown's emphasis on players with character.

The Lions won both the 1952 regular season (17-6) and championship games (17-7). They beat the Browns again in the 1953 title game (17-16) when Layne engineered a late 80-yard drive for a score, the payoff being a 33-yard TD pass to Jim Doran, who was primarily a defen-

SWEET REVENGE: After losing to Detroit in the 1952 and '53 championship games, the Browns annihilated the Lions in 1954. Curly Morrison scores the seventh touchdown on a 12-yard run in the third quarter of the 56-10 victory at Cleveland Stadium.

sive end, with what became Layne's signature: the two-minute drill. Doran had six receptions all season, but caught three on the drive.

Graham, with assistance from flanker Ray Renfro, avenged the two prior championship defeats in 1954. He scored three times on short QB sneaks and threw twice to Renfro and once to Pete Brewster for touchdowns as the Browns soundly trounced the Lions, 56-10.

The Lions and the Browns gave it a rest for two years, but went at it again in 1957. With Graham's successors, Tommy O'Connell and Milt Plum, playing with injuries and Layne on the injured reserve list, Tobin Rote dismantled the Browns, 59-14. The closest margin for the Browns was 17-7 after Jim Brown's 29-yard second-quarter touchdown run.

EARLY SUCCESS: Beginning in 1950, the Browns won the first eight games of their rivalry with Pittsburgh. Above, Ray Renfro makes a catch in a 29-28 win at Cleveland Stadium in 1952.

There is an old saying that "familiarity breeds contempt." Maybe it is the closeness (only a hundred miles by turnpikes). Or the similarity (both traditionally blue-collar, working-class cities). Whatever the reason, the rivalry between Cleveland and Pittsburgh is as heated and lengthy as any in the NFL. Through 1995, the Browns led the regular-season series, 52-40. However, the early Pittsburgh teams, with their single-wing offensive attack and hard-bitten players, once led Tom Landry of the Giants to remark, "We'd rather play the Browns twice than the Steelers once."

The Browns won 16 of the first 20 games. The Steelers never won until they ambushed the Browns at Forbes Field in 1954, 55-27. The Browns were not beaten at Cleveland Stadium until 1956, 24-16. Pittsburgh never swept the two-game series until 1959. Mostly Cleveland would win in Cleveland and Pittsburgh would win in Pittsburgh. Nothing illustrates this better than the years 1970-1985 when the Browns couldn't seem to beg, borrow or steal (although they attempted most of these tactics) a victory at Three Rivers Stadium.

Even when games went into overtime, the Steelers of Terry Bradshaw, Mean Joe Greene, Jack Ham, Jack Lambert, Franco Harris, Lynn Swann, Mel Blount, Rocky Bleier and John Stallworth would often come up with a gadget play to win. Changing hotels and travel itineraries, even pre-game meals, didn't help.

FRIENDS TO FOES: Above (l-r), Ray Renfro (26), Paul Brown, Chuck Noll and Billy Reynolds watch the action from the sideline in 1953. Noll and Bill Cowher (left) are former Browns linebackers who later coached the Pittsburgh Steelers. Each was groomed by successful Browns head coaches: Noll by Brown in the '50s and Cowher by Marty Schottenheimer in the '80s.

The Browns didn't leave Three Rivers with a victory until 1986 when they won, 27-24, behind Gerald "the Ice Cube" McNeil's 100-yard kickoff return and Earnest Byner's late touchdown. Head Coach Marty Schottenheimer said afterward, "I'm proud of the whole team. We set our goals in practice during the week and accomplished them on Sunday."

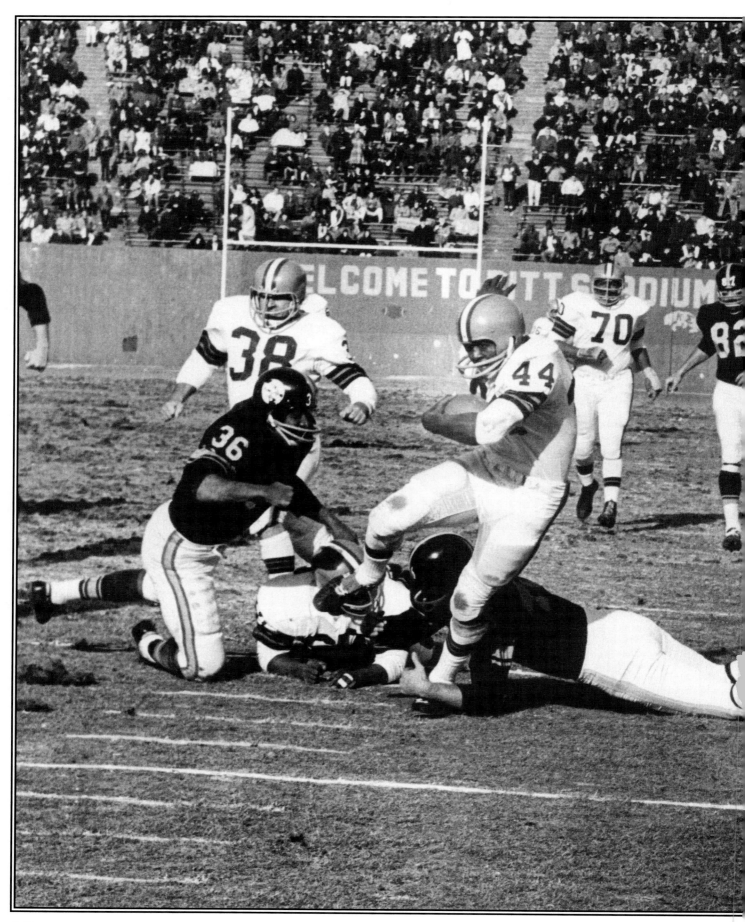

UNSTOPPABLE: The Browns dominated the Steelers rivalry in the 1960s, winning 15 of 20, including this 42-21 victory at Pittsburgh in 1965. Left, Leroy Kelly breaks loose on a 56-yard second-quarter punt return for a touchdown. Above, Bill Glass sacks Bill Nelsen while Jim Kanicki backs up the play.

Adding to the warmth of the rivalry is the fact that Cleveland native and former Browns guard and linebacker Chuck Noll coached the Steelers from 1969-91. When Noll wasn't too far into his regime, he said, "When I first came here, there was always more feeling for the Browns game than any other."

Following 1985, the Browns recaptured the series advantage, winning nine of 12 regular-season games from 1986-91. But Noll's successor in '92, Bill Cowher, another former Browns linebacker (1980-82), immediately put some sting back into the rivalry. Under Cowher, the Steelers beat the Browns seven of the next nine times, including the first-ever playoff game between the two teams after the '94 season.

The rivalry's most memorable contest in recent years occurred at Cleveland Stadium on Oct. 24, 1993, when Eric Metcalf nearly beat the Steelers singlehandedly. Speed was the big reason Metcalf was the Browns' No. 1 draft choice

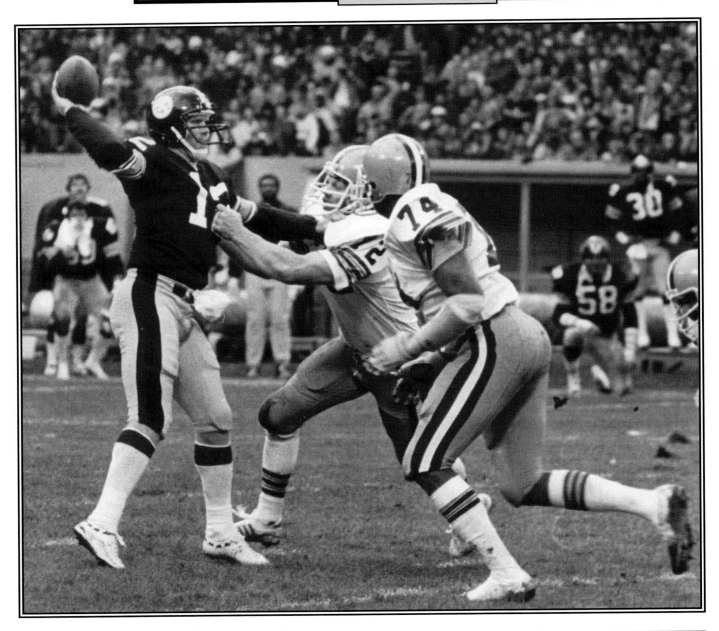

MORE THAN A HANDFUL: The Steel Curtain had the reputation, but the Browns' defense could make its own share of big plays in the rivalry. Above, Jerry Sherk (72) and Mike St. Clair (74) converge on Terry Bradshaw. Right, Dick Ambrose grabs Franco Harris while Bob Golic (79) provides reinforcement.

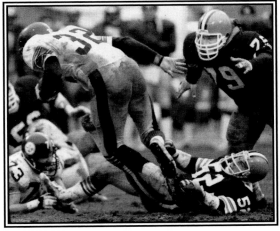

in 1989. Perhaps never did that decision pay a bigger dividend than against the Steelers on that day. Metcalf equaled an NFL record for punt returns for touchdowns in one game with two. His first was 91 yards in the second quarter to give the Browns a 14-0 lead. It broke the team record for longest punt return, set in 1986

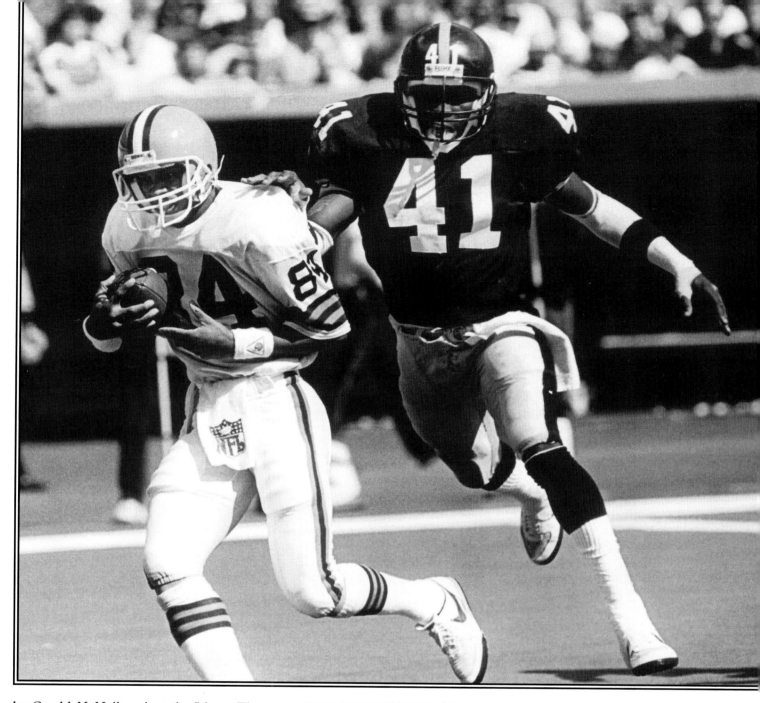

by Gerald McNeil against the Lions. The second was a 75-yarder with 2:05 to play that put Cleveland ahead, 28-23. The Steelers held the ball with 3:19 to play and a 23-21 lead, needing just one first down to run out the clock. James Jones stopped running back Barry Foster one yard short of the first down, and Pittsburgh was forced to punt.

Mark Royals got off a 53-yard punt to send Metcalf back to the Browns' 25. The blockers didn't hold anyone up at the line of scrimmage, but let the Steelers come downfield while a wall was being set up for Metcalf. Key blocks

END OF THE JINX: Sixteen years of frustration finally ended on Oct. 5, 1986, when the Browns won for the first time ever at Three Rivers Stadium. Webster Slaughter catches a 15-yard touchdown pass (above) to open the scoring in the 27-24 win.

by Ron Wolfley, Stevon Moore and Terry Taylor permitted Metcalf to sail down the right side to the open end of Cleveland Stadium. The score remained at 28-23 as Pittsburgh's final drive failed when strong safety Moore pulled the ball from the hands of wide receiver Dwight Stone, and linebacker Mike Caldwell recovered for the Browns.

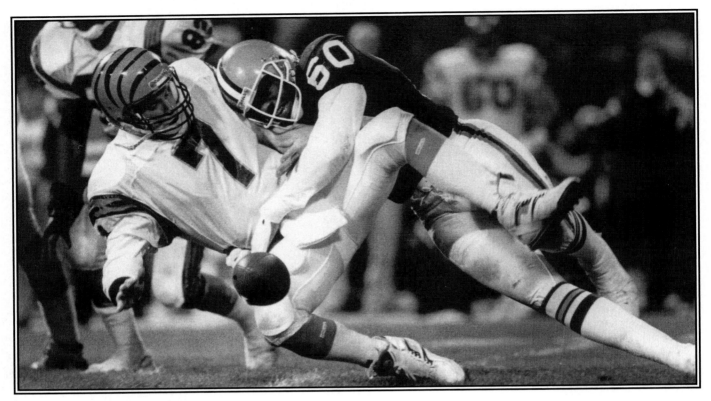

BENGAL BASHING: Al "Bubba" Baker slams Boomer Esiason to force a fumble recovered by the Browns. Beginning with a 30-27 Cleveland victory in 1970, the Browns-Bengals rivalry has never been short of close games and intensely-fought battles.

Two teams with the same first head coach and founder. If ever there was a natural rivalry, this was the one. Instate, intra-division and intense! Even the uniforms looked alike at first: Cincinnati's Paul Brown-designed orange and black attire greatly resembled the Brown-designed orange and brown Cleveland uniforms.

When the 1970 merger came about, Paul Brown lobbied to be able to play the Browns on an annual basis. Among other things, P.B. knew about rivalries. From the first year with both teams winning at home (Cleveland, 30-27; Cincinnati, 14-10), through coach Sam Wyche's ill-advised "You don't live in Cleveland" remark, there have been more than a few sparks flying. Only with the Bengals' fall on hard times during the '90s were the Browns able to pull ahead in the series, 27-24.

The combined point total is amazingly close for the 26-year series: Bengals 1,053, Browns 1,052. Individual game scores likewise reflect the closeness: 30-27, 14-10, 27-24, 31-27, 10-7, 13-10, 28-27, 20-17, 12-9, 14-13 and 29-26.

The feelings of Paul Brown toward beating the Browns in the early '70s were said to equal those toward the Eagles in 1950: He had something to prove. Other coaches on both sides of the field in succeeding years seconded Brown's emotions. Whether it was Brian Sipe hitting Ozzie Newsome on a key 18-yard pass to set up Don Cockroft's game-winner in overtime in 1978 (13-10), or Eric Thomas blocking Matt Stover's final-play field goal attempt to preserve a 1991 Bengals win (23-21), fans of both teams seem to always get their money's worth.

The most recent game of the series will forever be etched in the memories of Browns fans because it was the final home game at Cleveland Stadium—and the final Browns victory of their first 50 seasons. Played on Dec. 17, 1995, Cleveland won, 26-10, on Vinny Testaverde's two TD passes to Frank Hartley and Keenan McCardell and four Stover field goals.

Everything Old...

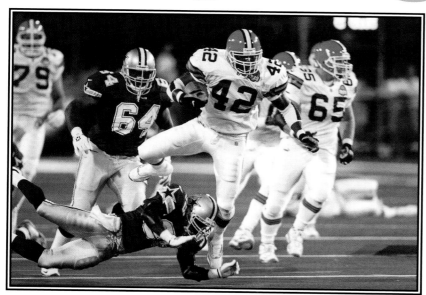

is New Again.

T he tradition has begun again. The Cleveland Browns are back. For those who followed the team during the first 50 years, the 1999 season is an opportunity to connect the old with the new. The following scenes from the past are combined with similar sights from 1999 to honor the return of the great football tradition on the lakefront.

Above: Leroy Kelly escapes Cowboy tacklers in the 1968 Eastern Conference title game. Left: Terry Kirby avoids a Cowboy in the 1999 Hall of Fame Game.

1

Head Gear

The helmet began as an all-white leather model. Then an orange version was introduced. Stripes were added, but never a logo. Simple and basic. Browns fans like it that way. After all, this is football, not fashion.

Opposite page: Jim Brown (1963). Clockwise from left: Dave Logan (1981), Hanford Dixon (1986), Clay Matthews (1991) and Tim Couch (1999).

III

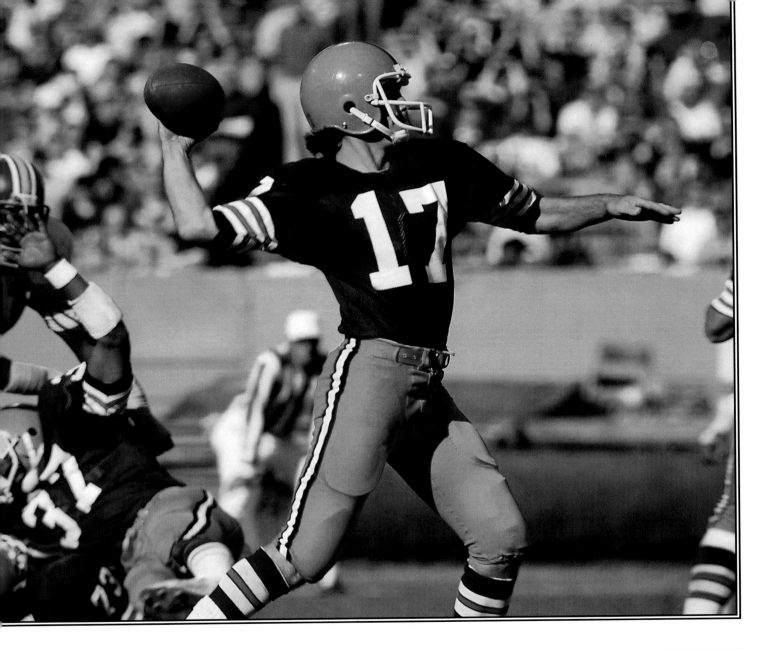

From the beginning of the dynasty era with Otto Graham, the offense has featured a strong passing game. There has been a tradition of top-flight quarterbacks to capture the imagination, interest and loyalty of Browns fans everywhere.

Above: Brian Sipe delivers against Washington in 1975. Right: Tim Couch does likewise in the 1999 Hall of Fame Game versus Dallas.

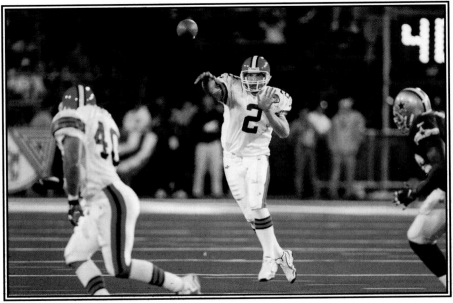

Aerial Artistry

Clockwise from left: Frank Ryan, Bill Nelsen and Bernie Kosar represent the winning tradition. Each led the Browns to championship games.

Critical Catches

Great pass receivers and game-breaking receptions are forever a part of the memories of those who follow Cleveland Browns football.

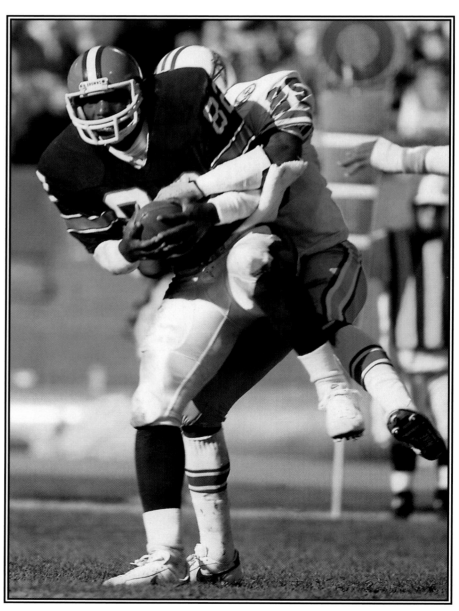

Clockwise from above: Reggie Langhorne hangs on versus Cincinnati. Damon Gibson makes the first TD catch in Cleveland Browns Stadium. Paul Warfield outraces a Cowboy to the end zone. Ozzie Newsome pulls in a pass against Houston.

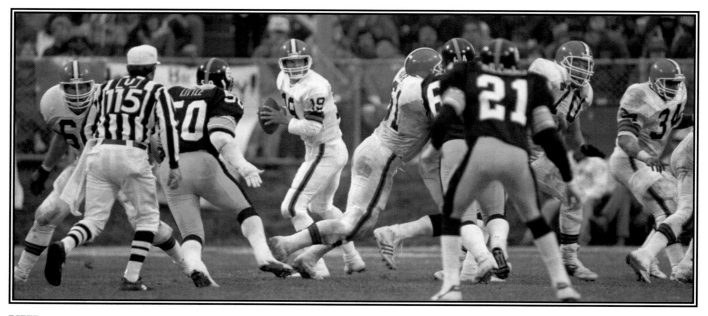

Beat the Steelers!

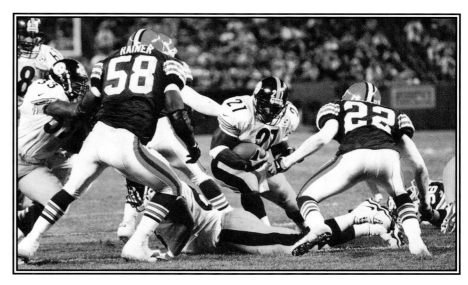

It's the ultimate rivalry. Two teams from football-loving working-class cities slugging it out on the gridiron twice a year.

Clockwise from left: Jim Brown grinds out yardage in 1965. Bernie Kosar sets up and spots a target. Carl "Big Daddy" Hairston nails Walter Abercrombie. Bob Golic (79) chases Franco Harris. Wali Rainer (58) and Tim McTyer (22) converge on Amos Zereoue in the 1999 opener at Cleveland Browns Stadium.

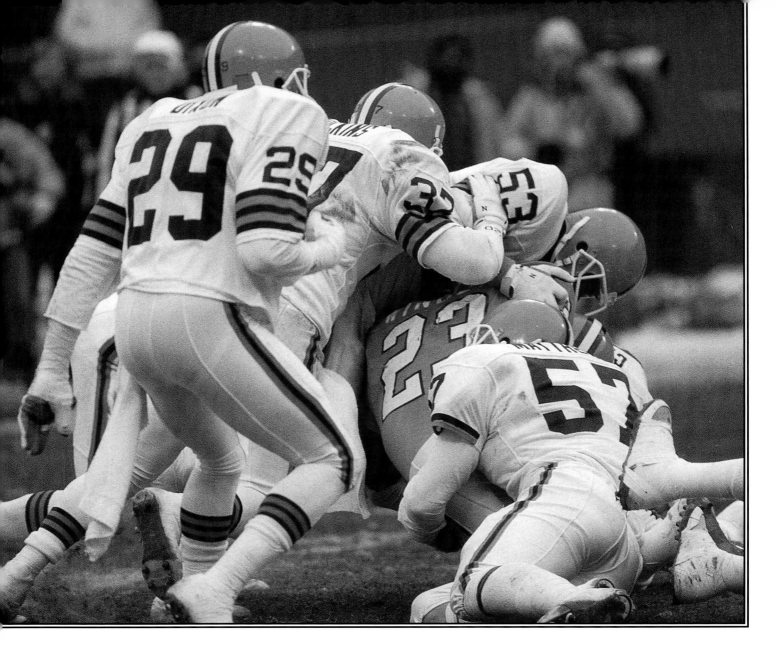

The hallmark of a solid defense is teamwork. The greatest Browns defenses worked together as a cohesive unit to help maintain a winning tradition.

Above: Hanford Dixon (29), Chris Rockins (37), Anthony Griggs (53) and Clay Matthews (57) smother Sammy Winder in the 1986 AFC title game. Right: Mike Howell (34), Marvin Upshaw (84) and Dale Lindsey (51) restrain a Lion in '69.

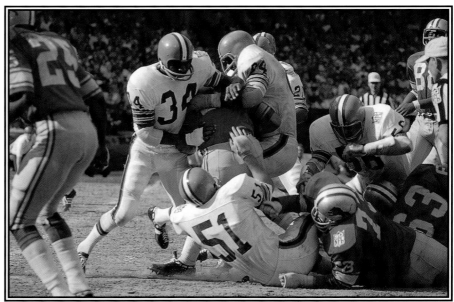

Gang Tackles

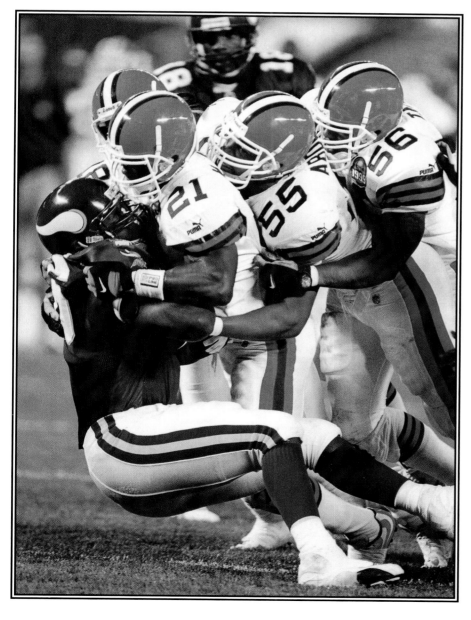

Clockwise from left: Marquis Smith (21), Rahim Abdullah (55) and Ryan Taylor (56) push back a Viking in the first game at Cleveland Browns Stadium in August, 1999. Dick Ambrose and Clinton Burrell (49) crush a Chief in 1980 while Ron Bolton (28) adds reinforcement. Jerry Sherk (72), Walter Johnson (71) and Jack Gregory sack quarterback Daryle Lamonica in a Monday night game versus Oakland in 1971.

Behind the Line

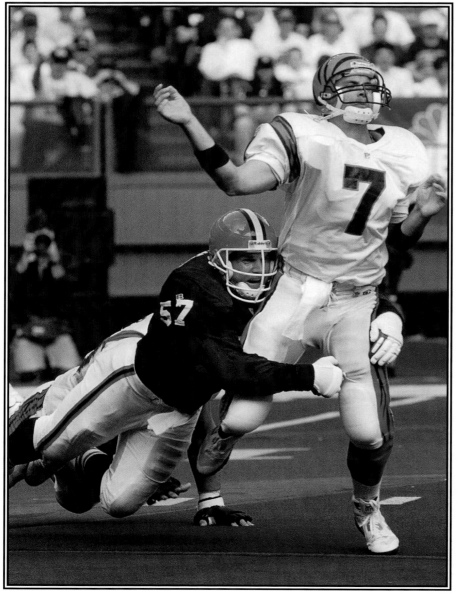

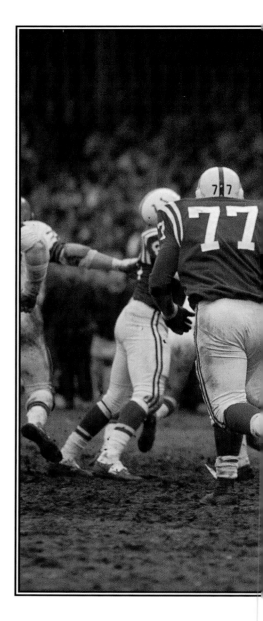

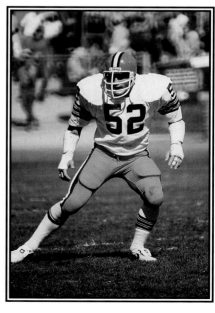

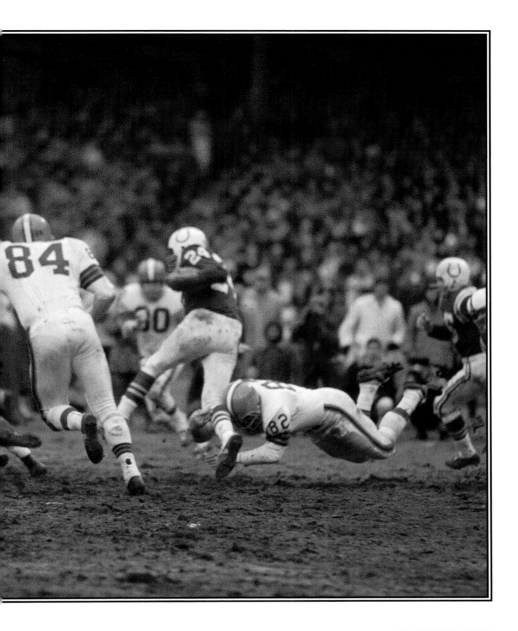

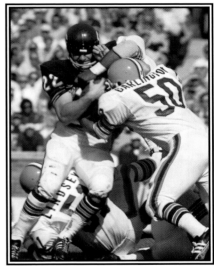

Browns fans appreci-
ate the tradition of
excellence at linebacker.
Some of the very best in
the business have worn
orange and brown.

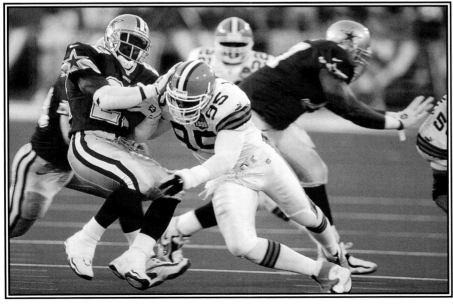

*Clockwise from left: Jamir Miller
tackles Emmitt Smith in the 1999
Hall of Fame Game. Dick Ambrose
focuses on the play. Clay Matthews
sacks David Klingler. Jim Houston
trips up the Colts' Lenny Moore in
the 1964 title game. John Garlington
stuffs the run against the Bears.*

Classic Kicks

Clockwise from above: Gary Collins booms a long punt in 1966. Paul McDonald holds for Matt Bahr's soccer-style boot in 1981. With Brian Sipe holding, Don Cockroft utilizes his customary straight-on kicking style in 1978.

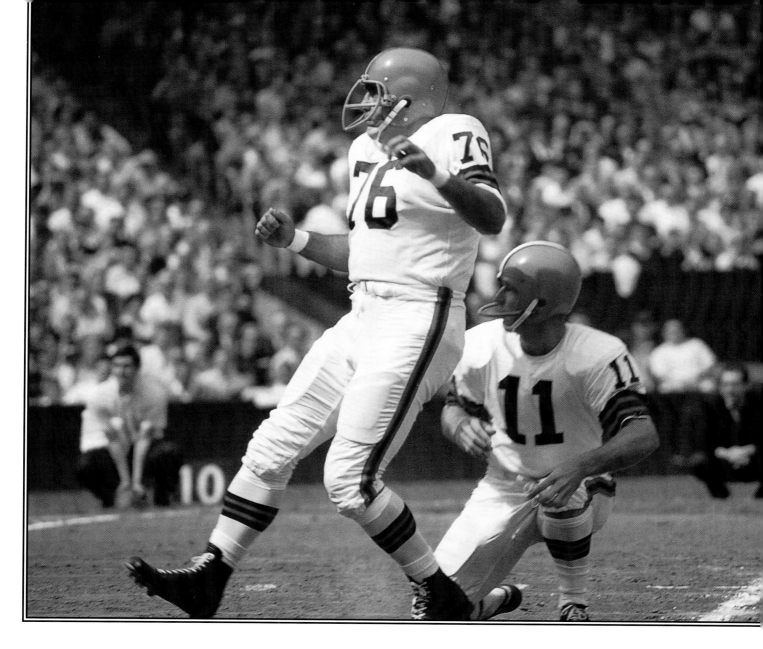

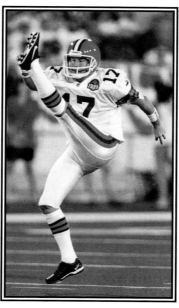

Above: Lou Groza and holder Jim Ninowski watch a field goal cross the uprights in 1966. Left: Place-kicker Phil Dawson (4) and punter Chris Gardocki (17) get a leg up on the action for the 1999 Browns.

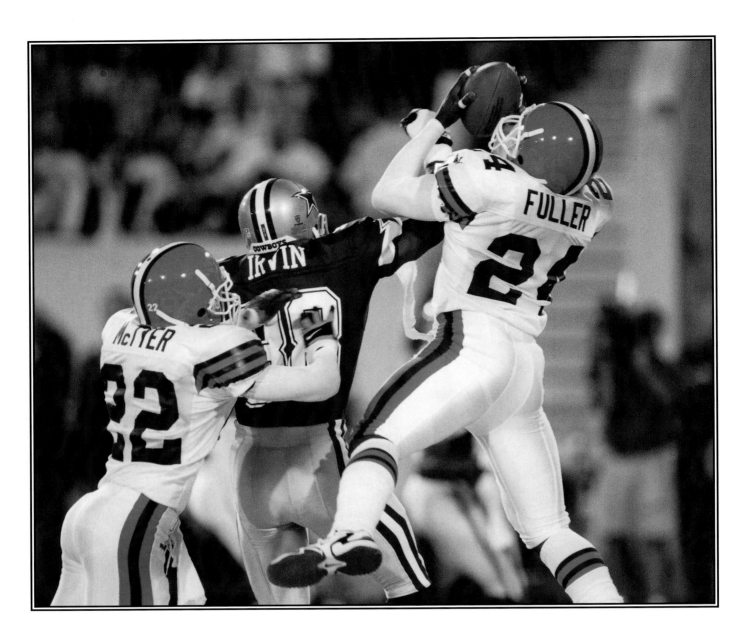

Up for Grabs

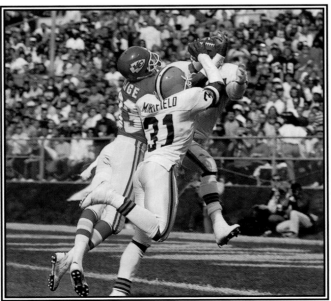

The Corner Brothers, Frank Minnifield and Hanford Dixon, were all-time fan favorites, but winning Browns football has always featured strength in the secondary.

Left: Frank Minnifield (31) and Chris Rockins surround the Chiefs' Stephone Paige in 1986. Above: Corey Fuller (24) outmaneuvers the Cowboys' Michael Irvin for an interception in the 1999 Hall of Fame Game.

Head Coaches

When discussing the history of the Cleveland Browns, the various eras comprising their first 50 years are defined by the head coaches who guided them through those eras. First there was Paul Brown—the organizer, innovator, taskmaster and Hall of Famer—who took the team to 11 title games in the first 12 seasons of his 17-year tenure. Then there was Blanton Collier, Brown's longtime former assistant who calmly led the team to four more title games in the 1960s. Later there was Sam Rutigliano and Marty Schottenheimer, the successful guiding forces behind the Kardiac Kids and the Kosar-led contenders, respectively, of the 1980s.

Through 50 seasons, the Browns employed only 10 head coaches. And for most of those seasons, the words "stability," "longevity" and "success" could be applied to the team's coaching fraternity. It all began with Paul Brown.

In 1948, the Browns were the ill-respected All-America Football Conference champions. It would take another two years before they were able to reach into the hearts of head coach Greasy Neale's Philadelphia Eagles and rip out the NFL's respect. To some, that might have seemed like an impossible dream in 1948. But to Paul Brown, it was a reality for which he had already begun planning. One of pro football's great visionaries, Brown not only knew the AAFC-NFL merger was imminent, he knew which team the Browns would likely play once they joined the established league.

"Paul would say to us in those early days, 'We'll be so good, we'll make 'em take us,'" said

Paul Brown and Lou Groza discuss strategy in 1953.

former Browns guard Lin Houston in a 1995 interview. "And by God, that's what happened."

Houston, an original member of the Browns who played from 1946-53, died at age 74 at his Canton, Ohio, home in September 1995, just

JUBILATION: Paul Brown rides John Yonakor's shoulders amidst happy fans at Cleveland Stadium after the Browns beat the New York Yankees for the 1946 AAFC championship.

eight days before the 45th anniversary of the Browns-Eagles matchup on Sept. 16, 1950.

The Browns went 52-4-3 and won all four AAFC titles from 1946-49. Off the field, Brown had his eyes fixed on Philadelphia. The Eagles won the NFL title in 1948 and 1949. Brown had studied them every step of the way. He had scouts at their games, he analyzed films of their games, and even went so far as to work on the Eagles in practice as early as 1948. Brown was leaving nothing to chance. His team had been taunted and teased relentlessly for playing in the "inferior league," and for its wide-open style of offense. Even NFL Commissioner Bert Bell had joined in the criticism.

"This was a league that was laughed at by the NFL for four years," said Joe Horrigan, curator of the Pro Football Hall of Fame. "The NFL sort of patted them on the head and said, 'Go get a ball and we'll play you.'" Brown's rage burned inside all the while. But on the outside, he was cool as usual.

"Paul was smart," Otto Graham remembers. "He never said a word. He'd just pin all those negative articles on the bulletin board so we had a chance to read them every day."

When Brown discovered his team would open its first NFL season in Philadelphia, he wrote letters to each of his players. He told them to come into training camp in top shape, and explained why. "When we found out we were playing the Eagles in Philadelphia in that first game, everybody said we'd get beat 40-0," Houston said. "We said the heck we will."

In 1995, Houston smiled at the memory of that Saturday night in 1950. He still wore the championship ring he earned in the Browns' 30-28 win over the Rams that season, but the stunning 35-10 rout of the Eagles was what he most remembered. "If you ever saw a personality fit a situation perfectly, it was Paul Brown and that game," Houston said. "He had us so high for that game. I don't think any team in the country, as good as there ever was, would have beaten us that night. I had never seen perfection until that game, or after that game. But in that game, it was perfection."

Graham agrees. "I guarantee no team was ever, ever more emotionally ready for a football game than we were that day," said Graham, whose passes to Dante Lavelli, Mac Speedie, Dub Jones and Rex Bumgardner frustrated the famed "Eagle Defense" for three quarters while setting the stage for powerful fullback Marion Motley to grind out the final quarter.

"After hearing everyone bad-mouth us for four years, we would have played those guys for a keg of beer, or in my case a chocolate milkshake," Graham said. "We just wanted to prove we were a good football team."

After the game, Greasy Neale was less than gracious in his remarks on the Browns. Steve Van Buren, the NFL's leading rusher in 1945 and 1947-49, missed the game with a foot injury and speedy halfback Bosh Pritchard was out as well. "Why, all [the Browns] do is pass and trap," Neale said. "They're like a basketball team the way they throw the ball around."

Brown loved it, especially when Bell came into the Browns' dressing room after the game and called the Browns "the greatest team ever to play the game." In his autobiography, *PB: The Paul Brown Story*, Brown wrote, "I knew we had embarrassed the National League, and I was quite pleased."

Brown led the Browns to six more championship games after 1950, winning two, before

CHALK TALK: Paul Brown developed and taught strategies that overwhelmed the AAFC and defeated the champion Philadelphia Eagles in the Browns' first NFL game in 1950.

being fired by owner Art Modell following the 1962 season. His record with the Browns was 167-53-8 (.759), including records of 14-0 in 1948 and 11-1 in 1951 and 1953. His only losing season was 1956 (5-7).

"Paul Brown took a part of what America was all about at the time and capitalized on it," Horrigan said. "He took a lot of young, disciplined men who were goal and task oriented, most of whom had been in the service, and won a lot of games with structure and preparation."

Brown was the first to hire a full-time, year-round coaching staff and the first to use note-

Paul Brown *1946-62*

books and classroom techniques extensively. He was the first to use intelligence tests and the first to do statistical film-clip studies and grade his players from individual film clips.

"George Halas was a real taskmaster and a big believer in game film before Brown was, but Brown brought classroom to the game of football in the strictest sense," Horrigan said. "Like the great ones, Paul took a lot of existing ideas and retooled and improved on them."

Brown also invented the first single-bar face mask and was the first to create the messenger-guard system so he could call plays from the sidelines. He and his coaching staff invented or refined many of the standard plays in today's professional game, such as the screen pass, the draw and the trap plays.

"Paul Brown could anticipate the answer before you asked the question. He was just that

TWO STRAIGHT: Paul Brown congratulates owner Mickey McBride after the Browns won their second straight AAFC title over New York in 1947. Behind Brown is guard Bob Gaudio (34). Also pictured are (l-r) Bill Willis, Horace Gillom, Lou Groza, Lou Rymkus, Tom Colella, Marion Motley and Ed Ulinski.

kind of guy," said Houston, who played for Brown at Massillon Washington High School, Ohio State and the Browns.

Brown tried to instill that quality in his players. Each year, he made his players write out their assignments and keep them in a notebook. The notebook then became a player's most treasured possession, if he knew what was good for him.

Sportswriter Hal Lebovitz remembers the day punter-wide receiver Horace Gillom didn't have his notebook in order: "Paul was very tough and he'd look at you steely-eyed," said

A PRO'S PRO: Paul Brown brought high standards to professional football. His players were taught in a classroom, kept notebooks and abided by a strict dress code. Here they analyze the Detroit Lions prior to the 1952 championship game.

Lebovitz, sports editor of the *Cleveland Plain Dealer* at the time. "He looked at Gillom and said, 'Horace, you're like an apple on a tree. You get too ripe, you'll fall off.'"

Ken Coleman was hired to do the Browns' radio play-by-play in 1952. Brown was the man who hired him, and the man who told him what his duties would be.

"My contract said I had to be at Hiram College and [remain] there for the entire training camp," Coleman said. "I had complete access to all the coaches meetings, and I'll never forget the detail and sophistication that Paul Brown brought to the game."

Coleman also remembers the day Brown took his knack for detail to an unheard of level. "During his opening day speech at Hiram, he said, 'Just so you know, since we're using pencils, the pencil sharpeners are located by rooms 102, 125, 155, whatever,'" Coleman said. "He had gone down the halls to see where the pencil sharpeners were."

There was nothing the Browns did that Paul Brown didn't have a hand in. He even distributed the players' game tickets because he didn't want the wives and girlfriends sitting next to each other.

"We had great chemistry on our team, and Paul wouldn't let anything get in the way of that," Graham said. "We'd get two tickets for each game, and they were scattered all over the stadium because he didn't want Lavelli's wife or Speedie's wife sitting up there with my wife complaining because I wasn't throwing the ball to their husbands."

Brown's policies began to rub some players the wrong way as his tenure reached the 1960s. That, coupled with his crumbling relationship with Modell, led to his firing.

Wide receiver Gary Collins, a rookie in Brown's final season, said he was one of the players who felt Brown was tough, but fair with the players. "He's probably what's lacking in today's world across the board," Collins said. "He demanded discipline on the job and discipline in the family."

Like Houston, former Browns cornerback Tommy James first met Brown at Massillon, where Brown posted an 80-8-2 record and outscored opponents 3,202-339 from 1932-40. "I was 14 years old and I looked at him in total awe," said James, who also played for Brown at Ohio State. "Sometimes you absolutely hated him. But you always respected him."

Chuck Heaton covered the Browns either part-time or full-time from 1946 through 1992. He said Brown was the most cooperative coach with the media the team has ever had.

Horrigan also points out that Brown does not get the credit he deserves for signing the AAFC's first black players, Hall of Famers Marion Motley and Bill Willis, in 1946. That was the year before Jackie Robinson broke the color barrier in major league baseball, and only

> **Brown is back to the drawing board in December 1958 after the Giants beat the Browns in the season finale to force a playoff for the Eastern Conference championship. Receiving instructions are (l-r) Warren Lahr, Gene Hickerson, Lou Groza and Pete Brewster.**

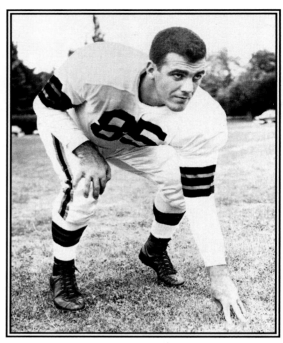

COACHING CRADLE: Paul Brown was mentor to many future head coaches, including linebacker Lou Saban (above photo, left) who coached Buffalo to American Football League championships in 1964 and '65, and halfback Ara Parseghian (right photo) who won two national titles at Notre Dame.

a month after the Rams made Kenny Washington and Woody Strode the first black NFL players since the Chicago Cardinals' Joe Lillard and the Pittsburgh Pirates' Ray Kemp played in 1933. "Paul Brown's willingness and open-mindedness to invite Bill Willis and Marion Motley to what was then an all-white AAFC was quite a risk," said Horrigan. "I think lost in the positive results of that move are the risks Brown took to bring them into the league."

Brown, however, was a remarkable judge of talent, and there was no doubt Motley and Willis were talented players. And so was Horace Gillom, another black player, who joined the Browns in 1947. Brown wanted to surround himself with good people and knew Motley, Willis and Gillom would be able to handle the challenge awaiting them in each AAFC city.

Said Graham: "Paul ran a high-class organization. He surrounded himself with high-class coaches. If a guy was a drunk or chased women, Paul didn't want him. And when it came to the players, he changed the image there too. He changed it from a lot of big potbellied guys with big black cigars to more like a college team."

Brown was not a great athlete, but he got the most out of what he had. Born Sept. 7, 1908, in Norwalk, Ohio, he moved to Massillon with his family when he was 12. Despite never weighing more than 120 pounds, Brown quarterbacked the Tigers two years. He enrolled at Ohio State, but when it became clear he wasn't going to play for the Buckeyes, he transferred to Miami University (of Ohio) where he was an above average passer and good runner.

When he returned to Massillon as head coach and athletic director, Brown rebuilt Massillon's sports teams. His last six football teams were a combined 58-1-1 with six straight Ohio state championships. His 1940 team, arguably the best in school history, was 10-0 and out-scored its opponents 477-6.

Brown then moved on to Ohio State where, from 1941-43, the Buckeyes were 18-8-1. His 1942 team was his best—becoming national champions after finishing 9-1 Brown's players included future Browns Lin Houston, Tommy James, Dante Lavelli, Bill Willis, Gene Fekete, Lou Groza and Les Horvath.

In 1944, Brown enlisted in the Navy. He became a lieutenant and was appointed athletic officer at the Great Lakes Naval Training Center outside of Chicago. As head coach of the football team, he went 15-5-2 from 1944-45. His 1945 team, with Motley at running back, upset Notre Dame, 39-7.

Five years after parting with the Browns, Brown resurfaced as founder and head coach of the expansion Cincinnati Bengals. Three seasons later, in 1970, the Bengals became the first third-year expansion team ever to win a division title, the AFC Central. Brown stepped down as head coach in 1975 so he could concentrate on his duties as general manager and vice president. The Bengals reached the Super Bowl twice, losing to San Francisco both times following the 1981 and 1988 seasons.

Brown experienced success every step of his career by keeping things simple and working hard on fundamentals. He maintained that philosophy until he died at age 82 on Aug. 5, 1991, 24 years to the day after his induction into the Pro Football Hall of Fame in 1967.

"Paul was a great, great teacher," Graham said. "He stressed repetition, repetition all the time. It wasn't anything real fancy. We ran the same plays over and over and over until we ran them perfectly. He was as good as any coach in history, not because he knew more about football. He was just better organized."

Originally drafted by the Detroit Lions in 1944, Graham chose instead to become the first player ever to sign a contract with the Browns. Sometimes, he wonders what might have been had he not picked Cleveland. "I was very lucky to have signed with Paul Brown," Graham said. "If I had signed with Detroit, you wouldn't be

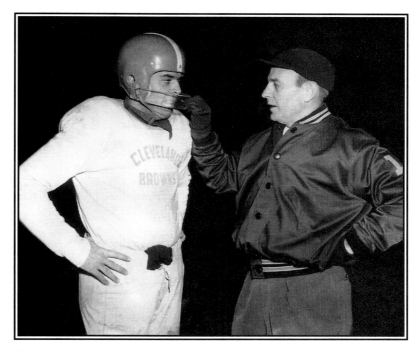

INNOVATOR: Paul Brown's many inventions included the single-bar face mask, devised for Otto Graham (left) in 1953. The first version was a narrow plastic bar, but a clear plastic version was also tested to enable greater field vision.

calling me today. And no one would have remembered who Otto Graham was."

During his career, Brown was the mentor to many future successful head coaches. Included were four Pro Football Hall of Famers. Weeb Ewbank, Brown's tackles coach from 1949-53, won championships with the Colts and Jets. Chuck Noll was a Browns linebacker and messenger guard from 1953-59 before coaching the Steelers to four Super Bowl titles. Don Shula began his pro career as a Browns defensive back from 1951-52 before leading the Colts and Dolphins to titles. Bill Walsh was an assistant coach with Brown at Cincinnati before moving on to Super Bowl crowns with the 49ers.

Three early Browns also later won championships: Tackle Lou Rymkus (1946-51) led the Houston Oilers to the first two American Football League titles in 1960 and '61. Linebacker Lou Saban (1946-49) coached the Buffalo Bills to AFL crowns in 1964 and '65. Halfback Ara Parseghian (1948-49), won two national championships at Notre Dame.

HAPPY DAYS: Blanton Collier coached the Browns to four NFL title games, including the 1964 victory over Baltimore. His 1963-65 backfield featured (left to right) fullback Jim Brown, quarterback Frank Ryan and halfback Ernie Green.

"You could say things. Paul was an organizer and an administrator. Blanton was a teacher."

Under Brown, Collier focused on defensive strategy, particularly pass defense. But he also helped to refine the skills of Otto Graham and developed a grading system based on film study of each player's performance. Each off-season, Collier would take the films home to Paris, Ky., to analyze every player.

"Blanton was an important man to Paul," Lebovitz said. "In fact, Paul once told me he'd rather lose his right arm than lose Blanton."

Collier's first year brought out the best in fullback Jim Brown. In 1963, Brown had 1,000 yards through eight games and finished with a then-record 1,863 in a 14-game season. The Browns were second in the Eastern Conference at 10-4, but would win the conference title four of the next seven years under Collier.

After Jim Brown dominated in 1963, Collier came back for the 1964 championship season with the team's most dangerous passing attack in years. Quarterback Frank Ryan and receivers Collins and Paul Warfield were a perfect balance for Brown and the ground attack.

Brown shocked the sports world in 1966 by retiring at age 30, but Collier's offense never slowed as Leroy Kelly rushed for 1,141 yards and Ryan threw an NFL-high 29 TD passes.

But in 1968, Collier benched an ineffective Ryan after the team lost two of its first three. He turned to former Steeler Bill Nelsen and the Browns won eight straight en route to the Century Division title. They advanced to the NFL Championship game, but were shut out by the Baltimore Colts, 34-0.

The Browns again made it to the title game in 1969, but were defeated by the Minnesota Vikings, 27-7. Collier then coached his final team to a 7-7 finish in 1970, which was only good for second place behind Cincinnati in the newly-formed Central Division of the American Football Conference.

Collier died March 22, 1983, of cancer. He was 76. Modell stayed within the organization when he replaced Collier by naming assistant Nick Skorich as head coach. Skorich had previ-

Then, of course, there was Blanton Collier, a Brown assistant for nine seasons in Cleveland.

Collier was a member of Brown's staff from 1946 until he left for the head coaching position at the University of Kentucky in 1953. He returned in 1962 to coach the offensive backfield, then at age 56 was given his first NFL head coaching opportunity as Brown's successor in 1963. Despite his years of working with Brown, Collier's coaching style was dramatically different from Brown's.

"Paul had the players scared," said Hal Lebovitz. "They didn't always like him, but they respected him. Blanton was more like a sweet father to the players."

Known as a kind, gentle man and one of the great teachers of the game, Collier probably spent more time on individual instruction than any other head coach. He was as close to the players as any coach in Browns history.

"Under Blanton, there was more freedom within the locker room, more input by the players as far as strategy," said wide receiver Gary Collins, who played for both Brown and Collier.

Blanton Collier *1963-70*

Nick Skorich
1971-74

Sensing the Browns needed discipline, Modell turned in 1975 to his offensive line coach, Forrest Gregg, an offensive tackle under football's ultimate disciplinarian, the Packers' Vince Lombardi. It was Gregg's first chance as a head coach after five seasons as an assistant in Green Bay, San Diego and Cleveland.

"After reading Lombardi's book, *Run to Daylight,* and then listening to Forrest, I thought it was dejavu, because some of his quotes were almost verbatim," Dieken said. "He was just a tough, tough guy."

Gregg was a rugged Texan only five years removed from a Hall-of-Fame playing career. He was 6-foot-4, 240 pounds with a booming voice. And if that wasn't enough to convince the players they were in for the workouts of their lives, then all they had to do was read the part in Lombardi's book where he called Gregg, "the finest player I ever coached."

Gregg's practices were brutally demanding. And so was everything else in Browns camp from the day Gregg was hired until the day he was fired with one game left in the 1977 season.

"He preached toughness and actually meanness," Dieken said. "If you talk to the Steelers, they still blame all the fights we had with them on Forrest Gregg. They think it was him teaching us some of the techniques that were ticking them off."

Gregg's first team in 1975 began at 0-9 and finished 3-11. When they were 0-8 and heading to Oakland to play the powerful Raiders, Gregg was so distraught that he brought in a motivational speaker to preach to the team the power of positive thinking.

"I'll never forget the speech," Dieken said. "It was, 'If you put your mind to it, you can do it too.' That was the guy's speech. The team thought it was just a little bit overdone. We lost out in Oakland, 38-17."

Gregg's demanding personality eventually came down the hardest on running back Mike

ously coached the Philadelphia Eagles to a 15-24-3 record from 1961-63. In Cleveland, he coached the defensive line and later became offensive coordinator. Skorich lasted four seasons, posting a 30-26-2 record, including two playoff defeats. His first team in 1971 went 9-5 and won the Central Division before losing to Baltimore in the playoffs, 20-3. In 1972, Skorich directed the Browns to a second-place finish in the Central before losing a 20-14 playoff battle with the Miami Dolphins team that went 17-0 and won the Super Bowl that season.

Skorich's last two teams failed to make the playoffs, setting up a string of seven consecutive seasons without a playoff appearance for the Browns. The 1974 team went 4-10.

Doug Dieken, who played left tackle from 1971-84, was a rookie during Skorich's first season. He said he could feel the team slipping. "Nick took over an established team that had won a lot of games," Dieken said. "He had been a buddy to a lot of the players when he was an assistant, so when he became head coach, let's just say the inmates were somewhat running the prison."

Dick Modzelewski *1977*

Forrest Gregg
1975-77

Pruitt, the Browns' No. 1 draft choice in 1976. "Mike Pruitt and Forrest didn't see eye-to-eye," Dieken remembers. "One time during a film session, he yelled out something about Mike Pruitt. Mike said something to him and boom, Forrest threw the projector across the room."

Players had a tough time escaping Gregg's disciplined ways. The rules included an 11 p.m. curfew, not only on Saturday nights, but also on Thursdays and Fridays. "He and his wife would drive around to see if your car would be in your driveway," Dieken said. "If it wasn't, he'd call you. If you weren't there, he'd fine you."

Dieken laughs about it as he looks back at those days. "The thing is I got along with the guy," he said. "But some guys, the ones who rejected discipline, had a lot of problems."

Under Gregg, the Browns were 9-5 in 1976, but it was only good for third place in the AFC Central. They opened the '77 season at 5-2, but lost five of six thereafter and Gregg was fired. Assistant Dick Modzelewski, a Browns defensive tackle from 1964-66, finished the season by coaching his only NFL game, a loss at Seattle.

"Mo gave the best pregame speech I'd ever heard in the pros," Dieken said. "Mo was just a good old guy, and he just basically laid it out on the line, saying this is my only chance. He was almost in tears. You really wanted to go out and play for the guy."

Next, Modell went outside the organization for the first time in 1978 and gave 46-year-old New Orleans Saints assistant Sam Rutigliano his first NFL head coaching job. He was the antithesis of Gregg. An 11-year assistant who had spent most of his years on the offensive side of the ball, Rutigliano instantly became one of the team's most popular head coaches. He was a gambler with a boundless enthusiasm and a

Sam Rutigliano
1978-84

son in Browns history. The "Kardiac Kids" of 1980 finished 11-5 as they made fans come to expect breathtaking comeback victories.

The Browns defeated the Super Bowl champion Pittsburgh Steelers en route to the AFC Central Division title, but lost to the Raiders, 14-12, on a bitterly cold afternoon in Cleveland on January 4, 1981. Sipe's interception in the waning moments overshadowed an NFL MVP season, as well as Rutigliano's banner year as NFL Coach of the Year.

Rutigliano never held back his feelings for the players. After Sipe threw the interception against Oakland, Rutigliano hugged him and said, "I love you Brian."

"I also remember Sam telling us in Pittsburgh before a game that he loved us," Dieken said. "I'm sitting there thinking, 'Great, [linebacker] Jack Lambert will kick my teeth out, but Sam loves me.' But that's just the kind of guy Sam was."

Rutigliano's 1981 team flopped to 5-11. The 1982 squad slipped into the playoffs at 4-5 during the strike-shortened season. In 1983, Sipe's last year before jumping to the ill-fated United States Football League, the Browns went 9-7 and missed the playoffs.

With Paul McDonald, the five-year veteran, quarterbacking the team in 1984, the Browns opened the season at 1-7. A 12-9 loss in Cincinnati on Oct. 21 finally cost Rutigliano his job.

Modell then went back within the organization and gave the Browns' 41-year-old defensive coordinator, Marty Schottenheimer, his first head coaching opportunity. An emotional optimist, a devoted teacher of the game and a stickler for detail, Schottenheimer rested somewhere between the demanding Gregg and the more laid-back Rutigliano.

Schottenheimer led the Browns to a 4-4 finish in 1984 and back into the playoffs at 8-8 in 1985. His defense, however, couldn't protect a 21-3 halftime lead over the Miami Dolphins in the opening round of the playoffs that year. Miami won 24-21.

With Lindy Infante, the new offensive coordinator, juicing up the offense in 1986, quarter-

fabulous personality. He was close to the players and eventually established the team's "Inner Circle" to help deal secretly with players' personal problems.

"Sam was a fun guy who made playing football a little more relaxing," Dieken said. "Plus he utilized the personnel pretty well. He came up with the offensive schemes that allowed us to put all those points up on the board.

"Sam wasn't afraid. He was out there saying 'Let's throw it!,' all the way down to Red Right 88," Dieken added.

Red Right 88, the Brian Sipe-to-Ozzie Newsome pass that was intercepted in the end zone by Oakland Raiders defensive back Mike Davis, brought to a close the most exciting sea-

back Bernie Kosar and the Browns scored 391 points to win the Central Division with a 12-4 mark, the Browns' best-ever NFL victory total.

Schottenheimer's teams could never make it past Denver in back-to-back AFC Championship games after the 1986 and '87 seasons. "The Drive," John Elway's last-minute, 98-yard march through Schottenheimer's defense helped beat the Browns, 23-20, in 1986. In 1987, "The Fumble," Earnest Byner's forced turnover at the three-yard line as he was going in for the tying score late in the game, eliminated the Browns, 38-33, in Denver.

The next year, the Browns lost to Houston in a Wild Card game in Cleveland. Afterward, Schottenheimer was asked to make changes in his coaching staff and give up his role as offensive coordinator, which he seized when Infante left for the Green Bay head coaching position.

Schottenheimer, who was criticized for his play-calling in 1988, chose to resign rather than bend to Modell's pressure. He left with a 46-31 record and three division titles in four full seasons. He was hired by Kansas City and coached the Chiefs to a winning record (8-7-1) in 1989 after the team had suffered losing seasons in 1987 and '88. Over the next six years, the Chiefs went 64-32 under Schottenheimer, making the playoffs each year.

After Schottenheimer's resignation, Modell went outside the organization and hired New York Jets assistant coach Bud Carson, a long-time NFL assistant who had never been given a head coaching opportunity despite having designed the Pittsburgh Steelers' "Steel Curtain" defense in the 1970s. Modell said he was thrilled to have landed "a defensive genius."

"I have never been involved in a more exhaustive talent search for a coach," Modell said at the time. "We wanted to make sure we studied the whole field, and when we did, Carson became the clear-cut choice."

Modell also said he expected the 56-year-old Carson to be the last head coach he would ever hire. But after the team's self-proclaimed "Season from Hell" in 1990, Modell called the Carson hiring a mistake.

Carson led the '89 Browns to a Central Division championship and another AFC title game in Denver. The Broncos won easily, 37-21, touching off a streak of losing seasons that wouldn't end until the 1994 season (11-5). Carson was fired the day after nearly 78,331 fans turned their backs and left the Browns following a 42-0 loss to Buffalo during the ninth week of the 1990 season. The Browns fell to 2-7 en route to a franchise-worst 3-13. Assistant Jim Shofner finished the season as the Browns lost six of their last seven.

Modell once again looked outside the organization in 1991 and gave yet another defensive coordinator his first head coaching chance. Bill Belichick, a 38-year-old who was coming off his

Marty Schottenheimer
1984-88

Jim Shofner
1990

Bud Carson *1989-90*

second Super Bowl victory as defensive coordinator of the New York Giants, became the Browns' eighth full-time head coach. A no-nonsense coach, he jumped headfirst into rebuilding the team to fit what he had seen succeed in New York. He began building a strong defense and an aggressive special teams unit. In 1995, he entered his fifth training camp with four players remaining from the 1991 Browns.

After a 6-10 record in 1991, Belichick put together consecutive seasons of 7-9 in 1992 and '93 before returning the Browns to the playoffs with an 11-5 record in 1994. But his squad went 0-3 against the Steelers in '94, including a 29-9 loss at Pittsburgh in the first-ever playoff game between the longtime rivals.

In five seasons, Belichick became the most unpopular head coach in the history of the franchise. His seeming disdain for the media resulted in the media returning the sentiment. The losing seasons, combined with the 1993 release of Bernie Kosar, turned off the fans.

Only Modell remained on Belichick's side: "I'm expecting big things from him," Modell said after the '94 season. "He took this franchise when it was in an all-out tailspin and rebuilt it in a way that will last. The man is an outstanding judge of talent, a very dedicated man, and an extremely hard worker. I will be very, very disappointed if he does not become one of the great coaches this league has seen."

But for Belichick and Modell, the "all-out tailspin" began anew in 1995 when the Browns dropped to 5-11, fourth in the AFC Central.

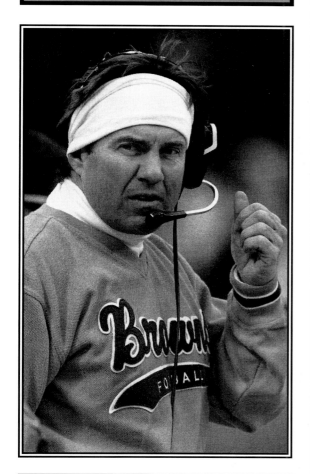

Bill Belichick *1991-95*

Chris Palmer
1999

When the building process began for the 1999 Browns and the upcoming college draft featured several outstanding quarterbacks, it became clear that the Browns would most likely aim for one of the "franchise" signal callers with their first selection—the No. 1 pick overall. Thus, as the interview process unfolded to hire a head coach, offensive-minded candidates moved to the top of the list.

Among them was 49-year-old Chris Palmer, Jacksonville's offensive coordinator, who was considered one of the best in the game at developing young quarterbacks. In 1998, the AFC's Central Division champion Jaguars won at least one game with five different quarterbacks, all of whom received tutelage from Palmer: Mark Brunell, Steve Matthews, Jamie Martin, Rob Johnson and Jonathan Quinn.

Palmer was hired in January to become only the 11th head coach in franchise history.

Prior to joining the Jaguars in 1997, Palmer had spent four seasons on Bill Parcells' staff at New England where he helped Drew Bledsoe improve to lead the Patriots to Super Bowl XXXI.

Palmer had 27 years of coaching experience before joining the Browns. His first professional position was with Montreal of the Canadian Football League in 1983 where he was offensive line coach. Another stop was New Jersey of the USFL where he was offensive coordinator and quarterbacks coach for an offense that included Brian Sipe, Doug Flutie and Herschel Walker. Palmer's first NFL job was in 1990-92 as Houston's wide receivers coach.

Otto Graham awoke the morning of the 1955 NFL season opener and decided he would change his style after playing in nine title games in nine seasons. No longer would he eat the team's bland pre-game food. And no longer would he worry himself to the point where he "had to go to the bathroom every five seconds."

After all, the Browns needed him, not the other way around. Graham had retired follow-

ing the 1954 championship game and was back only because head coach Paul Brown said he couldn't find a suitable replacement. The normally nervous Graham was calm, and unusually hungry, on the morning of the 1955 season opener. He bribed a waitress into bringing him "the biggest pre-game meal in history."

With the Graham of old back the following week, the Browns beat the 49ers, 38-3, en route to six straight victories, a 9-2-1 record and their 10th consecutive conference title.

The Browns then defeated the Los Angeles Rams in the L.A. Coliseum, 38-14, for their third NFL championship as Graham threw for two touchdowns and ran for two more. This time, at age 34, Graham retired for good.

In 1956, without Otto Graham, the first pro player Paul Brown ever signed, Cleveland went 5-7, its first losing season in franchise history. Brown couldn't coax Graham out of retirement a second time. The first time had been difficult enough. "When I retired in 1954, I told Paul I would come back for one more year if I had to, but I really didn't want to," Graham explained. "I promised him that if he lost a quarterback or somehow became shorthanded, that I would help him out."

Quarterbacks

Then he left the locker room without visiting the bathroom once. "I said to myself, 'I'm doing these guys a favor.' Why should I get all excited?" Graham recalled.

The 10-year veteran quarterback had hoped the new attitude would work, but it didn't. The Browns were smashed, 27-17, by the visiting Washington Redskins that day. "I played the worst game of my life," Graham said. "I realized that if you aren't afraid of getting the job done, you aren't going to be successful."

Brown, of course, knew just how difficult it would be to replace his star quarterback. Graham had led the Browns to all four All-America Football Conference titles from 1946-49. He led them to a championship in their first NFL season, 1950, and to defeats in the NFL title games of 1951-53 before winning two more crowns in 1954 and '55.

"At the time, they had drafted a quarterback named Bobby Freeman of Auburn in the third round," said Graham. "But the guy signed a contract with Paul Brown and the CFL [Canadian Football League]. They went to court and the CFL won."

UNBEATABLE OFFENSE: Otto Graham throws past four New York Yankees defenders in a 34-21 win at Yankee Stadium in Nov. 1948. The victory was the Browns' 14th straight during their 29-game unbeaten streak that extended from 1947-49.

So Brown then contacted Graham while the Browns were on a two-week preseason trip to California. "Paul called to remind me of my promise," Graham recalled. "I said 'Paul, I still don't want to come back. While you're on the West Coast, try to get yourself a quarterback. When you come back, if you don't have a quarterback, I'll come back.' Years later, I finally realized Paul didn't try very hard."

When Graham retired permanently, he took with him a 114-20-4 record, nine All-League and five NFL Pro Bowl selections. With a delicate passing touch, a very cool head, a running attack featuring Marion Motley and an exceptional receiving corps of Mac Speedie, Dub Jones and Dante Lavelli, Graham's teams averaged nearly 28 points per game over 10 years.

He finished his career with 1,464 completions on 2,626 attempts (55.7) for 23,584 yards and 174 touchdowns. He was elected to the Pro Football Hall of Fame in 1965.

"In 1946, we didn't think we would be that good, but we had a group that wanted to win," said ex-Browns guard Lin Houston in a May '95 interview, four months before his death in September. "Otto instilled the desire to win right there on the field."

Besides his leadership qualities, Graham had an uncanny knack to see the game in slow motion while playing it full speed, especially important in the Browns' innovative pass-oriented offense. An intelligent player with outstanding coordination, he picked defenses apart like a safecracker.

When the NFL announced its 75th anniversary all-time team in 1994, Graham was on the roster with Sammy Baugh, Johnny Unitas and Joe Montana. "My wife says Joe Montana was the first quarterback whose style ever reminded her of me," Graham said. "I ran a lot, threw on the run and all that stuff. Joe was a great athlete and I was a great athlete."

Graham first met Paul Brown when Brown was the head coach at Ohio State and Graham was a single-wing tailback for Northwestern. That was in 1942. Several years later, Brown called Graham and asked him if he'd like to be the first Cleveland Browns player.

"Paul was coaching at the Great Lakes Naval Training Center while I was a Navy air corps cadet just outside of Evanston, Ill.," Graham recalled. "He told me he would give me a $1,000 bonus if I would sign right away, a two-year contract worth $7,500 and also $250 a month starting immediately. As a cadet, I was making $75 a week, so $250 a month was like finding a gold mine. The war only lasted four or five more months, but it was a heck of a deal."

Graham's only experience in the T formation was one year at the Chapel Hill Pre-Flight School in North Carolina. "We had copied the Chicago Bears' playbook that year," Graham said. "One of our assistants was a man named Bear Bryant. Of course, no one knew him from Adam back then. I basically learned the T formation by looking at the playbook and teaching it to myself."

Brown wanted Graham as his quarterback based on one play he had seen the quarterback make against his Buckeyes in 1942. "I was the tailback in a single-wing offense," Graham said. "On one play, I ran around left end one time, stopped and threw the ball back to the right. Paul thought that took an awful lot of ability, so he liked that."

Graham credits his success as a quarterback in the T formation to his basketball experience. In 1945-46, Graham played for the champion

Otto Graham
1946-55

Rochester Royals of the National Basketball League (the forerunner of the NBA). When he won the AAFC title with the Browns in 1946, he became the only player to win championships in two different professional sports in the same year.

"I've always said the best athletes in the world are basketball players," Graham said. "I was lucky to be born with more coordination than most people."

"When you talk quarterbacks, give me Otto over anyone else," said right end Dante Lavelli. "Otto doesn't own one passing record today, but all he did was win championships."

The 1956 season, the Browns' first without Graham and last with Lavelli, was disastrous for the quarterback position. Graham's old

Tommy O'Connell *1956-57*

George Ratterman
1952-56

backup, George Ratterman, started the season, but injured a knee in the fourth game against the Redskins and was lost for the rest of the year. He later retired. Ex-Green Bay Packer Vito "Babe" Parilli was next, lasting three games before separating a shoulder. In desperation, the Browns signed former Chicago Bear Tommy O'Connell, who had not played in the NFL since 1953.

Under O'Connell, a former Big Ten passing champion at Illinois, the Browns won three of their final six games, but a loss to the Chicago Cardinals on the final day of the season gave the Browns their first-ever losing record.

In 1957, the Browns wanted to draft Purdue quarterback and future Hall of Famer Len Dawson, but they lost a coin flip to the Steel-

ers, who selected Dawson. The Browns, shut out of quarterback choices in a first round that also included Paul Hornung and John Brodie, "settled" for a guy named Jim Brown.

Ironically, the Steelers and the Browns both had shots at another Hall-of-Fame quarterback, but both rejected the talents of a young former Louisville signal caller named Johnny Unitas. The Steelers, who had drafted Unitas in 1955, released him before the start of the season, prompting Unitas to call Paul Brown for a tryout. But Brown now had Otto Graham back for another year and didn't need one more backup. The tryout request was denied, although Brown invited him to camp for '56. By then, of course, Unitas had become a Baltimore Colt on his way to winning back-to-back NFL championships in 1958 and '59.

1957 Quarterback Candidates

Left to right: Joe Clarke, John Borton, Bob Garrett, Milt Plum, Bobby Freeman, Tommy O'Connell

With O'Connell and Milt Plum, a second-round draft choice from Penn State, as the top candidates, Paul Brown held a special three-day quarterback "school" in July of '57, prior to the opening of training camp in Hiram, Ohio. Also participating were John Borton of Ohio State, Bobby Freeman of Auburn, Joe Clarke of Santa Clara and Bobby Garrett of Stanford.

Garrett, the Browns' bonus pick in the 1954 draft, had been dealt to Green Bay before the '54 season, but now was returning for a second try after Brown reacquired him in a deal that sent Babe Parilli, Carlton Massey, John Petitbon and Sam Palumbo to the Packers. By the opening of the season, however, it was back to O'Connell, backed up by Plum and Freeman.

With the Browns' 1957 offense increasingly centered upon Jim Brown, Cleveland recaptured the Eastern Conference. But O'Connell broke an ankle in late season and Plum pulled a hamstring prior to the title game in which the Browns were beaten by Detroit, 59-14.

O'Connell retired following the season and Plum assumed full-time duties in 1958, a position he held through 1961.

Dawson eventually made it to Cleveland in 1960-61 as a backup to Plum. Dawson threw 28 passes as a Brown, completing 15 for 109 yards, one touchdown and three interceptions. Then in 1962, he moved on to the AFL's Dallas Texans whom he led to the '62 championship in a double-overtime win over Houston. After the Texans became the Kansas City Chiefs in 1963, Dawson won two more AFL titles: 1966 and 1969, the latter resulting in a victory over Minnesota in Super Bowl IV.

Jim Ninowski *1958-59,'62-66*

Len Dawson
1960-61

Plum's backup in 1958-59, Jim Ninowski, was dealt to the Lions in 1960, but then was traded back to the Browns in 1962 for Plum. The deal also brought defensive end Bill Glass and the former Heisman Trophy winner from Ohio State, Howard "Hopalong" Cassady.

The trade occurred in the spring of 1962, exactly 40 days after Plum had criticized Paul Brown's offensive coaching methods in a story in the *Cleveland Plain Dealer*, saying the team was in a rut and morale was low. Plum had been the NFL's highest-rated passer in 1960 and '61, but like the rest of Paul Brown's quarterbacks, had no authority to call plays.

The deal would have received more media scrutiny had the Browns been champs under Plum, but the 1961 team had dropped to third place in the Eastern Conference—the worst finish since a fourth-place tie in 1956.

Ninowski was considered ready to assume the full-time role, but a dislocated shoulder and fractured collarbone suffered in Game 7 versus Pittsburgh opened the gate for Frank Ryan to take over. Ryan, acquired from the Los Angeles Rams prior to the 1962 season, remained the starter in 1963 and then came into his own in 1964 with the help of an outstanding offensive line, a legend named Jim Brown and receivers Gary Collins and rookie Paul Warfield.

Ryan continued in the starting role through 1967. He was intelligent, too, holding a doctorate degree in mathematics and working as an assistant professor of mathematics at Case Western Reserve University during his playing

Milt Plum *1957-61*

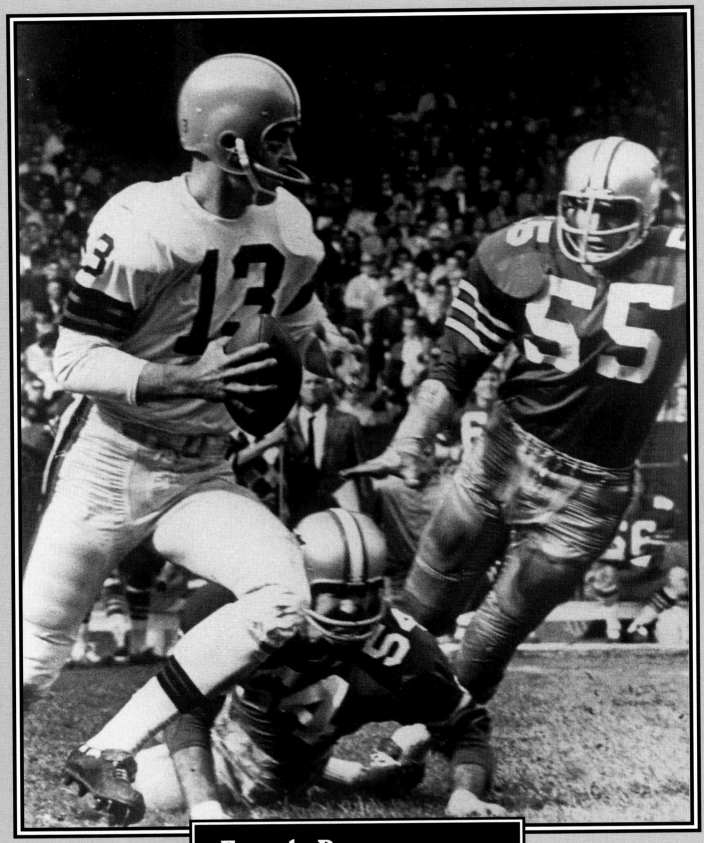

Frank Ryan *1962-68*

days. In 1964, Ryan led the NFL with 25 touchdown passes and then threw three more to Collins as the Browns upset the Colts, 27-0, in the NFL Championship game.

"I'm sure Otto Graham and Brian Sipe have all the records, but Frank did a great job in his own right," Collins said. "He was surrounded by a lot of great players, but Frank made a lot of great plays. He wasn't the prettiest player to look at, but he made a lot of clutch plays."

Ryan led the Browns in passing from 1962-67, throwing for 20 or more touchdowns in all but the 1962 and '65 seasons. He threw for an NFL-high 29 touchdowns and 2,974 yards in 1966, the year after Jim Brown retired. Ryan's 907 completions on 1,755 attempts are third behind Brian Sipe and Bernie Kosar on the Browns' all-time list. His most prolific passing

performance was a five-touchdown effort in a 52-20 romp over the New York Giants in the 1964 regular-season finale.

"People talk about that 1964 team all the time like it was the only good year Frank and the rest of us had," Collins said. "Heck, we were in it just about every year back then. In fact, the 1965 team that lost to Green Bay in the NFL title game was as good, if not better than the 1964 team. And to tell you the truth, I think the 1966 team that finished second to Dallas in the division and missed the playoffs was our best team of all."

In 1967, Ryan hurt his arm. A year later, the Browns lost two of their first three games and Ryan was benched by head coach Blanton Collier. Former Steeler Bill Nelsen stepped in on

Bill Nelsen
1968-72

Mike Phipps
1970-76

never considered more than a temporary solution. The Browns were looking for a healthy, high-profile quarterback who could lead them through their first decade in the former AFL—renamed the American Football Conference.

Thus in 1970, the Browns made the most controversial trade in team history by dealing Paul Warfield to Miami for the right to select Purdue quarterback Mike Phipps as the third overall pick of the 1970 draft. Phipps had set 24 Purdue career, season, single-game and Big Ten passing records. He had started 27 games and the Boilermakers had won 22.

Phipps began as winner with the Browns as well, but ultimately he was not the answer. It wasn't until two years after Phipps was drafted that the Browns finally did acquire their quarterback of the decade—and did so without having to send a future Hall of Famer to Super Bowl glory elsewhere. In the 13th round of the 1972 draft, they picked San Diego State's Brian Sipe, the national passing champion in '71.

Taking over for Nelsen after the Browns lost the 1972 opener to Green Bay, Phipps had what would be his best season with 1,994 passing yards and 13 touchdowns. The Browns finished second behind Pittsburgh in the AFC Central (10-4) to earn a Wild Card berth, then lost to Miami in the playoffs.

With Phipps still at the controls, the Browns dropped to 7-5-2 in 1973, then lost five of their first six in 1974. That's when Sipe gave his first indication of things to come when he replaced Phipps in the fourth quarter of a contest against the Denver Broncos at Cleveland Stadium on Oct. 27. Trailing 21-9, Sipe rallied the Browns for two touchdowns, both of which he scored, in the final six minutes for a 23-21 victory that snapped a four-game losing streak.

Sipe assumed the full-time role in 1976 and the Browns finished with their first winning record (9-5) since 1973. Phipps was traded to the Bears for a first-round pick in 1978. The Browns then traded that selection and a fourth-rounder from Washington to Los Angeles for the Rams' No. 1 choice. They used it to select Alabama wide receiver Ozzie Newsome.

his gimpy knees and led the Browns on an eight-game winning streak and into the playoffs at 10-4. Nelsen and the Browns beat Dallas, 31-20, to reach the NFL title game, but lost to Baltimore, 34-0, one step short of Super Bowl III.

A 10th-round draft choice from Southern California in 1963, Nelsen had been the Steelers' starter since 1965, but missed parts of the next three seasons with knee injuries. Turning to a younger, healthier Kent Nix, the Steelers traded Nelsen to the Browns for quarterback Dick Shiner and defensive tackle Frank Parker.

Nelsen played on his bad knees with determination, courage and a large measure of success. But in spite of leading the Browns to Eastern Conference titles in 1968 and '69, he was

It became a payback of sorts. The Browns had sacrificed one Hall-of-Fame receiver, Paul Warfield, to acquire Phipps. But trading Phipps resulted in another Hall of Famer coming to Cleveland in Newsome.

Sipe continued to grow in his role as starter as the Browns again grew to contender status. Then in 1980, Sipe became one of the most beloved athletes in Cleveland sports history. The year of the "Kardiac Kids" and their last-minute victories electrified the city. It also gave the Browns an 11-5 record and their first playoff appearance since 1972.

Sipe was at the center of it all, leading the Browns past the defending Super Bowl champion Pittsburgh Steelers in the AFC Central. He completed 61 percent of his passes, throwing for a team-record 4,132 yards, a team-record 30

touchdowns and only 14 interceptions in 554 attempts. He won the NFL's MVP award.

Brian Sipe
1974-83

"Brian had that special charisma, that kind of presence that assured you things would be all right," said ex-Browns offensive tackle Doug Dieken. "When you were down by two touchdowns, he was the guy who would be loose. He was never uptight. He'd always say, 'We got them right where we want them.' He also was the guy who wasn't afraid to take the chance to make the play. You know how Larry Bird would throw the pass that most people wouldn't throw because they didn't think they could? Well, Brian was that way in football."

Sipe's finest season ended against the Oakland Raiders in a gray way on a dismal, bitterly

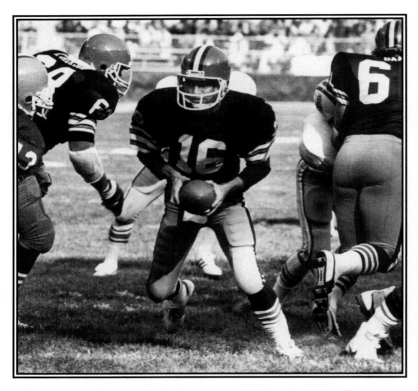

Paul McDonald
1980-85

cold Jan. 4, 1981, afternoon at Cleveland Stadium. It was the day "Red Right 88" became synonymous with the frustrations of a city and its team. With the Browns trailing, 14-12, and well within field goal range during the playoff game's waning moments, a Sipe pass to tight end Ozzie Newsome was intercepted in the end zone by defensive back Mike Davis.

Sipe left the Browns for the United States Football League following the 1983 season. He took with him nearly every passing record in Cleveland history. He still holds the Browns' career records in, among many others, passing yardage (23,713), touchdowns (154), completions (1,944) and attempts (3,439).

Paul McDonald succeeded Sipe in 1984, but the Browns lost seven of their first eight and Sam Rutigliano lost his job. McDonald lasted the season, but soon he was on his way out.

That was because in 1985, Bernie Kosar Jr. basically dictated to the NFL which team he wanted to play for. And that team was the Browns, whom he had followed while growing up in nearby Boardman, Ohio.

On Jan. 15, 1985, Bernie Kosar Sr. called the NFL office for a clarification on the supplemental draft rules. On March 14, he called a news conference for his son to announce he was passing up the remaining two years of his college eligibility at the University of Miami.

On April 9, the Browns traded their first and third picks in the 1985 regular draft and their first and sixth picks the following year for Buffalo's first pick in the 1985 supplemental draft. On April 24, Kosar announced he would

skip the regular draft, graduate from school early, and make himself available for the supplemental draft.

The Browns had their man. They signed Kosar to a series of five one-year contracts, then watched as the quarterback who had won a national championship as a freshman at Miami helped lead them to five straight playoff appearances. The 1986, 1987 and 1989 teams all came within a game of the Super Bowl, losing to Denver each time.

GUNSLINGER: Brian Sipe was unafraid to take a chance to make the big play. It resulted in record-setting passing statistics and the spectacular Kardiac Kids seasons of 1979 and '80.

The 1986 Browns team was Kosar's best. It finished at 12-4, the Browns' best mark in the NFL, as Kosar threw for 3,854 yards. A year later, he led the Browns back to the AFC Championship game when he threw 22 touchdown passes and only nine interceptions as he completed an NFL-best 62 percent of his passes.

Bernie Kosar *1985-93*

Kosar, 6-5, 215, was able to use his intelligence and excellent vision to overcome his physical deficiencies. He had slow foot speed and an awkward sidearm throwing motion. And making it tougher was the fact he played during an era in which the defensive players became both faster and bigger, as well as more specialized. Nickel and dime defensive backs, designated speed rushers and 300-pound tackles who ran sub-5.0 40-yard dashes were some of the obstacles Kosar had to overcome during his prime in Cleveland.

"Sipe and Kosar were a lot alike," Dieken said. "Things happen real fast in football, but people like Brian and Bernie saw them a little slower. They were able to diagnose what people were doing. They're pretty sharp as to what was actually happening [on the field]. If the defense was doing something unexpected, a Kosar or a Sipe could break it down, see what they were doing and do something else that worked."

Unfortunately, the end of Kosar's career in Cleveland was not as happy as the beginning. On Nov. 8, 1993, head coach Bill Belichick ended his rocky relationship with Kosar when he released the fan favorite.

Kosar had lost his starting job to former college teammate and ex-Tampa Bay Buccaneer Vinny Testaverde earlier in the season, but Testaverde was sidelined with a shoulder injury and the Browns were in first place with a 5-3 record at the time of the release. For Browns fans, the timing was difficult to comprehend.

The Sunday following Kosar's release, he started for the Dallas Cowboys in their 20-15 win over the Phoenix Cardinals. Troy Aikman, the Cowboys' regular starting quarterback, was sidelined with an injury.

Kosar picked up a Super Bowl ring as Aikman returned to health and led the Cowboys to the championship. Kosar then signed a two-year deal with Miami in 1994 and remained Dan Marino's backup until his retirement following the 1996 season.

Testaverde, the 1986 Heisman Trophy winner, completed 207 of 376 (55.1) for 2,575 yards and 16 touchdowns in 1994. Dating back to

Vinny Testaverde
1993-95

1993, he had thrown at least one touchdown pass in 19 of his last 23 games. His most memorable performance was on Dec. 26, 1993, when he set an all-time NFL single-game record for completion percentage (91.3) when he went 21 for 23 in a 42-14 victory over the Rams.

The first person hired by the NFL for the new Browns franchise of 1999 was Joe Mack as director of scouting. Mack made it clear that the No. 1 priority for him and his staff would be to find a quarterback for the owner of the new club, whomever that would be. Mack's job was made reasonably easy by the abundance of outstanding passers in college football in 1998.

Kentucky's Tim Couch, Central Florida's Daunte Culpepper, Washington's Brock Huard,

Ty Detmer
1999

back regarded as the best prospect since Georgia's Herschel Walker in the early 1980s, the top brass for the Browns seemed little swayed away from their course to get a quarterback first.

They appeared, however, to be wavering on Couch. Smith so impressed every scout with his athletic prowess that there were hints Smith had pulled ahead of, or at least even with, Couch in the Browns' estimation. In the end, though, the club went with instinct and drafted Couch No. 1.

A native of the coal-mining town of Hyden, Ky., Couch set virtually every passing record at the University of Kentucky, plus conference and national marks along the way. Couch completed 72 percent of his passes as a junior and 67 percent for his career. He had 73 touchdown passes to only 34 interceptions in his last two years for the Wildcats and totaled 8,159 passing yards over that time.

Couch was 6-4 and 227 pounds and turned 22 years old on July 31, 1999. He skipped his senior season to enter the draft and openly admitted he wanted to play for the Browns. But until Couch was ready to step in and be a starting quarterback, the Browns acquired seven-year veteran Ty Detmer from the 49ers to keep the seat warm for the rookie. Detmer, a graduate of Brigham Young and the Heisman Trophy winner in 1991, had played for the Eagles and Packers before the Niners. He had played in 44 NFL games with 19 as a starter.

At BYU, Detmer set 59 NCAA records, including touchdown passes (121), passing yardage (15,031) and completions (958), yet he was drafted in Round 9 by the Packers. His height (6-0) and weight (194) were considered insufficient to make an impact in the NFL.

Acquired as a rookie free agent was Mike Cook, who had thrown for 7,285 yards, 62 TDs and just 23 interceptions at William & Mary.

Midway through training camp, the Browns also added Jamie Martin, a six-year veteran who played under Browns head coach Chris Palmer in 1998 when Palmer was the offensive coordinator at Jacksonville. Martin, 6-2, 210, from Weber State, had backed up Mark Brunell.

UCLA's Cade McNown and Syracuse's Donovan McNabb had excellent seasons in 1997 and were considered sure-fire stars of the future in the NFL. Add to that list Oregon's Akili Smith, who seemed to arrive out of nowhere to have a superb year and launch himself to the top of the mountain in the eyes of NFL scouts.

Couch was considered the finest of the lot, and it was an article of faith that the Browns, now in the hands of owner Alfred Lerner and CEO Carmen Policy, would take Couch with the first overall selection of the college draft. Despite strong support among a few for Heisman Trophy winner Ricky Williams, a running

Tim Couch *1999*

Running Backs

Training camp for the Cleveland Browns already had started by the time Jim Brown's bright red corvette pulled into Hiram College in August 1957. It had been a long overnight drive from Chicago where Brown had played sparingly for a team of pass-happy ex-college seniors that lost to the defending NFL champion New York Giants in the College All-Star Game.

"I remember him looking more intimidating than any player I had ever seen," said writer Chuck Heaton, who covered the Browns for the *Cleveland Plain Deale*r at the time. "He wasn't happy that he hadn't been used much in the All-Star Game, and he had driven all night to get to Hiram. Normally, the rookies were razzed a little bit by the veterans. I don't remember anyone picking on Jim when he got there."

Brown, of course, was special. And everyone could sense it from Day 1. "I had players come up to me and talk about Jim even early on in his career," said Ken Coleman, the former long-time radio and television voice of the Browns. "They'd say, 'You know, I hope my grand kids believe me when I tell them one day that I played football with Jim Brown.'"

Brown didn't play much in his first exhibition game, a 20-10 loss in Detroit. But a week later in the Akron Rubber Bowl, he gave a preview of the future. With 26,669 fans looking on, he was spectacular in the Browns' 28-13 win.

Jim Brown avoids a tackler on a long gain against the St. Louis Cardinals.

PEAK PERFORMANCE Jim Brown's greatest rushing season was 1963 (above) when he led the NFL in attempts (291), yardage (1,863), average per carry (6.4) and touchdowns (12). His yardage total set an all-time league record that stood until O.J. Simpson broke the 2,000-yard barrier with 2,003 in 1973.

In fact, after a dazzling 48-yard touchdown run, head coach Paul Brown, who always was reluctant to start first-year players, was overheard telling his rookie, "You're my fullback." Nine years later, Jim Brown stepped away from the game having never let another player start in his place.

Brown played in 118 straight games, carrying the ball 2,359 times for 12,312 yards (5.2 average) and 106 touchdowns. He also had 20 TDs receiving on 262 receptions.

Brown left the game with all of its major rushing and scoring records. He led the NFL in rushing eight of nine seasons, running for more than 1,200 yards seven times, and made the Pro Bowl all nine seasons. And at age 30, there was no doubt Brown could have continued. Coming off an NFL MVP season in 1965 and a three-touchdown effort in the 1966 Pro Bowl, Brown retired July 14, 1966, while on the set of his first movie, "The Dirty Dozen," in England. Cleveland had attempted to get him to report to training camp on time, but Brown would not be forced to leave the set early.

Even after his records began to be broken two and three decades later, many still consider him the greatest football player of all time. In 1979, several of the greatest running backs in history were surveyed on a variety of subjects. When asked to name the best running back ever, Chicago Bears Hall-of-Famer Gale Sayers said, "I've said many times, and I will always say, Jim Brown is the best—and he will still be the best long after all his records are broken."

Another Hall-of-Famer, Paul Hornung of the Green Bay Packers, simply said, ". . . give me Jim Brown over anybody at anything."

The NFL had never seen anything like Brown. He was a powerfully built 6-foot-2, 228 pounds, but ran with a sprinter's speed. He ignored pain, showing up every week despite stacked defenses with guys like Huff, Nitschke and Schmidt all programmed to punish him.

"Everybody remembers the long runs, but I thought one of the most impressive things about Jim was the way he could grind out a game," Coleman said. "If you were leading by seven points with five minutes left, there were 80,000 people, especially the 11 people on the other side of the line, who knew that Jim was going to get the ball. But he'd still go and grind it out. He'd go five yards, seven yards, two yards, 12 yards, whatever it took."

Brown was always a great athlete. He once scored 55 points in a high school basketball game at Manhassett High in Long Island, N.Y. And as a sophomore at Syracuse University, he placed fifth in the nation in the decathlon championships, surpassing the previous marks of the great Jim Thorpe in six of 10 events. Brown also was an All-America in lacrosse at Syracuse, and an avid golfer. During a pro-am tournament in Cleveland in 1963, he shot a 79 while playing with Jack Nicklaus.

Boxing promoter Norman Rothschild once begged Brown to turn to boxing. In January 1964, the year after Brown rushed for a career-high 1,863 yards and outgained runner-up Jim Taylor of Green Bay by 845 yards, Rothschild wanted Brown to fight Sonny Liston or Cassius Clay for millions of dollars. Brown was smart enough to stick with football, saying he'd much rather "play three straight days against the Giants, Bears and Packers than to get in the ring with those guys."

THE BEST: Jim Brown led the NFL in rushing eight of his nine seasons, gaining over 1,000 yards seven times. He led the league in touchdowns five times and recorded 58 100-yard games. He finished with 12,312 rushing yards on 2,359 carries (5.2 average) and 106 rushing touchdowns in 118 games.

There were two things for which Brown was regularly criticized: that he was not a topflight blocker and that he did not practice hard. It upset Paul Brown, who later admitted he considered trading Brown before the 1962 season because his attitude might have been hurting the team. Two years later, ex-Browns quarterback Otto Graham said Brown should be traded because of his failure to block or fake. "The Browns will not win anything as long as Brown is in there. Now chew on that awhile."

FINAL FLOURISH: Jim Brown completed his career in 1965 (above) by setting Browns single-season marks in touchdowns, (21) and points (126). His 17 rushing touchdowns, equaling his career high set in 1958, is also an all-time Browns record.

The Browns, of course, went on to win the NFL championship that year. They also went to the title game in Brown's rookie season, 1957, losing to the Lions, and in his final season, 1965, losing to the Packers.

Years later, Brown answered his critics. "I was not a great blocker," he admitted. "But if I couldn't run the way I did, I would have been the best blocker going."

Brown, simply, was a devoted runner. "He would study films of the great runners, which I don't think a lot of people knew about," said Coleman, who hosted a television show with Brown during the 1960s. "I know he looked at the old Eagles running back, Steve Van Buren. And I believe he even looked at Red Grange. There were others, too, which he would look at to see what made them successful."

Paul Brown wasn't looking for a fullback in that 1957 NFL draft. He wanted a quarterback. But when he lost a coin flip with Pittsburgh to determine who would make the fifth selection, Brown watched as the Steelers took their quar-

terback, Purdue's Len Dawson. At that point, Brown settled for the "best available" player: Jim Brown.

After Jim Brown was selected, Paul Brown signed him to a $12,000 contract and gave him a $3,000 bonus, which at the time was the most ever given to a Cleveland rookie. "He's worth it," Paul Brown said at the time.

From 1958-61, Jim Brown shared the backfield with another future Hall of Famer. Bobby Mitchell started 48 consecutive games at half-

back for the Browns, scoring 38 touchdowns and gaining 2,297 yards rushing.

Also an outstanding kick returner and pass receiver, Mitchell was traded to Washington in 1962 in the deal that brought ex-Syracuse running back Ernie Davis to Cleveland. But Davis never played in the NFL after learning the week of the 1962 College All-Star Game that he had leukemia. He died in May of 1963.

Mitchell's service duties had limited him to a game-day player only. The Redskins, mean-

SCORING THREAT: Bobby Mitchell breaks free on a 65-yard touchdown run against the Eagles in 1959. He scored 38 TDs in his four-year Browns career (1958-61): 16 rushing, 16 receiving, three on punt returns and three on kickoff returns.

while, were getting pressured to sign their first black player. Mitchell's best years came in Washington where he played primarily as a receiver and returner through 1968. His 1,436 receiving yards in 1963 were a team record. He was elected to the Hall of Fame in 1983.

RAMPAGING BULL: Marion Motley gained 4,712 yards on 826 carries in his eight-year Browns career (1946-53). His 810 yards led the NFL in rushing in 1950. He also returned kicks.

Helping to pave the way for Jim Brown, Bobby Mitchell, Leroy Kelly and all black players was a 6-foot-1, 238-pound bone-crushing fullback by the name of Marion Motley. He and teammate Bill Willis were the first black players signed to play in the AAFC in 1946.

"The reason you hear so much about Jackie Robinson breaking the color barrier in baseball and not so much about a guy like Motley is because of the times," said Joe Horrigan, curator of the Pro Football Hall of Fame. "Pro football wasn't that big back then. Baseball was king. But the courage shown by guys like Motley, Willis and Paul Brown was admirable."

Brown had coached black players at every level going back to his days at Massillon Wash-

ington High School. His philosophy was simple, said former Browns quarterback Otto Graham: "If you didn't like playing with a black man, get out of here."

In 1946, Motley and Willis did not play in a game in Miami because they received death threats. That's the same year the manager at the hotel where the Browns were staying tried to keep Motley and Willis from staying.

"We walk in and the manager says the black guys couldn't stay there, that they had to stay at another place," Graham recalled. "The next thing you know, we're all walking out the door. The manager yells, 'What are you doing?' Paul turned around and said, 'It's very simple. If the black guys don't stay, none of us will stay.' The manager changed his mind real quick."

Motley led the All-America Football Conference in rushing all four years of its existence, rushing for 3,024 yards, 26 touchdowns and a 6.2-yard average on 489 carries.

In 1950, the Browns unseated Philadelphia as NFL champions and Motley unseated Eagles fullback Steve Van Buren for the rushing title. Van Buren had won the crown four of the five previous seasons. Motley gained 810 yards on 140 carries for a 5.8-yard average. No player since 1950 has led the NFL in rushing with 140 carries or less. Of course, Motley was known for getting the most out of the fewest number of carries. His combined AAFC-NFL career totals from 1946-53 included 4,712 rushing yards and a 5.7 average on 826 carries.

"Until Marion came along, it was Bronko Nagurski whose name came up when someone said fullback," Horrigan explained. "After Marion played, it was Bronko Nagurski and Marion Motley. Those two are the ones that defined what it is to play fullback."

Unlike Brown, Motley was also a devastating pass blocker. So devastating, in fact, that he helped the Browns catch the league off guard in the ways they used the fullback position. The Browns became known as the "pass and trap" team because just when teams were certain Graham was going to throw to Dante Lavelli, Mac Speedie or Dub Jones, he'd drop back and

secretly slip the ball to a raging Motley, who would burst through the line of scrimmage. Motley also became one of the first backs in NFL history to become a receiving threat.

"The screen pass and the trap play existed at the time, but they really weren't being used much," Horrigan said. "The way it was born is Marion was so good a blocker, he would deliver his blow and then roll off. At that time, teams weren't used to seeing outlet passes to the full-back. Imagine how they felt when Marion got the ball and got a full head of steam going."

Graham doesn't like to imagine what kind of player he would have been without Motley to block and keep defenses honest. Asked what he would have done without Motley, Graham said, "Nothing. I'd have been dead. He saved my life many times, which is good because I don't remember ever completing a pass lying flat on my back."

DOWN THE SIDELINE: Marion Motley charges through a pack of Chicago Bears in 1951. Paul Brown called him the best running back he ever coached, and that included Jim Brown.

Brown saw what kind of player Motley was when Brown's Massillon teams played Motley's Canton McKinley teams in the 1930s. Brown's Tigers handed Motley's Bulldogs their only loss for three straight seasons, but Brown developed a great admiration for Motley.

During World War II, with Motley in the service and Brown coaching at the Great Lakes Naval Training Center, their paths crossed once again. Motley became the fullback on the team Brown used to beat Notre Dame, 39-7, in 1945.

"Marion just happened to be passing through Great Lakes one day," Horrigan explained. "He had orders to go somewhere else, but Brown found out he was there and went to the commander and said he had to have Motley on his

"Special Delivery" Edgar Jones
1946-49

team. He was close to leaving. In fact, they literally went out and pulled his bags off the train."

Long after Brown retired from coaching, he called Motley the best running back he ever coached, and that included Jim Brown. Motley was elected to the Pro Football Hall of Fame in 1968. He died on June 27, 1999, of prostate cancer at age 79.

Motley's backfield mate during the AAFC days was Edgar "Special Delivery" Jones from the University of Pittsburgh. After spending four years in the Navy during World War II, Jones joined the Browns' original starting backfield in 1946 along with Graham, Motley and halfback Don Greenwood.

Jones, who played one game for the Chicago Bears in 1945, became a short-yardage specialist in key third-down situations. In four seasons, he gained 1,509 yards on 289 carries (5.2-yard average) with 18 touchdowns. He was a receiving threat as well, with 32 receptions for 635 yards (19.8-yard average) and 10 touchdowns.

In the Browns' four AAFC championship games, Jones scored in three: on a 4-yard run against the Yankees in 1947; a 3-yard run and a 9-yard pass versus the Bills in '48; and a 2-yard run against the 49ers in '49.

But Jones did not accompany the Browns when they entered the NFL in 1950. He had severely dislocated a shoulder in a 61-14 victory over the Los Angeles Dons in October 1949. Following medical advice, he retired at age 29 to avoid the risk of permanent damage.

Rex Bumgardner *1950-52*

Instead, the Browns paired Rex Bumgardner and Ken Carpenter with Motley for their first three seasons in the NFL. Bumgardner, a 5-11, 193 pounder from West Virginia, had been acquired from the Buffalo Bills after the AAFC folded along with guard Abe Gibron and defensive tackle John Kissell. Carpenter, 6-0, 195 pounds, was the Browns' No. 1 draft choice in 1950 from Oregon State.

Bumgardner was in the backfield when the Browns faced the Eagles in the 1950 opener. He gained 231 yards on 67 attempts that season and scored a touchdown on a 14-yard pass from Otto Graham in the fourth quarter of the 1950 championship game.

Carpenter took over in 1951 with 402 yards on 85 attempts and followed that with 408 yards on 72 carries in '52. Like Jones and Bumgard-

ner, Carpenter was a receiving threat. He also led the Browns in punt returns in 1951 and '52—and in kickoff returns from 1951-53.

Ken Carpenter
1950-53

As Motley neared the end with increasingly aching knees, fullback Harry "Chick" Jagade saw increased playing time in 1952-53 before moving on to Green Bay in 1954. Jagade, a 6-0, 213-pounder from Indiana, had played with the AAFC's Baltimore Colts in 1949.

Following Motley's departure, the backfield remained in transition until Jim Brown and Bobby Mitchell joined forces in 1958. Included in the 1954-57 mix were Billy Reynolds, Chet Hanulak, Maurice Bassett, Fred "Curly" Morrison, Lew Carpenter, Preston Carpenter, Ed Modzelewski and Milt Campbell.

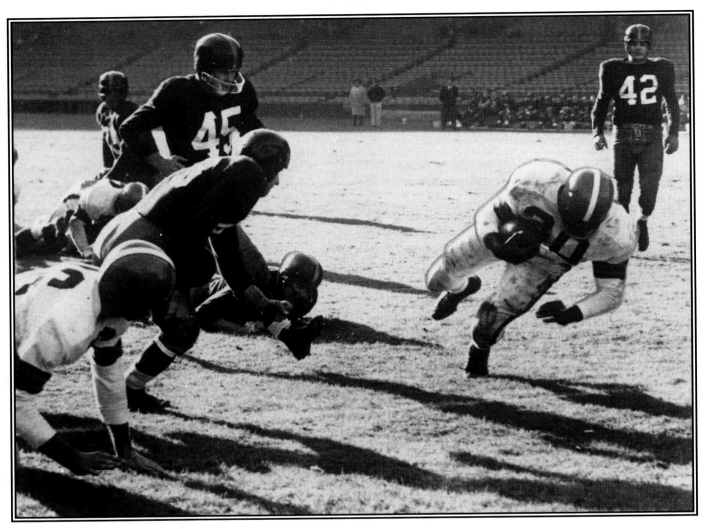

Maurice Bassett
1954-56

Bassett, a 6-1, 230-pound battering runner from Chickasha, Okla., became the full-time fullback in 1954 and led the Browns in rushing with 588 yards on 144 carries and six touchdowns. A third-round draft choice in '54 from Langston University, Bassett won the job in a battle with Morrison, a former Ohio State star and Chicago Bear, after Bassett demonstrated the superior pass blocking ability for Graham.

The following two seasons, Bassett shared duties with Ed Modzelewski, a former Steeler and brother of Giants defensive tackle Dick Modzelewski, who joined the Browns in 1964.

Morrison's best season was 1955. He gained a team-high 824 yards on 156 attempts, the top yardage performance since Motley's 810 in '50.

Nicknamed "Billy the Kid" and also "The Rock," Reynolds was a second-round choice in 1953 from Pittsburgh. He divided playing time with Dub Jones at halfback during his first two seasons while also returning kicks and punts. He then spent two years in the Air Force before returning to the Browns in 1957 primarily as a return specialist.

Reynolds was traded to Pittsburgh in 1958 where he saw limited action. Out of football in '59, he tried a comeback with the fledgling Oakland Raiders of the American Football League in 1960, but after six games and one rushing attempt, his career was over.

Preston Carpenter was a No. 1 draft choice in 1956 from Arkansas. He led the Browns in rushing with 756 yards as a rookie, then succeeded Dante Lavelli at right end in '57.

Billy Reynolds *1953-54,'57*

Preston Carpenter
RB-WR • 1956-59

With the Browns' offense increasingly centered upon Jim Brown and the ground attack, Carpenter led the team in receiving in 1958 with 29 catches for 474 yards, the second lowest leading totals in franchise history.

Carpenter and defensive back Junior Wren were traded to Pittsburgh in December 1959 for wide receiver Gern Nagler and quarterback Len Dawson. Carpenter enjoyed a lengthy, but traveled career with stops in Washington, Minnesota and Miami before retiring in 1967.

Lew Carpenter, one year older than brother Preston, joined the Browns in 1957 in a trade with Detroit. Carpenter was a starter in the Lions' backfield in 1954 and '55 before spending all of 1956 in the Army. He joined the Browns' backfield midway through the 1957 season, gaining 315 yards on 83 attempts, then was traded to Green Bay for wide receiver Billy Howton.

Milt Campbell was a sixth-round choice from Indiana in 1956 who also was a track star. In high school, he qualified for the 1952 Helsinki Olympics in the decathlon, finishing second to Bob Mathias. He later won the event in Melbourne in 1956. Campbell came to Cleveland in 1957 after his release from the Navy. Hampered by injuries in what was his only NFL season, he saw limited backfield time, but did lead the Browns in kickoff returns.

Chet Hanulak was a 5-10, 191-pound halfback whose two-year career was interrupted by two years in the Air Force. He finished second in rushing both seasons (1954 and '57), but is best remembered for his nickname: "The Jet."

CONTINUED EXCELLENCE: After Jim Brown retired in 1966, Leroy Kelly picked up the slack with three straight 1,000-yard-plus seasons from 1966-68 and six consecutive Pro Bowl trips from 1967-72. He was elected to the Hall of Fame in 1994.

Shortly before Jim Brown shocked the professional football world with the announcement of his retirement, he wrote head coach Blanton Collier a letter. It wasn't a farewell letter as much as it was a forecast of great things to come for Leroy Kelly, the Browns' third-year running back from Morgan State. "I told Blanton he would not have to worry because he still had a great running back," Brown said. "Leroy was the man. He was ready."

Brown was correct. After two seasons performing as an outstanding kick returner and downfield tackler on the special teams, Kelly averaged 5.5 yards per carry as he rushed for 1,141 yards and a league-high 15 touchdowns in 1966. Only the Bears' Gale Sayers had more yards rushing that season.

PAYDIRT PROWESS: Leroy Kelly races across the baseball infield at Cleveland Stadium for a touchdown against the New York Giants. He scored 90 touchdowns in his 10-year career, second only to Jim Brown's 126 on the Browns' all-time list.

Kelly followed that effort with back-to-back rushing titles and a league-high 120 points on 20 touchdowns in 1968. He rushed for 1,205 yards and a 5.1-yard average in 1967, followed by 1,239 yards and a 5.0-yard average in 1968.

When Kelly retired, the five-time all-league selection, six-time Pro Bowl pick and future Hall of Famer (inducted in 1994) ranked fourth in career rushing behind Brown, Jim Taylor and Joe Perry. Kelly, a 6-foot, 205-pounder with quick feet, slashing style and long strides, spent 10 seasons in the league and scored 90 touchdowns. He compiled 12,329 total yards and his 7,274 rushing yards rank second to Brown on the Browns' all-time career list.

Kelly's three consecutive 1,100-yard seasons were even more impressive when considering he did them before the hash marks were moved in to 23 yards, one foot, nine inches in 1972. From 1966-68, only 10 NFL running backs broke the 1,000-yard barrier and Kelly did it three times. In 1972, the first season the hash marks were moved in, 10 players ran for more than 1,000 yards.

"Leroy was like a cat," said Ernie Green, the only player to start alongside both Brown and Kelly. "So was Jim, only a bigger cat. It's difficult to knock a cat off his feet. Jim and Leroy also were similar in that they had the same seriousness about their play."

Ernie Green *1962-68*

Bo Scott
1969-74

Green, acquired from Green Bay for a draft choice during training camp of 1962, began his career as a halfback alongside Jim Brown, then converted to fullback in 1966 to complement Kelly. The 6-2, 212-pounder from the University of Louisville possessed excellent speed and great maneuverabilty in the Browns' backfield from 1962-68. Versatile and dependable, Green had his best season in 1966 when he set career highs in rushing yards (750), receptions (45) and receiving yards (445).

After Green retired, Kelly's backfield mates included Reece Morrison, Bo Scott and Ken Brown. It would not be until the late 1970s that the Browns again would have a consistent running-back combination.

Kelly's career had run its course by 1973 as nagging knee problems limited his effectiveness. He was released the following year to make room for a speedy water bug-type runner named Greg Pruitt, a 1973 second-round pick from Oklahoma. Pruitt, however, didn't get much of an opportunity to run the ball his first two years in Cleveland under head coach Nick Skorich.

"Nick thought I was too small," said Pruitt, whose playing size was 5-10, 190 pounds. "That was tough to take because although I may have been small, but I looked down on Nick Skorich. Then when Forrest Gregg was hired in 1975, he

> Leroy Kelly's quickness, slashing style and ability to stay on his feet kept NFL defenders on the chase for 10 seasons.

Mike Pruitt *1976-84*

Cleo Miller *1975-82*

called me at home and told me I would be getting the opportunity I had been crying for. He said be sure you're in shape, and I was."

Although the Browns went a combined 18-24 from 1975-77, "Do-It" Pruitt became one of the most exciting players in the NFL. Before the league outlawed the tear-away jersey, Pruitt probably went through more No. 34 jerseys than any player in NFL history. From 1975-77, Pruitt ran for 1,067, 1,000 and 1,086 yards.

At the height of Greg Pruitt's success, the Browns sought another Pruitt. Purdue's Mike Pruitt, no relation to Greg, was the team's No. 1 pick in 1976. For two-and-a-half years, Mike Pruitt was basically considered a first-round bust. "Forrest and Mike didn't see eye-to-eye," said former Browns offensive tackle Doug Dieken. "Forrest just didn't like Mike."

Sam Rutigliano, however, did. After becoming the head coach in 1978, he worked the 6-foot, 225-pound Pruitt into the workhorse role in a 41-20

Greg Pruitt
1973-81

victory over Buffalo on Oct. 29, 1978. He ran for 173 yards, including a 71-yard TD run.

Prior to Mike Pruitt, a variety of performers shared the Browns' backfield with Greg Pruitt from 1974-77. Included were Ken Brown, Hugh McKinnis, Billy Pritchett and Cleo Miller.

After Greg Pruitt suffered a knee injury in 1979, Mike Pruitt led the Browns in rushing from 1979-83, picking up 1,000-yard seasons four times. He had 1,294 yards and nine TDs in 1979 and 1,184 yards and 10 TDs in '83. For the 1980 Kardiac Kids, Pruitt led the team in both rushing and receiving (63 catches).

Earnest Byner
1984-88, '94-95

In 1985, the Browns again returned to the roots of professional football when they emphasized the running game with a solid backfield combination. Kevin Mack (1,104) and Earnest Byner (1,002) became only the third pair of teammates in NFL history to rush for over a 1,000 yards in the same season.

With the exception of Eric Metcalf's 633 yards in 1989, either Mack or Byner led the Browns in rushing from 1986-92, but neither one broke the 1,000-yard barrier. Mack led five times during that span.

From 1986-95, the Browns failed to produce a 1,000-yard performance. The closest was by Leroy Hoard whose 890 yards on 209 attempts in 1994 earned him a Pro Bowl berth.

Mack, a 6-0, 224 pounder from Clemson was acquired in 1984 after the Browns traded four late-round draft picks to Chicago for the Bears' three picks in the supplemental draft, one of which was used to claim Mack. He had played for the Los Angeles Express of the defunct United States Football League in '84.

In nine seasons, Mack gained 5,123 yards on 1,291 attempts with 46 touchdowns. He played only four games in 1989 after a substance abuse charge resulted in a 30-day jail sentence. He later returned to score the winning touchdown in a division-clinching contest against Houston in the season finale.

Mack retired prior to the 1993 season, then un-retired before Game 4. He returned, but was used sparingly by head coach Bill Belichick, who kept him mostly on the practice squad.

Kevin Mack *1985-93*

Tommy Vardell *1992-95*

Leroy Hoard
1990-95

A 10th-round draft choice from East Carolina in 1984, Byner will remain attached in Browns lore to "The Fumble," in which he was stripped of the ball at the three-yard line while attempting to score the tying touchdown in the fourth quarter of the 1987 AFC Championship game at Denver. But Byner is also remembered for scoring six post-season touchdowns, tying him with Gary Collins for most in team history.

At 5-10, 215 pounds, Byner had five productive seasons in Cleveland before being traded to Washington in 1989 for running back Mike Oliphant. It came after a solid 1988 season in which Byner had identical yardage totals of 576 in rushing and receiving. The trade became one of the Browns' worst ever. Oliphant saw limited action for two seasons, while Byner rushed for over 1,000 yards in two of his five years with the Redskins. He returned as a free agent in 1994, then caught a career-high 61 passes in '95.

In seven seasons, Byner gained 3,364 yards on 862 attempts with 27 touchdowns. He also caught 276 passes for 2,630 yards and 10 TDs.

Leroy Hoard, Tommy Vardell and Eric Metcalf were the main running backs from 1991-95. Hoard's 890-yard Pro Bowl effort in '94 was the best performance. Vardell, a fullback and No. 1 draft selection in 1992, gained 644 yards in '93 before knee problems took over. Metcalf was used primarily as a receiving back, tying for the team lead with Michael Jackson in 1992 with 47, then following with a team-high 63 in '93.

Sedrick Shaw *1999*

The Browns chose no big-name running backs in the 1999 expansion draft, waiting until their 25th pick (out of 37) to take one. Drafted were Michael Blair (Packers), Ronald Moore (Dolphins), Clarence "Pooh Bear" Williams (Bills) and Jerris McPhail (Lions).

Two experienced backs arrived later. Terry Kirby, a seven-year veteran who had previously played for the Dolphins and 49ers, was signed as an unrestricted free agent on March 9. His best season rushing was in 1996 when he gained 559 yards (4.2 yards per carry) for the 49ers. For his career, Kirby had 2,272 yards rushing (4.0 per carry) with 21 touchdowns and 246 catches for 2,498 yards and eight touchdowns.

Sedrick Shaw, who had played two seasons for the Patriots, was traded to the Browns on April 22 for past considerations. Shaw had no rushing attempts as a rookie. In his second season in the NFL he gained 236 yards on 48 carries for 4.9 yards per try.

The Browns drafted Madre Hill of Arkansas in the seventh round. Hill had been dynamite for the Razorbacks as a sophomore, gaining 1,387 yards, averaging of 115.6 yards a game and scoring 16 touchdowns (15 rushing, one receiving). Knee injuries forced him to sit out 1996 and '97. In 1998 he gained 669 yards on 160 carries and scored seven TDs.

Malcolm Thomas, who had spent time on the Giants' and Jaguars' practice squads, was signed as a free agent. For fullbacks, the Browns traded with the 49ers on draft day to get Marc Edwards and picked Tarek Saleh from Carolina in the expansion draft.

Marion Motley *1946-53*

The Legacy of
Running
Backs

*A strong backfield has been a
Browns tradition for 50 years.
These four became Pro Football
Hall of Famers.*

Bobby Mitchell *1958-61*

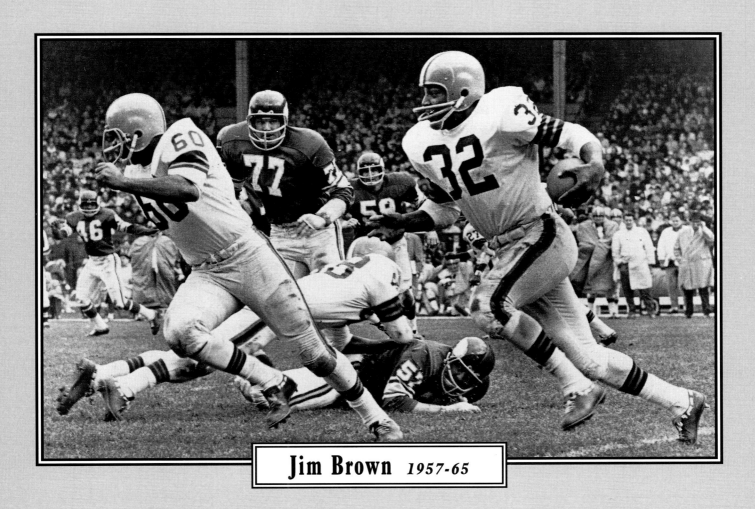

Jim Brown *1957-65*

Leroy Kelly *1964-73*

Frank Kuchirchuk

Before pass catchers were renamed "wide receivers" by the National Football League, Hall of Famer Dante "Glue Fingers" Lavelli was the Browns' right end and one of Otto Graham's dependable targets when the team went to 10 championship games from 1946-55. Lavelli's sidekicks were left end Mac Speedie, who led the league in receptions in 1952, and Dub Jones, a halfback with exceptional speed who often would go in motion.

When Graham was passing the ball from sideline to sideline and occasionally deep in the All-America Football Conference and the Browns' early days in the NFL, it was these three players who helped overwhelm defenses that at the time were mostly geared toward stopping the run. The era's six-man fronts and three-man secondaries often were of little resistance to Graham and his receivers.

Lavelli was the very best of the bunch. "My greatest strength was my hands," he said when characterizing the skills that made him a Pro Football Hall of Famer.

"My other strengths were deceptive moves and my quickness in the first 20 yards [of the route]. I also had great timing to go up in the air to catch the ball between defenders."

The hands—with those glue fingers—are what forever make "Lavelli" a legendary name in Cleveland Browns history.

"[Lavelli] has the strongest hands I've ever seen," said Paul Brown in a 1949 *SPORT* magazine article. "When he goes up for a pass and a defender goes up with him, you can be sure Dante will have the ball when they come down. Nobody can ever take the ball away from him once he gets his hands on it."

Glue fingers and a strong will helped Dante Lavelli make critical catches.

Later in Brown's autobiography, *PB: The Paul Brown Story*, he described Lavelli's hands as having "an almost liquid softness which seemed to slurp the ball into them."

Lavelli stuck with the Browns for 11 seasons (1946-56), never losing his starting right end position—a mark of longevity and consistency seldom seen then, and not likely to be seen in the NFL's current era of specialization and free agency.

"I was always in condition," he explained. "I played basketball in the winter and softball in the summer. I could just run perpetually and never get tired."

Lavelli feels his greatest contribution to the Browns' innovative pass offense was developing the "sideline pass down and out."

Receivers

"When I came back from overseas [after World War II], I saw the Washington Redskins play the Giants in New York. The Redskins had a little halfback named Steve Bagarus who would flank out, run downfield, stop and turn right angles to the sideline. We started using it to get eight or 10 yards. We called it a Z-in and Z-out. We would stay after practice and get it perfected to where Otto could tell by my shoulder pads which way I was going to go."

Throughout Lavelli's career, the Browns remained consistently confident in their passing attack. Speedie was replaced by Pete Brewster and Jones was succeeded by Ray Renfro, but it made little difference. "We felt that as long as we had a quarterback like Otto, even if we were 10 or 14 points behind, we could always catch 'em by throwing the ball," Lavelli said.

"Glue Fingers"
Dante Lavelli
RE • 1946-56

Graham also feels the same way about Lavelli. "If I had to throw to get a first down and I had to pick any receiver in history, it would be Dante," Graham said. "He wasn't the fastest or the quickest, but he had the best hands the game has ever seen. And he had such tremendous desire to go up and get the ball. He'd go up biting, scratching, doing anything to get the football.

"Many times in my career, I'd be roaming around back there and hear that voice, 'Otts! Otts! Otts! Otts!' and I'd turn and throw the ball at his voice," Graham added.

Lavelli was nicknamed "Glue Fingers" by Browns radio voice Bob Neal one summer during training camp at Bowling Green State Uni-

versity. The name stuck. "One year, I had 40 passes thrown to me and I caught every one of them," Lavelli said. "And in my career, I think I fumbled once. Some guy hit me in the back of the head and about knocked me out."

Paul Brown had known of Lavelli's ability to catch the football long before "Glue Fingers" became popular. "I was a freshman at Ohio State in 1941 and I was playing halfback on the freshman team," Lavelli recalled. "One day, we were playing a pickup game before school started and I was catching everything in sight. Paul was on the sideline watching quietly. He moved me to wide receiver from that day on."

Lavelli ended up playing only three games for Ohio State. He was injured as a sophomore in the Southern Cal game, and by the time he recovered, he was fighting in World War II. Lavelli's time in the Army found him involved in some of the war's fiercest battles in France, Belgium and Germany.

"There was a lot of heavy fighting," Lavelli said. "You never really talked about it, but you didn't really realize how lucky you were to be alive until you got home. And I was very, very lucky. My squad, there were 12 of us, is the only one that survived from my platoon."

Lavelli also remembers some of the few lighter moments he enjoyed in the Army: "We were in England waiting to go across the Channel," Lavelli said. "We were playing football with an aluminum canteen. You'd put the cover on the canteen and throw it like a football."

When the war ended, Lavelli knew he could play pro football. His first love was baseball, but when he saw a former Ohio State third-string receiver named Sam Fox playing for the Giants, Lavelli knew football was his best bet.

Brown was forming the Browns in the AAFC and he remembered Lavelli from Ohio State. Lavelli, however, was the least experienced of the five players trying out for the right end job. One was a tested professional, former Chicago Cardinal Alton Coppage. Two were ex-college stars who were standouts on the service teams. The fourth was John Yonakor, a "can't miss" 6-5, 225-pounder from Notre Dame.

Although Coppage was the starter in the 1946 season opener against Miami, Lavelli later took over, caught one touchdown pass and never looked back until retiring in 1956. Yonakor, meanwhile, became a productive defensive end through 1949. Coppage moved on to the AAFC's Buffalo Bills.

Lavelli led the AAFC in receiving in 1946 and caught the game-winning touchdown pass in the Browns' 14-9 championship game win over the New York Yankees. In 1950, the year the Browns won the championship in their first NFL season, Lavelli caught 11 passes and two TDs in the title-game victory over the Rams.

In 1955, the year the Browns beat the Rams, 38-14, for the championship in Otto Graham's final performance, Lavelli caught three passes for 95 yards and a touchdown.

Lavelli played just one season longer than Graham, although he would have played more under different cirmcumstances. Only 20 of his 386 career receptions were thrown by someone other than Graham.

At age 34, Lavelli reluctantly retired prior to the 1957 season. "We weren't getting any new quarterbacks who could throw the ball," he said. "Then Jim Brown came in and we went to the running game. I wanted to switch to defensive back, but Paul Brown wouldn't let me. So I decided to retire."

No doubt the huddle became quieter.

"Lavelli was a loud mouth in the huddle," said Lin Houston, the late former Browns right guard. "He'd yell 'Otto, Otto, Otto, Otto, Otto! Give me the ball, give me the ball, give me the ball.' Otto would find a way, but it might not be that play. And Lavelli would keep on yelling."

Never liking to stick with the basic program, Lavelli would often break his pass routes when he saw an opportunity. In a game against the Eagles in 1954, he grabbed a goalpost on the final play, swung around, ran the opposite direction and caught a pass for the game winning touchdown. The final score: 6-0.

In those days, receivers needed many more tricks in their bag. It wasn't until 1978 that the National Football League restricted the con-

tact between the receiver and defender five yards beyond the line of scrimmage.

"When I played, they could tackle you at the line of scrimmage," Lavelli said. "That's how the flanker came about. We used to line up close to the linemen, but they would tackle you at the line. That's when receivers were moved out so that there was more room to operate. Today, you can't even blow on a receiver. He gets to do whatever he wants."

Elected in 1975, Lavelli was the only receiver from the Otto Graham era to become a Hall of Famer. But he certainly was not Graham's only weapon during those early days.

Mac Speedie, a 6-3, 205-pounder, lined up on the left side opposite Lavelli. And while

Mac Speedie
LE • 1946-52

DUB'S BIG DAY: With Marion Motley blocking, Dub Jones scores the first of his six touchdowns versus the Chicago Bears in a 42-21 win at Cleveland Stadium on Nov. 25, 1951. In NFL history, only Chicago Cardinal Ernie Nevers (1929) and the Bears' Gale Sayers (1965) have equaled Jones' performance.

Lavelli possessed speed and those glue fingers, Speedie was known for deceptive moves, this despite a childhood disease that affected his left hip joint and caused his left leg to be an inch shorter and two inches less in diameter than his right. Yet Speedie became a track star at the University of Utah, setting conference records in the 220-yard low hurdles and 120-yard high hurdles.

Speedie played in Cleveland from 1946-52. He led the Browns in receptions with 42 in 1950 and again in '52 with a league-high 62. No Browns receiver has led the NFL in receiving before or since.

"Mac Speedie should be in the Hall of Fame with Lavelli," said former Browns defensive back Tommy James. "I covered the guy every day in practice. I never saw a better receiver than Mac Speedie."

Halfback Dub Jones was an equally dangerous receiver out of the Browns' backfield. The prototype of the "flanker," he often went in motion before the play started, causing problems because of his size (6-4, 205). The former Tulane football and track star was acquired from the AAFC's Brooklyn Dodgers after the 1947 season for the draft rights to Michigan All-America Bob Chappuis. Originally a defensive back, Brown switched Jones to offense where he remained through 1955.

Dub Jones HB-WR • 1948-55

Darrell "Pete" Brewster LE • 1952-58

Jones will forever be remembered for one of the greatest offensive performances in NFL history on Nov. 25, 1951, against the Chicago Bears at Cleveland Stadium. It is difficult to believe, considering all the offensive stars on the Browns in the early 1950s, that one man could score six touchdowns in one game. But Jones did it in the 42-21 victory.

It's also difficult to believe that entering the 1999 season, this NFL record has been equaled only once. Jones tied the standard set by the Chicago Cardinals' Ernie Nevers in 1929. Gale Sayers of the Bears did it in 1965.

Jones scored on runs of two, 12, 27 and 42 yards and on passes from Otto Graham of 34 and 43 yards. The Browns led 21-0 at one point and 42-7 before yielding the final two touchdowns of the game to the Bears.

The Browns were well prepared for Mac Speedie's exit to the Canadian Football League after the 1952 campaign. Purdue's Darrell "Pete" Brewster, who was a rookie in 1952 after being acquired in a post-draft trade with the Chicago Cardinals, took over in 1953 and held the position through 1958.

Brewster led the Browns in receiving from 1955-57. He caught one of Otto Graham's three touchdown passes in the 1954 championship victory over the Lions, but his best-ever performance occurred one season earlier—on Dec. 6, 1953, when his seven catches against the Giants netted 182 yards, fourth highest on the Browns' all-time single-game list, nine yards short of Ozzie Newsome's 191 against the Bears in 1984.

Ray Renfro *WR·1952-63*

Rich Kreitling WR • 1959-63

Likewise, the Browns were equally prepared for a successor to Jones. Ray Renfro, a fourth-round draft choice from North Texas State in 1952, started the '52 title game against Detroit when Jones was unable to play due to injury. By 1954, Renfro was firmly established in Jones' former flanker position, catching two touchdown passes in the '54 title game. He remained the starter through 1962.

Arguably the fastest halfback in the league early in his career, Renfro used his speed mainly as a punt returner as a rookie. The first time he touched the ball as a member of the Browns, he returned a punt 58 yards for a touchdown in a preseason game against the Packers.

Renfro, 6-1, 185 pounds, was a football and track star in college. He was a perennial 100- and 220-yard dash champion in the Gulf Coast Conference. His time of 9.5 seconds in the hundred-yard dash set a record at the North Texas State Relays.

In 1999, Renfro still ranks second on the Browns' all-time career receiving yardage list with 5,508 on 281 receptions (19.6 average). He also caught 50 touchdowns. He led the team in receptions once (1961).

Johnny Brewer TE-LB • 1961-67

Finding an able successor to Dante Lavelli was not quite as simple. Preston Carpenter took over in 1957 and led the team in receiving in '58, but after losing his job to Billy Howton in 1959, Carpenter was dealt to Pittsburgh in 1960. The deal brought Gern Nagler, who shared the position with Rich Kreitling in 1960. Nagler then became the full-time starter in 1961.

In 1962, the Browns introduced the "tight end" position to the receiving attack. Johnny Brewer and Leon Clarke filled the slot while Renfro and Kreitling became the outside receivers. In 1963, Gary Collins took over for Renfro while Kreitling remained.

The mid '60s and the dawning of the Blanton Collier era brought a new crop of receivers

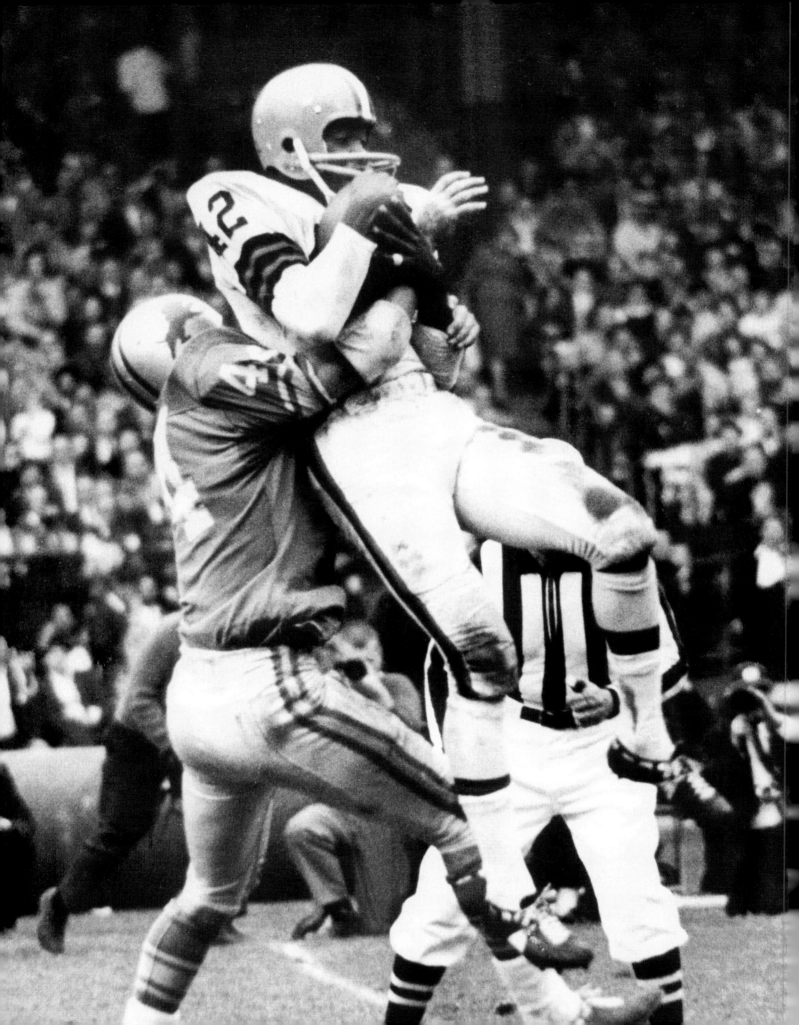

and another then-future Hall of Famer in Paul Warfield. One of the greatest pure athletes in the history of pro sports, the 6-foot, 188-pound Warfield was fast, smooth, precise in his routes, surehanded and an excellent blocker.

As a rookie on the 1964 NFL championship team, the former All-America halfback at Ohio State led the Browns with 52 receptions for 920 yards and nine touchdowns. He also led the Browns in 1968 with 50 catches and an NFL-high 12 touchdowns. His 1,067 yards receiving for a 21.3-yard average that season also marked the first time in Browns' history that a receiver topped the 1,000-yard mark.

Warfield was traded to Miami in 1970 in the deal that brought Purdue quarterback Mike Phipps to Cleveland. The Browns attempted to fill the void with Homer Jones, acquired from the New York Giants in the 1969-70 off season. But Jones was gone by 1971 and Fair Hooker became the primary starter through the early years of the decade.

Warfield returned to the Browns in the twilight of his career after helping lead the Dolphins to an unbeaten season in 1972 and back-to-back Super Bowl titles. He also played for Memphis in the World Football League before coming back to Cleveland in 1976-77.

Although he played for two run-oriented offenses in Cleveland and Miami, Warfield still caught 85 touchdown passes and averaged 20.1 yards per catch. The eight-time Pro Bowler had 427 receptions, but who knows how many he would have had if he had not gone to a Miami offense featuring a ground attack led by Larry Csonka and Jim Kiick. In Miami's 17-0 season of 1972, Warfield only caught 29 passes.

"In Super Bowl VII [a 14-7 win over Washington], we only threw the ball eleven times the whole game," Warfield said. "The next year, in Super Bowl VIII [a 24-7 victory over Minnesota], we threw it only seven times and completed six. I caught five passes in those two Super

Bowls, but it never bothered me. Winning was all that mattered back then."

Warfield always was a fantastic athlete. He set the Warren Harding (Ohio) High School record with a time of 9.7 seconds in the 100-yard dash. He long jumped 23 feet, nine inches and also set the state mark in the 180-yard low hurdles at 18.1. At Ohio State, he starred for three seasons at both halfback and defensive back. In track, he once leaped 26-2 and represented the United States in a meet against the Soviet Union.

While Warfield was flashy, 6-foot-4 Gary Collins was, as he likes to say, "the lunch pail guy who showed up and made all the crappy plays." Collins did, however, manage to lead the

Paul Warfield
WR • 1964-69, '76-77

> **Surehanded Paul Warfield leaps to pull down a pass against the Lions.**

Gary Collins
WR • 1962-71

Browns in receptions in 1963, 1965-66 and 1969. He was voted to the Pro Bowl after the 1965 and '66 seasons.

"If I were playing today, I'd make a lot of money as the guy who would come in on third down and catch the football," Collins said. "I wasn't fast and I ran OK pass routes. But there was one thing I could do better than 99.9 percent of the people out there, and that was catch the football."

Something Collins could also do was make the "post-pattern" play a memorable feature of the Browns' offense in the mid '60s. In the days when the goalposts still stood on the goal line, Collins would often break downfield and cut or "slant" behind the goalposts in time to catch a touchdown pass from quarterback Frank Ryan.

Through 1995, Collins ranked second on the Browns' all-time receptions list with 331. But even he realizes the three catches for which he will forever be remembered are the touchdown passes from Ryan in the Browns' 27-0 upset win over Baltimore in the 1964 NFL Championship game at Cleveland Stadium. Ryan and Collins hooked up for touchdowns of 18, 42 and 51 yards that afternoon.

"When I die, they'll say: 'Gary Collins, dead at whatever age.' And underneath, they'll say: 'Caught three touchdown passes in the 1964 championship game,'" Collins said. "I had a lot of great seasons after that game, and to tell you the truth, I wasn't that good in 1964. But at least I'll be remembered for something."

Collins also will be remembered as the guy who predicted the Browns' upset of the Colts

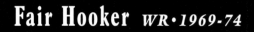

Fair Hooker *WR • 1969-74*

Milt Morin
TE • 1966-75

every day for two weeks leading up to the game. "I'd drive to work with some of my buddies like Dick Schafrath, and I'd say, 'You know what? I think we're going to kick those guys' butts,'" Collins laughed. "I told a guy from Channel 8, John Fitzgerald, the Thursday or Friday before the game the same thing. And I also said, 'Get me the ball, too.'"

Collins doesn't buy the argument that players from his generation couldn't play the game today because the athletes are bigger and stronger. "Somebody said to me recently that I couldn't play in today's game. I said wait a minute, this guy couldn't play in my game in the 1960s. When I played, defensive guys would hit you all the way down the field.

"It didn't matter if you had the sprinter's speed of Bob Hayes, the elusiveness of Paul Warfield or my strength, that gave you problems. That's why I think it's so unfair to compare different eras."

Milt Morin succeeded Johnny Brewer at tight end as Brewer closed out his career in 1966-67 as a linebacker. The Browns used their first-round choice to select the 6-4, 240-pounder from the University of Massachusetts. When healthy, Morin was a starting tight end for most of his 10-year career.

Entering 1999, Morin ranked eighth on the team's all-time receptions list with 271 catches for 4,208 yards. In 1968, his first injury-free season, Morin became one of the best tight ends in the NFL. Big and strong with soft hands and fine speed, Morin caught 43 passes for 792 yards (18.4) during what was the first of two Pro

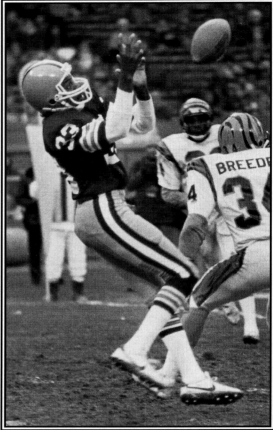

Reggie Rucker *WR•1975-81*

Dave Logan
WR•1976-83

Bowl seasons. He caught six passes for 133 yards in the win over the Washington Redskins that clinched the 1968 Century Division title.

After Morin retired in 1975, the Browns used Oscar Roan and Gary Parris as tight ends in 1976 and '77. Then came the 1978 college draft. Gary Collins' team reception record stood on firm ground until the day Sam Rutigliano said he had to have Alabama All-America wide receiver Ozzie Newsome as his next tight end. Rutigliano got his wish when the Browns made a trade and picked up a second first-round pick in the 1978 draft. In the best first round in team history, the Browns selected linebacker Clay Matthews as their first choice and Newsome as their second pick.

Years later, the Browns could say the 1970 Phipps-for-Warfield trade was not a complete failure. Phipps was dealt to Chicago for a draft choice that was later traded to the Rams as part of a deal that landed Cleveland the pick that ended up being Newsome.

Newsome was not thrilled about being converted to tight end. But little did he know at the time that he, Rutigliano and Brian Sipe would redefine the position in the 1980s. "Sam told me I could be a good receiver or a great tight end," Newsome said. "That sort of made my ears perk up a little bit."

In 1980, when Brian Sipe threw for a team-record 4,132 yards, Newsome was one of five players with 50 or more receptions: Mike Pruitt (63) Reggie Rucker (52), Dave Logan (51), Newsome (51) and Greg Pruitt (50).

Ozzie Newsome *TE•1978-90*

Reggie Langhorne *WR·1985-91*

Brian Brennan WR•1984-91

Webster Slaughter
WR•1986-91

Newsome led the Browns in receiving from 1981-85. Only once during that time did he have fewer than 62 catches. In 1981, he set the team single-season receptions record with 69 and then broke it with back-to-back 89-catch seasons in 1983-84. He also had two 1,000-yard seasons: 1,002 in 1981 and 1,001 in 1984.

As the Browns went from the Rutigliano era to Marty Schottenheimer and Newsome passed his prime, the passing game was turned back over to the wideouts. Newsome retired after the 1990 season with 662 receptions, the most by a tight end in NFL history. He was elected to the Pro Football Hall of Fame in 1999.

During the middle 1980s, the Browns drafted three receivers who would hook up with quarterback Bernie Kosar during the Browns' run of five straight trips to the playoffs.

In 1984, the Browns drafted Brian Brennan of Boston College in the fourth round. Brennan led the Browns in receptions in 1986 (55) and caught 315 passes from 1984-91, fourth on the all-time receptions list.

In 1985, Reggie Langhorne from Elizabeth City College was drafted in the seventh round. Though he never led the Browns in receptions, he became Kosar's favorite target on those hard-to-make, over-the-middle passes. After departing the Browns via Plan B free agency, Langhorne did lead the AFC in receptions as a member of the Colts in 1993.

Webster Slaughter, a second-round pick from San Diego State in 1986, was the flashiest of the three. "Web-Star," as he was called, led

Michael Jackson *WR•1991-95*

Derrick Alexander
WR•1994-95

the Browns in receiving from 1989-91. In '89, Slaughter had 65 catches for a team-record 1,236 yards and six TDs. On consecutive weeks in October that season, he caught eight passes for 186 yards against the Bears and four for 184 yards versus the Oilers, good for second and third place on the Browns' single-game yardage list behind Ozzie Newsome's 191 versus the Jets in 1984.

The Bears game, a 27-7 victory on Monday Night Football at Cleveland Stadium, featured the longest pass play in team history—a 97-yard touchdown reception from Bernie Kosar.

Contract problems in 1992 found Slaughter declared a free agent and he signed with Houston. In six seasons, he ranks sixth in both receptions (305) and yardage (4,834) on the Browns'

all-time receiving lists. The Browns of the Bill Belichick era were unable to find a receiver to match Slaughter's productivity, style and ability to excite a crowd. From 1992-95, in fact, the best receiving outputs were by running backs: Eric Metcalf's 63 catches in 1993 and Earnest Byner's 61 in '95.

Michael Jackson, a sixth-round draft choice in 1991 from Southern Mississippi, provided a deep threat, leading the team in receptions in 1992 with 47. Derrick Alexander, a first-round pick in 1994 from Michigan, became the first rookie to lead the Browns in receiving yardage since Paul Warfield in 1964. His 828 yards on 48 receptions ranked second behind Cincinnati's Darnay Scott (866 on 46 catches).

In 1999, Damon Gibson was the fourth player selected in the expansion draft. He repre-

Kevin Johnson *WR·1999*

sented perhaps better than anyone the Browns' strategy of youth and potential over proven veterans who might be past their primes. Gibson, 23, as a rookie for the Bengals, had 19 catches for 258 yards and three touchdowns, a 21.9 average on 17 kick returns and an 8.1 average on 27 punt returns, including a 65-yard TD.

The draft also brought wide receivers Justin Armour (Broncos) and Fred Brock (Cardinals).

In free agency came Leslie Shepherd, a five-year veteran, from Washington. Shepherd, who had a career-high 43 catches for 712 yards and eight touchdowns in 1998, had been the Redskins' touchdown leader in '98 with nine (one rushing) and was their No. 2 receiver.

In April's college draft, the Browns spent their second pick on speedy Kevin Johnson, an All-American from Syracuse (60 catches, 894

yards and nine touchdowns in 1998) and fifth-round pick on Darrin Chiaverini, who had caught 52 passes in a run-oriented offense at Colorado.

Free agent wide receivers signed were Jermaine Ross (a five-year veteran released by the Jaguars), five-year veteran Mark Seay, Ronnie Powell, Curtis Marsh, Sylvain Girard, Joseph Nastasi and Corey Bridges.

Irv Smith, a large (262 pounds) tight end with six years of experience, was acquired in a trade with the 49ers. Smith had had some good years with the Saints (86 receptions in 1994-95), but had lost his starting job with the Niners midway through 1998.

The only other veteran tight end acquired was Aaron Laing, a free agent from the Rams.

Strength in the offensive line has been a trademark of the Browns throughout their first 50 seasons. In the early days, Paul Brown's offensive strategies required quality linemen to protect Otto Graham or to open holes for Marion Motley. Later, Jim Brown and Leroy Kelly followed the lead of Gene Hickerson or John Wooten on many long runs. In the late '70s and early '80s, Doug Dieken, Tom DeLeone, Joe DeLamielleure and others gave Brian Sipe the protection to set Browns passing records during the Kardiac Kids era. Likewise,

in the mid 1980s, Mike Baab, Cody Risien and Dan Fike helped to keep Bernie Kosar in the pocket long enough to lead the Browns to three AFC Championship games.

When the 1999 Browns began building for the future, the offensive line received top priority. Guard Jim Pyne was the first pick in the

Jones (1991-95) had anchored the starting left tackle position for longer than two seasons.

In 1971, Dieken was 22 years old and now admits he "didn't have a clue" when it came to playing left tackle in the NFL. Listed at 6-5, 236 as a University of Illinois tight end, Dieken gained 18 pounds between his senior season and the opening of the '71 campaign. Drafted by the Browns with the intention of converting him to tackle, the reality of the switch first hit home when a team equipment manager handed

Offensive Linemen

him a jersey with the number 73 on it. "I knew right then I was doomed," Dieken recalled.

He was working his way into the lineup ahead of 34-year-old Dick Schafrath when the Browns hosted Atlanta on Halloween, 1971. It turned out to be a rather frightening experience because the Falcons' outstanding pass rush was coming to Cleveland Stadium. "I remember looking up and seeing [defensive end] Claude Humphrey, in his prime," Dieken said. "At that point, I'm thinking to myself, 'Oh my God, what have I gotten myself into?'"

The Browns were crushed that day, 31-14, in Dieken's seventh game as a pro. Dieken did, however, survive to play in a team-record 203 consecutive games during a 14-year career.

It was fitting that the person who brought Dieken and the Browns together was Groza.

expansion draft and tackles Orlando Brown and Lomas Brown, plus center Dave Wohlabaugh were early free agent signings.

Two Browns linemen are Pro Football Hall of Famers: center Frank "Gunner" Gatski and right tackle Mike McCormack. Another, left tackle Lou Groza, is likewise enshrined, but primarily as a place-kicker.

Groza, however, is the beginning link to the longest legacy in Browns offensive line history. Through the first 50 seasons, only Groza (1948-59), Dick Schafrath (1960-71), Doug Dieken (1971-84), Paul Farren (1985-90) and Tony

"Gunner"
Frank Gatski
C · 1946-56

Abe Gibron *G · 1950-56*

In the AAFC, Jim Daniell and Ernie Blandin handled the left tackle spot in the first two seasons. Groza moved in during the 1948 campaign and played the position until 1959. Signed by Paul Brown because of his talents as a place-kicker, Lou "The Toe" Groza proved he was a pretty dominating tackle as well, protecting Otto Graham's blind side during the dynasty years.

Scouts weren't exactly beating a path to Dieken's door, but Groza showed up and liked what he saw. He was working as a part-time scout for the Browns and a part-time insurance salesman. "I didn't come back and guarantee he could be the next left tackle for the Browns," Groza said. "I just said I think he could be a good blocker with capabilities to play that position. Doug was a tight end at the time, and he might get mad at me, but I think what hindered him there was his speed."

Dieken was selected in the sixth round with a pick the Browns received from the Chicago Bears for wide receiver Eppie Barney. So thanks to Groza, the Browns extended their legacy at the left tackle position into what would become a fifth decade as Dieken's career continued until his retirement following the 1984 season.

In 1960, Groza's back problems forced him into a one-year retirement. When he returned in 1961 as a place-kicker only, Dick Schafrath was in his second full season as the starting left tackle. Groza said he saw a lot of himself in Schafrath, a fellow former Ohio State Buckeye.

"Dick was a very intense player who really hustled," Groza said. "There wasn't much difference between us. I just got old quicker."

The left tackle position remained in capable hands in 1995. Tony Jones, a 1988 free agent from Western Carolina University, was the only player to start every game at one position since Bill Belichick was hired as head coach in 1991.

Lin Houston G • 1946-53

Lou Rymkus T • 1946-51

Groza, Dieken and Schafrath—"The Big Three" as Schafrath refers to them—smiled when they looked at Jones. He is the new-breed of tackle at 6-foot-5, 300 pounds.

"In my era, the line coach wanted guys with long arms, and he didn't want anybody who weighed over 260 pounds," said Dieken, whose playing weight remained in the 250-255-pound range. "If you were over 260 pounds, you were fined. Now in the 1990s, if you aren't 290, you're on a Greyhound bus out of town."

Groza's playing weight was listed at 250, but he says he played a number of games at 235. Of course, as Groza points out, 235 pounds made for a rather large person in the '40s and '50s.

"It was important back when I played that the tackles and the offensive linemen could run," Groza said. "So much of the game was based on speed in those days. We had to pull out and lead sweeps, or you had to release from the weak side and get downfield in front of plays to the other side of the field."

The late Lin Houston, the Browns' right guard from 1946-53, said coaches didn't have to break down the running drills into groups for the linemen and skill players back when he played. "Our guards were faster than the backs in those days," explained Houston, who Paul Brown used to call the fastest guard he ever coached. "Bill Willis and I played right guard on offense and middle guard on defense in the early days, and we'd always beat the backs. Paul wanted size and speed in his linemen, but if he had to choose one over the other, he took the speed."

As late as 1971, the NFL placed a greater emphasis on speed at the tackle positions. "My rookie year, I was covering kickoffs and punts," Dieken said. "Today, you basically have your 11 hired guns to handle the special teams."

Size, however, became more of an important commodity for NFL offensive linemen

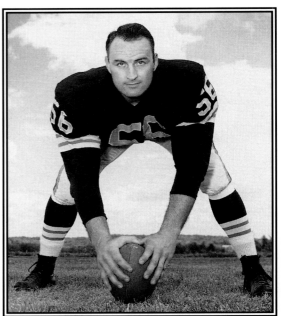

when the NFL's defensive players began to get bigger, faster and more specialized during the 1970s. "I remember a scout by the name of Mike Nixon talking to us down at the Senior Bowl," Dieken said. "They were weighing us and measuring us, and I'll never forget him telling me to stand up straight because that extra inch probably would be worth an extra $1,000 dollars. Today, that extra inch is probably worth $100,000, if not more."

Midway through Dieken's career, he began to experience the dawning of a new era for NFL defenses. "Because the passing picked up throughout the league, the defensive coaches wanted to increase the speed coming off the quarterback's blind side," Dieken said. "They

started widening the ends, and it got to be a footrace to see whether they could get to the quarterback before the offensive tackles could get out there to get a piece of the guy."

That's one reason left tackle became more of a glamourous position in the 1990s. When free agency was unveiled in '93, left tackles became millionaires because of the difficulty of playing the position and the importance of protecting the blind side of the era's high-profile, highly-paid quarterbacks. Jones earned $2 million in 1994 and was not the highest-paid left tackle in the league. "Today, I read in the papers where they give special recognition to the left tackle," Groza said. "We never got that. No one even looked at us unless we got called for holding."

When the defenses got bigger and faster in the 1970s, the league began loosening the rules for offensive linemen out of safety for the quarterback and the desire to keep scoring high. By the mid 1980s, offensive linemen not only were allowed to extend their arms, but they were also allowed to open their hands and push the defensive player. "Around 1986, they pretty much made it sumo wrestling," Dieken said.

Mike McCormack *T · 1954-62*

Gene Hickerson
G · 1958-60, '62-73

John DeMarie G-T · 1967-75

"I see guys today put both hands on a defensive player, grab him and fall down, and they don't call it," Houston said. "In my day, you had to knock the guy out of the way using your shoulders. If we even put one hand on the guy, it was a 15-yard penalty."

The best offensive line in Browns history might have been the one in the late 1950s and early-to-mid 1960s. In 1965, Jim Brown's final season, Cleveland led the NFL in team rushing with 2,331 yards. Then, in the first two years following the retirement of arguably the best running back in NFL history, the Browns still led the NFL in rushing with 2,166 yards in 1966 and 2,139 in 1967. Thirty years after his retirement, Brown still wondered why not one of the key linemen who blocked for the three Cleveland Hall-of-Fame running backs of that

era—Brown (1957-65), Bobby Mitchell (1958-61) and Leroy Kelly (1964-73)—is not also in the Pro Football Hall of Fame.

"How in the world can you have three Hall-of-Fame runners and not have anybody in from the line?" Brown asked. "Two runners who started together. Two runners who played back-to-back. You got to go directly to the commonality those players had."

Left guard John Wooten, right guard Gene Hickerson, left tackle Dick Schafrath and center John Morrow all started in front of Brown, Mitchell and Kelly. Together, they appeared in 16 Pro Bowls, led by Schafrath and Hickerson with six apiece. "We had the best downfield blocking in history," Brown said. "As I look at the game, there's no doubt in my mind I'd take Hickerson and Schafrath right now for my all-time team."

Hickerson, 6-3, 250 pounds, was a seventh-round "future" pick in 1957 from Ole Miss. He joined the Browns in 1958 as a messenger guard in Paul Brown's offense, a spot he held through 1962—the rest of Brown's tenure—although he missed the 1961 season with a broken leg.

Fred Hoaglin C·1966-72

Hickerson's notoriety came from leading the sweep around end. Following the 1965-70 seasons, he was voted to the Pro Bowl each time. When the NFL announced its 50th anniversary all-time team in 1994, Hickerson was named to the All-Sixties squad. His longevity is another testimonial to his greatness. Hickerson's 15 seasons in Cleveland is third behind Lou Groza's 21 and Clay Matthews' 16. He played in 202 games, fourth on the all-time list, including 165 straight from 1962-73.

Longevity was a factor for all the aforementioned blockers for Brown, Mitchell and Kelly. Each had pro careers in double figures. In addition to Hickerson's 15, there is Schafrath's 13, Wooten's 10 (nine in Cleveland) and Morrow's 10 (seven in Cleveland).

Schafrath was drafted in the second round from Ohio State in 1959. The Browns originally intended to use him as a defensive end, but when Groza was lost for the 1960 season with his back injury, Schafrath moved in at left tackle and remained there through 1971.

In 1999, Schafrath is best known as an Ohio state senator, an office he has held since 1985.

John Wooten G·1959-67

Wooten, a fifth-round draft choice in 1959 from Colorado, began as a right guard, then succeeded Jim Ray Smith on the left in '63 after Smith was traded to Dallas for right tackle Monte Clark.

Morrow was acquired from the Rams in a 1960 trade for the Browns' center, Art Hunter, and started until his career ended with a broken leg suffered midway through the 1966 season. When Fred Hoaglin, a sixth-round choice in '66, took over for Morrow, it was the beginning of an ongoing rebuilding process for the aging offensive line over several seasons.

John DeMarie, a sixth-round choice in 1967, succeeded Wooten at left guard in '68. Joe Taffoni replaced Clark in 1970. Dieken took over for Schafrath in 1971. DeMarie later moved to right guard when Hickerson moved to the left for his final two seasons of 1972-73.

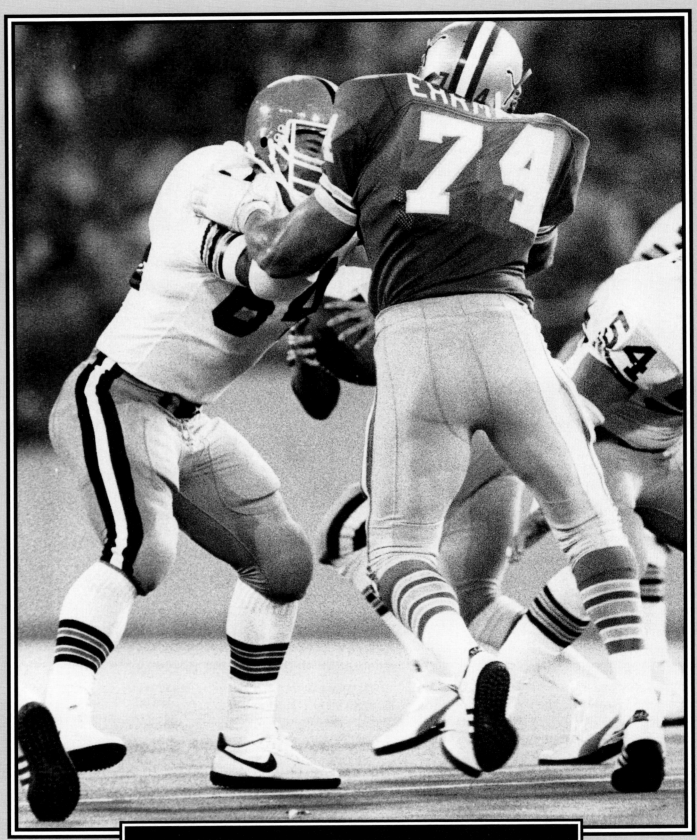

Joe DeLamielleure *G·1980-84*

Tom DeLeone C·1974-84

Robert E. Jackson G·1975-85

Regarding pass blocking, the 1980 Kardiac Kids would be difficult to top. It didn't set the team record for fewest sacks, but it did allow only 23 in 554 attempts. The only time the Browns ever attempted more passes was a year later when they threw the ball 567 times.

"When we had Brian Sipe, we were definitely in an era where we used the pass to set up the run," Dieken recalled. "You basically wanted offensive linemen who could keep the defense at arm's length from Brian. Now, it's more of a smash-mouth approach in football."

Playing with Dieken on that 1980 offensive line was Cody Risien at right tackle, Joe DeLamielleure at right guard, Tom DeLeone at center and Henry Sheppard at left guard. Except for DeLamielleure, who was picked up that season from the Buffalo Bills, the line had been together a few years.

Robert E. Jackson, who had gone to Duke University as a quarterback and converted to a guard, had been the starting right guard before DeLamielleure. Jackson moved back into the lineup in 1981 as a left guard and held the position through 1984.

Risien, had one of the better careers for a right tackle in Cleveland history. A seventh-round draft choice from Texas A&M, he played left guard as a rookie in 1979, then became the starting right tackle from 1980-83 and 1985-89. He missed the 1984 season with a knee injury.

Lou Rymkus (1946-51) and Monte Clark (1963-69) also were standouts at right tackle. Rymkus and Groza teamed up from 1948-51, dubbing themselves "Lou the Heel" and "Lou the Toe." The best right tackle of all, however, was Mike McCormack (1954-62). After one season on defense as Bill Willis' successor at middle guard, he played the balance of his career at right tackle, making the Pro Bowl five times. He was elected to the Hall of Fame in 1984.

Dan Fike *G-T • 1985-92*

Cody Risien
T • 1979-83, '85-89

Frank Gatski was an original member of the Browns in 1946 who became a starter at center in 1948 and held the position through 1956. He was a quiet man who never missed a game or a practice in 20 years of high school, college and pro ball. At 6-3, 240 pounds, Gatski was one of the strongest players on the team—and one of the toughest, having worked as a coal miner in West Virginia before going to Marshall to play college football.

After Gatski was traded to the Lions in 1957 for a third-round choice, Art Hunter, a pickup in 1955 from Green Bay, took over and held the position through 1959. Hunter was picked for the Pro Bowl in his final season before being dealt to the Rams for John Morrow.

The Browns have remained solid at center since Fred Hoaglin succeeded Morrow in 1966. Since then, the primary starters have been Bob DeMarco from 1972-74; Tom DeLeone from 1975-82; Mike Baab from 1983-87 and 1990-91; and Steve Everitt from 1993-95.

At right guard, Lin Houston (1946-53) and Dan Fike (1985-92) are names of distinction along with Hickerson. Houston, brother of ex-Browns linebacker Jim Houston, shared duties with Bill Willis through part of his career. Fike, a free agent who succeeded Joe DeLamielleure in 1985, provided quality and consistency until losing parts of 1989 and '90 with a major knee injury. He later started at right tackle.

At left guard, Abe Gibron (1950-56) and Jim Ray Smith (1956-62) were Pro Bowlers four and five times, respectively.

Dave Wohlabaugh C·1999

Orlando Brown T·1994-95, '99

Selecting Jim Pyne as the first choice of the 1999 expansion draft was a surprise to almost no one. He was still young, 27, and had started 54 games over the past four seasons. And he could play guard or center, having done both with the Lions and Buccaneers.

The Browns addressed the offensive line early and often. The No. 3 pick in the expansion draft was massive (6-9, 330 pounds) Scott Rehberg of the Patriots. Their fifth choice was center Steve Gordon of the 49ers. A week later they landed free agent Dave Wohlabaugh, who had been the Patriots' starting center since his rookie year of 1995.

After the Wohlabaugh signing, the Browns filled the tackle slots with a pair of "Browns": Orlando and Lomas. Orlando Brown came as a free agent from Baltimore. He had played for the Browns from 1994-95, and had started at right tackle for 69 consecutive games from 1994-98. Lomas Brown signed as an unrestricted free agent in March. He was a 14-year veteran who had failed to start in only one of 210 games with the Lions and Cardinals. Brown had played in six straight Pro Bowls from 1990-95.

With Pyne at left guard, Wohlabaugh at center and the two Browns at tackle, the only question for head coach Chris Palmer entering 1999 was who would win the right guard spot. The candidates were Rehberg, Orlando Bobo, a 6-3, 299-pound three-year veteran expansion choice from Minnesota, and Steve Zahursky, a 6-6, 305-pounder from Kent State who spent part of 1998 on Philadelphia's practice squad.

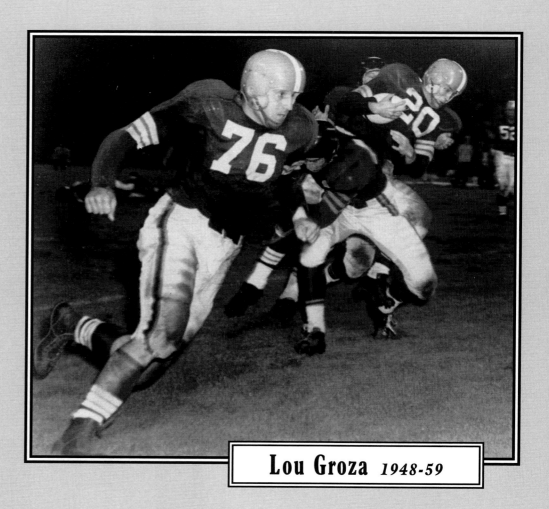

Lou Groza *1948-59*

The Left Tackle *Legacy*

Five players have been primarily in charge of this key quarterback-protection position. Beside their names are the years they started at left tackle.

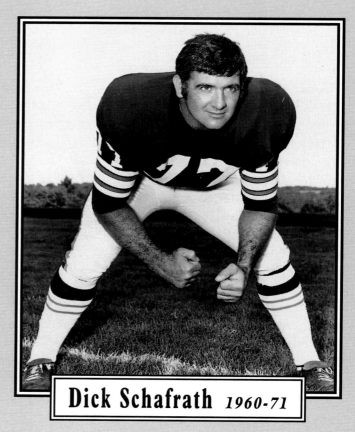

Dick Schafrath *1960-71*

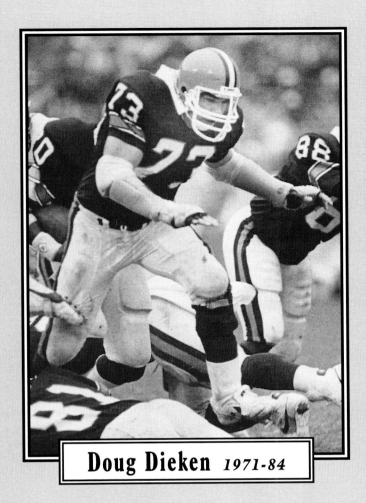

Doug Dieken *1971-84*

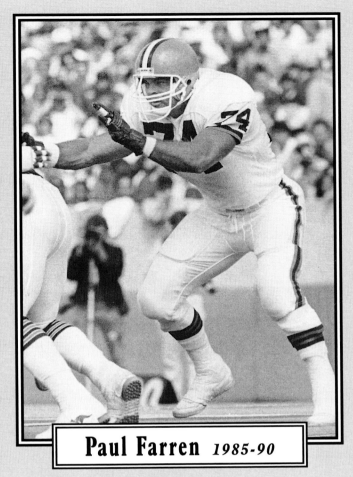

Paul Farren *1985-90*

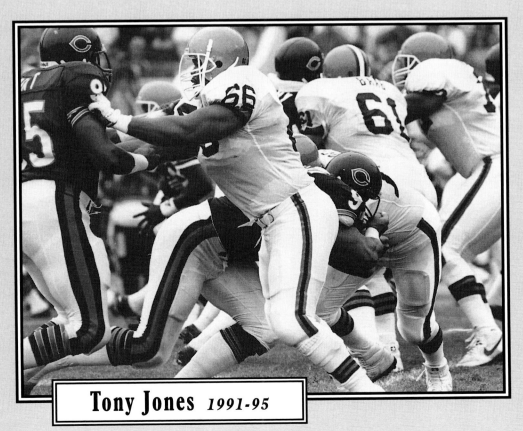

Tony Jones *1991-95*

The long history of Cleveland's fabled football franchise is one of names steeped in tradition, nostalgia and on-field excellence, including 14 Pro Football Hall of Famers. Except for Paul Brown, Bill Willis and Len Ford, the other immortals are linked to the offense. However, regardless of being outnumbered, the Browns' defenders, no matter the era, have been a vital part of the team's outstanding success over 50 years. Ford and Willis both played on the defensive line, Ford at end and Willis at middle guard. Willis would often drop back behind the line to take advantage of his speed and agility, enabling him to "go to the play" and thus creating a prototype of today's middle linebacker position.

"Dee-Fense" isn't new or unusual in Cleveland. The earliest Browns team knew that "the best offense is a good defense." Paul Brown went looking for skilled football players to start his team and many were great defenders. One of the early defenders was Tommy James, a halfback who played for Brown at Massillon and Ohio State. James, skilled as a two-way performer, played defensive halfback in Cleveland over eight seasons (1948-55).

Said James: "Everyone was playing a seven-diamond in those days—seven defensive linemen, just a middle linebacker, two defensive halfbacks, and only a single safety. Eventually, we got to a 6-2-2-1 and a 5-3-2-1. At about the time my career was winding down, the 4-3 was firmly established."

When the Browns took to the field in 1946, their lineup was one that wouldn't necessarily strike fear in the hearts of their opposition, at least not from a size perspective in comparison to today's behemoths. However, the defense's skill level was as good or better than anything its opponents could field.

> **Defensive end Bill Glass charges a scrambling Fran Tarkenton of the Vikings in the mid 1960s.**

The defensive ends were George Young of Georgia (6-3, 210), and John Yonakor of Notre Dame (6-5, 218). Tackles were Ernie Blandin of Tulane (6-3, 245), Chet Adams of Ohio U. (6-4, 228) and Lou Rymkus of Notre Dame (6-4, 230). The defensive guards were Eddie Ulinski of Marshall (5-11, 200) and Lin Houston of Ohio State (6-0, 205). Bill Willis of Ohio State (6-2, 206) was the middle guard who played nose to nose with the offensive center.

Defensive Linemen

James further discussed tactics: "Our ends in the seven-diamond played somewhat like linebackers in that they were wide, outside of the offensive ends, and had to protect against short passes. Also, you should know that even with a lot of platooning we had to know both offensive and defensive plays. We had to be ready to play on either side of the ball."

This explains why Yonakor caught seven passes (two for TDs). Why Young caught three passes. Why Otto Graham had five interceptions in 1946. Why halfback Tommy Colella ran the ball 30 times and had 10 interceptions in the Browns' first season of play.

With further specialization, the seven-diamond quickly gave way to a five-man line, with Willis still in the middle. Willis' main attribute was his cat-like quickness. His reflexes were so quick that he often shot between a center's legs

Bill Willis
MG • 1946-53

and grabbed a very surprised and bewildered quarterback before he could pull away with the snap from center.

Early Browns press books stated this advice: "Photographers need to set their shutter speed at 1/600th of a second to stop the action on Willis."

Because there is no such thing as a defensive guard in the NFL today, (even the nose tackle in the 3-4 doesn't quite fit the description), Willis is sometimes listed and thought of as a linebacker. True, he often played behind the line as defensive sets changed. But anyone who played against him, or saw him play very much, remembers him more as a middle guard, playing squarely on the nose of the opposing team's center.

Offensive centers remember Willis as well as, if not better than, the many ball carriers he tracked down over the years. Hall-of-Fame center Clyde "Bulldog" Turner of the Bears once said, "The first guy to convince me that I could not handle anybody I ever met was Bill Willis. He was skinny and didn't look like he should be playing middle guard, but he would jump right over you. The only way I could block him was to remain low in a squat after I snapped the ball, and when he tried to jump over me, I'd come up and catch him. That Willis was a warhorse, I'll tell you that."

Mike "Mo" Scarry, a center on the Browns and later a longtime assistant for Don Shula in Miami, may have been the first pro to witness Willis' speed and quickness firsthand. Scarry had played with the Cleveland Rams in 1944 and 1945, but elected to jump to the AAFC Browns in 1946 rather than go with the Rams to Los Angeles. He, too, was known for his quickness and was reputed to have "the fastest hands in football."

In Willis' first preseason scrimmage, he played head up on Scarry. This was kind of a tryout in that Willis wasn't yet under contract. On four successive plays, Willis blew by, over, or through Scarry and tackled Graham before the play could start. Finally, an unbelieving Scarry yelled, "Hey, check the offsides. Check this guy for offsides!"

Paul Brown had Blanton Collier, then an assistant, check. Everything was legal. Willis, who had made All-America as a tackle for the Buckeyes, was just too quick. Willis later told author Myron Cope in his book, *The Game That Was,* "What I had been doing, you see, was concentrating on the ball. The split second the ball moved, or Scarry's hand tightened, I charged. And I charged in a different way every time. I would go under him, then over him. I would bang off his left shoulder, then bang off his right shoulder. I caught Graham every time, usually before he had even begun to pull away from center."

After the practice, which P.B. called off early, Willis was summoned by the head coach. "Paul

offered me a four-thousand dollar contract." That's how the "color line" was broken in the AAFC. A few days later, Marion Motley also became a member of the Browns.

The first big change in the Browns' defensive line from a personnel standpoint was in 1950. When the Browns were folded into the NFL that year, several key players came from the defunct AAFC teams. None bigger, literally as well as figuratively, than 6-5, 260-pound Len Ford. Brown was familiar with Ford from his days at the University of Michigan. A fine two-way end with the Los Angeles Dons in 1948 and '49, Ford caught 31 passes in 1948 for 598 yards and seven touchdowns. The following year he gathered 36 for 577 yards.

Brown viewed Ford in a different light. He would be used exclusively as a defensive end. A native of Washington, D.C., he never saw a down of offense with the Browns, but did he play defense! He was inducted into the Hall of Fame in 1976 four years after his death at age 46 in 1972.

Len Ford
DE • 1950-57

Ford's ability allowed the Browns to adjust their defense at the time. Stationing linebackers behind the defensive ends, Ford could move even closer to the football, "crash"—as the pass rush was called then, and apply pressure to the quarterback. He may well have been the prototype for the L.A. Rams' Deacon Jones a generation later in the 1960s. Ford's old AAFC coach Jimmy Phelan said, "Len can become the best all-around end in history—he has everything."

Ford epitomized Paul Brown's "you play like you practice" theory. Lou Groza, who often

Chubby Grigg *DT • 1948-51*

Derrell Palmer
DT • 1949-53

lined up opposite Ford in practice, said, "He was always 'hell-bent for leather' anytime he stepped on a football field." Especially, if the "leather" was in the hands of a passer. Ford, like the Bears' Doug Atkins later, often leap-frogged blocks to nail an unsuspecting and unlucky quarterback.

In his first season in Cleveland, still in the leather helmet era before face masks were common, Ford caught Chicago Cardinals fullback Pat Harder's well-placed and well-timed elbow directly in the face. The damage report: several missing teeth, two fractured cheekbones and a broken nose. Plastic surgery was needed and it looked unlikely that Ford would play again that 1950 season. However, a specially-constructed helmet with a protective device allowed him to

play in the championship game against the Los Angeles Rams. Ford's all-out play was a factor in the stunning 30-28 victory.

Title games seemed to bring out the best in Ford. In the 1954 championship, 56-10 over the Lions, Ford made two interceptions. More than just a one dimensional pass rusher, Ford was solid against the run. He also recovered 20 fumbles in his relatively short Browns career.

Paul Wiggin, a youngster in Ford's final years, summed up what most feel about Ford, "He was a man among men." Ford, not entirely boastful, often said, "There is no one in this league who can take me on alone."

Joining Ford in Cleveland for the 1950 season, via the defunct AAFC Buffalo Bills, was defensive tackle John Kissell of Boston College. Kissell, one of several from a New Eng-

John Kissell *DT • 1950-52,'54-56*

Don Colo
DT • 1953-58

land family to play pro ball, was familiar to Paul Brown for two years. Like Ford, he filled a specific need on the team. His 247-pound bulk presented a formidable obstacle for teams to overcome. Much like tackle Art Donovan later allowed end Gino Marchetti of the Colts to freelance more as a pass rusher, Kissell gave Ford greater latitude in his play.

Forrest "Chubby" Grigg, not to be confused with latter-day Browns head coach Forrest Gregg, joined in 1948 after playing with the 1946 Buffalo Bisons and 1947 Chicago Rockets (the "Bisons" became the "Bills" in '47). Grigg provided 280 pounds of roadblock at tackle on the side away from Ford and Kissell.

Don Colo, who came from the Colts in a quality-for-quantity trade in 1953 that also brought Mike McCormack, established himself at right tackle after one season on the left. Colo, from Brown University, was a hard-bitten World War II veteran who represented the evolving player. He stood 6-3 and weighed 260—more in keeping with today's dimensions and proving out Tommy James' theory that "about every three years the players seemed to get an inch or two taller and ten or twenty pounds heavier." Colo was a good "hand fighter." He had the bulk and technique to battle blockers at the line of scrimmage and then "slide" to the point of attack.

During the 1950s, the Browns were unusually well stocked with outstanding defensive linemen. Len Ford and Bill Willis, of course, became Hall of Famers while wearing brown and orange. Four others, however, had Hall-of-

LINE OF DISTINCTION: The defensive line of the Browns' 1955 NFL champions (left to right): E Len Ford, T Don Colo, MG Bob Gain, T John Kissell and E Carlton Massey.

Fame careers after leaving Cleveland. One can't help but speculate on how much better the Browns would have been if these outstanding linemen could have worked long-term into the team's defensive system.

Art Donovan, a rookie in 1950, was traded to the New York Yanks as Brown elected to retain the more experienced Chubby Grigg at tackle. Doug Atkins (1953-54), Henry Jordan (1957-58) and Willie Davis (1958-59) were all dealt at various times as Paul Brown felt he had a surplus of defensive line talent.

Atkins played 12 seasons with the Chicago Bears, including the 1963 NFL championship team, and three with the New Orleans Saints, while Jordan and Davis anchored Vince Lombardi's Green Bay Packers defense of the 1960s. Donovan became a key member of the Baltimore Colts' defense that helped win back-to-back NFL championships in 1958 and '59.

At about the same time Don Colo arrived, another longtime Browns defender also came to Cleveland. Bob Gain, a native of Akron, had been a consensus All-America tackle at Kentucky under the coaching-legend-in-the-making, Paul "Bear" Bryant.

As a rookie in 1952, Gain (6-3, 250) started at left tackle. He then left the team to fulfill a military obligation in 1953, but was back in uniform in 1954. This time he was a swingman at both middle guard and left tackle, backing up Kissell, Colo and McCormack.

Doug Atkins DE·1953-54

Bob Gain
MG-DT·1952,'54-64

McCormack, who served in the military in 1952 and 1953 after an All-America career at Kansas and an early NFL career with the New York Yanks, was a middle guard, replacing the recently-retired Willis. In his own way, McCormack was every bit the "handful" that Willis was. Perhaps not quite as quick, but at 6-4, 248, bulkier. McCormack was a strong force in the 5-3 defensive front.

Howard Brinker, a Browns assistant coach from 1952-73, said this of McCormack's abilities: "No one took liberties in the middle with Mike when we turned him loose on a pass rush. He just crushed the middle with Kissell and Ford coming from the outside."

McCormack recalled this time in NFL history: "The five-three was evolving into the four-three. About thirty percent of the time, we'd hit and back out. The rest of the time, you stayed in and played as a lineman."

According to Chuck Noll, a Browns teammate of McCormack for six seasons (1953-59) before moving on to his long coaching career, "McCormack was fast for his size. He could really get around in that five-three. He made the Hall of Fame as an offensive tackle, but he could have gotten there on defense. This was at a time when you tended to put your best players on offense. You wouldn't do that now."

Gain was one who could stand his ground while reading the play and moving along the line of scrimmage. As Noll said, "He and Colo could 'parallel' and read." Eventually, added to technique was the tactic of penetrating across the line first and then "reading and reacting."

The surrounding cast on the defensive line changed during Gain's career. He broke in playing beside left end George Young, a link to the

Paul Wiggin
DE • 1957-67

With Walter Johnson (71), stopping Steeler Don Shy.

team's origins in 1946. He finished next to Paul Wiggin, who retired in 1967. Gain was a five-time Pro Bowler.

Gain remained in the '60s, but new faces began to appear. The 4-3 was now in vogue and ends were primarily pass rushers. Wiggin joined Bill Glass to give the Browns solidarity at the ends when Glass came over from Detroit in 1962 for Milt Plum in a deal that also brought the Browns quarterback Jim Ninowski.

Through 1995, Glass still owned the Browns records for most quarterback sacks in a season (14.5 in 1965) and most consecutive games with a sack (seven in 1966). He was a member of four Pro Bowl teams from 1962-67.

Through most of the '60s, Glass held forth on the field, and from the pulpit off the field. The Baylor All-America was also an ordained Baptist minister, active in the Fellowship of Christian Athletes. In 1965, Glass wrote a book, *Get in the Game,* that showed how it was possible to excel in pro football's violent world while maintaining an abiding sense of God's presence in everyday life.

Wiggin also became a multi-year Pro Bowler (twice). In fact, Paul Brown said, "The three greatest defensive ends in my time with the Browns were John Yonakor, Len Ford and Paul Wiggin." Both Wiggin and Glass could rush the passer and stop the run. Joining them at tackle in the 1964 championship season were old pro Dick "Mo" Modzelewski, a battle-tested veteran from the New York Giants and second-year

man Jim Kanicki, a 270-pounder. The pair gave the Browns a solid middle in the middle '60s—very tough against the run.

Talking about his technique, Modzelewski once said: "If you just fired off the ball, the play could be a cross-block or trap, so you had to think what you were doing or you simply would have gotten beaten all the time."

Modzelewski retired following the 1966 season at age 35. He rejoined the Browns as defensive line coach in 1968 and remained on the staff until replacing the fired Forrest Gregg as interim head coach with one game remaining in the 1977 season. The Browns lost that game to Seattle and Modzelewski was not retained by new head coach Sam Rutigliano in 1978.

Kanicki, a starter through 1969, was sacrificed to the Giants as part of the maneuvering around the trade of Paul Warfield to Miami in 1970 for the draft choice used to pick quarterback Mike Phipps.

In hopes of a quick fix to replace Warfield, the Browns traded Kanicki, running back Ron Johnson and linebacker Wayne Meylan to New York for veteran wide receiver Homer Jones, one of the NFL's better deep threats. Jones, however, never got rolling in Cleveland, catching only 10 passes in 1970 while being used mostly on kick-off returns. Johnson, the Browns' No. 1 draft choice in 1969, became an All-Pro, gaining over 1,000 yards in two of his first three seasons in New York. Kanicki, meanwhile, became a two-year starter on the Giants' defensive line.

Bill Glass
DE • 1962-68

Flying in front of Steelers quarterback Bill Nelsen.

Jim Kanicki DT·1963-69

Walter Johnson
DT·1965-76

Sacking Redskins quarterback Sonny Jurgensen.

Also making his debut in the mid 1960s was defensive tackle Walter Johnson. A former fullback from Taft High School in Cincinnati, Johnson grew to become a 6-4, 270-pound offensive guard and defensive middle guard at Los Angeles State.

In his second season of 1966, Johnson supplanted Modzelewski at left tackle. By 1969, Johnson was the well-established partner for Kanicki in the middle. But in the NFL Championship game at Minnesota, Johnson nearly lost three fingers on his right hand in the 20-below wind chill at Metropolitan Stadium.

Johnson had jammed the fingers in practice and received a Novacain shot to dull the pain. It

also dulled his sensitivity to cold until the fingers began to ache near the end of the first quarter. The pain increased and following the 27-7 defeat and trip back to Cleveland, Johnson was taken to a hospital where, for the next 24 hours, the possibility existed that the fingers would require amputation. The fingers, however, were saved and so was Johnson's career.

After Kanicki's departure, Johnson teamed with Jerry Sherk to once again give the Browns one of the best tackle tandems in the league. A three-time Pro Bowl selection (1968-70), Johnson never missed a game in his 12-year Browns career, playing 168 straight. He joined the Bengals in 1977 for his final season.

Johnson, who lived in Cleveland following his retirement, died at age 56 on June 30, 1999, of a massive heart attack.

Dick Modzelewski DT·1964-66

Jerry Sherk *DT·1970-81*

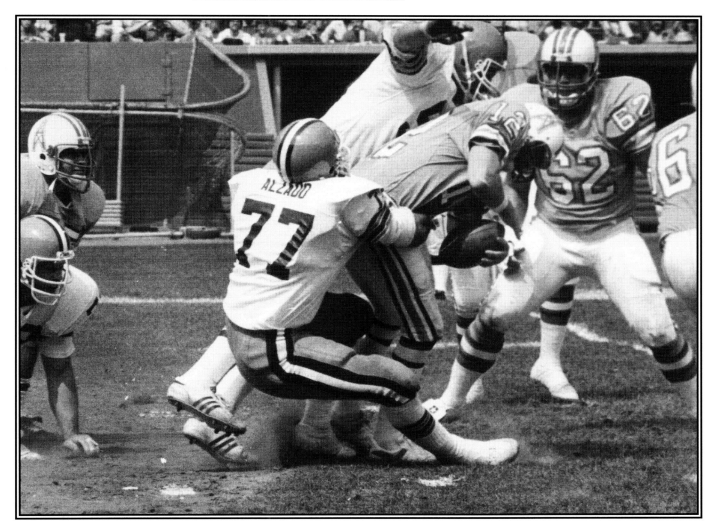

Jack Gregory would arrive at defensive end in the late '60s and play as well as anyone in the league. He made the Pro Bowl before being traded to the New York Giants in 1972. Gregory's forte was rushing the passer. His departure coincided with Jerry Sherk's arrival.

At 253, Sherk seemed light for a tackle, but he was active, quick and very tenacious. This last attribute won him the Mack Truck Bulldog Award as the AFC Defensive Player of the Year. During his prime in the mid '70s, Sherk was generally conceded to be "the game's best interior defensive lineman," if not the most decorated. In 1975, though, those who know (the NFL Players Association) voted him the best defender in the NFL.

Sherk's reputation outside of the Cleveland area suffered because a portion of his career was played in the middle-to-late 1970s when the Browns were only occasional contenders. His talents were often overlooked by the national media.

Lyle Alzado
DE•1979-81

Between Super Bowl flights with the Denver Broncos and Los Angeles Raiders, defensive end Lyle Alzado had a three-year layover in Cleveland, adding experience, fiery leadership and intensity to the defense of the "Kardiac Kids." Never one to underestimate himself, Alzado once said, "If me and King Kong went into an alley, only one of us would come out—and it wouldn't be the monkey."

When Alzado arrived in 1979, time and nagging knee injuries were taking a toll on Sherk. Then a staph infection suffered in Game 10 settled in a knee, nearly took his life and caused

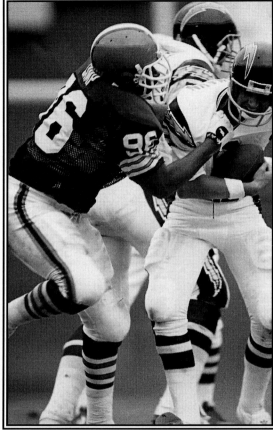

Reggie Camp *DE·1983-87*

Bob Golic
NT·1982-88

him to miss the rest of '79 and most of '80. He returned for one last try in 1981, but primarily as a backup in the new three-man front.

The most unselfish position in professional football is the nose tackle in a 3-4 defense. The position takes such a constant pounding that most teams use two or more players on a rotating basis. Using humor as an illustration, someone once said "being a nose tackle in a three-four is like being left to guard the camp during a rhinoceros stampede."

The dubious honor of handling the position alone first belonged to Henry Bradley, a compact 260-pounder from Alcorn State. By 1982 Bradley had begun sharing the job with Cleveland native Bob Golic.

One of the true characters of the NFL who would blossom into a full-blown celebrity later as a Raider, Golic took over the nose position in 1983 and held it through 1988. In 1989, the Browns went back to a 4-3.

Golic came into the NFL in 1979 with the Patriots as a 240-pound linebacker out of Notre Dame. The Patriots waived him in 1982 and he was claimed by the Browns. At the peak of his career, Golic weighed 265. His best year was 1986. He was selected to the Pro Bowl squad, but a broken arm kept him from playing. He was also elected after the '85 and '87 seasons.

A wrestler at Cleveland's St. Joseph's High School and at Notre Dame, Golic sometimes used grappling techniques to neutralize opposing centers and guards. Always quick with one-liners, Golic said of the demanding position he

Carl Hairston DE·1984-89

Michael Dean Perry DT·1988-94

played, "To play nose tackle you have to be either unemployed or crazy. So, I guess I was half qualified." He also said, "Contrary to popular belief, if I'd ever win the Ohio state lottery, I'd keep playing—until I got yelled at the first time. Then I'd buy the team and fire the coach who yelled at me."

Perhaps teammate Doug Dieken spoke best for Golic and the men in the trenches, saying, "Being a nose tackle is like being a fire hydrant at a dog show."

Golic said in a more serious vein about his position, "Sometimes coaches say you win or do your job just getting a standoff, and you're not supposed to make the tackle. But then there are plays when you fight through all those bodies and make a big hit, and that's pretty wild. It's an awfully tough position."

With only three players on the line, larger defensive ends were required for the 3-4. Reggie Camp, Elvis Franks, Keith Baldwin, and Sam Clancy all were in the 265-280 range. The Browns also got several solid seasons from 280-pound ex-Eagles defensive end Carl "Big Daddy" Hairston.

Although Hairston's well-traveled body may not have been built by Soloflex, head coach Sam Rutigliano put it all in perspective: "Carl is living proof that you don't have to have a body that resembles a Greek statue. I've seen a lot of guys like that working on the turnpike."

Hairston was a solid force on the defensive line during the Browns' five consecutive playoff appearances in the 1980s, first at right end in the 3-4 from 1985-88, and then at left tackle in

Rob Burnett *DE • 1990-95*

Anthony Pleasant
DE • 1990-95

'89 after the Browns returned to the 4-3. Hairston was joined by second-year tackle Michael Dean Perry and ends Robert Banks and Al "Bubba" Baker.

Perry arrived in 1988 as a second-round draft choice and garnered about every rookie honor one could. He led the team in sacks even though he was not a starter. Perry would later annex AFC and NFL honors for his spectacular play that season.

From the start, many NFL insiders thought that Michael Dean was a much larger talent, if not a much larger body, than his big brother William "the Refrigerator" Perry. The Fridge was 6-2, 335, while Michael Dean was 6-1, 285.

Said Nick Saban, Perry's defensive coordinator with the Browns, "He tried to play with-

in the scheme and a lot of people paid special attention to him. It helped some of the other guys to play better football."

While Perry and James Jones anchored the middle until both departed for Denver in 1995, Rob Burnett and Anthony Pleasant remained a pair of 280-pound pillars at end.

A fifth-round draft selection in 1990 from Syracuse, Burnett won All-Rookie honors that season, but was slowed by a foot injury in '91. He blossomed in 1992 and, following the 1994 campaign, was selected to his first Pro Bowl squad. From 1992-95, Burnett recorded 35 1/2 sacks—best among Browns defenders

Pleasant was likewise a sack artist. A third-round pick in 1990 from Tennessee State, he led the team in sacks in '93 with 11 as the Browns equaled their team sack record of 48 set in 1992.

Roy Barker *DE·1999*

Hurvin McCormack knew all about championships. He had been with the Cowboys when they won the Super Bowl after the 1995 season. But it wasn't the ring that led the Browns to make McCormack (6-5, 284) the second pick of the '99 expansion draft. He had career highs in tackles (28) and sacks (five) as a backup in '98.

Another defensive end, Roy Barker, came to Cleveland in February from the 49ers in a trade that also brought tight end Irv Smith. Barker (6-5, 290) was a seven-year veteran who had been a starter since 1993. He had 42 1⁄2 career sacks, including 12 in 1998.

A third defensive end arrived in April when the Browns signed free agent Derrick Alexander from the Vikings. Alexander (6-4, 286) had been a first-round draft pick, 11th overall, in 1995 and had started 51 of 57 games he had

played. He had a career high of 7 1⁄2 sacks in 1998.

Jerry Ball *DT·1993, '99*

The Vikings provided yet another lineman when tackle Jerry Ball, who had been with the Browns in 1993, signed in April. Ball, 34, had been a starter since his rookie year of 1987 and was named to the Pro Bowl while with the Lions in 1990. The 6-1, 320-pound 12-year vet played in Oakland before joining Minnesota.

The other projected starting defensive tackle signed via free agency was 31-year-old John Jurkovic from the Jaguars. Jurkovic, 6-2, 301 pounds from Eastern Illinois, was an eight-year veteran who had gone from being an undrafted free agent in 1990 to a practice squad player in 1991 to a starter for the Packers in 1992. He had started 86 of 104 games in his NFL career.

From the day there was just one in the seven-diamond, through the days of a troika in the 4-3, to a quartet in the 3-4, linebackers have been vital to a pro football team. They are the second line of defense, and in most alignments they should, and do, make the majority of a team's tackles.

Some of today's biggest names and biggest hitters are linebackers. Throughout the years, the Browns have had their share of men who policed the football field sideline to sideline. Certainly, few in recent years did it as long and as well as Clay Matthews. Jim Houston stood out among his contemporaries for a long while, and Tony Adamle and Walt Michaels had run-

Bill Willis was the nose man along with two tackles and two ends. The linebackers, Tony Adamle and Tommy Thompson on the outside, and Weldon Humble and Alex Agase splitting time on the inside, were formidable.

Strangely enough, the Browns' most devastating runner could have been their most devastating tackler, too: Marion Motley. Early in his career, he remained a part of the team's goal line defense. It was his skill at linebacking and fullbacking in his early days that led Paul Zimmerman to proclaim in his book, *A Thinking Man's Guide to Pro Football,* that Motley was "the greatest player" in pro football history.

No one can dispute Motley's great offensive ability, blocking and running, but Zimmerman

Linebackers

ners wishing they had never met in their time. In 1994, Pepper Johnson helped spark a strong defense that led the Browns to a playoff appearance. In 1999, Jamir Miller, Wali Rainer, John Thierry and Rahim Abdullah hoped to extend the tradition of excellence into the millennium.

In the late 1940s, unlike some teams, the Browns didn't linger too long with the seven-diamond defense. But before abandoning the old-fashioned way, Lou Saban, a much-traveled coach in later life, distinguished himself as the only linebacker on the field.

When the Browns moved to the 5-3, it featured a middle guard and three linebackers.

Eddie "The Assassin" Johnson stuffs the run against the Lions.

remembers his defense, too: "He backed up the line and I can still see him on one play, reaching out with one hand and grabbing Buddy Young by the seat of the pants and holding him up in the air for the crowd to see." In the same book, after giving it some thought years later, former Browns assistant coach Weeb Ewbank mused, "He [Motley] just might have been the greatest at that."

Tony Adamle is an interesting player. Like Willis, he played at Ohio State, then became a physician after he retired. Unlike latter-day players who attended medical school between seasons, Adamle waited until he retired to seriously pursue his medical career. He later attained a renewed celebrity when his son Mike became an NFL running back before finding his way to the broadcast booth.

Weldon Humble 1947-50

Tony Adamle
1947-51,'54

Dr. Tony, a rugged tackler, was, not surprisingly, a keen diagnostician of plays.

The other linebacker in the early years was Tommy Thompson of William & Mary (not to be confused with the Eagles' one-eyed quarterback of the same name and era). Thompson's career was relatively short (1949-1953) due to a combination of an injury and a business opportunity that was just too good to pass up.

Ex-Browns assistant Dick Gallagher shared the league's high opinion of him: "Tommy Thompson. . . Now there was a football player. He was a rugged blond guy, good lookin' son of gun. But tough as nails—also very smart. I was not surprised to see him so successful in business. He had a great mind for anything he did."

No matter who was playing in the middle, Humble or Agase, it was difficult making any headway through the center of the Browns' defense. Willis was right on the line and hard to get by, but if you did, Humble or Agase was right there to fill the hole.

Later, Willis would play off the line like a linebacker. His quickness and reactions gave him great range. Willis roamed far and wide in running down ball carriers. He could stay step for step with the fastest in the game, regardless of position. A Lions scouting report had this to say about Willis: "Pulls back very often and goes to the right 'hook' zone. Makes tackles all over the field."

Willis played eight seasons with the Browns (1946-53). He remained close to Paul Brown after retiring. In fact, knowledgeable fans would often pick him out sharing Paul Brown's owners box at Cincinnati Bengals games in the '70s and '80s (even if network sportscasters did not know who was on their screens).

In 1952, a new face appeared on the outside: Walt Michaels, a rough and tough guy from Pennsylvania's Anthracite Coal Region (Swoy-

Alex Agase *1948-51*

Tommy Thompson *1949-53*

ersville), who would play long and well for Cleveland through 1961. After a rookie season in Green Bay, he became a four-time Pro Bowl player, finishing with the 1963 New York Jets before embarking on a coaching career.

Michaels was such a student of the game and a motivator of men that he got the Jets to several playoffs, but was unable to duplicate Weeb Ewbank's success in getting the team to a Super Bowl. As bright as Michaels was, Mike McCormack remembers him for his toughness as well: "When Walter stopped them, they were stopped—period!"

Hal Herring (1950-52) was another intellectual player. He earned a doctorate and his doctoral dissertation was on "Defensive Tactics and Techniques in Professional Football."

Also in the 1950s, Tom Catlin brought his Oklahoma All-America credentials with him to man an outside position. If Michaels was a student of the game, Catlin was a full professor. Again, McCormack: "Catlin, I think, was the most intelligent linebacker I have ever seen. He just studied and analyzed everything. He wasn't too big—about 190 or 195 and he had to

fight to get up to 200—but he was tough. He just knew where to be, knew his defenses and knew his coverages."

Buddy Parker, head coach of the Detroit Lions when the Browns and Lions were getting ready to do battle in the 1953 NFL Championship game, said, "He's a little guy, but he is quick and slips between blockers rather than play through them." Sounds like a pretty smart linebacker to avoid those head-on collisions.

Catlin was so impressive in his knowledge of football that he would follow Chuck Knox for the better part of two decades, eschewing many head coaching opportunities to remain the architect and defensive coordinator of three division-winning playoff teams: the

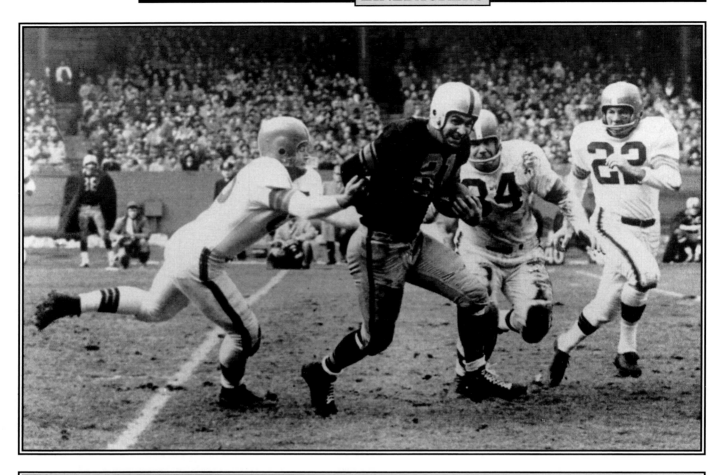

Chuck Noll *1953-59* • Walt Michaels *1952-61*

Noll (left), Michaels (34) and safety Ken Konz (22) surround Pittsburgh receiver Elbie Nickel.

Rams, Bills and Seahawks. When Catlin and crew played, defenses were quite simple compared to today—three or four alignments up front and two or three coverages in the secondary. Pass defense was mainly man to man, but with some zone.

Chuck Noll, a graduate of Benedictine High School in Cleveland, came to the Browns unheralded in 1953 as a 20th-round draft choice from Dayton. He spent his first two seasons as a "messenger" guard, but then crossed the line of scrimmage to play outside linebacker through 1957 before returning to the offensive line in 1958 and '59.

Noll was extremely intelligent and absorbed much of what Paul Brown had to offer as a teacher. Do you see a pattern developing in Browns players? They were tough with great character, skilled, but almost always highly intelligent. It's no coincidence. To be successful and productive in Brown's classroom approach to the game, a healthy intellect was required.

As smart as he was, Chuck Bednarik, the Philadelphia Eagles' Hall-of-Fame iron man center-linebacker, remembers a Noll who was also tough: "I got clobbered by a forearm while snapping for a punt. I got the number, 65. And I told the SOB I'd get him. Next year I did, on a kick return. He got up and told me he'd find me after the game.

"Sure enough, after the final gun, he comes over looking for me—helmet off. He started to say something and I just hit him cold-flush with a shot to the face. I mean, I powdered

Vince Costello *1957-66*

Galen Fiss *1956-66*

him. Only thing, [commissioner] Bert Bell was in the stands, saw it and fined me. Not only that, he told me to apologize to Chuck.

"Next time we played I found him before the game and said, 'I just want to apologize for what happened in Philly,' and stuck out my hand. Noll got up to me, face to face, and just said 'Bull!' I was stunned and started walking away. He grabbed me and said, 'Okay, I accept,' but after that we just kinda stayed out of each other's way."

Galen Fiss, a former Kansas Jayhawker, was a steady, heady linebacker in his era (1956-66). Fiss wasn't big at 6-0, 220, but he was a tough, analytical linebacker with a special knack for the big play. Jim Houston, a pretty good linebacker himself, said this of Fiss: "In the 1964 championship game with the Colts, Galen hit Lenny Moore something fierce and knocked him down. He hit [Johnny] Unitas, too."

Houston explained the significance: "That kind of thing determines how the defense will play; it was a spark. You see someone hitting a guy and all of a sudden, 'Hey, I wanna make sure I get my share.' Then your offense sees it and they wanna be a part of it, too."

Vince Costello's Browns career (1957-66) almost paralleled that of Fiss. Costello had delayed his pro football career to take a whack at professional baseball after leaving Ohio University, but then played in the middle and Fiss on the left or right from 1958-65. They were teamed first with Michaels and then with Houston.

Like Catlin and Michaels, Costello likewise became a coach, most notably as Paul Brown's linebackers coach on the early Cincinnati Bengals teams of 1969-73.

In 1962, young Mike Lucci hit town and nearly everything else that moved. A Western Pennsylvania type, Lucci began at the University of Pittsburgh and finished at Tennessee. He gained real notoriety with the Lions, but

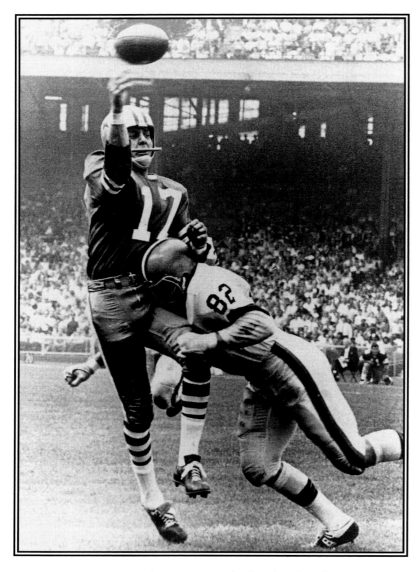

Jim Houston
1960-72

Putting a hit on Cowboys QB Don Meredith.

be there, wherever it is." Not a bad job description for an aspiring linebacker.

Jim Houston was another linebacker to impact the Browns' defense. Although he never thought much about it until he was about to play for the Browns, Houston was almost predestined to play in Cleveland. He is the younger brother of the late Lin Houston. He played at Massillon where the Paul Brown influence exists to this day. He played at Ohio State on an All-America level and as a youngster visited the Browns' camp with Lin. He met "Otto Graham, Mac Speedie, John Yonakor, Horace Gillom and all the greats the Browns had in those days."

The Browns never showed much attention toward Houston. But they did draft him No. 1 in 1960, right before the 49ers, who did show a great interest in him. Houston was very big for a linebacker in his day, even if he was stationed on the left or "strong" side. In fact, for probably the only time in NFL history, when he lined up behind tackle Dick Modzelewski, it was a case of the linebacker (243) outweighing the defensive tackle (239).

Because of Jim Brown, Leroy Kelly, Frank Ryan, Paul Warfield and Gary Collins, etc., the Browns' defense of the '60s probably didn't get the respect it deserved. When it did get some attention, it would come in the form of a left-handed compliment. The media dubbed the unit "the rubber band defense"—it stretched, but didn't snap. True, the Browns did give up yards, but were relatively stingy with points.

Regardless, it bothered Houston and his mates: "We didn't like to think of it in that sense. If a team runs the ball down your throat and continues to pile up yardage, well fine, so long as they don't score: that's their objective. Ours is to keep them from scoring."

Houston, who played defensive end when he first arrived, was very durable, playing 13 straight seasons. He trails only Clay Matthews (16), Doug Dieken (14) and Lou Groza (14) for consecutive seasons in a Browns uniform.

In 1966, Johnny Brewer, a tough old vet from Ole Miss, came over from tight end to

before leaving for Motown in the 1965 three-team trade that brought defensive back Erich Barnes to the Browns, Lucci played solid football.

In the short time he was a member of the Browns, Lucci impressed, among others, the Green Bay Packers' Hall-of-Fame quarterback, Bart Starr, who said of Lucci's Browns days, "He was strong, had good reactions and speed, and showed leadership potential, although sometimes his temper got him in trouble."

Lucci had an early awareness of the requirements of linebacking, saying, "The primary responsibility of a linebacker is to get to the ball and make the tackle. I've got to move and

Dale Lindsey *1965-72*

Bob Matheson
1967-70

In hot pursuit of Giants QB Fran Tarkenton.

play outside linebacker, and did quite well for two years. Brewer was part of a late-'60s transition period during which the Browns made room for new linebackers Dale Lindsey, Bob Matheson, John Garlington and Billy Andrews.

While this was going on, Houston sometimes found himself starting in the middle. Regardless of his position, Houston played at a Pro Bowl level or above for a number of years.

Dale Lindsey, from Western Kentucky, played primarily in the middle from 1965-72, but also spent some time on the outside during Bob Matheson's tenure. After a final season with New Orleans in 1973, Lindsey joined the Cleveland coaching staff in 1974. He absorbed well all the organization had to offer in the form of football knowledge and has been an NFL assistant for most of the past 25 years.

In 1995, Lindsey was passing along his know-how to all-pro Junior Seau and others as the AFC-champion San Diego Chargers' linebackers coach.

Bob Matheson was in the traditional Paul Brown mold: intelligent and tough. A 1967 No. 1 draft choice from Duke, Matheson was what scouts call a "tweener." His size (6-4, 240) was between that which is ideal for a defensive end, but a little bigger than what is needed for linebacker. With the Browns, however, he played primarily as a linebacker.

After playing four seasons with the Browns, Matheson was traded to Miami, where he really blossomed. Head Coach Don Shula later named one of his defenses, the "53," after Matheson's

John Garlington *1968-77*

Billy Andrews
1967-74

jersey number and deployed him in a manner that had him function as a defensive end in some sets and a linebacker in others. He was quite a weapon in that the opponents never knew what he was going to do and where he was going to do it.

Billy Andrews was primarily a right linebacker from 1967-74, but also played occasionally in the middle as the Browns tried various combinations of Andrews, Houston, Garlington, Matheson and Lindsey in the late '60s and early '70s. Somewhat undersized at 6-0, 225, Andrews was known for 110-percent effort.

Joining the mix in 1971 was Charlie Hall, a third-round draft choice. Hall was a quiet star. The Texan from Houston just did his job with little fanfare for a decade, playing strong on the

"strong" side. Hall was a transitional link in Browns history. He began his career as the remains of the 1960s Browns were finishing theirs, then retired in the midst of the Kardiac Kids era. His mates included Jim Houston in the beginning and Clay Matthews at the end.

Bob Babich returned to his Ohio roots via San Diego in 1973 and remained a force for six seasons. He had a fine career at Miami University (of Ohio) from which he was drafted in the first round by the Chargers in 1969. At the NFL draft meeting, a linebacker from a Mid-American Conference school going in the first round raised a few eyebrows, but Jack Butler of the BLESTO-V scouting combine said, "Don't worry, he's the real deal."

Babich started in the middle in 1973 and '74, then divided time with Dick Ambrose in

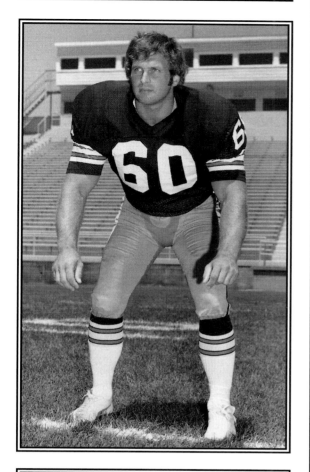

Bob Babich *1973-78*

Charlie Hall *1971-80*

1975 and '76. Although missing out as a Pro Bowl selection to the Steelers' Jack Lambert, Babich was a topflight linebacker in the 1970s.

At 6-0, 235, Dick Ambrose was a classic overachiever. Drafted 12th out of Virginia in 1975, he had one thing in mind that summer: "I went to camp prepared. I was determined to work as hard as I could and let the coaches make the decisions."

Ambrose, a strong silent type, was given the nickname "Bam Bam," because of the force of his hits (he literally broke his shoulder pads with the zealousness of his tackles) and the fact that his tackling was the only sound he made on the field. A couple of years later, Ambrose fought off the challenge of Robert L. Jackson, an All-America No. 1 draftee from Texas A&M. Jackson later became Ambrose's inside line-

backing mate at the time the Browns switched to the 3-4 alignment in 1980 during the "Kardiac Kids" era.

Ambrose said this regarding his football philosophy: "People aren't all that unequal. Anybody can do almost anything if he puts time and effort into it. Sooner or later, he'll get results."

When Clay Matthews left sunny Southern California for Lake Erie in 1978, the Browns were still a 4-3 team. After a one-year apprenticeship, Matthews, a No. 1 draft choice from the University of Southern California, moved into a regular position at right outside linebacker in 1979. He remained there through most of the '80s as the team went to a 3-4 in 1980. Except for a two-year stint on the left

Dick Ambrose *1975-83*

side (1989-90) when the Browns returned to the 4-3, Matthews was the team's right outside linebacker through 1993.

Matthews came from a pro football family. Father Clay Sr. was a defensive end with the 49ers in the early '50s and brother Bruce was a perennial All-Pro interior lineman with the Oilers, in the '80s and '90s.

As durable as he was skilled, Matthews owns the Browns' record for most games played (232) and his 16 seasons with the team ranks second only to Lou Groza's 21. He moved on to Atlanta via free agency in 1994 and retired after the '96 season at age 40. Matthews' 278 games played in 19 seasons is the most by a linebacker in pro football history.

Bill Muir, a longtime NFL assistant coach who was once the offensive line coach of the

Baltimore Colts, said, "I'll tell you, when the Browns were in that 3-4, Matthews was as good as you get. Lawrence Taylor and a couple of others got the attention of the media, but Matthews got the attention of his peers. I know we wanted to know exactly where he was on every play. He was the complete package, the consummate linebacker. He was tough against the run, tough against the pass—just tough on every play. When Chip Banks was also on top of his game, Matthews and Banks were the best outside combination anyone had, maybe ever had."

A typical performance by Matthews was a 1986 victory, 34-3, over the Bengals. He led a

Clay Matthews
1978-93

Stripping the ball from Colts QB Jeff George.

Eddie Johnson *1981-90*

Tom Cousineau *1982-85*

Chip Banks
1982-86

Making the grab on Oilers QB Warren Moon.

defense that limited 1,000-yard rusher James Brooks to 43 yards on 12 attempts. A scouting report on Matthews before the playoffs that season read: "Matthews has played very well and because of his smarts and experience is never out of position."

Matthews again proved the above when in the 1989 playoffs he made a game-clinching interception in a 34-30 victory over Buffalo.

In the middle '80s, paired with Matthews, Chip Banks, another blue-chipper from USC, gave the Browns as good a tandem at outside linebacker as any team in the league. Although traded after the 1986 season, Banks was a Pro Bowl selection in four of his five years with the team. There are those inside the NFL who, at the time, would have told you just as Bill Muir previously said, "Banks is among the best in

the game at his position: in a class with Lawrence Taylor."

While still in the 3-4 mode through the 1988 season, the Browns featured several solid inside linebackers to complement Matthews and Banks.

Prodigal Tom Cousineau, from Lakewood's St. Edward High School and Ohio State, returned from the Canadian Football League and played four seasons (1982-85).

Durability and consistency marked the career of hard-tackling Eddie "the Assassin" Johnson, who held down an inside linebacker position in the mid '80s. The seventh-round draft choice from Louisville missed just one game in his 10-year Browns career.

Pepper Johnson *1993-95*

Mike Johnson
1986-93

Mike Johnson, a former Hokey from Virginia Tech, emerged as a solid force in 1987. Johnson started at right and left inside early in his career, but became a fixture in the middle after the Browns returned to the 4-3 in 1989.

With Matthews and Mike Johnson forming two-thirds of the new alignment in 1989, the Browns tried several candidates at the remaining spot through 1992. Included were David Grayson, Van Waiters and David Brandon.

In 1993, the Browns signed ex-Giants linebacker Pepper Johnson and brought him back to Ohio where he had been Defensive Player of the Game 16 times in his Ohio State career.

Johnson, whose first name is Thomas, was nicknamed "Pepper" after sprinkling the spice on his cereal as a youngster. A rookie with the Giants in 1986, he became a star in 1987 and remained so throughout his Giants career. He played in Super Bowl XXI and was All-Pro in 1990 on the Super Bowl XXV champions.

Large at 255, Johnson was always a big hitter. Johnson not only responded on the field, but by 1994 was considered the motivational leader of the playoff-bound defense.

In 1999, linebacker was expected to be one strength of the new Browns, primarily because solid veterans would man each position.

The leader in the middle would be Chris Spielman. No one who ever saw Spielman play could doubt his intensity and dedication. The question was, after a vertebrae fusion and a year and a half off from the game, could he still make an impact. The Browns traded with the

Jamir Miller *1999*

Rahim Abdullah
1999

Bills for Spielman, 33, in February for past considerations. The former Massillon Tiger and Ohio State Buckeye had been to five Pro Bowls in his career, which began in 1988 with the Lions. Spielman had never failed to start the 148 NFL games in which he played.

Ultimately, however, Spielman did not get the chance to become the much-needed emotional leader of the expansion Browns' defense. In the fourth preseason game against Chicago, he took a solid hit to his neck, briefly lost feeling is his arms and legs, then walked unsteadily off the field. On advice from team doctors, Spielman retired the following Monday rather than risk more hits and possible permanent damage to his spinal cord. Replacing Spielman would be Wali Rainer, a 6-2, 235-pound fourth-round draft choice in 1999 from Virginia.

A major signing coup was Jamir Miller, a right outside linebacker formerly with the Cardinals who signed in May. A first-round draft choice in 1994, Miller had started 57 games in five seasons with 473 tackles and 13 1/2 sacks.

John Thierry, an outside linebacker and the Bears' No. 1 draft choice (11th overall) in 1994, was signed in February. Thierry had been unhappy in Chicago where he was used as a defensive end. The Browns made it clear they wanted Thierry as a linebacker.

In addition to Rainer, the college draft produced outside linebacker Rahim Abdullah of Clemson in the second round. An All-Atlantic Coast Conference first team selection in 1998, Abdullah was fifth in the ACC with 7.5 sacks.

Defensive Backs

They're often called "the last line of defense." If a defensive back makes a mistake, the result can be a quick-strike touchdown for the other guys. Fortunately for the Browns—from Tommy James, Warren Lahr and Cliff Lewis, through Hanford Dixon and Frank Minnifield, to the 1995 cast headed by Antonio Langham, Stevon Moore and Eric Turner—the tertiary (the third line) has usually been a strong one. One of the key factors in the Browns' playoff-bound resurgence in 1994 was the play of Turner at free safety, Moore at strong safety, and Langham and Don Griffin at the corners.

By his fourth season, 1994, Turner was firmly established as one of the NFL's best young safeties. No one had more interceptions (9) in the NFL than Turner in '94. Perhaps his most memorable play, though, was the game-saving hit he put on the Dallas Cowboys' Jay Novacek inches from the goal line as time was running out in the dramatic 19-14 victory at Texas Stadium on Dec. 10.

Turner was simply fulfilling a prediction of a survey of coaches and personnel men who said of him, "Definitely playing at an All-Pro level. He can really sting and he likes the attention that comes with making big hits." When Turner was a rookie in 1991, his first hit was a "big" one—he bent Cincinnati Bengal running back James Brooks' face mask on his first official tackle in the NFL.

In the beginning, the defensive secondary was a three-man gang. While some teams put a gridiron version of the Three Stooges on the field, the Browns had some of the AAFC's very best in the lineup.

Tommy Colella, while seeing considerable action as an offensive halfback, made 10 interceptions in 1946. No one in pro football—AAFC and NFL—made more. It is still a Browns single-season record, although tied by Thom Darden in 1978. Cliff Lewis and Don Greenwood were other early secondary standouts. And remember, Otto Graham also contributed five interceptions that first year.

Because of the seven-diamond alignment, the secondary deployed as two "defensive halfbacks" and one "safety." In 1948, the Browns were infused with two future greats—Tommy

Tommy James *CB·1948-55*

Warren Lahr *CB-S·1948-59*

James and Warren Lahr. They would give the team a solid set of defensive halfbacks.

James, of course, played for Paul Brown at Massillon and at Ohio State. Lahr was from Western Reserve. James played for the Lions in 1947 and "welcomed the change" in coming to Cleveland. Through 1951, the Browns' trio was James and Lahr at the corners and Cliff Lewis at safety. No quarterback took many liberties with this combo.

James reflected on the time: "We were all young and quick. Warren [Lahr] was quick and heady. He knew where to be and how to play the receiver. Same for Cliff [Lewis]. He was a quarterback at Duke—he could think, tackle and cover."

As to tactics, James said, "We used zone and man to man, and some combinations. But you

Don Shula CB • 1951-52

Ken Konz
S • 1953-59

had to be careful not to tip your hand. If you were in 'combo,' you had to disguise it. A quarterback didn't need to be an Otto Graham to figure out where the 'man' coverage was and go to that receiver—eventually, he'd be open. We had good personnel and were well-schooled."

As the '50s progressed, so did NFL defenses. The 5-3 evolved into the 4-3 and gave rise to a four-man secondary. After the 1951 season, Lewis retired and the Browns entered a transition period in both personnel and formation. Lahr and James continued at the corners in 1952, but rookie Bert Rechichar succeeded Lewis at safety. Second-year man Don Shula saw limited playing time in James' position.

Then in 1953, Paul Brown engineered the largest trade in NFL history, a 10-for-five swap with Baltimore that sent, among the 10, both

Shula and Rechichar to the Baltimore Colts, a new franchise that needed players. This, combined with the Browns switching to a four-man secondary in 1953, left the team with two major holes.

They were filled by a pair of Kens: Ken Gorgal, a second-year man from Purdue, and Ken Konz, a rookie from Louisiana State. Konz, James and Lahr each had five interceptions in 1953's inaugural season of the four-man secondary. James had three in one game, on Nov. 1 in a 27-3 victory over Washington.

Don Paul
CB • 1954-58

practice on rainy days was to 'hit a home run.' He'd stand where home plate was on the infield part of the Stadium, knock an imaginary ball over the wall and then slide into each base as he shouted the play-by-play. He'd be covered with mud before we even started practice. It really cracked up the players, but I don't think P.B. appreciated it all that much."

But as long as Don Paul made the Pro Bowl (1957-59), Paul Brown put up with his antics. Later, a Browns publication rated Paul "the Browns' greatest defensive back in the short term." In the long run, Warren Lahr earned "the greatest" label.

Paul later documented his life in the NFL and lifestyle in general in his autobiography entitled, *I Went Both Ways, The Adventures of the NFL's Joyboy During the Fabulous Fifties.*

Ex-Notre Damer John Petitbon moved in at right safety in 1956 before being traded to the Packers in '57. Not to worry—Lowe "Junior" Wren, a second-year man from Missouri, took over and started for three seasons before being dealt to Pittsburgh.

Lahr, "as heady a player as I've ever seen," according to James, moved to safety in 1959, his final season. That was the year two new-comers joined the starting secondary: corners Bernie Parrish and Jim Shofner.

Parrish was not only an All-America from Florida, but also a talented baseball player. At the time, baseball paid more and Parrish signed a $30,000 bonus contract with the Cincinnati Reds. But after two years of long, tiring bus rides in the minors, Parrish wanted to compete at a major league level, even if in a different sport.

He wrote a "bread & butter" letter to Paul Brown saying, "Being drafted by the Browns [No. 9 in 1958] was the greatest honor I ever received in football." Although an offensive standout, Parrish told P.B., "I like running the ball, but I think my best position may be defensive back." He was right. Parrish played in a couple of Pro Bowls and set an interception return record of 92 yards in 1960 that lasted until Najee Mustafaa went 97 in 1993.

Konz remained a dependable starter through 1958 and was the yearly leader, or tied for the lead, in interceptions five times. He also punted and returned punts during his seven-year Browns career. Gorgal, meanwhile, moved on to the Chicago Bears in 1955.

Don Paul, sometimes confused with a villainous Rams linebacker of the same name and vintage, joined the mix in 1954 and allowed James to move to safety where his savvy was still valuable. Paul was a free spirit obtained from the Chicago Cardinals. Ex-Browns assistant coach Dick Gallagher recalled how Paul would break the tedium during practice, if not endear himself to Paul Brown: "He was really a character. One of the things he would do before

Bernie Parrish CB·1959-66

Jim Shofner CB·1958-63

To say Parrish was outspoken is to say Jim Brown could run with the football. Parrish was a leader of the players union and a burr under management's saddle. He also had many suggestions for his defensive coaches, but he was instrumental in the defense of the 1964 championship Browns.

Threatening to retire in 1966, head coach Blanton Collier made Parrish a player-coach that year, saying, "Bernie knows as much or more about football than any other player in the NFL, and this year he will be coaching the defensive backs as well as playing with them." But Parrish said he seldom had any coaching input. If getting even for the slight was on Parrish's mind, he did to some extent.

In 1971, he authored a controversial book, *They Call It A Game*. Some looked at Parrish as an ingrate; others as a visionary. The book was publicized as "an indictment of the pro football establishment," and it did ruffle more than a few feathers, especially in the Cleveland area.

During the seven seasons (1959-65) that Parrish started at left cornerback, he was paired for the first five on the right with Texas Christian's Jim Shofner. A running back at TCU, Shofner led the Southwest Conference in rushing his senior season and was drafted No. 1 by the Browns in '58. Converted to cornerback, Shofner adapted so successfully that he tied Bobby Franklin for the team lead in interceptions in 1960 with eight. He still utilized his running skills, however, as he returned punts for portions of his Browns career.

Ross Fichtner
S • 1960-67

Drafted in the 28th round by the Chicago Cardinals in 1959 with a year of eligibility still remaining, Fleming did not give pro football much thought and was going to give baseball a shot. However, his Florida roommate, Parrish, convinced the Browns that he could be a good defensive back and they traded for his rights.

Fleming did not disappoint as he became a starter immediately. In his first professional game in 1960, he intercepted Norm Van Brocklin twice—it was the season the Dutchman led the Eagles to their last NFL crown. Parrish likened Fleming to Pro Football Hall of Famer Larry Wilson in size and temperament: "Don was angular and lean like Wilson and a relentless hitter. He was a good student of the game."

Paul Brown agreed: "Don Fleming will be one of the stars of this game." But tragedy struck on June 4, 1963. Working on a construction project (both Fleming and Parrish were building construction majors in college), the young defensive back was electrocuted.

Bobby Franklin of Ole Miss was another 1960 addition. He had been a fine quarterback in college, but like many offensive stars of the two-way era in college, he found himself learning how to back-pedal and knock down passes in the pros.

Franklin and rookie Lowell Caylor from Miami University (of Ohio) were starting right safeties in a very young Browns secondary in the 1964 championship campaign. Second-year men Larry Benz and Walter Beach were the primary left safety and right cornerback, respectively. Benz moved in following an injury to fifth-year man Ross Fichtner. Parrish, at left corner, had the most NFL experience.

In an era when the NFL looked down its collective nose at the AFL, Beach caused a stir. He was cut by the AFL's Boston Patriots, one of the rival league's weaker teams, and became a starter for the Browns. Go figure!

Cornerback Erich Barnes arrived in 1965 as part of a three-team deal involving the Browns, Giants and Lions. The Browns traded linebacker Mike Lucci to Detroit, who shipped quarterback Earl Morrall to New York. The

Shofner later coached at TCU in the '60s and '70s. He returned to the Browns for two separate assistant coaching stints, 1978-80, and in 1990, the latter of which resulted in his serving as interim head coach after Bud Carson was fired with eight games remaining.

The Browns have retired just five jersey numbers over the years. Graham's and Groza's are obvious. One that may not be so, outside of Browns followers, is No. 46, Don Fleming's. He was a safety with the Browns from 1960-62. In his short time he made quite an impression. He went to Florida from Shadyside, Ohio, a mill town not too far from Groza's Martins Ferry. He began his Gators career as a 180-pound two-way end, but made his reputation as a receiver.

Erich Barnes *CB-S•1965-71*

Mike Howell CB-S•1965-72

Ernie Kellermann
S•1966-71

Giants traded guard Darrell Dess to Detroit and Barnes to Cleveland. Barnes was the prototype for today's bigger defensive back: 6-3, 198, fast and tough. It was said that Barnes was "good at pushing and shoving before the bump-and-run was used." He began his Browns career at right corner. Then, after Parrish retired, he moved to the left for five years before finishing at right safety in 1971.

Ernie Kellermann, who produced big yards as a quarterback at Miami University (of Ohio), joined the Browns in 1966 and played safety with distinction. The baby-faced assassin gave the Browns quality service through 1971 before moving on to Paul Brown's Cincinnati Bengals in 1972 and to the Buffalo Bills in 1973.

Mike Howell of Grambling played both corner and safety from the mid '60s through 1972. He led the Browns in interceptions in 1966 with eight (tied with Ross Fichtner) and in 1969 with six.

Cornerback Ben Davis joined the team in 1967. He became a starter almost immediately and, with the exception of missing the 1969 season due to injury, provided steady play through 1973. In his second season, 1968, he set a team record for most consecutive games with an interception: seven.

He did it between Oct. 20 and Dec. 1, 1968, for a streak of seven games as the Browns finished the season with a 10-4 record and the Eastern Conference title. He had eight interceptions in the regular season and one against Dallas in the conference championship game.

Walt Sumner CB-S·1969-74

Ben Davis
CB·1967-68,'70-73

Davis' rise to pro football stardom was meteoric. Born in Alabama, he attended high school in Fair Lawn, N.J., via sponsorship by the Quakers. It wasn't to play football, but to play the cornet in the Fair Lawn High School band. He spent a post-graduate year at Bridgton (Maine) Academy. Bridgton had no band, so Davis joined the football team. He attended Defiance College, an NCAA Division III school in northwestern Ohio where, as a running back, he gained 1,815 yards on 288 carries (6.3 yards a carry) and scored 23 touchdowns.

In his first season with the Browns, Davis led the NFL in punt return average (12.7 yards per return) and returned kickoffs (26.2 average, seventh in the league).

Walt Sumner, a seventh-round draft choice from Florida State, was another versatile defensive back. From 1969-74, he logged playing time at safety and corner. Davis' injury in 1969 propelled Sumner into a starting cornerback slot as a rookie prior to the opening of the season. He moved to safety in 1971 and played effectively despite a nagging knee injury.

At Kansas State, Clarence Scott played well enough to warrant being the Browns' No. 1 pick in 1971. All he did after that was give the Browns 13 solid seasons in the secondary. As knowledge replaced speed as his number one asset, Scott moved from cornerback to strong safety to free safety, but the important thing is that he played at a level that allowed him to remain in the lineup longer than any defensive back in Browns history.

Clarence Scott *CB-S•1971-83*

Ron Bolton CB·1976-82

Thom Darden
FS·1972-74,'76-81

Thom Darden left Michigan in 1972 as a No. 1 draft choice and brought great range to the free safety position through 1981. He had actually been a "Wolfman," or roving linebacker for the Wolverines. By this time, zones were prevalent and right safeties were "free" to roam and play the ball. Darden played "centerfield," as it was called, as well as anyone in the game at the time.

Darden led or tied the Browns in interceptions six times. Through 1995, his 10 interceptions in 1978 and 45 in his career were both all-time Browns records.

Scott and Darden manned the two safety positions for head coach Sam Rutigliano's 1980 Kardiac Kids, while Ron Bolton and Clinton Burrell were the cornerbacks. Said Rutigliano: "For a team to be successful, it must have a solid corps of veterans to provide leadership. We were very fortunate to have had a guy like Thom Darden. He was a leader and a winner."

Darden prepared for success after football by getting corporate and business experience during his playing days. He said, "If I had my druthers, I would play the rest of my life. But there's no way I can physically or mentally."

Hanford Dixon out of Southern Mississippi arrived in 1981 as a first-round draft choice and immediately impressed NFL observers. But it wasn't until Frank Minnifield came over from the ill-fated United States Football League in 1984 that the Browns had a dominant young pair of cornerbacks for their playoff run of five straight seasons (1985-89).

Hanford Dixon *CB·1981-89*

Felix Wright S·1985-90 · Frank Minnifield CB·1984-92

The originator of the "Dawg" moniker that became the "Dawg Defense" and the "Dawg Pound," Dixon became a three-time Pro Bowl selection in his nine-year career. Minnifield played through 1992 and was a four-time Pro Bowl pick.

For a short time (1984-85), they were augmented by safety Don Rogers, an All-America from UCLA and first-round draft choice. Tragically, Rogers died of a drug overdose.

Minnifield, a 5-9, 180 pounder from Louisville, intercepted 20 passes in nine seasons with the Browns, including three in a 40-7 victory at Houston on Nov. 22, 1987.

He clearly favored his cohorts in the Dawg Pound over his opponents on the field: "Aside from those on our team, they are the scoundrels of the earth," he once said about wide receivers.

"Throughout the game they try to be your friend. Then they catch a pass and they want to go through this Indian war dance and spike the ball on you. You're nothing but a scoundrel when you do something like that."

Dixon intercepted 26 passes, tied with Felix Wright and Tommy James for seventh place on the Browns' all-time list. Following the 1989 season, he was left unprotected as a Plan B free agent. Head Coach Bud Carson felt that Dixon's play had slipped in '89 and the Browns signed another veteran corner, the Patriots' Raymond Clayborn, as a replacement. Dixon signed with San Francisco, but did not make the team.

Eric Turner S·1991-95

Don Rogers
S·1984-85

Felix Wright, an undrafted free agent safety from Drake in 1985, moved into the starting lineup in 1987 and led or tied for the team interceptions crown four consecutive seasons, including an NFL high of nine in 1989.

Wright replaced Chris Rockins in Game 7 of the strike-shortened '87 season, then proceeded to start 55 consecutive games until leaving for Minnesota as a free agent in 1991.

The departures of Dixon and Wright, plus the eventual release of Minnifield in 1993, left Bill Belichick with a secondary in transition after he assumed head coaching duties in 1991. New names appeared and disappeared, including Randy Hilliard, Steven Braggs, Harlon Barnett, Vince Newsome, Terry Taylor, Najee

Mustafaa and Everson Walls. But by 1995, the quartet of Don Griffin and Antonio Langham at the corners, and Stevon Moore and Eric Turner at the safeties, appeared set.

That proved to be untrue, however, when Turner missed the second half of the '95 season with a back injury. The Browns' No. 1 draft choice in '91 from UCLA, the 6-1, 207-pounder had earned his first Pro Bowl berth following the 1994 playoff season.

A first-round choice in 1994 from Alabama, Langham started all 16 games as a rookie to win consensus All-Rookie honors, plus the Defensive Rookie of the Year award from the NFL Players Association and *Football Digest*. Langham, who played with San Francisco in 1998, was picked again by the Browns in 1999 as the final selection of the expansion draft.

Daylon McCutcheon CB•1999

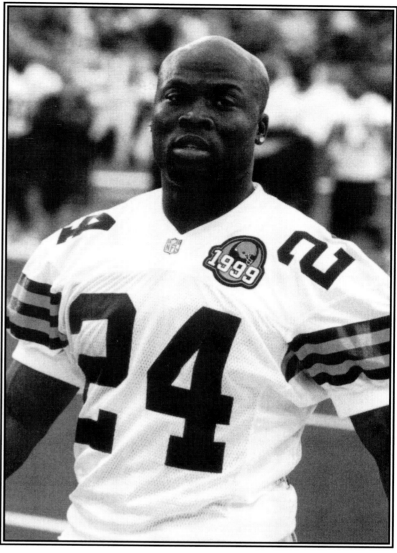

Corey Fuller
CB•1999

After the Browns were moved to Baltimore in 1995, Langham never became the player he appeared to be after his rookie campaign. He started only six games for the 49ers in 1998 after signing a hefty free agent contract. Langham wanted to rejoin the Browns, and said he would play for less than the $3.02 million he made with the 49ers in 1998.

Other free agent corners added to the 1999 roster were Corey Fuller, a four-year starter with the Vikings, and Ryan McNeil from the Rams, who led the NFL with nine interceptions in 1997.

Fuller had started 43 consecutive games for Minnesota and had 10 interceptions and 317 tackles over four seasons. He recorded 14 tackles in 1997 versus Detroit, second best all-time by a Vikings defensive back.

In April's college draft, the Browns selected cornerback Daylon McCutcheon (Southern California) and strong safety Marquis Smith (California) as their two choices in the third round.

McCutcheon, an All-Pac 10 first-team selection in 1998, made his presence felt quickly in the preseason when he intercepted two passes in the Hall of Fame Game against Dallas in August, then picked off another at Tampa Bay the following weekend. By Game 2 of the 1999 season, he had moved ahead of Langham in the starting lineup.

Smith was likewise an All-Pac 10 first-team choice in 1998, starting every game at strong safety. His four-year totals included 247 tackles and five interceptions.

Kickers & Punters

When the Browns first started playing in 1946, little emphasis was placed on what was then very loosely defined as "the kicking game." Kicking, returning, covering kicks—now known as special teams—just weren't that special. It was simply a case of who was on the field rather than utilizing specialists for particular phases of the game. Once again, however, Paul Brown showed the way.

The precision place-kicking of Lou Groza and the cloud-seeding punting of Horace Gillom (despite what one writer called "the worst form and the best punts in pro football") gave the Browns a couple of early specialists before most pro football teams even thought of such luxuries.

In the first years of the AAFC, Groza and Gillom really weren't luxuries. Groza was a regular left offensive tackle—good enough to start in six Pro Bowls during his career—in addition to doing all the place-kicking.

After 1946, the punting was left to Gillom, who was used as an offensive and defensive end. In his career (1947-1956), he caught 74 passes for 1,083 yards, but had only five receptions in his last three seasons. He backed up both Dante Lavelli and Mac Speedie, leading Paul Brown to remark after the Browns were admitted to the National Football League in 1950, that Gillom could be a starter with all the other NFL teams.

Tommy James, a fine defensive back of the late '40s and '50s, and Groza's longtime holder, said: "If we didn't have Lavelli and Speedie, Horace would have been a starting offensive end—and a good one."

Groza would remain an All-Pro tackle until a back injury reduced him to kicking specialist

only after sitting out the 1960 season. Like the offensive left tackle spot (featuring Groza, Dick Schafrath and Doug Dieken from 1947-1984), the history of the Browns' kicking game can nearly be told by simply detailing the careers of Groza and his three primary successors—Don Cockroft, Matt Bahr and Matt Stover.

Former assistant coach Dick Gallagher shed some light on why the Browns were unique with one primary kicker and punter when many other teams took a committee approach: "Remember that in 1946 a lot of players were products of the old single-wing where the tailback was a 'triple threat'—run, pass, kick. We had players like Tommy Colella, Mac Speedie and Dippy Evans, who could kick and punt pretty well—but none like Groza and Gillom. Other teams weren't as lucky. It was not uncom-

STAYING STRAIGHT: Groza and holder Tommy James practice in 1948 with the six-foot guide tape designed to keep the Browns' kicker properly aligned. The tape was later ruled illegal by the NFL before the Browns joined the league in 1950.

mon to see a half-dozen or so different players figure in another team's season stats. Without specialists, it was just a case of who was in the game when the occasion arose."

Even the Browns practiced a little kicking by committee in 1946. Groza took 47 extra-point attempts (making 45) while two-way end John Rokisky and Speedie were good on each of their only attempts. By 1948 Groza was the man. He took every PAT and field goal attempt.

Like many of the Browns, Groza had played for Paul Brown at Ohio State, but only as a freshman. World War II interrupted and Groza served three years in the South Pacific, including on Okinawa. It was said that Groza kept his kicking skills sharp by kicking coconuts over palm tree goalposts. An amusing story, but one that wilted under closer scrutiny. However, between military duties, Groza did get some kicking time in, using balls and shoes sent to him by Brown.

Asked if he thought Brown singled him out for his kicking potential, the Hall of Famer replied, "No mention was made. I felt he signed me as a football player. You have to remember

there was no real specialization then. In those days, kicking was incidental to playing. Horace Gillom was an end and his punting was incidental, too. But he did it well and helped our football team to win."

Groza's straight-on kicking style—with the same square-toed, high-top shoe he had employed since high school—looked simple enough, but in reality it required every bit as much focus, concentration and dedication as any other aspect of professional football.

Constant practice of time-honored techniques culminated to allow the toe to do its job. Groza adapted Paul Brown's four-point system of football fundamentals to his own practice regimen: stance, approach, contact and follow-through.

"In the stance, I looked at the goalpost and squared my shoulders to the uprights," Groza explained. "I then lined up two and a half walking strides from where the ball was going to be placed and lined my toe up with a spot on the ground."

Groza would actually draw a line in the turf with his cleats to properly align himself with the uprights. Then in 1946, his first holder with the Browns, Don Greenwood, suggested using tape instead. They developed the "guide tape," a 72-inch roll of adhesive Groza would unravel to the right of, and parallel to, his kicking path. It included a small crosspiece to spot the point of contact and extra inches beyond the crosspiece to mark the area of follow-through.

"We'd lay down the tape, I'd square my shoulders and take a short jab step when the ball was in the air," Groza said. "When the ball was on the ground my eyes would transfer from the spot on the ground to the spot on the ball. I'd try to see my toe hit the spot—that's the approach. The contact was when my foot hit the ball right below center—my heel down to give the ball loft.

"The follow-through occurred when my foot came down to the front of the spot from where the ball was kicked. Whenever I missed one I'd look to where my foot came down. Invariably it would be more than a shoe width from the extended tape line. It meant I was swerving rather than keeping my balance and going straight through."

Groza continued to employ the guide tape through 1949, but the device was banned by the NFL when the Browns joined in '50.

Groza's focus on techniques enabled him to remain calm before every kick. Even when the game was on the line, he seemed almost nonchalant while taking his stance. He was, instead, completely confident his techniques would pay off. "I never thought I'd miss one," he said. "I used to say that if I ever missed one it would be the holder's fault."

He was kidding, of course, but with Groza's record of consistency, it was also believable. "One time I missed one when Jim Ninowski

TOP FORM: Proper follow-through (left) was the fourth of Lou Groza's four points of successful place-kicking. At right, he cleans his square-toed shoe during the 1957 season in which he led the NFL in scoring with 77 points on a league-high 15 field goals on 22 attempts and 32-for-32 on PATs.

was the holder. As we were coming off the field, Paul Brown was giving him hell, wondering what he did wrong holding the ball for me."

During the season, the Browns did not practice on Mondays or Tuesdays, so Groza practiced primarily after offensive (Wednesday) and defensive (Thursday) drills.

"But we always had fellas with weight problems assigned to chase my kicks after practice. They'd be on my case not to kick too many," he said. "As a result I really didn't do too much kicking after practice."

BETWEEN TOES: Sam Baker performed kicking duties in 1960 during Lou Groza's one-year absence. He also punted in '60-61. His blocker and holder above is safety Bobby Franklin.

Sam Baker P-K•1960-61

Groza seldom practiced kicking on Fridays or Saturdays. "I didn't want to lose the natural snap in my leg by kicking too many," he said.

He still considers his last-minute 16-yard field goal, the margin of victory over the Rams in the 1950 championship game, "my biggest thrill in pro football."

After sitting out the entire 1960 season with a back injury, Groza returned in 1961 to kick seven more years. He was exclusively a kicker by then, but still among the game's best.

Including Groza's AAFC totals, "the Toe" scored 1,608 points on 264 field goals, 810 extra points and one touchdown.

Although his field goal kicking percentage (55%) is not as lofty as today's kickers, several things need to be kept in mind. First and foremost, the goalposts were on the goal line at the time, not the end line (10 yards further back) as they are today. If the Browns had the ball on their opponent's 40 yard line or closer, Groza could try a 47-yard kick. If he made it, three points. If he missed, the opponent got the ball at their 20. No big deal!

Today, it would come out to the 40 on a miss—a nice bonus for the opposition. The philosophy seemed to be then: cross midfield and we'll try a field goal from anywhere we bog down. Thus, while the kicks today may actually be longer in relation to the scrimmage line and goalposts, the penalty for a miss is now greater. Consequently, many coaches are reluctant to try a kick from far out. No longer can NFL teams automatically think "three points" as soon as midfield is crossed. A more realistic place to try a field goal today is from the 20- or 25-yard line on in. Only in desperate situations are teams likely to take anything other than a "chip shot." This helps modern percentages.

Another thing to keep in mind is that development of sophisticated blocking schemes—protection for the kicker—was not as intense in Groza's day. There was a larger chance of a "leaker" sifting through to block an attempted kick. An incident in which a 6-6 Big Daddy Lipscomb would hoist a 6-4 Don Burroughs on his shoulders to block a kick attempt would no longer be allowed by today's rules.

Today's kickers benefit from closer hash marks, too. Groza and his contemporaries had a much more difficult angle when kicking from the hashes. All this doesn't mean Groza could not match today's kickers at times. In 1953 he boomed 23 of 26 field goal attempts through the pipes, 88.5%, the best season in Browns history until Matt Stover broke the mark with 26 of 28 (92.8%) in 1994.

Late in Groza's career he had to contend with a new phenomenon, the kamikaze. By the mid 1960s in the NFL, rookies and hellbent-for-leather younger players were assigned to kick-coverage and return teams, where they just streaked downfield on kickoffs and tried to tackle the returner, separating him from the

OLD RELIABLE: After a one-year retirement due to a back injury, Groza returned in 1961 to kick the winning field goal in a 20-17 victory over the St. Louis Cardinals in Game Two. His second retirement would not come until age 43 in 1967.

ball if possible, if not separating his head from his shoulders.

Ike Kelley, a linebacker for the Philadelphia Eagles at the time, took it a step further. As part of the kick-return team, he wasn't as interested in blocking for the return man as he was in taking out Groza, the kicker. He would seek out Groza, who by this point in his career was not so intent on getting downfield to make a tackle, and try to wipe him out. Usually, the younger man prevailed, but Groza never shied away from the confrontation. Ironically, Kelley was a fellow Buckeye, having played at Ohio State for Woody Hayes.

Despite being a pioneer specialist, Groza still kicked over 50% of his field goals when the norm was closer to 30%. Ben Agajanian, a man who kicked for many years for many teams in many leagues, said of Groza, "Lou was the best of the olden days kickers. He kicked better

DUAL DUTIES: Don Cockroft punted and place-kicked during his 13-year career, one of the last in pro football history to perform both roles before special teams became more specialized. He is the Browns' all-time leader in punts (651) and is second behind Lou Groza in PATs (432) and field goals (216).

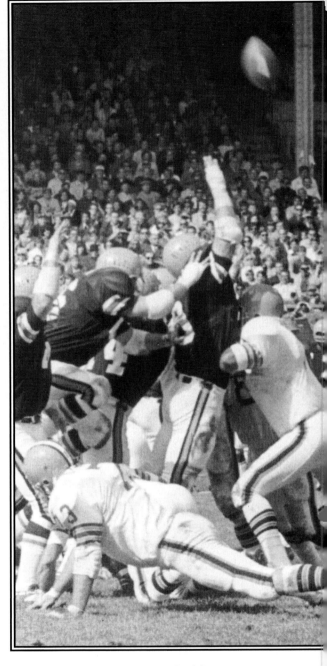

under pressure than anyone I know. I can't remember him missing a clutch field goal."

Paul Brown said it simply, succinctly and best: "Lou Groza shortened the football field for us from one hundred yards to sixty yards."

The year Groza sat (1960), Sam Baker filled in capably. Baker, a player who did nothing to dispel the image of kickers as flakes, led the NFL in PAT attempts and PATs made (46 and 44). The journeyman kicker was also good on 12 out of 20 field goals. For good measure, the eccentric Baker did the Browns' punting and compiled a 42-yard average.

The Browns were indeed fortunate in maintaining great continuity in their kicking game. Groza retired after the 1967 season. In 1968, after a year of learning and observing on the taxi squad, Don Cockroft took over. As a rookie, he converted 46 of 48 PATs and 18 of 24 field goal attempts.

The former Adams State kicker was also the Browns' punter. He continued to go against the flow of NFL mainstream thinking and did

both, saving the team a valuable roster spot, through the 1976 season.

In his 13-year career, Cockroft kicked 432 of 458 PATs and 216 of 328 field goals. This added up to 1,080 points, No. 2 on the Browns' all-time NFL-only list behind Groza's 1,349. In his nine seasons as a punter, Cockroft kicked 651 times, averaging 40.3 yards per kick.

By the time Cockroft came on the scene, no other team had the same person as their front line kicker and punter. Cockroft, whose 13 consecutive seasons is third behind Clay Matthews'

16 and Groza's and Doug Dieken's 14, represented a dinosaur in another way, too. He was a straight-on kicker. And by the end of his career, he would be a true throwback as the sidewinding soccer-stylists had made irreversible inroads in the NFL.

A superbly coordinated athlete, Cockroft had great power in his well-used leg, especially for a 190-pound straightaway kicker. His 57-yard field goal versus Denver in 1972 trails only Steve Cox's 60- and 58-yarders in the Browns' record book. Cox, primarily a thunder-footed

punter, was occasionally called on for long distance field goals. At least twice he delivered.

When Cockroft reached the end of his career in 1980, the team recycled former Steelers kicker Matt Bahr via a mid-season trade with the 49ers. A soccer player for his father, Walter, at Penn State, Bahr was the Browns' first soccer-style kicker. Like his brother, Chris, also a Penn Stater who enjoyed a fine and lengthy career with the Bengals and Raiders, Matt had played pro soccer before graduating from Penn State. NCAA rules allow a student-athlete to retain

Horace Gillom *P-E • 1947-56*

Tom Colella
P-DB • 1946-48

his or her amateur standing in a particular sport, even in light of signing a professional contract, as long as the sport in which the athlete "turned pro" is not the same one in which he or she attempts to still compete in college.

The smallish Bahr (5-10, 175) led the Browns in scoring eight times from 1981-89. Bahr's theory on kicking was simple: "Pressure is what you put on yourself. What's important is how you handle it. One thing you have to do as a kicker is to want to go out and kick. You live for the clutch situations. If you miss, you have to want to get out and try again."

However, during Bahr's tenure, injuries prevented him from always playing week after week. One who took up the slack was longtime Redskin Mark Moseley, the last of the straight-on place-kickers who was vital in the late-season drive of 1986, especially his winning field goal in the double overtime playoff win over the New York Jets.

Nevertheless, Bahr eventually became the Browns' most accurate field goal percentage kicker during his tenure. He converted 143 of 193 attempts for a 74.1 percentage. As was the case with Groza and Cockroft, the longevity factor also applies to Bahr. Joining the New England Patriots in 1995, Bahr played his 17th and final NFL season.

Two years after Bahr departed and a year after Jerry Kauric held kicking duties in 1990, the Browns settled on Matt Stover, a refugee from the Giants' injured reserve list, in 1991. The Louisiana Tech graduate proved to be an increasingly productive and accurate kicker. It was his fourth and final field goal of the game (a 45-yarder with :04 on the clock) that beat the Bengals in the third week of the 1991 season.

After making 26 of 28 in 1994 to raise his career percentage to 78.2%, Stover surpassed Bahr as the Browns' most accurate kicker.

Although Horace Gillom would become a great punter with the Browns for a number of years, he didn't join the team until he left the University of Nevada in 1947. Gillom was no stranger to Paul Brown. He played for him at Massillon's Washington High School before Brown went to Ohio State.

Until Gillom's arrival, the Browns passed the punting duties around. In their first season, Tommy Colella was the main punter—47 kicks for a 40.3 average, but Fred "Dippy" Evans and Mac Speedie punted eight and three times for a 38- and 28-yard average, respectively. From 1947 on, it was mainly Gillom's job, although Ermal Allen, Cliff Lewis and Warren Lahr would occasionally put instep to leather from punt formation.

Gillom brought a different style of punting to the game. He was the first to kick for height and distance. His 80- and 75-yard punts are still in the Browns' record book. Gillom was a proponent of "hang time" long before the term gained widespread usage. Gillom also stood much deeper than the average punter of his era. This cut down on the possibility of any of his punts being blocked. He took a 15-yard drop, while many others still kicked from 10 or 12 yards behind the line of scrimmage.

In addition, Paul Brown was beginning to spread the punting formation. Rather than bunching up to protect the kicker, Brown felt if Gillom would drop deeper the Browns could spread themselves a little thinner along the line. This allowed the cover men—mostly the ends at the time—to get downfield more quickly. That Gillom could be so deep and still average 45.5 or 45.7 in some seasons tells you just how much thunder there was in his foot.

When Gillom's career ended, Fred "Curly" Morrison, Ken Konz, Dick Deschaine, Junior

Gary Collins
P-WR•1962-71

Wren and Sam Baker handled the duties from 1956-61.

Baker, filling in for Groza as a place-kicker when Lou was injured in 1960, stayed on to punt only in 1961 and had another fine season with a 43.3-yard average.

Rookie No. 1 draft choice Gary Collins took over in 1962. Again, good fortune or good planning favored the Browns. Collins, a consensus All-America at the University of Maryland, was also a starting wide receiver and a good one.

Collins posed a threat to run or pass from punt formation. But mainly he was a strong kicker. His 46.7-yard average in 1965 led the NFL. Keep in mind that Collins would often be called on to punt after running downfield on a pass pattern on the previous down.

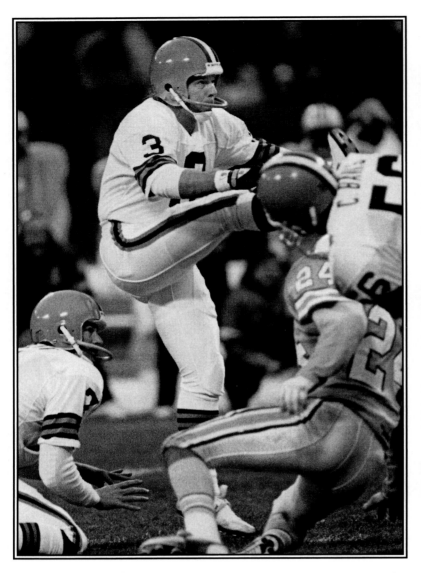

Mark Moseley
K•1986

The Browns often benefited from having a specialist who was more than that. The kicking phase of Cleveland Browns history is filled with names of players with multiple duties: Groza, tackle-kicker; Cockroft, kicker-punter; Fred "Curly" Morrison, fullback-punter; Collins, receiver-punter; Junior Wren, defensive back-punter; Johnny Evans, quarterback-punter; and Tom Tupa, quarterback-punter.

Cockroft replaced Collins in 1968 and held the job through '76. Then in 1977, the punting parade featured Greg Coleman, who later had a successful career with the Minnesota Vikings, followed by Johnny Evans (1978-80).

Steve Cox, whose strong leg often overshadowed the fact that he could place the ball out of bounds when needed, was the regular in 1981-82 and '84. Jeff Gossett was the choice in 1983 and 1985-87. He was followed by Max Runager (1988), Bryan Wagner (1989-90), Brian Hansen (1991-93) and finally Tupa (1994-95).

A rule that continues to affect punting averages, as well as punt return averages, is the one keeping cover men on the line until the ball is actually punted—earlier rules allowed the kicking team to send their kamikazes flying downfield at the snap.

Special teams are sometimes taught to leave at the thud of the kick—although more sophisticated coaching has the cover guys leaving on a certain count, knowing just how long after the snap the ball will be kicked. This is all well and good on a perfect snap, but if the ball is bobbled, an illegal procedure (leaving before the ball is kicked) penalty is almost automatic.

Each team now has several specialists who are important parts of the punting team in that

Phil Dawson *K • 1999*

Chris Gardocki *P • 1999*

they are the widely-placed cover men who attempt to get downfield in a hurry and down the ball, keep it from going into the end zone, or tackle the returner, whichever the case may be. Kick return teams counter by assigning two men, usually, to hold up the fleet "bomb squadders." As with other aspects of the game, for every new move by one unit a counter move is usually made—and made very quickly—by the other unit.

For 1999, the Browns acquired one of the best punters in the NFL when they signed free agent Chris Gardocki, a 29-year-old eight-year veteran with Chicago and Indianapolis. As a Colt in 1998, Gardocki was the league's fourth-leading punter with a 45.4-yard average on 79 punts. Gardocki had never had a punt blocked in his NFL career and ranked in the top five in gross average yardage the previous three seasons. He ranked second in '96, earning him Pro Bowl honors.

Place-kicking was considerably less settled for the new Browns as they tried out several candidates. Starting camp were Phil Dawson, who spent his rookie season of 1998 on New England's practice squad, and Danny Kight, who had tried out with several teams over several seasons before spending 1998 on Washington's non-football injury list.

Although Dawson kicked the winning field goal in the victory over Dallas in the Hall of Fame Game in August and Kight was later cut, Dawson found himself battling a late addition with two preseason games left—Chris Boniol, the Cowboys' kicker in Super Bowl XXX, who had been released by Philadelphia. Dawson, however, won the job and Boniol was released.

The Legacy of Kickers

In the Browns' first 50 seasons, the majority of place-kicking was done by these four players.

Lou Groza *1946-59, '61-67*

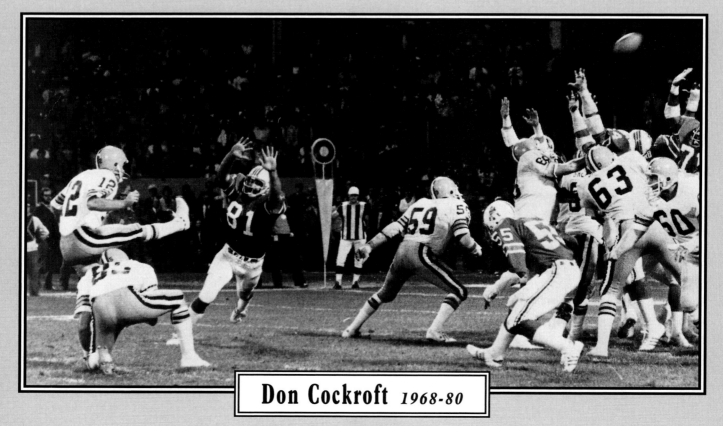

Don Cockroft *1968-80*

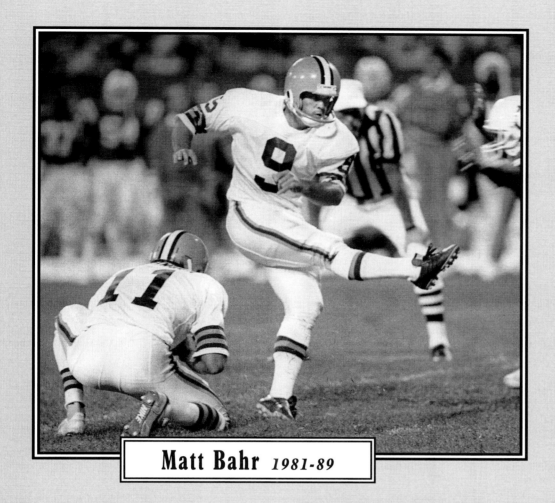

Matt Bahr *1981-89*

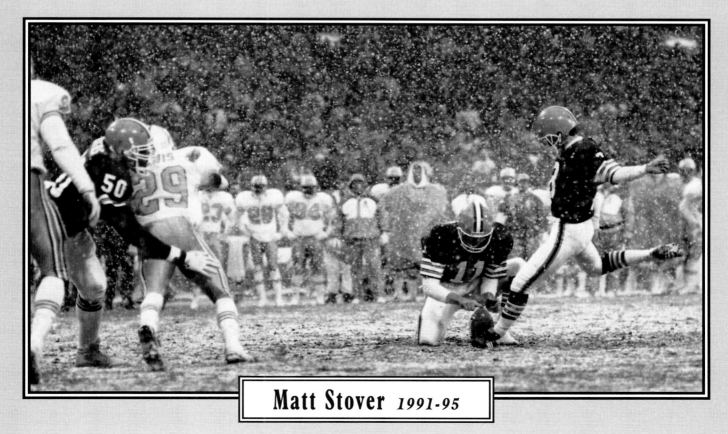

Matt Stover *1991-95*

Those who cover professional football have been known to remark of an electrifying performer, "He can change your field position quicker than anyone on the football field other than the referee." As often as not, the player they're talking about is a kick returner. There is no more dramatic example of this, nor of his value to the ball club, than what Eric Metcalf did on Oct. 24, 1993, before 78,118 at Cleveland Stadium. In a 28-23 victory over the Steelers, Metcalf turned the game on two monster plays.

His 91-yard punt return helped stake the Browns to a 14-10 lead. And with the Steelers leading, 23-21, at the midway point of the final quarter, the 190-pound "lightning bolt in a bottle" ripped through the Steelers' coverage, streaked down the right sideline, cut back, and scored on a 75-yard punt return to seal the victory for the Browns.

Statistically, the Steelers had the better of the game. But only one statistic really counts, the final score, and Metcalf put the Browns on the long end. It wasn't the only time the son of former St. Louis Cardinals "franchise" Terry

Returners

"Returning kicks was no big deal when we first started. If you were on the field, you did it."

A look at the figures proves the accuracy of Gallagher's statement. No less than seven different Browns players returned punts in 1946. Nearly double that number returned kickoffs. Who were the primary guys? A couple of Hall of Famers who did OK in other phases of the game: quarterback Otto Graham and fullback Marion Motley. Sound incredible?

Who would risk injury to a legendary quarterback today by having him perform what is arguably the most dangerous job in football? Certainly, the 49ers never even thought of asking Joe Montana to return punts. How many other rushing-leader, 240-pound fullbacks can you name who also led the team in kickoff

returns as Motley did? All of this just adds to what Gallagher said about it being "no big deal" in the days before specialization.

It was 1948 before Cliff Lewis took over for Graham as the front-line punt returner. However, Graham continued to return some punts a while longer. By the time the Browns joined the NFL in 1950, Motley, too, had turned over the return chores to others.

In the 1950s, teams began using younger runners for return duties, both punts and kickoffs. For the Browns it was players such as Ken Carpenter, Don "Dopey" Phelps, Bob Smith, Billy Reynolds, Ken Konz, Preston Carpenter and Olympic decathlete Milt Campbell.

By 1954, most NFL teams used twin rather than single safeties. Two players were deep, but either could, and did, return the kicks.

Metcalf had done that for the Browns. Metcalf's 91-yarder was the longest punt return in Browns history. He then broke his own record with a 92-yarder for a touchdown in the 1994 season opener versus the Cincinnati Bengals.

Four Browns have broken the 100-yard barrier on kickoff returns: Carl Ward (104) in 1967, Leroy Bolden (102) in 1958, Metcalf (101) in 1990 and Gerald McNeil (100) in 1986.

The emphasis placed on today's kick and punt return game is in dramatic contrast to professional football of the 1940s, when the Browns made their debut in the All-America Football Conference. Dick Gallagher, a Browns assistant coach from 1947-49 and 1955-59 said,

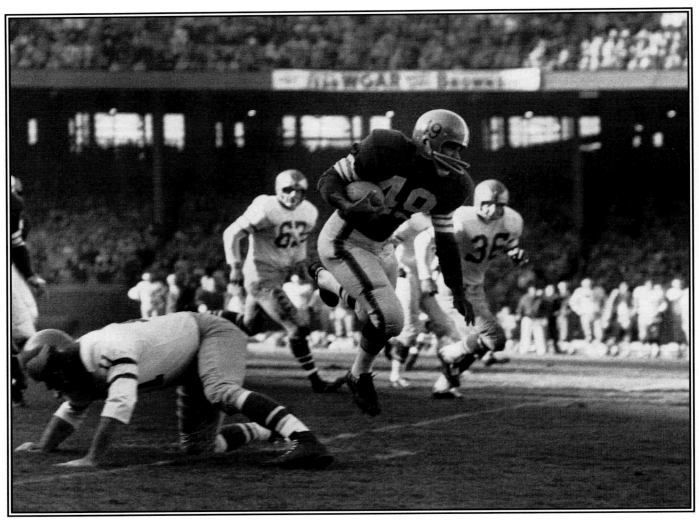

Bobby Mitchell
1958-61

An example was Reynolds and Chet "the Jet" Hanulak. Reynolds returned 25 punts and 14 kickoffs that season; Hanulak 27 punts and nine kickoffs. Interestingly, the Browns returned only 30 kickoffs all year. It was the days of kicking off from the 40-yard line when touchbacks were more the norm than the exception.

In the late '50s, Bobby Mitchell brought his special brand of magic to the game. Not only did he lead the Browns in punt and/or kickoff returns from 1958-1961, he ran like blazes from scrimmage and caught passes, too. During the time frame, Mitchell scored at least one touchdown on a punt or kickoff return each year, usually in the 90-yard category. There are those who will tell you that Mitchell made the Pro

Football Hall of Fame on his numbers as a prolific receiver with the Washington Redskins, but very few of them live in Cleveland. Paul Warfield, who knows about these things, said of Mitchell, "He really terrified defenders."

After Mitchell departed, the Browns utilized Howard "Hopalong" Cassady and Jim Shorter as punt returners in 1962 and '63, respectively. The Browns' primary kickoff returners were Tom Wilson in 1962 and Charley Scales in '63. Then came three of the best seasons in Browns return-man history.

From 1964-66, it was Leroy Kelly returning the punts and Walter "the Flea" Roberts returning the kicks. They formed arguably the best tandem in team history until Metcalf and Randy Baldwin shared duties in the 1990s. Roberts is generally recognized as the Browns'

first true return specialist: "The Flea" was a 160-pound flyer from San Jose State. He led the team in kickoff returns in each of his three seasons with the team (1964-66) before being taken by the New Orleans Saints in the 1967 expansion draft. Roberts' 25.9-yard return average ranks second behind Greg Pruitt (26.3) in the Browns' record book.

At about the time that Roberts and Kelly emerged, the trend was for teams to use different players for punts and kickoffs. The jobs evolved to where different skills were needed for each task.

Tommy James, who did both for the Browns in the early years, said, "For kickoffs, you could almost get by on speed alone. The field was more open and the tacklers weren't right on top of you. Punt returning is different.

Speed helps, but you gotta make sure you have the ball first, make the catch—even with a lot of people breathing down your neck. You just find yourself in congested traffic a lot sooner on punts."

> "The Flea"
> **Walter Roberts**
> *1964-66*

With Jim Brown still in the backfield, about all Leroy Kelly could do to get noticed was return punts. For the future Hall of Famer's first three seasons (1964-66) he led the team in punt returns, and when needed again in 1971, he turned in team-leading numbers, saying, "I'm willing to do whatever I can to help the team." Kelly led the NFL in 1965 with a sterling 15.6 yard average and two for touchdowns.

Jim Garrett, who would later become a Browns assistant coach, foresaw Kelly's great-

Leroy Kelly
1964-73

ness while the Morgan State youngster was still confined to return duties. Said Garrett at the time of Jim Brown's retirement, "Leroy Kelly will pick up where Jim Brown left off and not miss a beat." Kelly proved the knowledgeable Garrett a great prophet. In his first year as a full-time runner after Brown's departure for the silver screen in 1966, Kelly rushed for 1,141 yards, with a league-leading 5.5 yards-per-carry average, a league-long 70-yard scrimmage run and 15 touchdowns, an NFL high for the season.

With Roberts gone and Kelly in the backfield, the Browns turned to a variety of return men in the late '60s and early '70s. Cornerback Ben Davis handled both kickoff and punt returns in 1967, as did running back Charley Leigh in '68. Afterward, the jobs fell to a long list of performers, including Reece Morrison, Walt Sumner, Bo Scott, Ken Brown, Homer Jones and Bobby Majors. Then in 1973, the list shortened dramatically.

While waiting to become a 1,000-yard rusher, Greg Pruitt, a water bug running back from Oklahoma, became the primary Browns return man. His talent defied the conventional wisdom of the day that you couldn't do both—return punts and kickoffs. In 1973-75, Pruitt led the team in both categories each year, ranking at or near the top in NFL and AFC totals.

Helping Pruitt at this time was an all-out returner named Billy Lefear, who had no fear. When not laying the first block for Pruitt, Lefear returned kicks for well over 1,000 yards in his brief stay (1972-75).

Billy Lefear *1972-75*

Greg Pruitt
1973-81

Diminutive Dino Hall was the Browns' next established returner, and again proving the wisdom of the special teams coaches in the selection process, handled both jobs effectively from 1979-83. He led the Browns in kickoff and punt returns three times each. The 5-7, 165-pounder from Glassboro State was fearless and durable. Once after a brilliant day with Mr. and Mrs. Hall in the stands, teammate Dave Graf said, "I bet Dino's folks feel five feet tall."

During the time that the Bears' 300-pound-plus William "the Refrigerator" Perry became a national folk hero, Gerald McNeil brought his 140-plus pounds to the game. When looking for a suitable nickname in keeping with the appliance theme established by Perry, "the Ice Cube" seemed very appropriate for the tiny, slippery McNeil. He led the NFL in kickoff returns in

1986 and punt returns in 1989. In Pittsburgh, they still grumble about a 100-yard kickoff return that beat the Steelers on Oct. 5, 1986. One week earlier, he returned a punt 84 yards for a touchdown in a 24-21 victory over the Lions.

Following the 1987 season, McNeil became the first Browns return specialist voted to the Pro Bowl. In just four seasons, he amassed a team-record 1,545 punt-return yards. His best season was also a record: 496 yards in 1989.

Many observers still wonder how the Baylor mite was able to do it on the NFL level. "Never giving them too much of a target," is how he explained his survival and effectiveness.

During times when two roster spots were taken by two returners—one for punts and one

Dino Hall *1979-83*

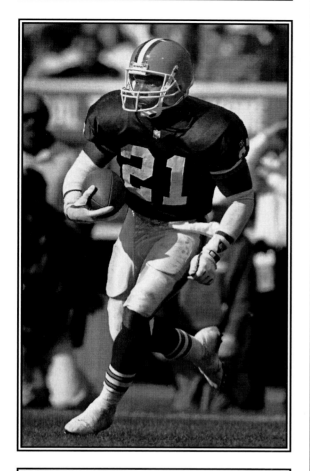

Eric Metcalf *1989-94*

for kickoffs, the Browns have been fortunate to have the Greg Pruitts, the Dino Halls and the Gerald McNeils to do both and give the team the opportunity to keep another player.

Eric Metcalf first returned kicks in 1989. Initially, he was used more on kickoffs than punts, but in 1992 he handled both and became the NFL leader with 44 punt returns for an AFC-leading 429 yards.

In 1990, Metcalf had his best season as a Browns kickoff returner, handling 52 for 1,052 yards and two touchdowns: 98 yards versus the New York Jets on Sept. 16 and 101 against the Houston Oilers on Dec. 9.

Randy Baldwin, a running back from Mississippi, took over for Metcalf as the primary kickoff man in 1992 and 1993 as the Browns worked Metcalf more into the regular offense.

Metcalf, however, continued to return punts. In 1994, Metcalf (punts) and Baldwin (kickoffs) again set the pace. Baldwin's 26.9-yard average was best in the AFC. But following the season, Metcalf was traded to Atlanta and Baldwin signed a free agent deal with the expansion Carolina Panthers, thus leaving the Browns' special teams with two pairs of shoes that were difficult to fill in 1995.

Metcalf departed as only the fourth player to crack the Browns' top 10 career yardage lists in rushing (2,229), punt returns (1,341), kickoff returns (2,806) and combined net yards (9,108). The other three are Bobby Mitchell, Leroy Kelly and Greg Pruitt.

"The Ice Cube"
Gerald McNeil
1986-89

The Pro Football Hall of Famers

OTTO GRAHAM

Quarterback • Inducted in 1965

PAUL BROWN

Head Coach • Inducted in 1967

MARION MOTLEY
Running Back • Inducted in 1968

LOU GROZA
Place-kicker-Tackle • Inducted in 1974

JIM BROWN
Running Back • Inducted in 1971

DANTE LAVELLI
Right End • Inducted in 1975

LEN FORD

Defensive End • Inducted in 1976

PAUL WARFIELD

Wide Receiver • Inducted in 1983

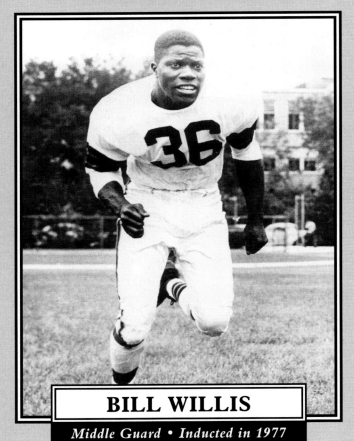

BILL WILLIS

Middle Guard • Inducted in 1977

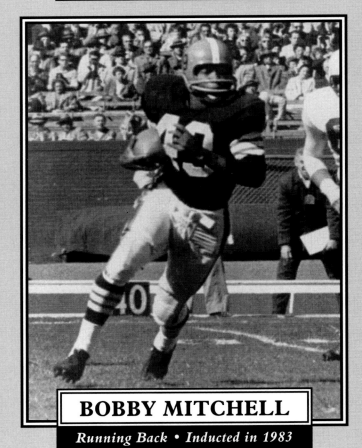

BOBBY MITCHELL

Running Back • Inducted in 1983

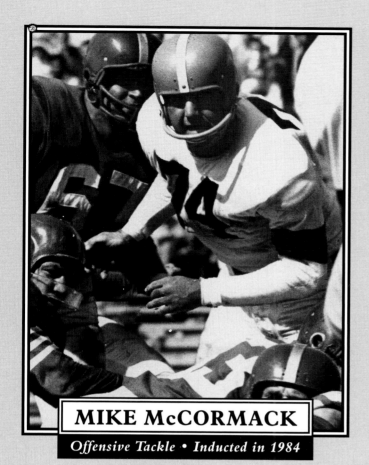

MIKE McCORMACK

Offensive Tackle • Inducted in 1984

LEROY KELLY

Running Back • Inducted in 1994

FRANK GATSKI

Center • Inducted in 1985

OZZIE NEWSOME

Tight End • Inducted in 1999

All-America Football Conference

Year	Conference	Division	W-L-T	Finish
1946	----------	Western	12-2	First
1947	----------	Western	12-1-1	First
1948	----------	Western	14-0	First
1949	---------- *	----------	9-1-2	First

National Football League

Year	Conference	Division	W-L-T	Finish
1950	American	----------	10-2	First-tie
1951	American	----------	11-1	First
1952	American	----------	8-4	First
1953	Eastern	----------	11-1	First
1954	Eastern	----------	9-3	First
1955	Eastern	----------	9-2-1	First
1956	Eastern	----------	5-7	Fourth-tie
1957	Eastern	----------	9-2-1	First
1958	Eastern	----------	9-3	First-tie
1959	Eastern	----------	7-5	Second-tie
1960	Eastern	----------	8-3-1	Second
1961	Eastern	----------	8-5-1	Third
1962	Eastern	----------	7-6-1	Third
1963	Eastern	----------	10-4	Second
1964	Eastern	----------	10-3-1	First
1965	Eastern	----------	11-3	First
1966	Eastern	----------	9-5	Second-tie
1967	Eastern	Century	9-5	First
1968	Eastern	Century	10-4	First
1969	Eastern	Century	10-3-1	First
1970	American	Central	7-7	Second
1971	American	Central	9-5	First
1972	American	Central	10-4	Second
1973	American	Central	7-5-2	Third
1974	American	Central	4-10	Fourth
1975	American	Central	3-11	Fourth
1976	American	Central	9-5	Third
1977	American	Central	6-8	Fourth
1978	American	Central	8-8	Third
1979	American	Central	9-7	Third
1980	American	Central	11-5	First
1981	American	Central	5-11	Fourth
1982	American	----------**	4-5	Eighth
1983	American	Central	9-7	Second
1984	American	Central	5-11	Third
1985	American	Central	8-8	First
1986	American	Central	12-4	First
1987	American	Central	10-5	First
1988	American	Central	10-6	Second
1989	American	Central	9-6-1	First
1990	American	Central	3-13	Fourth
1991	American	Central	6-10	Third
1992	American	Central	7-9	Third
1993	American	Central	7-9	Third
1994	American	Central	11-5	Second
1995	American	Central	5-11	Fourth

* AAFC played as one league with no divisions.
** NFL played without divisions in strike-shortened season.

League Championship Results

Year	League	Score				Date/Location
1946	AAFC	Browns	14	Yankees	9	12-22-46, Cleve.
1947	AAFC	Browns	14	Yankees	3	12-14-47, N.Y.
1948	AAFC	Browns	49	Bills	7	12-19-48, Cleve.
1949	AAFC	Browns	21	49ers	7	12-11-49, Cleve.
1950	NFL	Browns	30	Rams	28	12-24-50, Cleve.
1951	NFL	Rams	24	Browns	17	12-23-51, L.A.
1952	NFL	Lions	17	Browns	7	12-28-52, Cleve.
1953	NFL	Lions	17	Browns	16	12-27-53, Det.
1954	NFL	Browns	56	Lions	10	12-26-54, Cleve.
1955	NFL	Browns	38	Rams	14	12-26-55, L.A.
1957	NFL	Lions	59	Browns	14	12-29-57, Det.
1964	NFL	Browns	27	Colts	0	12-27-64, Cleve.
1965	NFL	Packers	23	Browns	12	01-02-66, G.B.
1968	NFL	Colts	34	Browns	0	12-29-68, Cleve.
1969	NFL	Vikings	27	Browns	7	01-04-70, Minn.

Conference Championship Results

Year	Conf.	Score				Date/Location
1950	American	Browns	8	Giants	3	12-17-50, Cleve.
1958	Eastern	Giants	10	Browns	0	12-21-58, N.Y.
1967	Eastern	Cowboys	52	Browns	14	12-24-67, Dal.
1968	Eastern	Browns	31	Cowboys	20	12-21-68, Cleve.
1969	Eastern	Browns	38	Cowboys	14	12-28-69, Dal.
1986	American	Broncos	23	Browns	20	01-11-87, Cleve.
1987	American	Broncos	38	Browns	33	01-17-88, Den.
1989	American	Broncos	37	Browns	21	01-14-90, Den.

Additional Playoff Results

Year	League	Score				Date/Location
1949	AAFC	Browns	31	Bills	21	12-04-49, Cleve.
1971	NFL	Colts	20	Browns	3	12-26-71, Cleve.
1972	NFL	Dolphins	20	Browns	14	12-24-72, Miami
1980	NFL	Raiders	14	Browns	12	01-04-81, Cleve.
1982	NFL	Raiders	27	Browns	10	01-08-83, L.A.
1985	NFL	Dolphins	24	Browns	21	01-04-86, Miami
1986	NFL	Browns	23	Jets	20	01-03-87, Cleve.
1987	NFL	Browns	38	Colts	21	01-09-88, Cleve.
1988	NFL	Oilers	24	Browns	23	12-24-88, Cleve.
1989	NFL	Browns	34	Bills	30	01-06-90, Cleve.
1994	NFL	Browns	20	Patriots	13	01-01-95, Cleve.
1994	NFL	Steelers	29	Browns	9	01-07-95, Pitts.

Browns Head Coaches

Coach	Years	Record
Paul Brown	1946-1962	167-53-8 (.759)
Blanton Collier	1963-1970	79-38-2 (.675)
Nick Skorich	1971-1974	30-26-2 (.536)
Forrest Gregg	1975-1977	18-23-0 (.439)
Dick Modzelewski	1977 (interim)	0-1-0 (.000)
Sam Rutigliano	1978-1984	47-51-0 (.480)
Marty Schottenheimer	1984-1988	46-31-0 (.597)
Bud Carson	1989-1990	12-14-1 (.463)
Jim Shofner	1990 (interim)	1-6-0 (.143)
Bill Belichick	1991-1995	37-45-0 (.451)

CLEVELAND BROWNS RECORDS AND STATISTICS

Team Records: NFL

Total Points
Season 415 (1964)
Game 62 (12-6-53 vs. Giants)
62 (11-7-54 vs. Redskins)

Touchdowns
Season 54 (1966)
Game 8 (12-6-53 vs. Giants)
8 (11-7-54 vs. Redskins)

Extra Points
Season 52 (1966)
Game 8 (12-6-53 vs. Giants)
8 (11-7-54 vs. Redskins)

Field Goals
Season 26 (1986, 1994)
Game 5 (10-19-75 vs. Broncos)

Combined Net Yards
Season 5,915 (1981)
Game 562 (10-25-81 vs. Colts)

Rushing Attempts
Season 559 (1978)
Game 60 (10-2-55 vs. 49ers)

Rushing Yardage
Season 2,639 (1963)
Game 338 (10-29-50 vs. Steelers)

Passing Attempts
Season 624 (1981)
Game 57 (9-7-81 vs. Chargers)

Passing Completions
Season 348 (1981)
Game 33 (12-5-82 vs. Chargers)

Passing Yardage
Season 4,339 (1981)
Game 444 (10-25-81 vs. Colts)

Interceptions
Season 32 (1968)
Game 7 (12-11-60 vs. Bears)

Punt Returns
Season 61 (1954)
Game 8 (11-7-54 vs. Redskins)
8 (11-28-54 vs. Giants)
8 (11-18-56 vs. Eagles)

Kickoff Returns
Season 75 (1979)
Game 9 (10-17-54 vs. Steelers)
9 (10-7-79 vs. Steelers)

Quarterback Sacks
Season 48 (1992, 1993)
Game 11 (11-18-84 vs. Falcons)

First Downs
Season 364 (1981)
Game 35 (11-23-86 vs. Steelers)

Fumbles
Season 50 (1978)
Game 9 (12-20-81 vs. Seahawks)
9 (12-23-90 vs. Steelers)

Penalties
Season 128 (1978, 1989)
Game 21 (11-25-51 vs. Bears)

Punts
Season 97 (1989)
Game 12 (12-3-50 vs. Eagles)
12 (11-19-88 vs. Chiefs)

Individual Records: NFL

Longest Plays

Running 90 Bobby Mitchell (11-15-59 vs. Redskins)
Passing 97 Kosar-Slaughter (10-23-89 vs. Bears)
Punt Ret. 92 Eric Metcalf (9-4-94 vs. Bengals)
Kick Ret. 104 Carl Ward (11-26-67 vs. Redskins)
Int. Ret. 97 Najee Mustafaa (10-10-93 vs. Dolphins)
Fmb. Ret. 89 Don Paul (11-10-57 vs. Steelers)
Punt 80 Horace Gillom (11-28-54 vs. Giants)
Field Goal 60 Steve Cox (10-21-84 vs. Bengals)

Scoring

Total Points
Career 1,349 Lou Groza (1950-59, '61-67)
Season 126 Jim Brown (1965)
Game 36 Dub Jones (11-25-51 vs. Bears)

Touchdowns
Career 126 Jim Brown (1957-65)
Season 21 Jim Brown (1965)
Game 6 Dub Jones (11-25-51 vs. Bears)

Extra Points
Career 641 Lou Groza (1950-59, '61-67)
Season 51 Lou Groza (1966)
Game 8 Lou Groza (12-6-53 vs. Giants)

Field Goals
Career 234 Lou Groza (1950-59, '61-67)
Season 26 Matt Stover (1994)
Game 5 Don Cockroft (10-19-75 vs. Broncos)

Combined Net Yards

Attempts
Career 2,650 Jim Brown (1957-65)
Season 353 Jim Brown (1961)
Game 39 Jim Brown (10-4-59 vs. Cardinals)
39 Mike Pruitt (12-3-81 vs. Oilers)

Yardage
Career 15,459 Jim Brown (1957-65)
Season 2,131 Jim Brown (1963)
Game 313 Jim Brown (11-19-61 vs. Eagles)

Rushing

Attempts
Career 2,359 Jim Brown (1957-65)
Season 305 Jim Brown (1961)
Game 37 Jim Brown (10-4-59 vs. Cardinals)

Yardage
Career 12,312 Jim Brown (1957-65)
Season 1,863 Jim Brown (1963)
Game 237 Jim Brown (11-24-57 vs. Rams)
237 Jim Brown (11-19-61 vs. Eagles)

Touchdowns
Career 106 Jim Brown (1957-65)
Season 17 Jim Brown (1958, 1965)
Game 5 Jim Brown (11-1-59 vs. Colts)

Receiving

Receptions
Career 662 Ozzie Newsome (1978-90)
Season 89 Ozzie Newsome (1983, 1984)
Game 14 Ozzie Newsome (10-14-84 vs. Jets)

Yardage
Career 7,980 Ozzie Newsome (1978-90)
Season 1,236 Webster Slaughter (1989)
Game 191 Ozzie Newsome (10-14-84 vs. Jets)

Touchdowns
Career 70 Gary Collins (1962-71)
Season 13 Gary Collins (1963)
Game 3 Eight times, most recent by
Eric Metcalf (9-20-92 vs. Raiders)

Passing

Attempts
Career 3,439 Brian Sipe (1974-83)
Season 567 Brian Sipe (1981)
Game 57 Brian Sipe (9-7-81 vs. Chargers)

Completions
Career 1,944 Brian Sipe (1974-83)
Season 337 Brian Sipe (1980)
Game 33 Brian Sipe (12-5-82 vs. Chargers)

Yardage
Career 23,713 Brian Sipe (1974-83)
Season 4,132 Brian Sipe (1980)
Game 444 Brian Sipe (10-25-81 vs. Colts)

Touchdowns
Career 154 Brian Sipe (1974-83)
Season 30 Brian Sipe (1980)
Game 5 Frank Ryan (12-12-64 vs. Giants)
5 Bill Nelsen (11-2-69 vs. Cowboys)
5 Brian Sipe (10-7-79 vs. Steelers)

Interceptions

Number
Career 45 Thom Darden (1972-74, '76-81)
Season 10 Thom Darden (1978)
Game 3 Eight times, most recent by
Frank Minnifield (11-22-87 vs. Oilers)

Yardage
Career 820 Thom Darden (1972-74, '76-81)
Season 238 Bernie Parrish (1960)
Game 115 Bernie Parrish (12-11-60 vs. Bears)

Touchdowns
Career 5 Warren Lahr (1950-59)
Season 2 Five times, most recent by
Thane Gash (1989)
Game 2 Bobby Franklin (12-11-60 vs. Bears)

Punt Returns

Number
Career 161 Gerald McNeil (1986-89)
Season 49 Gerald McNeil (1989)
Game 7 Six times, most recent by
Eric Metcalf (11-8-92 vs. Oilers)

Yardage
Career 1,545 Gerald McNeil (1986-89)
Season 496 Gerald McNeil (1989)
Game 166 Eric Metcalf (10-24-93 vs. Steelers)

Touchdowns
Career 5 Eric Metcalf (1989-94)
Season 2 Leroy Kelly (1965)
2 Eric Metcalf (1993, 1994)
Game 2 Eric Metcalf (10-24-93 vs. Steelers)

Kickoff Returns

Number
Career 151 Dino Hall (1979-83)
Season 52 Eric Metcalf (1990)
Game 9 Dino Hall (10-7-79 vs. Steelers)

Yardage
Career 3,185 Dino Hall (1979-83)
Season 1,052 Eric Metcalf (1990)
Game 172 Dino Hall (10-7-79 vs. Steelers)

Touchdowns
Career 3 Bobby Mitchell (1958-61)
Season 2 Eric Metcalf (1990)
Game 1 11 times, most recent by
Randy Baldwin (9-4-94 vs. Bengals)

Quarterback Sacks

Number
Career 76.5 Clay Matthews (1978-93)
Season 14.5 Bill Glass (1965)
Game 4 Jerry Sherk (11-14-76 vs. Eagles)
4 Mack Mitchell (11-20-77 vs. Giants)

Dick Schafrath

Cleveland Browns All-Time Roster

A

Abrams, Bobby	LB	Michigan	1992
Adamle, Tony	RB-LB	Ohio State	1947-51,'54
Adams, Chet	T	Ohio	1946-48
Adams, Pete	G	Southern Cal.	1974,'76
Adams, Stefon	DB	Auburn	1990
Adams, Vashone	DB	E. Michigan	1995
Adams, Willis	WR	Houston	1979-85
Aeilts, Rick	TE	SE Miss. St.	##1989
Agase, Alex	G	Illinois	1948-51
Akins, Al	RB	Wash. St.	1946
Aldridge, Allen	DE	Prairie View	1974
Alexander, Derrick	WR	Michigan	1994-95
Allen, Ermal	QB	Kentucky	1947
Allen, Greg	RB	Florida St.	1985
Alzado, Lyle	DE	Yankton	1979-81
Ambrose, Dick	LB	Virginia	1975-83
Amstutz, Joe	C	Indiana	1957
Anderson, Herbie	DB	Texas A&I	##1992
Anderson, Preston	DB	Rice	1974
Anderson, Stuart	LB	Virginia	1984
Andrews, Billy	LB	SE La.	1967-74
Athas, Pete	DB	Tennessee	1975
Arvie, Herman	T	Grambling	1993-95
Atkins, Doug	DE	Tennessee	1953-54

B

Baab, Mike	C	Texas	1982-87,'90-91
Babich, Bob	LB	Miami-Ohio	1973-78
Bahr, Matt	K	Penn State	1981-89
Baker, Al	DE	Colo. St.	1987,'89-90
Baker, Sam	P-K	Oregon St.	1960-61
Baker, Tony	RB	E. Carolina	1986,'88
Baldwin, Keith	DE	Texas A&M	1982-85
Baldwin, Randy	RB	Mississippi	#1991-94
Ball, Jerry	DT	SMU	1993
Bandison, Romeo	DL	Oregon	#1994,'95
Banker, Ted	G	SE Miss. St.	1989
Banks, Carl	LB	Michigan St.	1994-95
Banks, Chip	LB	Southern Cal.	1982-86
Banks, Fred	WR	Liberty U.	1985
Banks, Robert	DE	Notre Dame	1989-90
Barisich, Carl	DT	Princeton	1973-75
Barnes, Erich	DB	Purdue	1965-71
Barnett, Harlon	S	Michigan St.	1990-92
Barnett, Vincent	S	Arkansas St.	1987
Barney, Eppie	WR	Iowa St.	1967-68
Bassett, Maurice	RB	Langston	1954-56
Battle, Jim	DE	Southern U.	1966
Baugh, Tom	C	S. Illinois	1989
Bavaro, Mark	TE	Notre Dame	1992
Beach, Walter	DB	C. Michigan	1963-66
Beamon, Autry	DB	E. Texas St.	1980-81
Beauford, Clayton	WR	Auburn	1987
Bedosky, Mike	G	Missouri	#1994,'95
Belk, Rocky	WR	Miami	1983
Benz, Larry	DB	Northwestern	1963-65
Berry, Latin	DB	Oregon	1991-92
Best, Greg	S	Kansas St.	1984
Bettridge, Ed	LB	Bowling Green	1964
Beutler, Tom	LB	Toledo	1970
Biedermann, Leo	T	California	1978
Bishop, Harold	TE	LSU	1995
Black, James	RB	Akron	1984
Blandin, Ernie	T	Tulane	1946-47
Blaylock, Anthony	DB	Winston-Salem	1988-91
Bloch, Ray	T	Ohio	#1981
Boedeker, Bill	DB	No College	1947-49
Bolden, Leroy	RB	Michigan St.	1958-59
Bolden, Rickey	T	SMU	1984-89
Bolton, Ron	DB	Norfolk St.	1976-82
Bolzan, Scott	T	N. Illinois	#1985
Booth, Issac	DB	California	1994-95
Borton, John	QB	Ohio State	1957
Bosley, Keith	T	E. Kentucky	1987
Bostic, Keith	DB	Michigan	1990
Bradley, Harold	G	Iowa	1954-56
Bradley, Henry	DT	Alcorn St.	1979-82
Brady, Don	DB	Wisconsin	1995
Braggs, Stephen	DB	Texas	1987-91
Brandon, David	LB	Memphis St.	1991-93
Brannon, Robert	DE	Ark.-Fay.	1987
Braziel, Larry	CB	Southern Cal.	1982-85
Brennan, Brian	WR	Boston Col.	1984-91
Brewer, Johnny	TE-LB	Mississippi	1961-67
Brewster, Darrell	WR	Purdue	1952-58
Briggs, Bob	DE	Heidelberg	1971-73
Briggs, Greg	S	Tex. Southern	##1993
Brockman, Lonnie	LB	W. Virginia	##1991
Brooks, Clifford	DB	Tennessee St.	1972-74
Brooks, James	RB	Auburn	1992
Brown, Dean	DB	Ft. Valley St.	1969
Brown, Eddie	DB	Tennessee	1974-75
Brown, Jerome	DL	Mississippi St.	##1993
Brown, Jim	RB	Syracuse	1957-65
Brown, John	T	Syracuse	1962-66
Brown, John III	WR	Houston	##1992
Brown, Ken	RB	No College	1970-75
Brown, Orlando	T	S. Carolina St.	1994-95
Brown, Preston	KR	Vanderbilt	1984
Brown, Richard	LB	San Diego St.	1991-92
Brown, Stan	WR	Purdue	1971
Brown, Terry	DB	Oklahoma St.	1976
Brown, Thomas	DE	Baylor	1981,'83
Buben, Mark	DT	Tufts	1982
Buchanan, Charles	DE	Tennessee St.	1988
Buczkowski, Bob	DL	Pittsburgh	1990
Buddenberg, John	OL	Akron	##1989
Buehler, George	G	Stanford	1978-79
Bumgardner, Rex	RB	W. Virginia	1950-52
Bundra, Mike	DT	Southern Cal.	1964
Burnett, Rob	DE	Syracuse	1990-95
Burrell, Clinton	DB	Louisiana St.	1979-84
Burton, Leonard	OL	S. Carolina	#1991
Butler, Dave	LB	Notre Dame	1987
Butler, Ray	WR	Southern Cal.	#1989
Byner, Earnest	RB	E. Car.	1984-88,'94-95

C

Caldwell, Mike	LB	Mid. Tenn. St.	1993-95
Caleb, Jamie	RB	Grambling	1960,'65
Camp, Reggie	DE	California	1983-87
Campbell, Milt	RB	Indiana	1957
Capers, James	LB	C. Michigan	1987
Carollo, Joe	T	Notre Dame	1972-73
Carpenter, Ken	RB	Oregon St.	1950-53
Carpenter, Lew	RB	Arkansas	1957-58
Carpenter, Preston	RB	Arkansas	1956-59
Carreker, Vince	DB	Cincinnati	1987
Carrier, Mark	WR	Nicholls St.	1993-94
Carter, Alex	DE	Tennessee St.	1987
Carver, Dale	LB	Georgia	1983
Cassady, Howard	RB	Ohio State	1962
Catlin, Tom	LB	Okla.	1953-54,'57-58
Caylor, Lowell	DB	Miami-Ohio	1964
Charlton, Clifford	LB	Florida	1988-89
Cheroke, George	G	Ohio State	1946
Childress, Freddie	T	Arkansas	1992
Christensen, Jeff	QB	E. Illinois	1987
Clancy, Sam	DE	Pittsburgh	1985-88
Clark, Monte	T	Southern Cal.	1963-69
Clarke, Frank	WR	Colorado	1957-59
Clarke, Leon	WR	Southern Cal.	1960-62
Clayborn, Raymond	CB	Texas	1990-91
Cline, Ollie	RB	Ohio State	1948
Cockroft, Don	K-P	Adams St.	1968-80
Cole, Emerson	RB	Toledo	1950-52
Colella, Tom	P-DB	Canisius	1946-48
Coleman, Greg	P	Florida A&M	1977
Collins, Gary	WR-P	Maryland	1962-71
Collins, Larry	RB	Texas A&I	1978
Collins, Shawn	WR	N. Arizona	1992
Colo, Don	T	Brown	1953-58
Conjar, Larry	RB	Notre Dame	1967
Connolly, Ted	G	Tulsa	1963
Conover, Frank	DL	Syracuse	1991
Contz, Bill	T	Penn State	1983-86
Cooks, Johnie	LB	Mississippi St.	1991
Cooper, Scott	DE	Kearney St.	1987
Copeland, Jim	G	Virginia	1967-74
Coppage, Alton	DE	Oklahoma	1946
Cornell, Bo	RB	Washington	1971-72
Costello, Vince	LB	Ohio U.	1957-66
Cotton, Fest	DT	Dayton	1972
Cotton, Marcus	LB	Southern Cal.	1990
Cousineau, Tom	LB	Ohio State	1982-85
Cowan, Bob	RB	Indiana	1947-48
Cowher, Bill	LB	N. Carolina St.	1980-82
Cox, Arthur	TE	Tex. Southern	1991
Cox, Steve	P-K	Arkansas	1981-84
Craig, Neal	DB	Fisk	1975-76
Craig, Reggie	WR	Arkansas	1977
Craven, Bill	DB	Harvard	1976
Crawford, Mike	RB	Arizona St.	1987
Crawford, Tim	LB	Texas Tech.	1987
Crespino, Bob	WR	Mississippi	1961-63
Crews, Ron	DE	Nevada-L.V.	1980
Crosby, Cleveland	DE	Arizona	#1980
Cureton, Will	QB	E. Texas St.	1975
Cvercko, Andy	G	Northwestern	1963

D

Dahl, Bob	G	Notre Dame	1992-95
Daniell, Jim	C	Ohio State	1946
Danielson, Gary	QB	Purdue	1985,'87-88
Darden, Thom	DB	Mich.	1972-74,'76-81
Dark, Steve	TE	Mid.Tenn. St.	##1993
Darrow, Barry	T	Montana	1974-78
Davis, Ben	DB	Defiance	1967-68,'70-73
Davis, Bruce	WR	Baylor	1984
Davis, Dick	RB	Nebraska	1969
Davis, Gary	RB	Cal. Poly SLO	#1981
Davis, Johnny	RB	Alabama	1982-87
Davis, Oliver	DB	Tennessee St.	1977-80
Davis, Willie	DE	Grambling	1958-59
Dawson, Doug	G	Texas	1994
Dawson, Len	QB	Purdue	1960-61
DeLamielleure, Joe	G	Michigan St.	1980-84
DeLeone, Tom	C	Ohio State	1974-84

Dellerba, Spiro	RB	Ohio State	1947
DeMarco, Bob	C	Dayton	1972-74
DeMarie, John	G-T	Louisiana St.	1967-75
Dennis, Al	G	Grambling	1976-77
Dennison, Doug	RB	Kutztown St.	1979
Denton, Bob	DT	Col. of Pacific	1960
Deschaine, Dick	DE	No College	1958
Devries, Jed	OL	Utah State	##1994,'95
Devrow, Billy	DB	S. Mississippi	1967
Dewar, Jim	RB	Indiana	1947
Dickey, Curtis	RB	Texas A&M	1985-86
Dieken, Doug	T	Illinois	1971-84
Dimler, Rich	DT	Southern Cal.	1979
Dixon, Gerald	LB	S. Carolina	1993-95
Dixon, Hanford	CB	S. Mississippi	1981-89
Donaldson, Gene	G	Kentucky	1953
Douglas, Derrick	RB	La. Tech	1991
Dressel, Chris	TE	Stanford	#1988
Driver, Stacey	RB	Clemson	1987
Dudley, Brian	S	Beth. Cookman	1987
Dumont, Jim	LB	Rutgers	1984
Dunbar, Jubilee	WR	Southern U.	1974
Duncan, Brian	RB	SMU	1976-77
Duncan, Ron	TE	Wittenberg	1967

E

East, Ron	DE	Montana St.	1975
Echols, Donnie	TE	Oklahoma St.	1987
Edwards, Earl	DT	Wichita	1976-78
Elkins, Mike	QB	Wake Forest	#1991
Ellis, Ken	DB	Southern U.	1977
Ellis, Ray	S	Ohio State	1986-87
Engel, Steve	RB	Colorado	1970
Ethridge, Ray	WR	Pasadena City	1995
Evans, Fred	RB	Notre Dame	1946
Evans, Johnny	QB-P	N.C. State	1978-80
Everett, Major	RB	Miss. College	1986,#'87
Everitt, Steve	C	Michigan	1993-95

F

Fairchild, Greg	G	Tulsa	1978
Farren, Paul	T	Boston U.	1983-91
Feacher, Ricky	WR	Miss. Valley St.	1976-84
Fekete, Gene	RB	Ohio State	1946
Ferguson, Charley	DE	Tenn A&I	1961
Ferguson, Vagas	RB	Notre Dame	1983
Ferrell, Kerry	WR	Syracuse	##1993
Fichtner, Ross	DB	Purdue	1960-67
Figaro, Cedric	LB	Notre Dame	1991-92
Fike, Dan	G-T	Florida	1985-92
Fiss, Galen	LB	Kansas	1956-66
Fleming, Don	DB	Florida	1960-62
Flick, Tom	QB	Washington	1984
Flint, Judson	DB	Memphis St.	1980-82
Florence, Anthony	DB	Beth. Cookman	1991
Foggie, Fred	DB	Minnesota	1992
Fontenot, Herman	RB	LSU	1985-88
Footman, Dan	DE	Florida St.	1993-95
Ford, Henry	RB	Pittsburgh	1955
Ford, Len	DE	Michigan	1950-57
Forester, Herschel	G	SMU	1954-57
Franklin, Bobby	DB	Mississippi	1960-66
Francis, Jeff	QB	Tennessee	1990,#'92
Franco, Brian	K	Penn State	1987
Franks, Elvis	DE	Morgan St.	1980-84
Frederick, Andy	T	New Mexico	1982
Frederick, Mike	DE	Virginia	1995
Freeman, Bob	QB	Auburn	1957-58
Fullwood, Brent	RB	Auburn	1990
Fulton, Dan	WR	Neb.-Omaha	1981-82
Furman, John	QB	Texas-El Paso	1962

G

Gain, Bob	DT	Kentucky	1952,'54-64
Gainer, Derrick	RB	Fla. A&M	##1989,'90
Galbraith, Scott	TE	UCLA	1990-92
Garcia, Jim	DE	Purdue	1965
Garlington, John	LB	Louisiana St.	1968-77
Gartner, Chris	K	Indiana	1974
Gash, Thane	S	E. Tenn. St.	1988-90
Gatski, Frank	C	Marshall	1946-56
Gaudio, Bob	G	Ohio State	1947-49,'51
Gault, Don	QB	Hofstra	1970
Gautt, Prentice	RB	Oklahoma	1960
George, Tim	WR	Carson-Newman	1974
Gibron, Abe	G	Purdue	1950-56
Gibson, Tom	DE	N. Arizona	1989-90
Gillom, Horace	P-WR	Nevada	1947-56
Glass, Bill	DE	Baylor	1962-68
Glass, Chip	TE	Florida St.	1969-73
Goad, Tim	DT	N. Carolina	1995
Goebel, Brad	QB	Baylor	1992-95
Golic, Bob	DT	Notre Dame	1982-88
Goode, Don	LB	Kansas	1980-81
Goosby, Tom	LB	Baldwin-Wallace	1963
Gorgal, Ken	DB	Purdue	1950,'53-54
Goss, Don	DT	SMU	1956
Gossett, Jeff	P	E. Illinois	1983,'85-87
Graf, Dave	LB	Penn State	1975-79
Graham, Jeff	QB	Long Beach St.	##1989
Graham, Otto	QB	Northwestern	1946-55
Grant, Wes	DE	UCLA	1972
Graybill, Mike	OL	Boston U.	1989
Grayson, David	LB	Fresno St.	1987-90
Green, Boyce	RB	Carson-Newm.	1983-85
Green, David	RB	Edinboro St.	1982
Green, Ernie	RB	Louisville	1962-68
Green, Ron	WR	N. Dakota	1967-68
Green, Van	DB	Shaw	1973-76
Greenwood, Don	RB-DB	Illinois	1946-47
Greer, Terry	WR	Alabama St.	1986
Gregory, Jack	DE	Delta St.	1967-71,'79
Griffin, Don	CB	Mid. Tenn. St.	1994-95
Grigg, Forrest	DT	Tulsa	1948-51
Griggs, Anthony	LB	Ohio State	1986-88
Gross, Al	S	Arizona	1983-87
Groves, George	G	Marquette	1946
Groza, Lou	T-K	Ohio St.	1946-59,'61-67
Gruber, Bob	T	Pittsburgh	1986
Guilbeau, Rusty	LB	McNeese St.	1987

H

Hairston, Carl	DE	Md.-E. Shore	1984-89
Hairston, Stacey	DB	Ohio Northern	1993-95
Haley, Darryl	OL	Utah	1987-88
Hall, Charlie	LB	Houston	1971-80
Hall, Dana	S	Washington	1995
Hall, Dino	KR-RB	Glassboro St.	1979-83
Haller, Alan	DB	Michigan St.	1992
Hannemann, Cliff	LB	Fresno St.	1987
Hanulak, Chet	RB	Maryland	1954,'57
Hansen, Brian	P	Sioux Falls	1991-93
Harper, Mark	CB	Alcorn St.	1986-90
Harraway, Charley	RB	San Jose St.	1966-68
Harrington, John	DE	Marquette	1946
Harris, Duriel	WR	New Mexico St.	1984
Harris, Marshall	DE	Tex. Christian	1980-82
Harris, Odie	DB	Sam Hous. St.	1991-92
Hartley, Frank	TE	Illinois	1994-95
Harvey, Frank	RB	Georgia	##1994,'95
Haynes, Hayward	OL	Florida St.	##1991
Hawkins, Ben	WR	Arizona St.	1974
Helluin, Jerry	DT	Tulane	1952-53
Herring, Hal	LB	Auburn	1950-52
Hickerson, Gene	G	Miss.	1958-60,'62-73
Hilgenberg, Jay	C	Iowa	1992
Hill, Calvin	RB	Yale	1978-81
Hill, Jim	DB	Texas A&I	1975
Hill, Travis	LB	Nebraska	1994-95
Hill, Will	S	Bishop College	1988
Hilliard, Randy	CB	LSU	1990-93
Hoaglin, Fred	C	Pittsburgh	1966-72
Hoard, Leroy	RB	Michigan	1990-95
Hoggard, D.D.	CB	N. Carolina St.	1985-87
Holden, Steve	WR	Arizona St.	1973-76
Holland, Jamie	WR	Ohio State	1992
Holloway, Glen	G	N. Texas St.	1974
Holohan, Pete	TE	Notre Dame	1992
Holt, Harry	TE	Arizona	1983-86
Hooker, Fair	WR	Arizona St.	1969-74
Hoover, Houston	G	Jackson State	1993
Hopkins, Thomas	T	Alabama A&M	1983
Horn, Alvin	DB	UNLV	1987
Horn, Don	QB	San Diego St.	1973
Horvath, Les	RB	Ohio State	1949
Houston, Jim	DE-LB	Ohio State	1960-72
Houston, Lin	G	Ohio State	1946-53
Howard, Sherman	RB	Nevada	1952-53
Howell, Mike	DB	Grambling	1965-72
Howton, Bill	WR	Rice	1959
Humble, Weldon	LB	Rice	1947-50
Hunt, Bob	RB	Heidelberg	1974
Hunter, Art	C	Notre Dame	1956-59
Hunter, Earnest	RB	SE Okla. St.	1995
Hutchinson, Tom	WR	Kentucky	1963-65
Hutchison, Chuck	G	Ohio State	1973-75
Huther, Bruce	LB	New Hampshire	1981
Hynoski, Henry	RB	Temple	1975

I

Ilgenfritz, Mark	DE	Vanderbilt	1974
Ingram, Darryl	TE	California	1991
Irons, Gerald	LB	Md.-E. Shore	1976-79
Isbell, Joe Bob	G	Houston	1966

J

Jackson, Alfred	DB	San Diego St.	1991-92
Jackson, Bill	S	N. Carolina	1982
Jackson, Enis	CB	Memphis St.	1987
Jackson, Michael	WR	S. Mississippi	1991-95
Jackson, Rich	DE	Southern U.	1972
Jackson, Robert E.	G	Duke	1975-85
Jackson, Robert L.	LB	Texas A&M	1978-81
Jacobs, Dave	K	Syracuse	1981
Jacobs, Tim	CB	Delaware	1993-95
Jaeger, Jeff	K	Washington	1987
Jagade, Harry	RB	Indiana	1951-53
James, Lynn	WR	Arizona State	1991
James, Nathaniel	DB	Florida A&M	1968
James, Tommy	DB	Ohio State	1948-55
Jefferson, Ben	T	Maryland	##1989,'90
Jefferson, John	WR	Arizona St.	1985
Jenkins, Al	G	Tulsa	1969-70
Johnson, Bill	DL	Michigan St.	1992-94
Johnson, Eddie	LB	Louisville	1981-90
Johnson, Lawrence	DB	Wisconsin	1979-84
Johnson, Lee	P	BYU	1987-88
Johnson, Mark	LB	Missouri	1977
Johnson, Mike	LB	Virginia Tech	1986-93
Johnson, Mitch	T	UCLA	1971
Johnson, Pepper	LB	Ohio State	1993-95
Johnson, Ron	RB	Michigan	1969
Johnson, Walter	DT	Cal. State-L.A.	1965-76
Joines, Vernon	WR	Maryland	1989-90
Jones, Bobby	WR	No College	1983
Jones, Dave	WR	Kansas St.	1969
Jones, Dub	RB-WR	Tulane	1948-55
Jones, Edgar	RB	Pittsburgh	1946-49
Jones, Homer	WR	Tex. Southern	1970
Jones, James	DL	Northern Iowa	1991-94
Jones, Jock	LB	Virginia Tech	1990-91
Jones, Joe	DE	Tennessee St.	1970-71, '73,'75-78
Jones, Keith	RB	Nebraska	1989
Jones, Kirk	RB	UNLV	1987
Jones, Marlon	DE	Central State	1987-89
Jones, Reginald	CB	Memphis St.	#1994,'95
Jones, Ricky	LB	Tuskegee	1977-79

Reeves, Walter	TE	Auburn	1994-95
Renfro, Ray	WR	N. Texas St.	1952-63
Reynolds, Billy	RB	Pittsburgh	1953-54,'57
Reynolds, Chuck	C	Tulsa	1969-70
Rhome, Jerry	QB	Tulsa	1969
Rich, Randy	DB	New Mexico	1978-79
Richardson, Gloster	WR	Jackson St.	1972-74
Riddick, Louis	DB	Pittsburgh	1993-95
Rienstra, John	G	Temple	1991-92
Righetti, Joe	DT	Waynesburg	1969-70
Risien, Cody	T	Tx. A&M.	1979-83,'85-89
Rison, Andre	WR	Michigan St.	1995
Roan, Oscar	TE	SMU	1975-78
Robbins, Kevin	T	Michigan St.	##1989,'90
Roberts, Walter	WR	San Jose St.	1964-66
Robinson, Billy	DB	Arizona St.	1987
Robinson, DeJuan	LB	N. Arizona	1987
Robinson, Fred	G	Washington	1957
Robinson, Mike	DE	Arizona	1981-82
Rockins, Chris	S	Oklahoma St.	1984-87
Rogers, Don	S	UCLA	1984-85
Rokisky, John	DE	Duquesne	1946
Roman, Nick	DE	Ohio State	1972-74
Romaniszyn, Jim	LB	Edinboro St.	1973-74
Rose, Ken	LB	UNLV	1990
Rouson, Lee	RB	Colorado	1991
Rowe, Patrick	WR	San Diego St.	1993
Rowell, Eugene	WR	S. Mississippi	1990
Rucker, Reggie	WR	Boston U.	1975-81
Runager, Max	P	S. Carolina	1988
Rusinek, Mike	NT	California	1987
Ryan, Frank	QB	Rice	1962-68
Rymkus, Lou	T	Notre Dame	1946-51
Rypien, Mark	QB	Washington St.	1994

S

Saban, Lou	LB	Indiana	1946-49
Sabatino, Bill	DT	Colorado	1968
Sagapolutele, Pio	DL	Hawaii	1991-95
St. Clair, Mike	DE	Grambling	1976-79
Sandusky, John	T	Villanova	1950-55
Sanford, Lucius	LB	Georgia Tech	1987
Scales, Charley	RB	Indiana	1962-65
Scarry, Mike	C	Waynesburg	1946-47
Schad, Mike	G	Queens U. Can.	1995
Schafrath, Dick	G-T	Ohio State	1959-71
Schoen, Tom	DB	Notre Dame	1970
Schultz, Randy	RB	Iowa St. Teachers	1966
Schwenk, Bud	QB	Washington U.	1946
Scott, Bo	RB	Ohio State	1969-74
Scott, Clarence	DB	Kansas St.	1971-83
Sczurek, Stan	LB	Purdue	1963-65
Seifert, Mike	DE	Wisconsin	1974
Selawski, Gene	T	Purdue	1960
Sensanbaugher, Dean	RB	Ohio State	1948
Sharkey, Ed	G	Nevada	1953
Shavers, Tyrone	WR	Lamar	1991
Sheppard, Henry	G-T	SMU	1976-81
Sheriff, Stan	G	California Poly	1957
Sherk, Jerry	DT	Oklahoma St.	1970-81
Shiner, Dick	QB	Maryland	1967
Shoals, Roger	T	Maryland	1963-64
Shofner, Jim	DB	Tex. Christian	1958-63
Shorter, Jim	DB	Detroit	1962-63
Shula, Don	DB	John Carroll	1951-52
Shurnas, Marshall	WR	Missouri	1947
Sikich, Mike	G	Northwestern	1971
Sikora, Robert	T	Indiana	#1984
Simonetti, Len	DT	Tennessee	1946-48
Simons, Kevin	T	Tennessee	##1989
Sims, Darryl	DE	Wisconsin	1987-88
Sims, Mickey	DT	S. Carolina St.	1977-79
Sipe, Brian	QB	San Diego St.	1974-83
Skibinski, Joe	G	Purdue	1952
Slaughter, Webster	WR	San Diego St.	1986-91
Slayden, Steve	QB	Duke	#1988

Smith, Bob	LB	Nebraska	1955-56
Smith, Daryle	T	Tennessee	1989
Smith, Gaylon	RB	Southwestern	1946
Smith, Jim Ray	G	Baylor	1956-62
Smith, John	WR	Tennessee St.	1979
Smith, Ken	TE	New Mexico	1973
Smith, Leroy	LB	Iowa	##1992
Smith, Ralph	TE	Mississippi	1965-68
Smith, Rico	WR	Colorado	1992-95
Snidow, Ron	DE	Oregon	1968-72
Sparenberg, Dave	G	W. Ontario	1987
Speedie, Mac	WR	Utah	1946-52
Speer, Del	S	Florida	1993-94
Spencer, Joe	DT	Oklahoma St.	1949
Stams, Frank	LB	Notre Dame	1992-95
Staroba, Paul	WR	Michigan	1972
Steinbrunner, Don	DE	Washington St.	1953
Stephens, Larry	DT	Texas	1960-61
Steuber, Bob	RB	Missouri	1946
Stevenson, Rickey	CB	Arizona	1970
Stewart, Andrew	DE	Cincinnati	1989
Stienke, Jim	DB	SW Texas St.	1973
Stover, Matt	K	LSU	1991-95
Stracka, Tim	TE	Wisconsin	1983-84
Strock, Don	QB	Virginia Tech	1988
Sullivan, Dave	WR	Virginia	1973-74
Sullivan, Gerry	T-C	Illinois	1974-81
Sullivan, Tom	RB	Miami	1978
Summers, Fred	DB	Wake Forest	1969-71
Sumner, Walt	DB	Florida	1969-74
Sustersic, Ed	RB	Findlay	1949
Sutter, Ed	LB	Northwestern	##1992,'93-95
Swarn, George	RB	Miami-Ohio	1987
Swilling, Ken	LB	Georgia Tech	##1992

T

Taffoni, Joe	T	Tenn.-Martin	1967-70
Talley, John	TE	W. Virginia	##1989-91
Tamm, Ralph	G	W. Chester St.	1990-91
Taseff, Carl	DB	John Carroll	1951
Taylor, Terry	CB	S. Illinois	1992-93
Teifke, Mike	C	Akron	1987
Tellison, A.C.	WR	Miami	1995
Tennell, Derek	TE	UCLA	1987-89
Terlep, George	QB	Notre Dame	1948
Terrell, Ray	RB	Mississippi	1946-47
Testaverde, Vinny	QB	Miami	1993-95
Thaxton, Jim	TE	Tennessee St.	1974
Thomas, Johnny	CB	Baylor	1995
Thome, Chris	OL	Minnesota	1991-92
Thompson, Bennie	DB	Grambling	1994-95
Thompson, Tommy	LB-C	Wm. & Mary	1949-53
Thornton, John	DL	Cincinnati	1991
Tidmore, Sam	LB	Ohio State	1962-63
Tierney, Leo	C	Georgia Tech	1978
Tillman, Lawyer	WR	Auburn	1989,'92-93
Tinsley, Keith	WR	Pittsburgh	1987
Tomczak, Mike	QB	Ohio State	1992
Trocano, Rick	DB-QB	Pittsburgh	1981-83
Trumbull, Rick	OL	Missouri	##1991
Tucker, Travis	TE	S. Conn. St.	1985-87
Tupa, Tom	QB-P	Ohio State	#1993,'94-95
Turnbow, Jesse	DT	Tennessee	1978
Turner, Eric	S	UCLA	1991-95
Turner, Kevin	LB	Pacific	1982

U

Ulinski, Ed	G	Marshall	1946-49
Upshaw, Marvin	DE	Trin.-San Ant.	1968-69

V

Van Dyke, Ralph	T	S. Illinois	1987
Van Pelt, Brad	LB	Michigan St.	1986
Vardell, Tommy	RB	Stanford	1992-95
Verser, David	WR	Kansas	1987

W

Wagner, Bryan	P	Cal. St. N'ridge	1989-90
Waiters, Van	LB	Indiana	1988-91
Walker, Dwight	RB-WR	Nicholls St.	1982-84
Walls, Everson	DB	Grambling	1992-93
Walters, Dale	P	Rice	1987
Ward, Carl	DB	Michigan	1967-68
Warfield, Paul	WR	Ohio St.	1964-69,'76-77
Washington, Brian	S	Nebraska	1988
Watkins, Tom	RB	Iowa State	1961
Watson, Louis	WR	Miss. Valley St.	1987
Watson, Remi	WR	Beth.-Cookman	1987
Weathers, Clarence	WR	Delaware St.	1985-88
Weathers, Curtis	TE-LB	Mississippi	1979-85
Webb, Ken	RB	Presbyterian	1963
Weber, Chuck	DE	W. Chester St.	1955-56
Webster, Larry	DT	Maryland	1995
White, Bob	RB	Stanford	1955
White, Charles	RB	South. Cal.	1980-82,'84
White, James	DE	LSU	#1985
White, Lorenzo	RB	Michigan St.	1995
Whitlow, Bob	C	Arizona	1968
Whitwell, Mike	WR-S	Texas A&M	1982-83
Wiggin, Paul	DE	Stanford	1957-67
Wilburn, Barry	CB	Mississippi	1992
Wilkerson, Gary	DB	Penn State	##1989
Wilkinson, Jerry	DE	Oregon St.	1980
Williams, A.D.	WR	Coll. of Pacific	1960
Williams, Clarence	RB	Washington St.	1993
Williams, Gene	T-G	Iowa State	1993-95
Williams, Larry	G	Notre Dame	1986-88
Williams, Lawrence	KR	Texas Tech	1977
Williams, Sidney	LB	Southern U.	1964-66
Williams, Tony	T	Kansas State	1993
Williams, Wally	C	Florida A&M	1993-95
Willis, Bill	G-MG	Ohio State	1946-53
Wilson, Tom	RB	No College	1962
Wilson, Troy	CB	Notre Dame	1987
Wingle, Blake	G	UCLA	1987
Winslow, George	P	Villanova	1987
Winters, Frank	C	W. Illinois	1987-88
Wise, Mike	DL	Cal.-Davis	1991
Wiska, Jeff	G	Michigan St.	1986
Wolfley, Ron	RB	West Virginia	1992-93
Woods, Rob	OL	Arizona	1991
Woolsey, Rolly	DB	Boise State	1977
Wooten, John	G	Colorado	1959-67
Wren, Junior	DB	Missouri	1956-59
Wright, Alvin	NT	Jacksonville St.	1992
Wright, Felix	S	Drake	1985-90
Wright, George	DT	Sam Houston	1986
Wright, Keith	WR	Memphis St.	1978-80
Wycinsky, Craig	G	Michigan St.	1972

Y

Yanchar, Bill	DT	Purdue	1970
Yonakor, John	DE	Notre Dame	1946-49
Young, George	DE	Georgia	1946-53
Young, Glen	WR	Miss.	1984-85,'87-88
Youngblood, George	DB	Cal. St.-L.A.	1967
Youngelman, Sid	DT	Alabama	1959

Z

Zeier, Eric	QB	Georgia	1995
Zeno, Lance	C	UCLA	1992-93

\# On active roster but did not play in a game.
\## On practice squad, but did not play in a game.

Browns Retired Uniform Numbers

14	Otto Graham
32	Jim Brown
45	Ernie Davis
46	Don Fleming
76	Lou Groza

Clay Matthews & Bob Golic

BIBLIOGRAPHY

Books

Brown, Jim, with Myron Cope. *Off My Chest.* Doubleday, 1964.

Brown, Paul, with Jack Clary. *P.B.: The Paul Brown Story.* Atheneum, 1979.

Campbell, Jim. *Golden Years of Pro Football.* Crescent. 1993.

Cerbaro, Varo. *Twenty Years with the Cleveland Browns.* Varo Cerbaro, 1966.

Clary, Jack. *Great Teams, Great Years: Cleveland Browns.* Macmillan Publishing Co., 1973.

Clary, Jack. *Pro Football's Great Moments.* Sammis Publishing Corp., 1983.

Collett, Ritter. *Super Stripes.* Landfall Press, 1982.

Cope, Myron. *The Game That Was.* The World Publishing Co., 1970.

DeLuca, Sam. *The NFL Playbook.* Jonathan David Publications, 1972.

Eckhouse, Morris. *Day by Day in Cleveland Browns History.* Leisure Press, 1984.

Glass, Bill. *Get in the Game!.* Word Books, 1965.

Grosshandler, Stanley. *The Mighty Ones.* Vantage, 1969.

Huff, Sam, with Leonard Shapiro. *Tough Stuff.* St. Martin's Press, 1988.

King, Peter. *Football. A History of the Professional Game.* Oxmoor House, 1993.

King, Peter. *Inside the Helmet.* Simon & Schuster, 1993.

Kowet, Don. *Golden Toes.* St. Martin's Press, 1972.

Leuthner, Stuart. *Ironmen.* Doubleday, 1988.

Levy, Bill. *Return to Glory, The Story of the Cleveland Browns.* The World Publishing Co., 1965.

Levy, Bill. *Sam, Sipe and Company.* J.T. Zubal and P.D. Dole, 1981.

McGuire, Dan. *San Francisco 49ers.* Coward-McCann, 1960.

Owen, Steve. *My Kind of Football.* David McKay, 1952.

Parker, Raymond "Buddy." *We Play to Win.* Prentice-Hall, 1955.

Parrish, Bernie. *They Call It A Game.* Dial Press, 1971.

Rutigliano, Sam. *Pressure.* Oliver Nelson, 1988.

Riffenburgh, Beau and Jack Clary. *The Official History of Pro Football.* Crescent Books, 1990.

Schneider, Russell. *Cleveland Browns Memories.* Russell Schneider, 1990.

Slone, Kay Collier. *Football's Gentle Giant: The Blanton Collier Story.* Life Force Press, 1985.

Whittingham, Richard. *Giants in Their Own Words.* Contemporary Books, 1992.

Zimmerman, Paul. *A Thinking Man's Guide to Pro Football.* E.P. Dutton, 1970.

Record Books & Guides

AAFC Record Manual. All-America Football Conference, 1947-49.

Browns Media Guide. Cleveland Browns, selected years, 1946-99.

Neft, David S. and Richard M. Cohen, *Sports Encyclopedia: Pro Football.* Sports Products, Inc., 1987.

Riffenburgh, Beau. *The Official NFL Encyclopedia.* New American Library, 1986.

The NFL's Official Encyclopedic History of Professional Football. Macmillan Publishing Co., 1973.

The Official National Football League 1995 Record & Fact Book. National Football League and Workman Publishing, 1995.

The National Football League Official Record Manual. National Football League, selected years.

Treat, Roger. *The Encyclopedia of Football.* A.S. Barnes, 1952 & 1974.

Publications

Kable, F.T., *Pro Football Illustrated.* Elbak Publications, 1946-50.

PRO! NFL Properties, selected issues.

Pro Football Weekly. Pro Football Weekly, selected issues.

Street & Smith's Pro Football Annual. Street & Smith's, selected years.

PHOTOGRAPHY

Legend: T=top, B=bottom, L=left, R=right, TL=top left, TR=top right, BL=bottom left, BR=bottom right

AP/Wide World Photos: pages 29, 37, 141, 171 T, 177, 178, 181, 183.

Chance Brockway: pages 54, 56, 60, 62, 84 T, 244, 254, 279, 294 R, 319, 321 L, 341 TR, I T, II, III TL-BL-BR, IV T, V T-BL-BR, VI BL, VII, IX TR, X T-B, XI BR, XII, XIII TL-TR, XIV T-BL-BR, XV T.

Browns News/Illustrated: pages 41, 46 R, 52 L, 76, 78, 79, 80, 81, 82 L-R, 84 B, 86 T-BL-BR, 87 L-R, 89, 92, 93, 94, 95, 96 T-BL-BR, 97 L-R, 100, 101 TL-TR-B, 102, 103, 106, 107 TL-TR-BL-BR, 108 TL-B, 109, 110, 111 R, 112, 113 R, 127 L, 171 B, 174 B, 184 R, 190, 191, 192 L-R, 193 L, 197, 200 L-R, 201, 204, 205, 208, 209, 216, 223 L-R, 228, 229 L-R, 230, 231, 232 L-R, 235 T, 236, 241 R, 242, 243 R, 245, 247 R, 248 L-R, 249, 250, 251 L-R, 252 L-R, 256 L-R, 258 R, 259, 262, 263 L-R, 264 L-R, 266 B, 267 TL-TR-B, 273 R, 274, 275 R, 278 R, 280, 282 L-R, 283 L-R, 284 R, 291 L-R, 295 L, 296, 297, 299 L-R, 300 L-R, 304 L, 307 R, 308, 309, 310 L, 311 R, 313 L-R, 314, 316 R, 322 R, 328 L-R, 330 T-B, 331 T-B, 338, 339 L-R, 341 BR, 343 TL-BL, 351, VIII TL-TR-B.

The Cleveland Press Collection/Cleveland State University: pages 7, 10, 11, 15, 16, 20, 23, 25 T, 27, 32, 34 T-BL-BR, 35 T-B, 40 R, 45, 46 L, 47 L-R, 50, 68 R, 85, 140, 143, 146, 147, 166 B, 167 TR, 169, 170, 173, 180, 182, 184 L, 188, 189 R, 202, 217, 219, 222, 227 L, 234 B, 238, 239, 246, 260 L, 261 R, 266 T, 271, 273 L, 276, 277, 278 L, 290, 292, 305 R, 306, 310 R, 322 L, 323, 335, 336, 340 L, 341 BL, 342 TR-BR.

Cleveland Public Library: page 142.

Crow Collection: pages 2, 5, 12, 18, 187, 189 L, 198 R, 221 L-R, 227 R, 243 L, 257 L-R, 258, L, 260 R, 261 L, 270, 272 L-R, 275 L, 288 L-R, 289 L-R, 295 R, 304 R, 305 L, 307 L, 311 L, 326 L-R, 327, 337 L-R, 342 TL-BL, 346.

The Dallas Morning News: page 161.

The Dayton Daily News: page 156.

Diamond Images: pages 108 TR, 111 L, 113 L, 115, 116, 117, 118, 119, 120, 121, 122 T-BL-BR, 123, 129, 130 L-R, 131 L-R, 132 L, 233 R, 253 L-R, 265 L, 285 L-R, 301 R, 317 L-R, 329 L-R, III TR, VI T.

Pete Groh: pages 193 R, 210, 211, 265 R, VI BR, XI T, XVI B.

The Ohio State University Photo Archives: pages 8, 9 L-R.

PRO-File Collection: pages 214, 215.

RJM Collection: pages 49, 55, 57, 59, 61, 63, 65, 66, 67, 69, 70 T-B, 71, 72, 73, 74, 75, 83, 91, 98 B, 105, 126, 134, 155, 163, 168, 172, 174 T, 175, 176, 203, 206, 207, 213, 224, 225, 226, 247 L, 268, 281, 284 L, 286, 293 L-R, 294 L, 298, 303, 312, 315, 316 L, 324, 325, 332, 343 TR-BR.

Ron Schwane: pages 125, 128, 132 R, 133 T-B, 233 L. 301 L, I B, IV B, IX B, XI BL, XIII B, XV BL-BR, XVI T.

Transcendental Graphics: pages 39, 40 L, 42, 43, 51, 127 R, 167 TL-B, 185, 186, 198 L, 199, 241 L, 321 R.

UPI/Bettmann Newsphotos: pages 1, 13, 17, 19, 21, 22 L-R, 24, 25 B, 28, 30, 31, 33, 36, 44, 52 R, 53, 58, 68 L, 88, 98 T, 99, 137, 138, 144, 149, 150, 152 T-B, 153, 159, 164, 165, 166 T, 179, 194, 196, 218, 220, 234 T, 235 B, 240, 320, 334, 340 R, 341 TL.